Celts
art and identity

Edited by Julia Farley and Fraser Hunter

The British Museum

National Museums Scotland

This publication accompanies the exhibitions *Celts: art and identity* and *Celts* organized by the British Museum and National Museums Scotland.

Celts: art and identity at the British Museum is supported by

In memory of Melvin R. Seiden
Sheila M. Streek
Stephen and Julie Fitzgerald
Fund for the Future donors

Celts at the National Museum of Scotland is kindly sponsored by Baillie Gifford Investment Managers

The exhibition at the British Museum has been made possible by the provision of insurance through the Government Indemnity Scheme. The British Museum would like to thank the Department for Culture, Media and Sport, and Arts Council England for providing and arranging this indemnity.

The exhibition at the National Museum of Scotland has been assisted by the Scottish Government and the Government Indemnity Scheme.

First published in the United Kingdom in 2015
by The British Museum Press
A division of The British Museum Company Ltd
38 Russell Square, London WC1B 3QQ
britishmuseum.org

A catalogue record for this book is available from the British Library

ISBN 978 0 7141 2835 1 (hardback)
ISBN 978 0 7141 2836 8 (paperback)

Designed by Will Webb Design
Printed in Italy by Graphicom Srl

Prelim illustrations
Endpapers (hardback only): Detail of carpet page from St Chad Gospel, see fig. 198; detail from the Battersea shield, see fig. 26.
p. 1 Detail of the Witham shield, see p. 84.
p. 2 The Hunterston brooch, see p. 174.
p. 3 Detail of a gold torc from Blair Drummond, see p. 93.
p. 4 Detail of a crescent-shaped mount from Balmaclellan, see p. 125.

Exploring different worlds (left)

Celtic art takes the modern viewer back into very different worlds. The deliberate simplicity of this stylized, two-sided figure from south-west Germany is very striking, with a single arm and almost geometric, expressionless face. Stone statues are rare in Iron Age Europe. Some probably marked the graves of prominent people, but the two faces of this one suggest it was a god rather than a human. Their names and powers are entirely lost to us, but the protruding horns represent a headdress worn at this time by people (or gods) of special status.

Holzgerlingen, Baden-Württemberg, Germany 500–400 BC
Sandstone; H 2.30 m (excluding restored horns)
Württembergisches Landesmuseum, Stuttgart

Contents

Directors' Forewords

The collections of National Museums Scotland and the British Museum house a wealth of material which is of central importance for exploring the complex question of the Celts. Who were they? Why was this identity, this art style and this name such a persistent part of European history for over two millennia? Why does it still have such an enduring resonance today? The exhibition which accompanies this book explores these questions, reveals new insights and brings intriguing and beautiful objects together for the first time. The highlights of the Celtic-related collections from Edinburgh and London have been combined with a wealth of major finds from museums across Europe, providing an unparalleled opportunity for British audiences to explore the Celts and their influence in depth.

It is over forty years since the last British exhibition was mounted to consider the Celts on a European scale – another project which was shared between Edinburgh and London. The focus of the 1970 show was much narrower, however, with a concentration on the Iron Age. The current exhibition broadens the scope to include much new research and cover the early medieval period, which for many people today provided the epitome of Celtic art, with treasures such as the Hunterston brooch and the great illuminated manuscripts. It also considers the rediscovery and reinvention of the Celts and their influence from the sixteenth century to the present day. This broad perspective challenges any easy assumptions about a simple Celtic past, and reveals the complexities, the constant change and reinvention of this idea. The objects in the exhibition and the stories they tell show Britain's extensive connections with Continental Europe, and reveal how decoration with curvilinear and complex Celtic artistic forms gave objects a real power and significance. In these magnificent items we catch glimpses of an ancient world at key moments in Europe's early history.

I am delighted that this collaboration with the British Museum has allowed us to present a stronger, more rounded exhibition than either of the institutions could have achieved on their own. I am sure that audiences in Edinburgh and London, and the readers of this book, will find much to engage, enthuse and inspire them.

Finally, I would like to record our grateful thanks to Baillie Gifford Investment Managers for their generous support of *Celts*. An exhibition on this scale is not possible without the substantial assistance and enthusiasm of our sponsors and many other talented people in the team.

DR GORDON RINTOUL CBE
Director, National Museums Scotland

Celts: art and identity at the British Museum marks the first time that any exhibition has attempted to tell the story of the Celts from 500 BC to the present day. Yet this is not so much a show about a people as a show about a label, exploring how the name 'Celts' has been used and appropriated over the last 2,500 years. 'Celtic' is a cultural construct that has changed its meaning many times. The word was originally used by Greeks and Romans to describe their 'barbarous' neighbours to the north. It has been used at different points since in the history of western Europe, characterizing particular communities that produced objects reflecting a distinct, non-Mediterranean, non-metropolitan way of thinking about the world. 'Celts' has always been a word with a purpose: to label oneself or another as different.

While the Celts are not a distinct race or genetic group that can be traced through time, the word 'Celtic' still resonates powerfully today, all the more so because it has been continually redefined to echo contemporary concerns over politics, religion and identity. This word continues to strike a resonant chord both nationally and globally, among the populations of Ireland, Scotland and Wales, and their diaspora communities around the world.

Celts: art and identity has been organized in partnership between the British Museum and National Museums Scotland. The two exhibitions in London and Edinburgh are the result of many years of fruitful collaboration between our two houses. This rewarding partnership has given us the opportunity to tell a far richer story than would otherwise have been possible. I should like to thank all of our colleagues in Edinburgh for the generosity with which they have shared their knowledge, expertise and collection. This book, like the exhibitions which it accompanies, is very much a joint project. I should also like to express my appreciation to the lecturers and curators at the National Gallery of Scotland, University of Edinburgh and Cambridge Museum of Archaeology and Anthropology who have contributed not only to the catalogue but also to the exhibition itself, giving very generously of their time. This also extends to the many specialists at other institutions who have assisted the authors with their research.

The scope of the exhibition reaches across much of Europe and spans a period of over two and a half thousand years. An exhibition on this scale would not have been possible without the support of many other institutions from the UK and across Europe. In total 17 UK institutions and 10 international museums and art galleries have generously lent pieces from their collections to the British Museum exhibition. I should like to thank all of our lenders for their cooperation and trust.

No exhibition can happen without financial support, and we are grateful to an anonymous gift in memory of Melvin R. Seiden, and also Stephen and Julie Fitzgerald, the late Sheila M. Streek and our Fund for the Future donors. Their generosity has made this exhibition possible.

NEIL MACGREGOR
Director, The British Museum

Editors' Preface and Acknowledgements

The exhibitions that this book accompanies have had a long and complicated genesis. The idea of a collaborative show drawing together star pieces from the British Museum, National Museums Scotland, National Museum Wales and the National Museum of Ireland was first proposed in 2003, after a curatorial discussion at the British Museum led by J.D. Hill and Sam Moorhead. It had been several decades since the last major exhibition on the Celts in Britain, and Simon James's 1999 book *The Atlantic Celts* had brought the question of the relationship between modern Celtic identity and the ancient Celts firmly into the public eye. Although this exhibition never came into fruition, the proposal was revived and revised in 2010 by Jonathan Williams, Ian Leins, Fraser Hunter and Martin Goldberg. The exhibition has always been a collaborative venture. All of the contributors to this volume, and a great many others acknowledged below, have helped to shape the content of the exhibitions in London and Edinburgh and the ideas expressed in this book.

A project of this scale has incurred many debts of gratitude. For comments on earlier drafts of various chapters the editors and contributors would like to thank Alice Blackwell, Sue Brunning, David Clarke, Mary Davis, J.D. Hill, Vincent Megaw (who also kindly provided pre-publication access to his forthcoming *Early Celtic Art – a Supplement*), Tanja Romankiewicz, Lesley Taylor, Susan Youngs and Rosie Weetch. Any mistakes that remain are our own. Rosie, the Project Curator for the British Museum exhibition, deserves a very special thanks for her tireless and always cheerful work in bringing the exhibition into being, remaining undaunted in the face of the plentiful challenges that reared their heads along the way.

There are many people at our respective institutions to whom we owe our thanks. At the British Museum we are particularly indebted to our colleagues who have lent advice and encouragement, particularly Roger Bland, Sue Brunning, Jill Cook, J.D. Hill, Richard Hobbs, Ralph Jackson, Helen Ritchie, Judy Rudoe, Dora Thornton, Neil Wilkin and Jonathan Williams. Neil MacGregor and Joanna Mackle also gave invaluable guidance and support. Two contributors to this volume who worked as curators on the British Museum exhibition before moving on to other roles outside the museum deserve special thanks: Jody Joy and Ian Leins, the exhibition would not have been possible without you. The Department of Conservation and Scientific research helped with both the research for this volume and the conservation of objects ready for display. Thanks for conservation work and preventive work at the British Museum are due to Alex Baldwin, Jenny Bescoby, Hayley Bullock, Rachel Berridge, Hazel Gardiner, David Giles, Loretta Hogan, Denise Ling, Pippa Pearce, Julie Phippard, Jude Raynor, Ailsinn Smalling and Tracey Sweek. Thanks are also due to a great many in the exhibitions team including our project managers Rachel Brown, Philippa Edwards, Alistair Hood, Holly Peel, Sarah Terkaoui and Matthew Weaver, as well as Caroline Ingham and Carolyn Marsden Smith who have guided us through the process of putting on a major exhibition, our 3D designers from Real Studios, the team from New Angle who worked on our digital media, and Paul Goodhead, our 2D designer. Jill Maggs, Christopher Stuart and Joanna McAleer administered the loans for the exhibition, and Natalie Tacq arranged our reciprocal UK partnerships loans in conjunction with National Museums Scotland, with assistance from Angela Rowbottom. Thanks are especially due to all of the Museum Assistants who worked on making the exhibition a reality, and packing a large number of objects for transport to Edinburgh. Many others helped with other aspects of the show, including Helen Chittock, Sarah Scheffler, Rachel Wilkinson, Lydia Woolway, and Emily Glynn-Farrell, who assisted Rosie Weetch with the due diligence research, and too many other friends and colleagues to name them all here. We thank you all.

At the National Museum of Scotland, our foremost thanks are to Martin Goldberg, our co-curator on the shows. The exhibition process was managed by Sarah Teale with strategic guidance from Gordon Rintoul, Ruth Gill and Alison Cromarty, and support from Tom Chisholm and his team. Special thanks to our assistant curators Craig Angus and Jim Wilson, to Lucy Malcolm Clark and Caroline Murphy in the loans team, Claire Allan and Jane Miller from the learning and programmes team, and Elaine Macintyre for dealing with digital media aspects. The conservation support from Jane Clark, Åke Henrik-Klemens, Emmanuelle Largeteau and Charles Stable was invaluable, as was advice from our curatorial colleagues Alice Blackwell, George Dalgleish, David Forsyth, Lyndsay McGill and Jackie Moran. We are grateful to Bruce Blacklaw, Kerryn Fraser, Susan Gray and Alex Hinton in our marketing and communications department, and to Debbie Crawford in our development department for securing sponsorship.

Outside our own institutions, we owe great debts of thanks to all of our lenders,. We wish to thank colleagues at the Bodleian Library (Oxford), the British Library (London), DRAC Auvergne (Clermont-Ferrand), East Riding Museum (Hull), Glasgow Museums Service, The Gorsedd of the Bards, Historisches Museum Bern, the Hunterian Art Gallery (Glasgow), Keltenwelt am Glauberg, Kunsthistorisches Museum (Vienna), Lichfield Cathedral, Littlehampton Museum, Mansion House (London), McManus Galleries (Dundee), Musée d'Archéologie Nationale (Saint Germain), Musée Saint-Raymond (Toulouse), the National Library of Scotland, the National Museum of Denmark (Copenhagen), the National Museum of Ireland (Dublin), the National Museum (Prague), the National Museum (Sofia), the National Museum of Wales (Cardiff), the National Trust for Scotland, Norwich Castle Museum, Rheinisches Landesmuseum (Bonn), the Royal Collection (London), Scottish National Galleries (Edinburgh), the Society of Antiquaries of London, Statens Museum for Kunst (Copenhagen), the Treasure House (Beverley), the University of Edinburgh, the Victoria and Albert Museum (London), and Württembergisches Landesmuseum (Stuttgart).

Special thanks are due to many external colleagues for their support, guidance and insights which have helped to shape our thinking, as well as the volume which you hold in your hands, including Neal Ascherson, Barbara Armbruster, Sabine Bolliger, Mary Cahill, Barry Cunliffe, John Davies, Polly Devlin, Roy Foster, Nathalie Ginoux, Chris Gosden, Andrew Fitzpatrick, Katherine Forsyth, Adam Gwilt, Anette Hagan, Peter Halkon, Colin Haselgrove, Simon James, Flemming Kaul, Eamonn Kelly, John Koch, Tammy Macenka, David Marchant, Joseph Marshall, Michael Marshall, Felix Müller, Courtney Nimura, Raghnall Ó Floinn, Andrew O'Hagan, Laurent Olivier, Tim Pestell, Maria Reho, Vera Rupp, Pavel Sankot, Ralf Schmitz, Martin Schönfelder, Maeve Sikora, Mansel Spratling, Evelyne Ugaglia and Ludmil Vagalinski. We would particularly like to thank Thomas Hoppe for his enthusiastic support and the insights reaped from his own experience of putting on a big Celts show. Frances Fowle and Heather Pulliam both contributed not only to this volume, but also to researching and shaping both exhibitions, and we are hugely grateful for their help and expertise in areas beyond our ken.

This book would not have been possible without the assistance of a great many individuals. For the wonderful new photography of BM and NMS material, thanks are due to Stephen Dodd, Neil McLean and Saul Peckham. For the illustrations and tremendous practical assistance in obtaining them we are grateful to Stephen Crummy, Paul Goodhead, Craig Williams and Maggie Wilson. We owe thanks to many at British Museum Press, including Kate Oliver and Axelle Russo-Heath, freelancers Will Webb, Linda Schofield and Lisa Footitt, and most especially Coralie Hepburn, for her commitment and patience.

JULIA FARLEY AND FRASER HUNTER

Timeline

CHRONOLOGICAL PERIODS

Later Bronze Age

Earlier Iron Age/Hallstatt

Later Iron Age/La Tène

Roman period

ART STYLES

Early

Plastic/Sword

Mirror

Vegetal

Romano-Britis

British Late Iron Age styles

LANGUAGE

Development of Celtic languages since 3rd millennium BC

First surviving inscriptions in Celtic languages

1500 BC

1000 BC

500 BC

BC /AD

EVENTS IN EUROPE

Late Hallstatt rich burials & early towns

Oppida

Rich early La Tène burials

Greek colony at Marseilles c. 600 BC •

First Greek authors mention Celts

Death of Alexander the Great 323 BC •

Celtic war bands in Greek world, settlement in Tu

279 BC sack of Delphi •

• 123 BC Foundation of Roman
colony in southern France

Celtic invasions & settlement
recorded in Italy

Mythical foundation of Rome 753 BC •

Sack of Rome by Celts 390 BC •

Expansion of Roman Power

EVENTS IN BRITAIN & IRELAND

Roman occupa
of Britain

Roman invasion of Britain 43 •

Caesar in Gaul & Britain 58–51 BC •

BOOK STRUCTURE

CHAPTER 3

CHAPTER 5

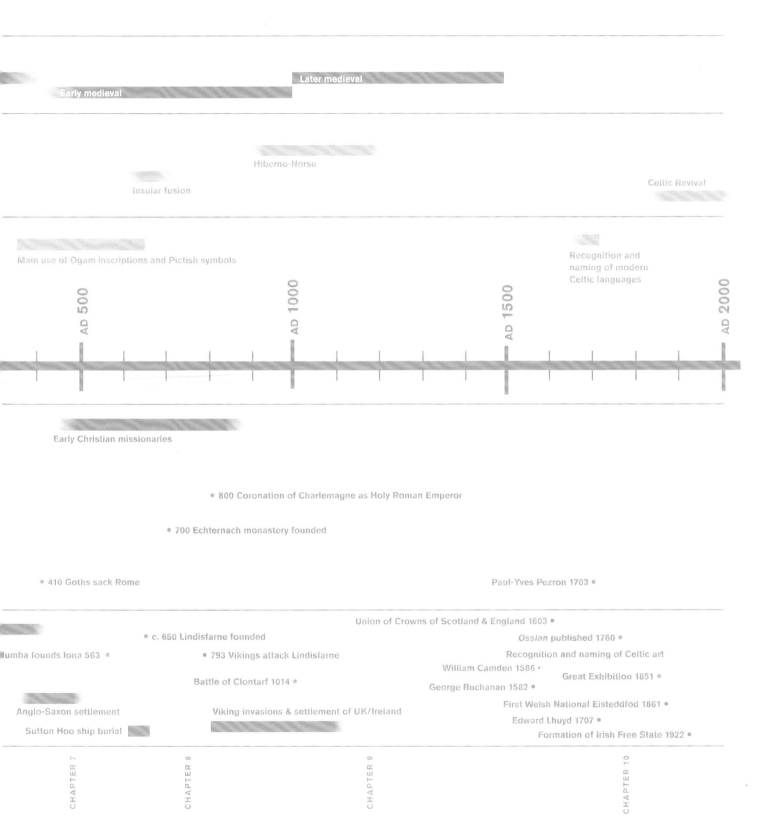

Later medieval

Early medieval

Hiberno-Norse

Insular fusion

Celtic Revival

Main use of Ogam inscriptions and Pictish symbols

Recognition and naming of modern Celtic languages

AD 500

AD 1000

AD 1500

AD 2000

Early Christian missionaries

● 800 Coronation of Charlemagne as Holy Roman Emperor

● 700 Echternach monastery founded

● 410 Goths sack Rome

Paul-Yves Pezron 1703 ●

Union of Crowns of Scotland & England 1603 ●

● c. 650 Lindisfarne founded

Ossian published 1760 ●

Columba founds Iona 563 ●

● 793 Vikings attack Lindisfarne

Recognition and naming of Celtic art

William Camden 1586 ·

Battle of Clontarf 1014 ●

Great Exhibition 1851 ●

George Buchanan 1582 ●

Anglo-Saxon settlement

Viking invasions & settlement of UK/Ireland

First Welsh National Eisteddfod 1861 ●

Edward Lhuyd 1707 ●

Sutton Hoo ship burial

Formation of Irish Free State 1922 ●

SHETLAND

St Ninian's Isle

ATLANTIC

OCEAN

Skye

High Pasture Cave

Hilton of Cadboll

Deskford

Tarnavie

Blair Drummond

Newbridge

Balloch Hill

Edinburgh

Dunaverney

Lisnacrogher

Torrs

Carlingwark

NORTH

SEA

Dronninglund

Gundestrup

Rødmose

Stanwick

Ballydavis

Wetwang Slack

Cerrig-y-drudion

Kirkburn

Eggeslevmagle

Gammelborg

BALTIC SEA

Ratcliffe-on-Soar

Witham

Snettisham

Eaton

Chiseldon

Thames

Chiswell Green

Weston

London

Chertsey

North Bersted

ENGLISH CHANNEL

Rhine

Saint-Amand-

Lens

les-Eaux

Eigenbilzen

Ribemont-sur-Ancre

MOSEL-RHINE

Amfreville

Seine

Gournay-sur-Aronde

Pfalzfeld

Glauberg

BOHEMIA

Roissy-en-France

MARNE

Goeblingen-

Echternach

Waldalgesheim

Hořovičky

Paris

Pleurs

Nospelt

Weiskirchen

Mainz

Prague-Šárka

Salon

Somme-

Basse-Yutz

HUNSRÜCK-

Plaňany

Cernon-

Bionne

Kleinaspergle

EIFEL

sur-Coole

Köngen

Chýnov

Holzgerlingen

Heubach

Roseldorf-

Alésia

Gäufelden-Nebringen

Eislingen

Manching

Sandberg

Trichtingen

Erms

Bibracte

Urach

Heuneburg

Munich-

Hallstatt

La Tène

Muri

Untermenzing

Thielle

THE

ALPS

Clermont-Ferrand

Tintignac

Fenouillet

Monte Bibele

Marseilles

MEDITERRANEAN

SEA

N

0   250 Miles

0   400 Kilometres

Cerveteri

Rome

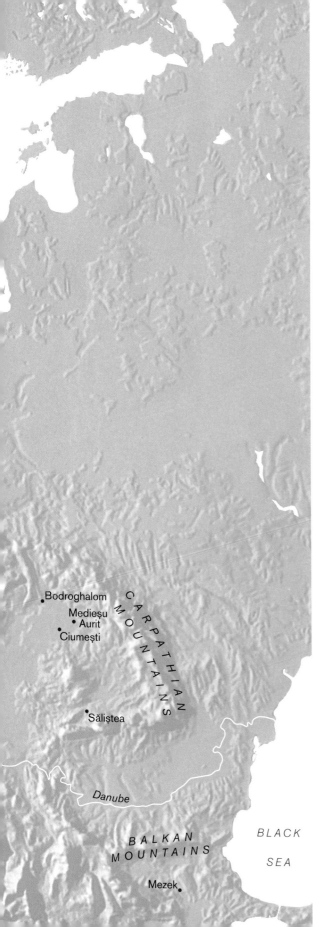

Map of Europe

Places referred to in the text
(see also p. 16).

Bodroghalom
Medieşu
Aurit
Ciumeşti

CARPATHIAN
MOUNTAINS

Sălıştea

Danube

BALKAN
MOUNTAINS

BLACK
SEA

Mezek

SHETLAND

Papil
St Ninian's Isle

Birsay • Westness
Skaill • ORKNEY
• South Ronaldsay

Rogart
Portmahomack
Nigg • Shandwick
• Gaulcross
Craig Phadraig • Auldearn
Torvean • Culloden
Parkhill

Castle Tioram
Bunrannoch • Tummel Bridge
Glendochart • West Grange of Conan
WEST • Crieff • Monifieth
HIGHLANDS • Iona • Dupplin
Antonine • Norrie's Law
Dunadd • Dunipace • Wall • Firth of Forth
Firth of Clyde • Cramond • Traprain Law
Langbank • Govan • Longfaugh
Hunterston • Stichill • Lindisfarne
• Stanhope
• Whitecleugh
HEBRIDES

Ballynagloch
Ballinrees
• Dooey
Ballinderry
Lochar Moss • Middlebie
Balmaclellan • Birrens • Hadrian's
Carlingwark • Wall
• Mote of Mark • Durham

NORTH

SEA

Grange
• Armagh
Tully Lough • Newry
Lough Ramor • Grousehall
Ardagh • Kells • Monasterboice
Rinnegan • Newgrange • Bettystown
Athlone • Lagore • Donore
Clonmacnoise • Durrow • Tara
• Dowris • Dublin
Faddon More

Glankeen
• Ballyspellan

Cork

Isle of Man

IRISH

SEA

Gosforth

South Cave

Witham

Ilam
Heckington • Snettisham
Deopham • Ashmanhaugh
Hallaton • Saham Toney • Crownthorpe
Desborough • Hockwold • Carleton Rode
Baginton • Westhall
Steane • Hildersham
Fenny Stratford • Barkway • Sutton Hoo
Rhayader • Welwyn • Colchester
Carmarthen • Abergavenny • Oldcroft • Oxford • Essendon
Seven Sisters • Uffington • Thames • London • Bredgar
Margam • Chiseldon • Avebury • Ruscombe • Faversham
Southbroom • Compton • Aylesford • Canterbury
Polden Hill • Winchester • Lullingstone
Hinton St Mary • Wickham
Maiden Castle • Hod Hill

Portland

St Keverne

ENGLISH CHANNEL

N

0   100 Miles
0   150 Kilometres

'To many, perhaps to most people ... "Celtic" of any sort is ... a magic bag into which anything may be put, and out of which almost anything may come ... Anything is possible in the fabulous Celtic twilight, which is not so much a twilight of the Gods as of the reason.'

J.R.R. TOLKIEN 1963, 29–30

'those singularly beautiful curves, more beautiful perhaps in the parts that are not seen than in those that meet the eye, whose beauty [is] revealed in shadow more than in form.'

JOHN KEMBLE 1863, 79

Map of the United Kingdom and Ireland

Places referred to in the text (see also pp. 14–15).

Fig. 1 **Decorated shield boss**

An ornate boss decorates the centre of a shield dredged from the River Witham, near Lincoln (see figs 9 and 67 and p. 85).

River Witham, Lincolnshire 300–200 BC
Bronze, coral; W of boss 16.5 cm
British Museum, London

Chapter 1

In Search of the Celts

Fraser Hunter, Martin Goldberg, Julia Farley and Ian Leins

The white marble catches the expression on the dying warrior's face (fig. 2). Leaning heavily on his right arm, he stares downwards, his hair tousled, his moustache drooping. Solid drops of cold white blood ooze from a chest wound. He is naked, sitting on his shield with his weapons scattered round him. Around his neck is a gold torc, its twisted wires and rounded terminals carefully teased from the marble. In the Greek world, where the original sculpture was carved around 200 BC, he was a Celt. To the Romans who made this copy some 150 years later, he was a dying Gaul: their name for the same people, those barbarians who lay to the north of their Mediterranean world.[1]

Fig. 2 **A classical view of the Celts**

This sculpture typifies Mediterranean views of these 'barbarians' to their north. They were seen as warlike, hairy and naked: very different from civilized Greeks and Romans. The original sculpture was made in the Greek world, in Asia Minor, in the late third century BC to celebrate victories over invading Celtic tribes. This Roman marble copy may have been made for Julius Caesar to commemorate his victories in Gaul.

Rome *c.* 50–1 BC
Marble; H 94 cm
Capitoline Museum, Rome

Fig. 3 **Self-image: the Glauberg statue**

This life-size figure looks very different from the naked barbarian of classical imagination. Here, the well-dressed warrior wears complex armour and ornate jewellery. His 'leaf-crown' headdress marks him out as a person of special status, perhaps a leader or someone who could mediate with the otherworld.

Glauberg, Hessen, Germany 450–400 BC
Sandstone; H 1.86 m
Keltenwelt am Glauberg

A red sandstone man stares impassively into the distance (fig. 3). He too is a warrior: heavily armed, his sword by his side, a shield held in front of him, ornate body armour for protection. His strong muscular legs mark an active life. His right arm, raised to his chest, bears a bangle and finger-ring. Around his neck is a prominent torc. He wears an ornate headdress, a mark of special status, with two swollen 'ears' like large leaves.[2] This was no artist's fantasy: excavation of a grave he once guarded at the Glauberg in Germany revealed just such a man, his headdress beside his body, his sword sheathed. The jewellery, so carefully picked out on the statue, was worn by the dead man, gleaming gold on his body. He lived perhaps 200 years before the marble Gaul, but to someone from the Mediterranean world he too would have been a Celt. Whether he thought of himself that way is impossible now to tell. He looks unfamiliar to us: stylized, staring, with alien headgear and clothing.

bgeneratio

Fig. 4 The Book of Kells

Early medieval interlaced decoration is seen today as typically Celtic. This page from the Book of Kells is one of the masterpieces of the period. It is the opening of the Gospel of St Matthew (folio 34r). The Greek letters χρι (chi-rho-iota), the first letters of Christ's name, are decorated with interlaced designs and complex scroll patterns. Birds, animals and humans lurk in them. The style fuses influences from Britain, the Germanic world and the Mediterranean.

Kells, Co. Meath, Ireland AD 750–850
Vellum; H 33 cm
Trinity College Dublin

The letters on the early medieval manuscript are all but hidden by the patterns (fig. 4). The first three letters of the word Christ in Greek are elaborated almost beyond recognition. Patterns snake around them, interlacing, stepping, coiling. On closer inspection these resolve into fantastical contorted beasts and convoluted human figures; in one corner, cats and mice play with a piece of bread.[3] To one later observer, writing in the twelfth century, such manuscripts were 'the work, not of men, but of angels'.[4] To many people today, this is the epitome of Celtic art. But its makers did not call themselves Celts.

The gift shop lies on Edinburgh's Royal Mile (fig. 5). Half a dozen languages are being spoken around you as tourists crowd round the display cases, full of items advertised as Celtic: jewellery, scarves, jumpers, mugs, key rings. Some of the labels include unfamiliar words in Gaelic. The label 'Celtic' sells a country and an ideal to outsiders. But this is not just commercial exploitation of ancient history. Being Celtic is a real element of people's identity in Scotland, Ireland, Wales, the Isle of Man, Cornwall, Brittany and across the world for people who trace their ancestry to these places. This modern Celtic draws on strands from the past, real and imagined, varying widely in space and time.

All these things are called Celtic, and many more: music, dance, languages, beliefs and attitudes. Celt and Celtic have meant different things at different times to different people. This wide scope creates many problems. There is no single history, no single people and no easy answer to basic questions: 'who was a Celt?' or 'what is Celtic?' We will review the history of these ideas, highlighting some of the problems, before looking at the two areas most commonly seen as Celtic: language and art. Our main focus here is the art or, rather, the objects that carried the art, why they were decorated and what this can tell us. But first we need to clear some preconceptions.

Fig. 5 Selling Celts today

Interlaced textile design inspired by Celtic art.

Edinburgh 2015

What's in a name? Ancient views of Celts

We have no real idea what words people in ancient Europe used to describe themselves because they have not left us any historical records of their own: this is *pre*history. Greek and Roman writers spoke of people they called Celts (or Gauls) in these northern barbarian lands, but 'Celt' is not a Greek or Latin word in origin, which suggests classical writers adopted an indigenous term for these groups.[5] However, what these people meant by it, whether a specific tribe, a general grouping or something else entirely, and how its meaning changed over time, is largely lost.

Greek and Roman writers were unreliable witnesses, with only partial views of an alien world. Around 450 BC the Greek historian Herodotus had a vague notion that Celts were to be found near the source of the great river Danube and in south-west Iberia.[6] Over the next five centuries both lands and peoples became more familiar to a Mediterranean audience. Increasingly this was through conflict as the legions of Rome advanced north. One of the most detailed commentaries comes from Julius Caesar, who led armies into France (Gaul) in the 50s BC, although he records a world that had already changed in response to the threat posed by Rome. Caesar says that Gaul was divided into three parts, only one of which was Celtic, and notes that these people were called Celts in their own language but Gauls in Latin.[7] There was no single, consistent meaning of 'Celt' in the ancient sources – indeed, there was considerable confusion over the terminology in the ancient world[8] – but the impact of these early writings remains with us today.

Britain and Ireland were never referred to as Celtic by classical authors in the surviving sources: they were Albion or the Prettanic Isles, Hibernia or Ierne; the people were the Brittanni or the Hiberni, or were given tribal names such as Iceni, Caledonii, Catuvellauni, Picti.[9] However, the historian Tacitus did note similarities between southern Britain and Gaul,[10] and the inhabitants of these isles were clearly connected to and aware of what was happening among their neighbours.

Rediscovery

After the Roman period, for over a thousand years, the word 'Celt' fell from use. It was not applied by medieval historians such as Bede, nor in the surviving early medieval literature of these islands, which speaks of Gaels and Scots, Picts and Britons, and a kaleidoscope of shifting territorial, dynastic and political groupings. With the Renaissance, scholars rediscovered classical texts talking of Celts which had survived in monastic libraries, and began to get new glimpses of an ancient past. One of the first was the Scottish scholar George Buchanan; in 1582 he connected place names recorded in classical sources to a series of imagined migrations, including the Celts.[11]

In the seventeenth and eighteenth centuries, scholars increasingly grappled with the question of Europe before written history. They were reliant on this mixed bag of fragmentary anecdotes and stereotypes surviving from Mediterranean sources, and a view shaped by the Bible where the world was populated by the sons of Noah after the Flood in 2348 BC.[12] But new types of evidence were coming to people's attention. Enlightenment scholars recognized similarities between the languages spoken on the edges of the newly united Britain – in Scotland, Ireland, the Isle of Man, Wales and Cornwall – and linked this to Breton. It must, they thought, mark an original ancient language shared between Britain, Ireland and France. In 1703 Paul-Yves Pezron, a Breton monk, associated this with the Celts who were mentioned by Julius Caesar and called the original language Celtic. He argued this was the earliest tongue spoken across Europe, the ancestor of all other European languages, and in a process of rather wishful word-association traced the Celts back to peoples named in the Bible.[13] Edward Lhuyd, Keeper of the Ashmolean Museum in Oxford, recorded these linguistic connections in the field. His 1707 publication noted the similarities, but he was hesitant to take the story as far across Europe as Pezron had. Yet Lhuyd and Pezron shared a similar logic. The people occupying Britain, Ireland and Brittany before written history must be the people mentioned by Caesar: the Celts. Their language would be given the name Celtic.

From this came further theories. The Celts were first recorded near the Mediterranean lands, so they must have invaded into the west. Thus was born a series of entirely imaginary Celtic migrations, which popular views have still not cast off. The language revealed links, the classical sources gave names and early antiquarians, struggling to understand prehistory, seized on this structure and terminology. They began to identify what they thought were Celtic objects or monuments (fig. 6). Remains of stone circles survived especially in western Britain and Ireland – the area where the classical authors mentioned mysterious priests called druids – so these must be druidical monuments.[14] These attempts to understand the past brought together pieces of evidence that we now know were thousands of years apart: the monuments were built long before the classical authors wrote of the druids. The story became increasingly complicated as more and more layers were built upon it. From the mid-nineteenth century ancient artefacts increasingly came into the picture, decorated with unfamiliar styles that came to be called Celtic art.

Fig. 6 **Stukeley and the Celts**

The antiquary William Stukeley (1687–1765) was the first to argue in print that the Celts were responsible for surviving ancient monuments in Britain. He referred to the great Neolithic stone circle and henge at Avebury as a 'Celtic Temple'. In fact, these stones were erected thousands of years before the ancient Greeks first wrote of people called Celts.

Stukeley 1743, plate XV
Paper
British Library, London

Critique

Yet the story was flawed. Many of the arguments were built on shaky foundations. Through most of the later nineteenth and twentieth centuries, linguists studied the clear links in languages across Europe, and trusted the archaeologists to provide a cultural and historical background. The archaeologists built on these theories of a linguistically connected Europe but were often talking about different things. Much of the problem came from a desire to build coherent histories out of prehistory. Different strands of evidence were mixed together and assumed to be related: classical sources, modern and ancient languages, art styles, burial evidence, hints of ancient religious beliefs from Roman inscribed altars, the myths of early Ireland and Wales. In truth, these were all telling different stories, of different times and places, overlapping at points but differing in others, as you would expect across a diverse continent over several thousand years of history.

A hot and at times bad-tempered dispute has been running since the 1980s. On one side are the so-called 'Celtomaniacs', scholars (and a large public) who follow the conventional view of a connected Celtic Europe in later prehistory, stretching from the Atlantic to the Danube and beyond. On the other side, and mostly from Britain, are the 'Celtosceptics', arguing that this was fatally flawed and concealed tremendous regional diversity and more complex histories.[15] Much of the debate has focused on Britain, where Celts have become and remain a key part of many people's identities. It has been much less heated on the Continent, where Celtic identity has little relevance to modern national identities and the Celts can be safely confined to prehistory. More extreme ends of the debate have been dying down recently, so what is left? There are both connections *and* differences over a very broad reach of time and space. You need to define what you mean: someone who studies the German Iron Age is not dealing with the same 'Celtic' as someone studying medieval Ireland.

So why do we still use this difficult word 'Celtic'? It is problematic, but familiar: a word that people use all the time. We should try to explain it, not just ignore it. It is best understood as a shorthand, but an ambiguous one: people know approximately what you mean, but you need to specify where and when you are talking about to understand it. From this muddle, two strands do indeed provide links over large areas. One is language, the other is art. What can these tell us about the idea of the Celts?

Language

Elements of ancient languages that we call Celtic can be recognized from Ireland to Turkey. The earliest hard evidence comes from inscriptions from south-west Iberia and northern Italy in the eighth to sixth centuries BC.[16] Brief hints of vocabulary and grammar in these ancient texts reveal

Original territory of the Celts

Zone of expansion of the Celts

Celtiberians

Direction of expansion

GERMANS

ATLANTIC

OCEAN

La Tène

Hallstatt

SCYTHIANS

VENETI

DACIANS

BLACK SEA

CELTIBERIANS

LIGURIANS

ETRUSCANS

IBERIANS

Rome

THRACIANS

GALATIANS

MEDITERRANEAN

SEA

Delphi

N

| 0 | | 400 Miles |
| 0 | | 600 Kilometres |

Fig. 7 **Celtic migrations
– the traditonal view**

For much of the twentieth century, it was argued that Celtic languages and Celtic art were spread from a central European homeland by migrating Celts. Whilst the classical sources do attest to ancient population movements, this traditional model of the Celts as a single people who migrated across broad swathes of Europe is now widely challenged.

languages related to ones still spoken in modern times in Brittany, Cornwall, Wales, Ireland and Scotland. But the evidence for these prehistoric languages is, by definition, very sparse. What little we know of their development takes us back beyond the cusp of history.

Celtic languages were long argued to have developed in central Europe and spread east and west with migrating Celts (fig. 7), but this view is being increasingly challenged.[17] One intriguing recent theory takes the freshly recognized evidence for an early Celtic language in Spain and argues that the Celtic language group developed in westernmost Europe, probably along the Atlantic seaways, during the Bronze Age between 3,000 and 4,000 years ago (fig. 8).[18] It was a branch of the Indo-European language family, a widespread language group spoken from India to the Atlantic. One theory sees Celtic as 'Indo-European spoken with an Iberian accent', created when people who were used to speaking Iberian (a non-Indo-European language)

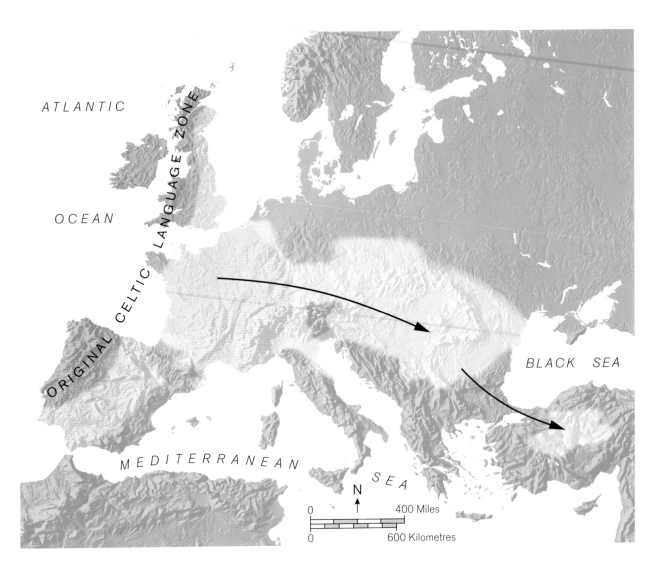

Fig. 8 **An alternative view of Celtic languages**

Current research proposes that what we call Celtic languages developed along the Atlantic seaways sometime in the Bronze Age (perhaps around 2000 BC), and subsequently spread across much of Continental Europe. Different colours represent the likely stages in the spread of the Celtic language in the Bronze Age (light orange) and Iron Age (yellow).

tried this new tongue.[19] Archaeological evidence shows there were widespread contacts up and down the Atlantic coasts of western Europe at this time, which implies an ability to communicate. Celtic may originally have spread as a *lingua franca* along the seaways, with regional versions diverging from one another over time.[20]

The languages had a core area in western Europe but were clearly widespread, extending at some periods across much of the Continent. We call them Celtic, but this does not link them to a single group called the Celts. The name has been applied to these languages only recently, and in any case a shared linguistic heritage does not equate to a single shared cultural identity. Not all English-speakers are English; not all Spanish-speakers are Spanish. Languages can be widespread owing to shared historical events and communication needs, but this does not create a single people. There may have been related languages across much of Europe, but they are unlikely to have been the only ones. Today most people in Britain speak only one language but this is unusual: in many parts of the world speaking several languages is the norm. And even this single language, English, can vary tremendously within one country. A person from Shetland and a person from Suffolk may struggle to communicate as their versions of English are so dissimilar. So too in the past: Europe would have been a patchwork of languages and dialects, spoken by different groups in different areas. The early Celtic languages themselves were probably a spectrum of dialects, shifting slightly from valley to valley and island to island. Languages may have common roots, but this does not make the speakers a common people.

At times when we have substantial evidence for these Celtic languages, it is their diversity that is striking, not their unity. Early medieval inscriptions illustrate the languages used in western and northern Britain and Ireland in the fifth to seventh centuries AD, and we see them in flux, changing dramatically over a few hundred years. People must have found ways to communicate, but their mother languages – Welsh, Irish, Pictish – were not mutually intelligible even though they lived close together and were in regular contact.[21] For instance, Saint Columba, travelling from the west coast of Scotland to the east in the sixth century, needed an interpreter.[22] Through the medieval period, as the nations of Ireland, Scotland, Wales and England were forming, there was no sense of linguistic or cultural unity: no Celtic nations.

The existence of this long-lived language group across Europe does not help much with our archaeological evidence. Language did not dictate what objects people used, how they chose to decorate them or why they decided to bury them. It is the objects, and the art styles that adorned them and made them potent, which are our key focus in this book.

Celtic art – a history

Our second strand of widespread connections is art. This shows clear similarities from the Atlantic to the Black Sea in the last few centuries BC. It seems stylized and ambiguous in contrast to naturalistic classical art, with only suggestions of human and animal forms. Complex, swirling, curvilinear shapes evoke twisting vegetation, entrancing or confusing the onlooker. It appears mostly on valuable objects of bronze and gold, and on restricted, powerful items, such as jewellery, weaponry, chariot gear and feasting equipment. Similar styles continued for a millennium or more. They were fused with other traditions from the Germanic and classical worlds to create the distinctive art style of early medieval Britain and Ireland, which adorned sculpture and manuscripts as well as valued metals. This art was more than just decoration, or art for art's sake (which is a very modern idea): it carried messages and gave these objects (and their users) a power and significance.

The recognition of this art has a long and convoluted pedigree. Early scholars did not consider art when they thought of the Celts. Their eyes were focused on language or on much older prehistoric material, such as stone circles, stone axes and bronze swords. But in the middle of the nineteenth century a series of scholars identified connected art styles as they began to organize collections in museums, and as more finds were brought from the earth by the disturbances of industrialization and agricultural improvement. This definition of a Celtic art was a British and Irish phenomenon, created by a group of scholars who clearly knew one another's work so closely that identifying the original spark is now difficult. In 1851 in Edinburgh, Daniel Wilson provided an early definition of Celtic arts and related these to interlace ornament and the early Christian arts of Ireland.[23] In Sheffield, John Obadiah Westwood wrote a section on 'Celtic art' for Owen Jones's influential 1856 *Grammar of Ornament*.[24] These writers focused on early medieval material, and Wilson traced the influences in Scotland through medieval and post-medieval times. But it was John Kemble in 1857 who realized that Iron Age material showed similar designs, especially a spiralling motif with a flared, trumpet-like terminal.[25] He was influenced by Augustus Franks at the British Museum, who had access to the latest finds from Britain and the Continent. Franks organized the plates and accompanying text for Kemble's posthumous publication *Horae Ferales* (figs 9–10).[26] The plates drew heavily on British Museum collections, much as Wilson had drawn on the Edinburgh ones, and the different strengths of these museums led to different foci: Franks on the Iron Age, Wilson on the early medieval. 'Celtic art' took on a broad meaning that spanned these two quite different periods. This definition of a Celtic art was largely a British phenomenon: Franks quoted Continental parallels, and Continental scholars were aware of this work,[27] but it was not widely adopted on the Continent until Joseph Déchelette's magisterial synthesis of the Iron Age in 1914.[28]

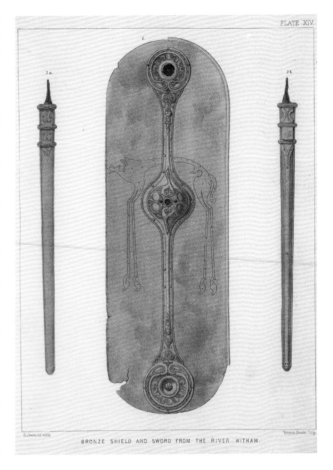

Fig. 9 **Rediscovering Celtic art:**
Horae Ferales

The publication of *Horae Ferales* in 1863 was a milestone in the recognition of Celtic art. Iron Age objects such as the bronze shield from the river Witham (Lincolnshire) were identified as Celtic for the first time. The figure of an animal was once attached to the front: rivet holes and differences in surface patina outline the silhouette of a long-legged male boar, which is clearly visible in this plate.

Kemble 1863, plate XIV
Paper; page H 31 cm

Many, not one – a view of Celtic arts

Most books on Celtic art seek to show continuity from prehistory up to the early medieval period; some extend this to the present day. It is traditional to trace a thread of development, waxing and waning over time. This view sees Celtic art starting across much of Europe *c.* 500–200 BC, but becoming largely restricted to Britain and Ireland in the last centuries BC. It was subdued under Rome but then re-emerged in the so-called 'Dark Ages' in Ireland and Scotland in the later first millennium AD. Here it was kept alive in the western edges of these Atlantic islands until it was reclaimed by modern resurgent Celtic nations.

This is not our story. We see not one style, but several; not one history, but many. There were links, but also dissimilarities. These Celtic arts – plural – need to be placed into their own histories. In the chapters of this book you will see different Celtic arts in different times and places, not one developing tradition. There were both widespread similarities and regional variations. These styles sparked to life at moments of contact with other cultures, which created a need for expression or influenced changes: in the fifth century BC through contact with the Mediterranean world; in the first century AD through Roman conquest; or in the seventh century AD with the conversion of Anglo-Saxon Northumbria to Christianity under Irish influence. No consistent style unites these arts across two and a half millennia: it would be surprising if it did. Rather, we see a repeated habit of synthesizing and modifying external sources of inspiration, transforming Mediterranean naturalism to more abstract styles, and drawing on and reinventing older motifs. These different Celtic arts were people's way of marking beliefs and expressing power, understanding their own heritage and their place in the world.

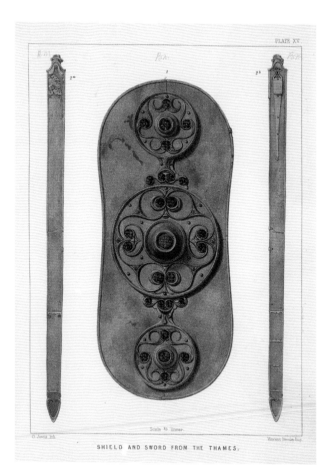

SHIELD AND SWORD FROM THE THAMES.

Fig. 10 **The power of publication**

A spate of discoveries in the nineteenth century prompted scholars to think about what this unusual material meant. The shield from Battersea was found in 1855; publications like *Horae Ferales* meant it became well known to scholars.

Kemble 1863, plate XV
Paper; page H 31 cm

We will look at five key periods:

The origins of an innovative non-naturalistic curvilinear art style during the later Iron Age, *c.* 450–150 BC, across much of temperate Europe (fig. 11). It is often called La Tène art after one of the key findspots, a lake in western Switzerland where large quantities of finds were discovered in the late nineteenth century. This is discussed in Chapters 3 and 4.

Object and art styles changed drastically across much of Europe at the end of the Iron Age (*c.* 150 BC–AD 50) as larger-scale societies developed and the growing power of Rome became a major influence. Earlier complex, very individual styles were replaced by more mass-produced items. Only in Britain and Ireland did curving, swirly styles continue and flourish. With the Roman conquest of much of Britain, styles of Celtic art exploded across the country. Initially this was a way for people to express resistance to Rome, but it became a distinctive part of life in Roman Britain (*c.* AD 50–250; fig. 12). This is covered in Chapers 5 and 6.

Emerging out of a Roman world in Britain and Ireland was a later Celtic art (*c.* AD 250–800). This was no throwback to earlier times, or mystical survival beyond Rome's heavy hand; the Roman world was the key crucible for its creation (fig. 13). It was a set of artistic tools for a new world shaped by the impact of Rome, and speaking to a newly Christian Europe. This was forged from a fusion of earlier Iron Age motifs reinvented in the Roman period, Anglo-Saxon art and classical Mediterranean designs (Chapters 7 and 8).

Fig. 11
Origins: early Celtic art

The curvilinear decoration on this bronze fitting from Brentford is typical of much early Celtic art. The design is based on tendrils and coils of vegetation, but the swirling lines have moved beyond naturalism to form intriguing patterns. The function of the object is unknown.

Brentford, Middlesex 350–250 BC
Bronze; D 8.3 cm
Museum of London

Fig. 12
The effect of the Roman world

This copper-alloy neck collar (torc) is typical of the local styles that flourished in Britain under Roman rule. The object type and its decoration drew on earlier Iron Age traditions but were reinvented in this newly Roman world.

Probably from Stichill, Scottish Borders AD 50–200
Copper alloy; D19.5 cm
National Museums Scotland, Edinburgh

Fig. 13
Fusing traditions: later Celtic art

The disc from Donore brings together art from two different cultural traditions. The swirls and scrolls in the outer circle developed from earlier Celtic art, while the interlacing beasts in the inner circle come from the Anglo-Saxon and Germanic world. A red-eyed beast in the centre grips the door handle.

Donore, Co. Meath, Ireland
AD 700–750
Copper alloy, tinned, glass inlays;
D 13.5 cm
National Museum of Ireland, Dublin

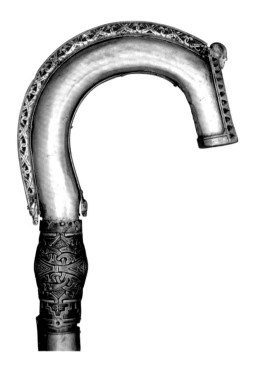

Fig. 14
Reinventing and preserving older traditions

This Irish crozier was an object of veneration for centuries. Around AD 900 an old yew-wood staff was encased in brass. Its interlaced decoration is a mixture between local and Viking art. The later covering of the handle is decorated in eleventh-century Viking style. A small chamber once held a saint's relic.

Ireland AD 900–1200
Copper alloy, silver, wood;
D of crook 22 cm
British Museum, London

Some of these earlier traditions were reinvented and preserved in medieval Scotland and Ireland (Chapter 9). From AD 800, raiding and settlement by Vikings along the western seaways led among other things to new art forms that mixed local and Scandinavian habits. These were dominated by interlaced designs. But there were also deliberate attempts by local leaders to preserve or (more often) adopt and reinvent the earlier traditions (fig. 14).

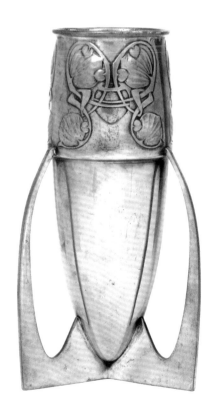

Fig. 15
Celtic revival

The Manx artist Archibald Knox designed this Celtic Revival vase for Liberty's of London. Its interlacing decoration was inspired by early medieval sculpture from the Isle of Man.

1906–9
Pewter; H 29 cm
Victoria and Albert Museum, London

A conscious and deliberate reimagining of the Celtic past took place within the context of a newly united Britain from the eighteenth century onwards, associated with artistic, literary and political revival (Chapter 10). This had different strands at different times, from the invented poems of the fake Gaelic bard Ossian, which sparked the imaginations of Romantic artists, to the flourishing Celtic Revival of the later nineteenth and early twentieth centuries, which was fuelled by new archaeological finds and a fresh appreciation of the value of this ancient art. This is ongoing in the modern Celtic nations, although we will stop our story in the early twentieth century (fig. 15).

A partial picture – deposition, survival and recovery

We should enter some cautionary words about our evidence. These fantastic artefacts decorated with Celtic art were highly valued: even the smallest brooch would have been a precious item. As a result, they were not just lost or thrown away. Finds come overwhelmingly from burials and hoards, not from everyday settlements, and these habits of burying objects varied according to the beliefs and needs of the time. Rich burials were most common in the sixth to early fourth centuries BC, at a key time of social change in Europe. This was not accidental: lavish funerals often occurred at times of change and uncertainty, when families and communities used them to show their status, cement their position or bring people together. From the later fourth century BC, burials became much plainer and more standardized: there was less individual expression and competition. Instead, many objects adorned with Celtic art from the later Iron Age come from hoards and other deliberate deposits. These may well be connected to the development of larger social groups, with shared sacrifices of wealth acting to bring smaller units together.[29]

Such habits varied both in time and space. In Britain, for instance, the bulk of our Iron Age burial evidence comes from East Yorkshire. In most of the country, bodies were presumably cremated and the ashes scattered, or left to decay and return to nature; they had no grand send-off with rich artefacts. The same is true elsewhere: large parts of France, for example, had no burial tradition for most of the Iron Age, and even areas that adopted rich burials in one period, such as north-east France in the fifth century BC, often changed their practices in later centuries.[30] In the early medieval period, the areas of Scotland and Ireland where this decorated material was manufactured had no tradition of lavish burials: it was alien to their newly Christian ways. Instead, many of the richest pieces of later Celtic art turn up far from their homelands, in the pagan graves of Anglo-Saxon England or Viking Norway where these exotica were highly valued.

Hoards and deliberate deposits were also a very varied habit (see pp. 103–5). In Yorkshire in the third century BC, for instance, swords are found in burials but never in hoards, while in northern Ireland and south-eastern Britain, they come only from watery deposits, never burials. The rest of Britain had no strong tradition of either burials or hoards at that time, so almost no weapons survive. Such choices made in the past – to bury an item or not – impose tremendous restrictions on our knowledge today. We see glimpses of Celtic arts only where people chose to bury them. These times and places are of great interest, and tell us that interesting and unusual things were happening there and then. However, we must remember that such material could have been in use elsewhere but not deliberately placed into the ground. Our picture of Celtic art objects is a picture of habits of burial and deposition, not how these things were employed in life (fig. 16).

Fig. 16 **Celtic art uncovered**

When one sees beautiful decorated objects, it is easy to forget that these were once buried as offerings to unknown gods or as grave goods. Excavations at North Berstead in 2008 uncovered a richly furnished grave, including a remarkable helmet with openwork decorated plates attached to it.

North Berstead, West Sussex 100–1 BC
Copper alloy

Why Celtic?

What we show in this book are not the arts of Celtic-speaking peoples: people can speak different languages just as they can use different objects, and language is learned, not biological. Nor are these the arts of a genetically related people, 'the Celts', because art is not genetically determined. Populations mixed and moved in prehistoric Europe.[31] They carried their languages with them, taught them to their children and learned to communicate with others, just as they carried objects with them, inherited, gifted and exchanged them. There never was a single pan-European ancient people called the Celts; there was no single culture; there was no single language. There were relations and connections, but the certainties of a Celtic Europe rapidly unravel under the sharp scrutiny of critical scholarship. It is a more complicated story than the history of a single people and a more fascinating one because of it. This book will explore the story of the decorated artefacts that these peoples made, used, exchanged and deposited. We focus on the period from *c.* 500 BC to AD 800, but extend our story in Britain and Ireland almost to the present day. The objects are beguiling, the art fantastic, but this is not just a book about beautiful things. This was not art for art's sake, but art with a meaning, a power and a story. It is a tale of Europe's first complex art style, how and why it was created, what it was used for and what it might have meant. How it was constantly reinvented at times of contact and change, as worlds collided and different cultures came into contact. And how and why elements of this shared style lived on for over 2,000 years.

Chapter 2

Fig. 17 **Detail of the Battersea shield**

Some of the decoration on the front of the
Battersea shield can be seen as otherworldly
faces. Depending on which way up and from
which angle you view the design, the same
elements resolve into different creatures,
some strange and menacing. This way up, the
enamelled roundels under the main central boss
resemble a wide-eyed bull with bulbous-ended
horns. Bulls or cows are also depicted on
similar parts of the Witham shield (see p. 1).

River Thames at Battersea 350–50 BC
Bronze, glass; D of panel 16.9 cm
British Museum, London

Approaching Celtic Art

Jody Joy[1]

To our eyes Celtic art can look strange, unnatural, yet entrancing. Its meanings are mostly lost to us, but we can appreciate its power and complexity, even if it seems to come from a different world. In fact there is no single Celtic art. Instead a range of different 'Celtic arts' may be observed over a period of around 1,500 years through the Iron Age, Roman and early medieval periods, their influence continuing to the present day. While the persistent use of curvilinear motifs gives the illusion of homogeneity and the impression of threads of continuity from 500 BC to AD 800 and beyond, we look back on these objects from a privileged position and establish connections that would have been impossible for people to make in the past. These objects do not form a single homogenous group. Instead we can see a series of different Celtic arts, varying greatly in terms of the types of objects that are decorated and the materials used to make them.

Different ways of seeing

From 500 BC, around the same time as the emergence of early Celtic art, a very different kind of art was being developed in Greece: a realistic style that tried to accurately re-create nature. It was used especially on sculpture and painted pottery, and was a forerunner of the classical art of Rome.[2] It still dominates how we perceive art today in the Western world, where naturalism and realism are often seen as key features of 'good art'. Only in the last 150 years or so has this approach been challenged with the introduction of more impressionistic or abstract aesthetics such as Cubism.

Fig. 18 **A face or a mask?**

Brooches with the heads of humans, animals or fantastical creatures are known as 'mask' fibulae and are some of the most common artefacts decorated in the earliest styles of Celtic art.

Chýnov (Bohemia), Czech Republic 450–400 BC
Bronze; L 6.8 cm
National Museum, Prague

Fig. 19 **Openwork bronze belt-clasp**

Does the decoration on this belt-clasp show pairs of fantastical creatures on either side with a human head in the centre, or the left- and right-hand sides of the same beast with a front view of its human-like face?

Weiskirchen (Rhineland), Germany 450–400 BC
Bronze, coral; W 6.6 cm
Rheinisches Landesmuseum, Trier

Fig. 20 **Model canoe prow ornament**

In the Trobriand Islands, elaborately carved and decorated sea-going canoes carry people on voyages to neighbouring islands to engage in a traditional trading system called the Kula. The quality of the decoration on the vessels enhances their owners' personal prestige and the standing of their village. The carvings on objects like this prow ornament are considered to play an active role in the encounter. The complex designs are intended to intimidate or even mesmerize potential trading partners. In a similar way, the sinuous designs on ancient Celtic art may have been believed to hold magical properties, drawing in the eye and captivating the viewer.

Kiriwina, Trobriand Islands, before 1919
Wood; L 22.5 cm
British Museum, London

Classical realism was very different from Celtic art, and embodied contrasting ways of seeing the world. Celtic art was more ambiguous and harder to read. This was probably the intention of its makers: these were not 'primitive' artists unable to re-create their world accurately, and their art was just as important as classical art to the early history of Europe.[3]

Recent attempts to understand Celtic art have sought to explore its ambiguity. It has been seen as a *technology of enchantment*,[4] much like the complex art found in parts of the Pacific (fig. 20) or among Maoris, that was able to beguile and dazzle the uninitiated viewer through its highly skilled manufacture and complexity, to the extent that they could not understand how it was made or the meaning of its decoration. Complicated interlocking designs with no obvious beginning or end 'trapped' the attention by leading the eye in different directions.[5] Representations of semi-human creatures, mythical beasts or hints of vegetation[6] blurred the boundaries between myth and reality (fig. 18). Such enigmatic designs sparked the curiosity of the viewer and engaged the imagination;[7] stylized animals and humans might evoke fantastical creatures and deities. Pairs of animals depicted side by side (fig. 19) are perhaps attempts to show the left- and right-hand sides of the animal simultaneously, indicating a different way of representing the world.[8]

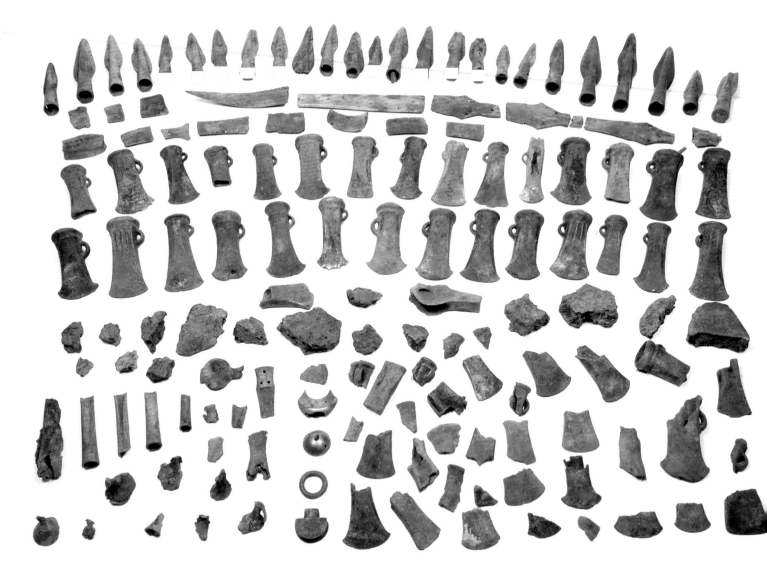

Patterns over time and space

The Celtic arts explored in this book were used in diverse ways and took various forms in different times and places, spanning much of Europe over 1,500 years. The earliest Celtic art was very different from that which had gone before. In the later Bronze Age and earlier Iron Age (c. 1250–600 BC), decoration consisted of simple geometric patterns (fig. 37). Across Europe at this time, thousands of virtually identical objects, particularly axes, were made. Many were deposited together in hoards that might contain hundreds of individual items (fig. 21). Some of these objects were poorly made and many were unused. It is thought that these hoards were in part intended as offerings to the gods.[9] Whatever the motivation, the emphasis was on the quantity of objects rather than their quality: they did not hold the eye for close inspection.[10]

Fig. 21 **The Eaton II hoard**

This late Bronze Age hoard includes socketed axes, spearheads and gouges. The vast majority of the 145 objects are of standardized form and may have been buried as an offering to the gods.

Eaton, Norwich, Norfolk 950–750 BC
Bronze
Norwich Castle Museum

In contrast, during the later Iron Age (*c.* 500 BC–AD 50) much of the art was extremely well made and detailed: individual, bespoke items with an emphasis on the quality of manufacture rather than quantity. One of the most spectacular examples is the 'Great Torc' from Snettisham (fig. 22). This is a technical masterpiece manufactured from just over a kilogram of a gold-silver alloy. The neck-ring comprises eight 'ropes', each formed of eight hand-hammered wires twisted together. To achieve consistency and evenness of twist the diameter of each wire needed to be virtually identical. The two terminals, which would have been worn at the front, are hollow and were made using the 'lost wax' technique: they were modelled in wax, covered in clay and then heated to melt out the wax, leaving a void behind. This was a perfect mould of the wax model, ready to take the molten metal. Each terminal was cast directly onto the neck-ring. The person who did this was highly skilled and supremely confident in their abilities: a mistake in the casting could ruin days of work. The cast decoration on the terminals (fig. 30) was sharpened up by hand with very fine tools. The individuality of these objects was ensured by the techniques and methods employed to make them (see pp. 106–7). The great investment of time and effort, together with the lost wax casting technique (where the moulds can be used only once), means that the Snettisham Great Torc is a unique object and exact replication of it would have been virtually impossible.

Fig. 22 **What is a torc?**

Torcs are neck-rings with elaborate terminals; the hoop is often made from twisted wires. They come in a range of sizes and were worn by both sexes and possibly even children. Put on at an angle, one terminal was pulled forward to widen the gap.

Snettisham, Norfolk 100–50 BC
Gold-silver alloy; D 20.0 cm
British Museum, London

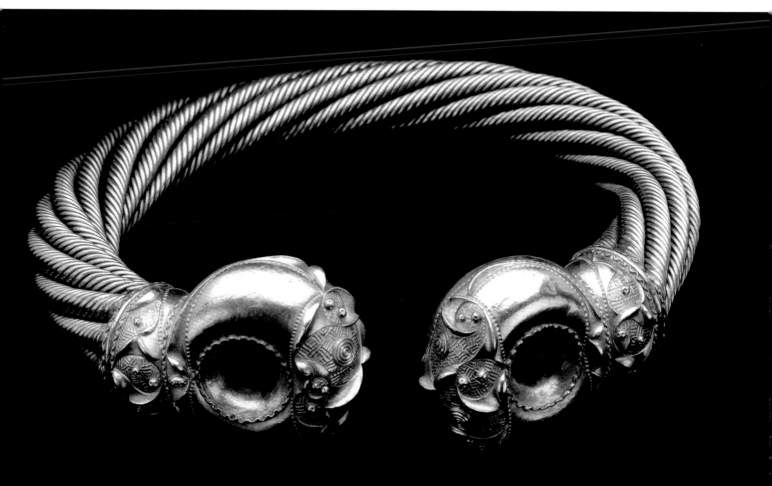

A very restricted range of metals was embellished with Celtic art during the Iron Age: predominantly gold alloys and bronze (an alloy of copper and tin). Many different techniques were used to enhance the effect of the patterns, such as inlays of red coral and glass to contrast with bronze, or inscribed and raised decoration to form subtle and intricate designs (see figs 17 and 95).[11] Everyday materials such as iron, stone, wood and pottery rarely featured such complex curvilinear motifs.

This Iron Age trend for highly crafted, individual objects was later reversed, with the emphasis once more on the quantity of artefacts produced rather than their uniqueness. On the Continent this took place from the second century BC as societies became more centralized and developed stronger links to the Roman world. In Britain it occurred slightly later, when much of the island became part of the Roman empire during the first century AD.[12] While we still find some extremely well-made items, a significant proportion were quite crudely manufactured and poorly decorated. However, this did make versions of Celtic art more widely available on smaller, less showy objects such as everyday brooches (fig. 24),[13] or as motifs on typical Roman artefacts like seal boxes and bronze vessels.[14] Standardized techniques of manufacture were used, for example die-stamped decoration, where a die was made and thin strips of metal hammered over it to create raised patterns. These dies could produce many identically decorated objects, including metal plaques applied to wooden boxes and caskets.[15]

During the Roman period new metals such as brass (an alloy of copper and zinc) and decorative techniques like enamelling were used (fig. 23).[16] These gave objects a very different look and feel; the enamels were

Fig. 23 **A colourful strap fitting**

Strap fittings like this one were made for horse harness. They are often lavishly ornamented on the front with glass or enamel, and have loops at the back to take the leather strap. This example is decorated with red, blue and white enamel.

Westhall, Suffolk AD 1–100
Copper alloy, enamel; L 8.2 cm, W 7.8 cm
British Museum, London

Fig. 24 **Art of the everyday**

In the Roman period, simple brooches often carried designs from Celtic art. This disc brooch has a triskele (triple-legged pattern) hammered out from a thin copper-alloy sheet which is fitted over the front.

Brough Castle, Cumbria AD 100–200
Copper alloy, enamelled and tinned; D 3.1 cm
British Museum, London

Fig. 25 **Brooches from the St Ninian's Isle treasure**

These twelve brooches were part of a larger hoard of twenty-eight silver-gilt, decorated objects. Found in 1958 by Douglas Coutts, a schoolboy working on excavations at a medieval church, the treasure was contained in a wooden box, buried under a slab marked with a cross.

St Ninian's Isle, Shetland AD 750–825
Silver; central brooch D 10.8 cm
National Museums Scotland, Edinburgh

multicoloured, while brass is more yellow than bronze and has a gold-like sheen. In contrast to the Iron Age, gold itself was rarely utilized.

As Roman power waned from the fourth century AD onwards, new versions of Celtic art adorned key parts of small, often personal objects, such as brooches and pins.[17] Their two-dimensional designs were enhanced with coloured enamel. Most were bronze, but some were of silver: a valuable material that became available in northern Britain in the fourth to sixth centuries AD from the recycling of Roman objects (see fig. 142).

Around AD 700, these new styles of Celtic art fused with other influences from the Anglo-Saxon and classical worlds. The resulting style (termed the 'Insular fusion', see pp. 178–9) was applied to a markedly wider variety of materials: not just copper alloys and silver, but stone and parchment as well. It appeared over a range of different scales too: massive stone crosses dominated the landscape, while fine decorative panels on brooches or books demanded close scrutiny. Manuscripts were often embellished in minute detail, in a variety of colourful pigments. Occasionally, very exotic imported materials were used. For example, the cover of the psalter (book of psalms) found in 2006 in a bog at Faddan More in central Ireland is lined with papyrus from the eastern Mediterranean, probably Egypt.[18]

New techniques were adopted for enhancing metal, such as inlaying semi-precious stones like amber or garnets, and creating patterns by soldering small wires or balls onto the surface (techniques known as filigree and granulation respectively). Decoration on some metal objects mimicked the texture of sharp-edged chips chiselled out of wood (so-called 'chip-carving'). Coating the surface of more common metals like bronze with gold (gilding) also became increasingly widespread. For example, the early medieval hoard from a church on St Ninian's Isle in Shetland includes brooches that are very similar to each other in size, shape and design (fig. 25).[19] Several of them may derive from the same original model, but each was finished with different panels of decoration, gilding and gem settings to create variety. Gilded interlace mimicked the gold filigree of more luxuriously embellished ornaments such as the Hunterston and Tara brooches (figs 166 and 182).[20]

On Christian objects, art was again used to create highly individual pieces, whether stone monuments, fine metalwork or religious manuscripts. The time and effort that went into making these Christian devotional objects was itself an act of religious piety. Our knowledge of Christian beliefs and iconography allows us to understand the meanings behind this art in ways that are simply not possible for earlier periods (see Chapter 8).

How was the art used?

For much of the time that Celtic arts were made and used we have no written texts to inform us about their significance or provide clues about meaning. As a result we are almost wholly reliant on the objects themselves and the contexts in which they are found to try to answer these fundamental questions. It is therefore virtually impossible to be certain what this art meant. By looking carefully at the objects and reflecting on the activities in which they were used we can make more progress, especially if we ask two simple questions: what does the art do, and why decorate?[21]

Although there were different Celtic arts across Europe from 500 BC to the early medieval period, it is possible to draw some connections. Celtic art objects can be categorized into five major areas of social importance or 'arenas': warfare, eating and drinking, personal appearance, horse and chariot gear, and religion (see Chapter 4). These varied in importance through time. In the Iron Age, for instance, specifically religious items are rare, although much of the art probably had a religious meaning (see Chapter 3). With the widespread adoption of Christianity by AD 700, many decorated objects had a particular religious role in Christian practices, while art virtually disappeared from weaponry and feasting gear. These changes through time tell us about wider social concerns, as well as providing clues about what Celtic art did, why it was made and how it was used in different periods. We will return to these themes throughout the book.

Decorating an object is one way to make it stand out and so give it the power to impress and influence audiences in a variety of social arenas. Ornamented weaponry, especially sword hilts and scabbards, includes some of the finest examples of Celtic art made during the Iron Age and Roman periods (see figs 60, 61, 69 and 116). Such objects make it clear that being a warrior was an important part of being a man across Europe (see Chapter 4, note 4), as can be seen from the Glauberg statue (fig. 3), thought to represent a warlike 'hero',[22] and the rare 'display' shields recovered from watery contexts in Britain, of which the Battersea shield is probably the finest example (fig. 26). Given its excellent condition and intricate designs, it is unlikely to have been used in the heat of battle. Perhaps it was intended for elaborate display and posturing, to create the appearance of an impressive warrior. This might have been just as important as practical skill in battle (see Chapter 4). In contrast, decorated military equipment is rare from the early medieval period, or perhaps the conditions did not exist for such objects to survive. While Anglo-Saxon burials often included weapons, people in northern and western Britain and Ireland (where Celtic art was most common at this time) were not buried with their belongings.

It is not surprising that many of the objects decorated with Celtic art were items of jewellery or containers utilized in the consumption of food and drink: people wanted to impress onlookers through their appearance or to influence others at social occasions. For example, stave-built wooden

Fig. 26 **Made for showing off?**

Held aloft in flamboyant display, the highly polished bronze of the Battersea shield with its raised decoration and red glass inlay would have been a great spectacle.

River Thames at Battersea, London 350–50 BC
Bronze, glass; L 77.7 cm
British Museum, London

tankards from the later Iron Age and early Roman period (*c.* 50 BC–AD 150) often have beautifully ornamented handles; some are encased in bronze (fig. 27). These are large vessels with capacities of around two litres, which were used to hold alcoholic beverages, probably ale. Perhaps they were passed among a small group, each taking a turn to drink. Where wooden parts of tankards survive, analysis shows they were made from yew, which is poisonous. This means that the alcohol could have been tainted, making drinking from these vessels an act of bravado as well as endurance.[23]

A distinctive group of early medieval copper-alloy bowls have decorated mounts with hooks for suspension, which give them the name 'hanging-bowls' (fig. 28). On first inspection these seem to be designed to be suspended over a fire but the metal is too thin and light to survive this. Instead it is likely that they were for serving drink at feasts or for ritual hand-washing. Most were made in Scotland but they are primarily found in Anglo-Saxon burials, often old, well used and repaired: these far-travelled objects must have been very desirable.[24] Like the tankards, they were prized artefacts, probably featuring in ceremonies or rituals. Their decoration was an important way to signal status, wealth or connections.

Fig. 27 **Trawsfynydd tankard**

Encased in bronze sheet, the yew staves and circular base of this tankard are well preserved due to its burial within peat. The cast bronze handle includes an openwork S-shaped design.

Trawsfynydd, Gwynedd 50 BC–AD 75
Bronze, wood; H 14.2 cm, D 18.4 cm
National Museums Liverpool

Fig. 28 **Hanging-bowl from the
Sutton Hoo ship burial**

The largest of three hanging-bowls from the
burial, it was probably made somewhere in
northern Britain but may have been in southern
England for some time because it was repaired
using silver patches decorated with animals in a
style typical of Anglo-Saxon art.

Sutton Hoo, Suffolk AD 610–40
Bronze, enamel; D 29.8 cm
British Museum, London

Decoration also serves to animate objects. The raised pattern found
on an Iron Age iron and copper-alloy cauldron from Chiseldon is in the
form of a cow's or bull's head. When illuminated from below by the
flickering firelight, different features would have been picked out, such as the
horns and flaring nostrils, acting to bring the animal to life. Cauldrons were
used at feasts when people came together for special occasions.[25] Eating
food prepared in and served from the cauldron with its special decoration
would have added to the drama and theatre of these events.

Theatre and interaction were fundamental to Celtic art. The purpose
of any three-dimensional raised decoration is to interact with light, shifting
its shape and form. This was especially important for early medieval stone
crosses. These religious symbols stood outdoors, where the play of sunlight
moving across the relief-carved stone animated the object and highlighted
different elements of the decoration depending on the time of day,
illuminating the message on one side while the other was in shadow (fig. 206).

Reading the art

A further question to ask is, who was the audience for Celtic art? The way in which it is often portrayed in popular books can be misleading, making the ornament seem more prominent than it actually was. For example, the mount from Stanwick, decorated like a horse's head (fig. 29) and originally part of a wooden bucket, is only 100 millimetres high, yet it frequently appears as a full-page picture.[26] To fully understand much of this art, a close encounter with the objects was required.[27] Techniques such as inscribing, stippling or raised decoration acted to break up smooth surfaces, making objects highly tactile.[28] This texturing also meant that the art caught the eye from a distance, even with a fleeting glimpse. Yet those who experienced such art from afar saw mere hints of raised and broken surfaces when the bright metalwork caught the light. Only those with privileged access could touch and feel the objects, and spend time unravelling the complexity of the designs. As Mansel Spratling has observed, 'you could not have seen much of the harness of a horse without proffering it an apple nor much of a chariot's fittings as it sped by at a maximum speed of about 20 mph … nor much of a brooch's design or a torc's ornament without being invited to come close, so close as would otherwise transgress private space'.[29] Sometimes the decoration was hidden, as on the backs of early medieval brooches, or disguised; to appreciate the ornate handle of the Battersea shield or the finely engraved birds on the Wandsworth shield boss (fig. 31) would have required very intimate encounters with objects that seem designed primarily for wider public display. Perhaps the very fact of their embellishment gave these objects a powerful or protective quality, whether the design could be seen by others or not.[30]

In Christian art, the range of scale of decoration, from large stone monuments to smaller portable objects, suggests that the items were intended for different audiences and to communicate a variety of messages. The fifty-six interlocking trumpet-scroll triskeles on the Hilton of Cadboll cross-slab (see fig. 170 and pp. 198–200) are symmetrically arranged in a square panel almost a metre wide, whereas the same motif measures only centimetres across on a bronze disc (fig. 32) or millimetres when painted on manuscripts (fig. 4). On stone, the art could be appreciated from a distance and conveyed Christian messages to wider communities. On parchment, art highlighted important moments in a text that only the literate priesthood could read: sacred words and messages in Latin.

We should also consider the overall visual environment in the past. The majority of objects we discover through archaeological excavations – pots, bones and ironwork – are brown, plain and drab. While it is possible that objects that do not survive well, such as textiles or wood, were more brightly coloured, this is a very different visual context to the one we encounter today, where we are bombarded with images and colour through advertising, television and the internet.[31] Celtic art should be understood

Fig. 29 **The Stanwick horse mask**

This small model of a horse's head is made from sheet bronze and would originally have adorned a wooden bucket. It is shown here life-sized. It is depicted face-on and appears to be flaring its right nostril.

Stanwick, Melsonby, North Yorkshire AD 40–80
Bronze; L. 10.0 cm
British Museum, London

Fig. 30 **An eye for detail**

The decoration of the
Snettisham 'Great Torc' has
raised edges and hatching on
the cast-on terminals, which
has been worked using fine
tools (see pp. 106–7).

Snettisham, Norfolk 100–50 BC
Gold-silver alloy; terminal D 5.7 cm
British Museum, London

Fig. 31 **Circling birds**

The repoussé decoration on
this shield boss defines two
stylized birds flying around the
rim. Further birds have been
engraved on the flange and
boss (see also fig. 62).

River Thames at Wandsworth, London
300–200 BC
Bronze; D 33 cm
British Museum, London

Fig. 32 (opposite) **Complex scrolls**

The interlocking trumpet-scrolls and pelta shapes on this disc form a complex interlocking pattern that was laid out by compasses and then finished freehand. Tinning creates a silvery effect to the surface, with designs cutting through this to create a colour contrast. It was probably the support for a door handle.

Donore, Co. Meath, Ireland AD 700–750
Copper alloy, tinned; D 13.1 cm
National Museum of Ireland, Dublin

Fig. 33 **A ceramic shoe**

This shoe-shaped pot is decorated with stamped circles, lines and crosses. It gives a glimpse into the lost world of decorated leather objects.

Jíkov, Bohemia, Czech Republic 450–400 BC
Ceramic; L 16 cm
National Museum, Prague

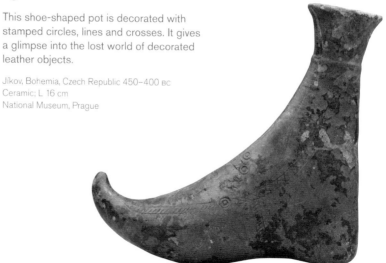

Fig. 34 **Weaving comb**

Antler and bone weaving combs often have ring-and-dot patterns. Many are worn from use and the majority are perforated at the end, probably for suspension from a person's belt. These are highly personal objects and no two are decorated in the same way.

Danebury, Hampshire 300–100 BC
Antler; L 14.0 cm
British Museum, London

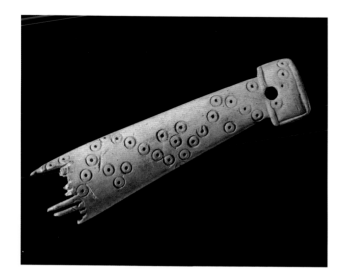

from this perspective. The art would have had a far greater impact on past peoples against their relatively plain visual environment.[32]

Celtic art stands out when compared to other contemporary decorative traditions. For example, during the Iron Age simple geometric patterns created from rectangles, triangles and circles are found on certain types of pottery. Ring-and-dot patterns also feature on bone and antler artefacts like weaving combs (fig. 34) and pottery (fig. 33).[33] These decorative techniques draw on traditions from the Bronze Age and early Iron Age.[34] Even where there was a desire to embellish, Celtic art was used only in particular circumstances, such as on high-status metalwork. It may have been reserved for these special objects because it carried important messages, which it was rarely relevant or desirable to include on more everyday objects.

Approaching Celtic art

Celtic art was designed to draw in and enchant the viewer while carrying messages about beliefs and ideas about the natural, human and other worlds.[35] It was not static. Techniques and technologies, as well as the types of object that were decorated and the meaning and significance of the art, changed significantly over time. It is more correct to understand it as a series of 'Celtic arts' rather than a single, homogenous tradition. But together they give us glimpses into how people saw their world in Iron Age and early medieval Europe, and how they used decoration to reflect beliefs and ideas about that world, and to show off their status and connections. These ideas run through the rest of the book.

Fig. 35 **The Basse-Yutz flagons**
These two locally-made wine flagons are decorated in complex Early-Style Celtic art. They were found with two Etruscan wine-mixing vessels (see pp. 54, 60–61).

Basse-Yutz, Lorraine, France 400–360 BC
Bronze, coral, glass; larger flagon H 40.6 cm
British Museum, London

Chapter 3

A Connected Europe, *c.* 500–150 BC

Fraser Hunter and Jody Joy

Late in November 1927 a team of road-builders unearthed two bronze wine flagons and two Etruscan bronze wine-mixing vessels at Basse-Yutz in north-east France. At first they thought they had found an unexploded First World War bomb and dived for cover. Eventually they plucked up courage to investigate further, and one of the labourers took all four vessels away with him in a sack. After being offered unsuccessfully to a number of museums in France, they were acquired by the British Museum in 1929.[1] The Basse-Yutz flagons are masterpieces in a new art style that developed in Europe north of the Alps in the fifth century BC. It used complex curvilinear designs and stylized or seemingly abstract representations of humans and animals. By 300 BC elements of this art style, which we call Celtic art, had spread east as far as the Black Sea, west to the Atlantic and south into the Iberian peninsula. Celtic art remained in use on the Continent for over 300 years, but during the second century BC simpler, more realistic, mass-produced decoration became popular instead. However, in Britain and Ireland recognizably related curvilinear styles continued to develop into the Roman period.

The fineness of the craftwork and decoration of Celtic art objects like the Basse-Yutz flagons and the wide geographical connections they embody can tell us a great deal about their world. The people who made and used Iron Age Celtic art lived in small communities. Farming was the basis of their lives. Yet these groups included craftworkers able to make complicated artefacts from materials sourced from distant areas, such as coral from the Mediterranean or amber from the Baltic. Some of the styles they used were shared from Ireland to the Danube, while others were much more local. Stylistic influences came from the Mediterranean, the Near East and the steppes of central Asia, directly or indirectly. How did these remarkable objects arise?

Fig. 36 **The Dunaverney flesh-hook**

The birds decorating this implement are typical of late Bronze Age and early Iron Age styles across Europe.

Dunaverney, Co. Antrim 1000–900 BC
Bronze, wood; hook end L. 27 cm
British Museum, London

Older traditions

First we need to consider the background of art in Europe around this
time.[2] During the late Bronze Age and early Iron Age (*c.* 1100–500 BC)
geometric patterns and stylized representations of people and animals
were widespread across Europe. For example, the bronze flesh-hook from
Dunaverney used to pluck meat out of cauldrons at feasts was decorated
with swans, cygnets and what are probably ravens (fig. 36). Stamped pottery
from south-west Germany bears geometric patterns, often painted red and
black (fig. 37).[3] Further east, in central and south-east Europe, vessels and
belt plaques made from sheet metalwork were embellished using dot-
punched, raised or stamped decoration to create narrative scenes with
figures of people and animals.

Stylistic Variation in Early Celtic Art

Jody Joy

One of the defining characteristics of Iron Age Celtic art is its diversity through space and over time, with local forms of decoration, types and uses of artefacts. Consequently, the art has been categorized into a series of Styles or Stages.

Overlapping with the Early Style, the so-called 'Waldalgesheim' or 'Vegetal' Style was in use throughout the fourth century BC. Named after a lavishly furnished female grave from the middle-Rhine region in Germany (see pp. 68–72; figs 50–53), the typical pattern of this style is formed of a sinuous line with flowing tendrils (above), loosely inspired by Greek designs.

As we have seen with the Basse-Yutz flagons (figs 35, 40 and 41), the so-called 'Early' Style, dating to the fifth and early fourth centuries BC, mixes geometric elements from earlier Iron Age artefacts with motifs and patterns influenced by Greek and Etruscan art, such as the lotus flower. The central band of the design on a sheet gold mount from Eigenbilzen (Belgium; above) uses modified versions of vegetal designs (palmettes and lotus flowers) derived from Greek art such as the frieze on a pot from Cerveteri in Italy (below). Objects like flagons, brooches and belt fittings were decorated with highly stylized human and animal faces or masks (figs 18, 19, 42, 43, 46 and 48).

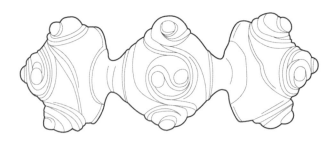

Two further styles, the 'Plastic' and 'Sword' Styles, follow on from the Waldalgesheim Style and are broadly contemporary, dating from the third century BC. The Plastic Style (above) is a three-dimensional form of art with exaggerated raised surfaces. It is found especially on artefacts of personal adornment such as arm- and ankle-rings (figs 54–9).

By the late third and early second centuries BC, Celtic art became much more regionalized across Europe, and art in Britain began to differ markedly from that on the Continent. One striking regional style is the British 'Torrs-Witham-Wandsworth' Style of the third century BC (below and figs 31, 39, 62, 67 and 86).

The relatively small number of Celtic art objects that survive across a wide geographical spread means that these styles are only really useful at a general level. Recent work has shown how decorative motifs were sometimes shared across styles. As each new style emerged, the repertoire of motifs from which to draw upon increased, and some styles overlapped in time. The Torrs-Witham-Wandsworth Style is a good example of this, as it combines elements of both the Plastic and Vegetal styles. This means that dating objects based purely on their style of decoration is highly problematic.

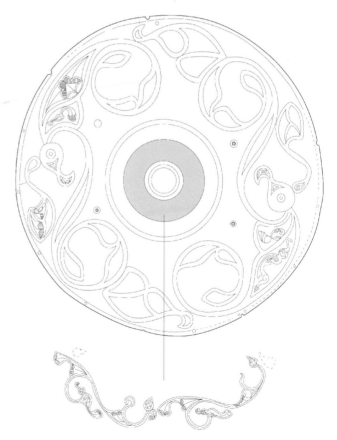

The Sword Style (above) is a more two-dimensional, engraved style. It comprises diverse curvilinear designs, often with hints of plants and animals in them, and is most often found on the mouths of sword scabbards (figs 60, 61 and 69). Both styles are widely distributed from Britain and France to Hungary and the Balkans.

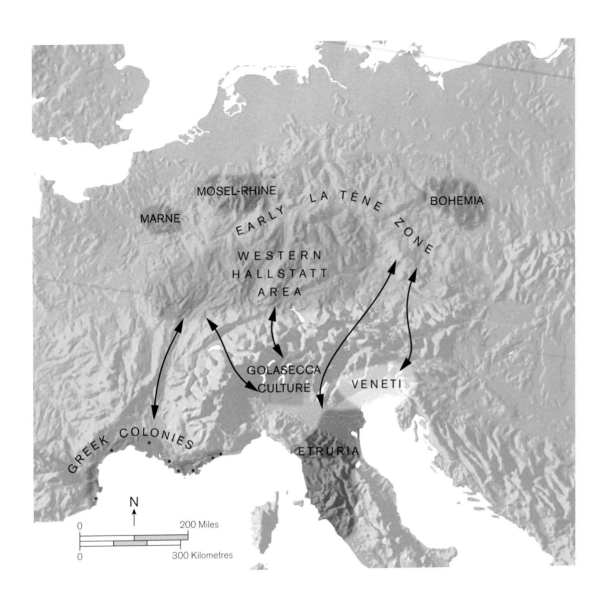

Fig. 38 **Changing power-centres in temperate Europe**

The western Hallstatt area developed complex societies with rich burials and Mediterranean connections in the sixth and early fifth centuries BC. In the later fifth century BC, Celtic art emerged in a series of regional centres to the north of this, known as the early La Tène core areas. The arrows show trade connections between these Iron Age power-centres and the Mediterranean world.

Fig. 39 **Abstract and ambiguous**

The simple curving lines at the top of this shield boss suggest an expressive human face, while the swirling decoration in the centre takes the form of two stylized birds' heads, similar to those on another shield boss found nearby (see figs 31 and 62).

River Thames, Wandsworth, London 300–200 BC, Bronze; L 37 cm
British Museum, London

The fifth century BC – a time of change

In the sixth and fifth centuries BC there were extensive connections between the Mediterranean world and an area stretching from eastern France through southern Germany to Switzerland, known to archaeologists as the western Hallstatt zone after one of the key findspots (fig. 38). Objects, including exotic materials like coral, glass and elephant ivory, were imported north of the Alps from Greece, Greek colonies such as Marseilles, and the Etruscan cities of northern Italy.[4] A few select people in this western Hallstatt area were buried in very rich graves with valuable objects such as gold neck-rings. Some burials included rare imported bronze and ceramic vessels, which were used for the consumption of wine at feasts and other social gatherings. The first large-scale centres of population north of the Alps, a form of early town, developed in eastern France and southern Germany during the sixth century BC. The groups that built these fortified settlements seem to have grown wealthy from links with the Mediterranean world, perhaps controlling trade in sought-after items including amber, gold and tin from the northern and western parts of Europe.[5]

But the fifth century BC saw marked change, and by about 400 BC a zone of wealthy burials marking new power-centres lay north of the old heartlands (fig. 38). These burials included finds decorated with an innovative style: Celtic art. This art had no single point of creation. Several regions across Europe developed versions of it: the earliest was probably in the Moselle–Rhine area of western Germany and the Marne in northern France, but versions also evolved along the Atlantic façade of France (and perhaps westwards into Britain), and in eastern Europe either side of the Danube in Bohemia, Austria, Hungary and Slovakia.[6] The spread of this style (usually termed 'Early-Style' Celtic art) shows east–west connections between Iron Age societies across temperate Europe that were stronger than the north–south links with the Mediterranean. Shared ideas were expressed, but with regional differences.[7] In northern France, the preference was for openwork compass-drawn ornament (fig. 44) and flowing plant designs, in contrast to the more broken-up plant motifs of the Mosel–Rhine area of Germany. Figures of animals and mythical beasts were common from Germany eastwards, especially on brooches (figs 18 and 42), but were almost absent from France.

This new style utilized ideas and motifs from the classical world taken from imported Mediterranean objects such as bronze vessels. External designs were adapted, deconstructed, rearranged and mixed with local ones to create fresh styles with their own aesthetic sense and internal logic that we now recognize as distinctively Celtic: abstract, ambiguous, shape-shifting and sinuous (fig. 39).

Back to Basse-Yutz

The decoration of the Basse-Yutz flagons distils these influences. Many elements were adapted from the Mediterranean world. Their form originates from Etruscan 'beaked' jugs. Their bases and 'throats' are enhanced with lavish quantities of coral, originally a vivid red colour, probably from the Gulf of Naples.[8] The curved geometric patterns of coral inlays around the bases are reminiscent of designs on fifth- and fourth-century BC Etruscan cups.[9] The palmette shape found on the necks and handles was widely used in Etruscan and Greek art, and ultimately derives from palm fronds depicted in Egyptian art.[10] At the base of each handle are highly stylized faces with moustaches, large round eyes and prominent eyebrows (fig. 41). The inspiration for these too came from Etruscan vessels, which featured much more naturalistic faces on their handles.[11] There were also technological links to the south: the stoppers are embellished with red glass that was probably made in the eastern Mediterranean.

Stylistic influences from even further afield can also be detected. Designs similar to the engraved decoration on the spouts and mouths occurred from the Marne in France to the Black Sea.[12] The animal-shaped handle, probably a dog or wolf guarding her cubs on the rim (fig. 40), is a

Fig. 40 **A Celtic menagerie**

The fierce beasts and fleeing duckling on top of the flagons must represent some lost myth or story. When the flagon was poured, the duckling would appear to be paddling along a river of wine.

Basse-Yutz, Lorraine, France 400–360 BC
Bronze, coral, red glass; flagon D 19.5 cm
British Museum, London

Fig. 41 **Faces on the flagon**

The face on the bottom of the handle is based on Etruscan prototypes, but the artist has deliberately stylized it to create a pattern of curves and bulging eyes.

Basse-Yutz, Lorraine, France 400–360 BC
Bronze, once inlaid with coral and red glass
face; W 6.7 cm
British Museum, London

feature commonly seen in more easterly art across the central Asian steppe. Versions of the S-curves and spirals so typical of Celtic art can also be found throughout much of temperate Eurasia around this time.

There were more local links too. The duckling positioned on each spout continued an earlier tradition of birds on items such as brooches or flesh-hooks (fig. 36). Their position made the ducklings appear to be swimming on a river of wine as it was poured.

Exploring the earliest Celtic art

The Basse-Yutz flagons bring together local, Mediterranean and eastern influences. Peter Wells has argued that Celtic art studies focus too heavily on Mediterranean links. He sees the far-flung similarities as revealing wider developments in complex art throughout Eurasia: in the Near East, among steppe peoples such as the Scythians, and extending as far as China. This places Iron Age Europe into a much bigger changing world.[13] However, the evidence is hotly disputed. Eastern links clearly had an impact on Early-Style Celtic art but evidence of direct contacts is elusive. They could have come indirectly via the classical world: for instance, Greek craftworkers around the Black Sea created fine artefacts for Scythian groups.[14]

While the mechanisms behind such connections are controversial, this new Celtic art style shows knowledge of much wider worlds. But why was it created? The answers lie in politics and social change. One theory argues that there was a power struggle during the early fifth century BC. Ambitious groups immediately north of the traditional heartlands were keen to obtain more direct links to the Mediterranean. They challenged the control of the older centres, building their own contacts to wider exchange networks. These new centres were well placed to bring desirable raw materials to the markets of Greece and Italy (fig. 38), as they lay closer to sources of salt, gold, tin and amber.[15]

But there are other possibilities. Mediterranean contacts were clearly one spark for this new art style that emerged around 450 BC, but there are surprisingly few imports in contemporary settlements and burials (in contrast to the 'proto-towns' and rich burials of the sixth and early fifth century BC). Many contacts were probably indirect, through groups in northern Italy.[16] The societies creating and using early Celtic art were also rather different from what went before. There were not many substantial centralized hillfort settlements; most of the proto-towns of the previous century had been abandoned or were in decline.[17] The majority of people lived in modest, scattered farming settlements. Cemeteries were also small with only a few rich burials; these were widely spread, not concentrated around major centres as in the previous century.[18] This points to small-scale communities competing with one another for status and connections, not big power blocks controlling large swathes of territory. It implies an unstable, fluid system where an individual could win and lose power by their personal qualities and deeds, their charisma and connections, and their abilities to influence others or forge deals. Such environments encouraged rich burial rites because families used these to show off their connections and wealth to the rest of society. They also stimulated innovative means of display. Earlier generations had been content with lavish imports. Now these served as a starting point for self-confident local creations: an inspiration for this new style of art, which was deliberately unlike anything preceding it. Celtic art became a powerful way for people to show that they were someone special.

Meanings?

Fig. 42 **A contorted menagerie**

This tiny brooch has people, animals and fantastical creatures staring from every side. Each element is part of one or more faces. The drawing shows where to find the various beasts.

Heubach-Rosenstein, Baden-Württemberg, Germany
450–400 BC
Bronze; L 5 cm
Württembergisches Landesmuseum, Stuttgart

The emergence of Celtic art may also have been connected to changes in beliefs or how they were expressed. Art frequently has a religious or ritual significance. The mysterious scenes on many Early-Style objects, such as the Basse-Yutz flagons or the stark two-faced stone figure from Holzgerlingen, hint at a world of myths, impossible now for us to understand (see p. 6).[19] Often they include fantastical creatures. A tiny brooch from Heubach in south-western Germany, barely fifty millimetres long, crams in a contorted series of ten human and animal faces: birds of prey, ducks, and rams with

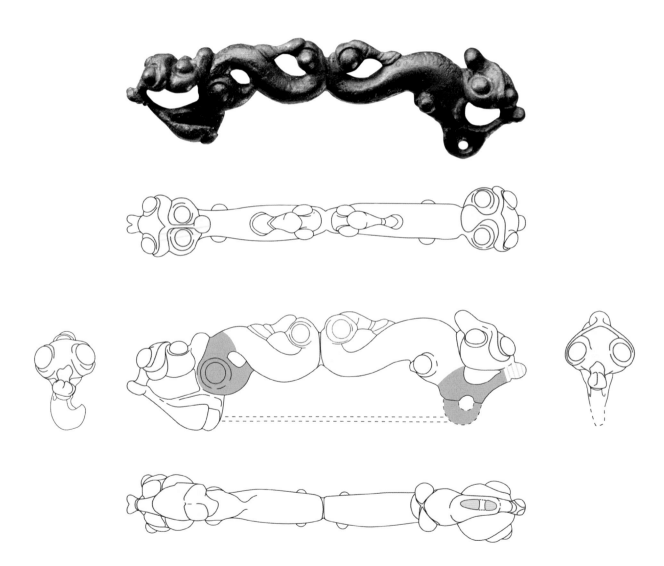

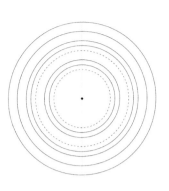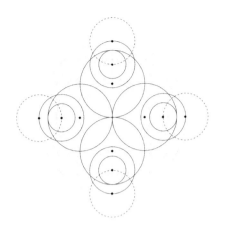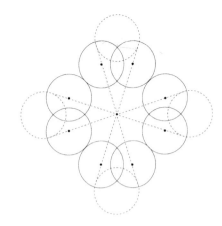

half-human faces and fish-like bodies (fig. 42).[20] Such brooches were widespread from France to Slovakia[21] and may have been amulets: many accompanied the dead to their graves. The striking images and their use in burials strongly suggest this art had a magical role.

This new ambiguous and abstract art was restricted to certain kinds of objects: personal ornaments, feasting gear, chariot fittings and weaponry.[22] The body, the battleground, the journey and the feast were the areas in which people competed to show their importance and connections.

Burial finds give a glimpse of how this art was used. People often expressed their ideas, beliefs and aspirations in the items that they buried with their dead. Only a small proportion of burials included Celtic art. From Somme-Bionne in north-eastern France comes a rich burial, probably of a man given the presence of a warrior's gear: the grip of a lost shield and an iron sword in a decorated scabbard (fig. 64).[23] This was suspended from a belt by bronze rings, fastened with an openwork hook showing two animals either side of a central disc (fig. 43). The motif of paired beasts (often flanking a human) was widespread, especially on warrior gear, and was probably seen as protective.[24] A single plain gold ring marked him as a man of stature: gold was rare in French graves. The burial was accompanied by Mediterranean imports: a Greek painted pottery cup and an Etruscan bronze flagon. Local elements were also included: an ornamented gold sheet may have come from a drinking horn, while a locally-made pot, a knife and iron meat-skewers completed the feasting gear so that he could play host in the afterlife. But the most spectacular item was a chariot, heavily embellished with bronze fittings. The ornate horse harness included a series of bronze discs with complex openwork decoration, carefully laid out using compasses (fig. 44): a striking feature of the art of this area.[25] The design shows advanced geometrical knowledge: powerful, impressive and rare skills in a society that relied on memory, not books.

Fig. 43 **Protective animals**

Decorated belt hooks were designed to catch the eye. Often they carried pairs of animals. Here two fantastical creatures, perhaps griffins, have their heads turned back and their hooked beaks open. The central disc and the rows of dots below their feet may be sun symbols. One end of the fitting curves into a fastening hook; the tang would have fastened to a broad leather belt.

Somme-Bionne, Marne, France 450–400 BC
Bronze; L 6.3 cm
British Museum, London

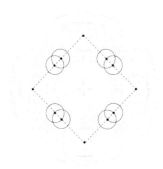 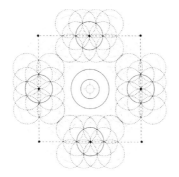 

Fig. 44 (above and right) **Complex compass-work**

The decoration on this harness ornament was prepared using complex compass-drawn patterns. Drawings reconstruct how the design could have been laid out (working from left to right above). It shows tremendous expertise and a knowledge of geometric principles that is often attributed to Greek mathematicians such as Pythagoras. Were such skills another part of the influences spreading from the Mediterranean, or were they developed independently in this area of France?

Somme-Bionne, Marne, France 450–400 BC
Bronze: D 6.9 cm
British Museum, London

Fig. 45 **The Kleinaspergle burial**

The rich finds from this burial include Mediterranean imports (the two wine-mixing buckets and painted cups) and local items (the flagon, drinking horns and gold mount).

Kleinaspergle, Baden-Württemberg, Germany
450–400 BC
Bronze, gold, ceramic; flagon H 45.3 cm
Württembergisches Landesmuseum, Stuttgart

Fig. 46 (opposite above) **Inspiration and modification**

Two bronze vessels from the Kleinaspergle burial show how Mediterranean styles influenced local craftworkers. The human-like head with ornate beard and pointed ears on the locally-made flagon was inspired by the human figures on the handle of the Etruscan wine-mixing vessel.

Kleinaspergle, Baden-Württemberg, Germany
450–400 BC
Bronze
Württembergisches Landesmuseum, Stuttgart

A burial from Kleinaspergle in south-western Germany, 300 kilometres to the east, shows many of the same features, emphasizing the shared ideas among ambitious fifth-century BC groups (fig. 45).[26] It was full of ornate feasting gear: an indigenous bronze cauldron and wooden container, and bronze vessels from Italy used for mixing wine or other drinks. These were served in an elaborate locally-made flagon, the human or demonic heads on its handle modelled on ones from Etruscan vessels (fig. 46). The drink was consumed from different styles of vessels: a pair of drinking horns with gold ram-headed terminals and two painted Greek cups. As in some other rich burials of this time, the feasting and drinking set was for two people although

it seems only a single person was buried. A guest was expected in the afterlife; or did this symbolize a powerful person's role as a giver of hospitality?[27] The body did not survive in the Kleinaspergle burial, but evidence from similar graves suggests this was a part played by influential women.

The handles of the Greek cups had snapped off and been repaired with gold mounts (fig. 47). This is a tantalizing hint of a Greek drinking game called *kottabos*, where the players spun their cup on a finger, swirling the dregs of wine before launching them at a target; over-enthusiastic participation often led to breakage.[28] Not only objects but also habits were imported from the Mediterranean, it seems.

The drinking game may be a direct import, but in general these people only borrowed Greek and Etruscan practices that suited them, and adapted them to local taste. They were not aspiring to be Greeks; instead they were creating a new visual world that fused and expanded the indigenous and the exotic. The decoration on the gold repairs embodies this: the gold sheet bears Early-Style Celtic art motifs, blending this with the Greek object beneath.[29]

The Kleinaspergle flagon has stylized images of humans on its handle. Human heads are a recurring feature of Celtic art. Earlier researchers saw this as a cult of the head, and argued for a morbid fascination with heads and head-hunting.[30] Recent work shows this interpretation to be too simple. There was nothing particularly 'Celtic' about an obsession with heads; they remain significant for cultures all across the world.[31] Iron Age head-hunting could involve real heads – of ancestors, removed during burial rites, or of enemies, taken in or after battle – but images of heads were also important. These carried a variety of meanings. Some were probably symbols of a warrior's prowess; others were displayed to mark sacred places. Often they were used as symbols of fertility, vital for the community's future: a reminder of the ancestors who brought success by defeating the enemy and ensuring the group's survival. There was no single 'head cult'.

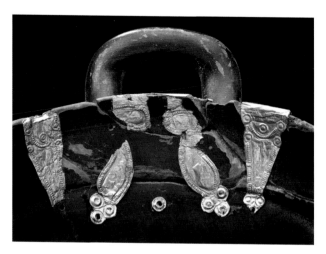

Fig. 47 **Greek and Celtic**

This Greek cup was repaired locally using gold mounts decorated in typical Early Style with geometric and leaf motifs.

Kleinaspergle, Baden-Württemberg, Germany
450–400 BC
Gold, ceramic; handle W 4.5 cm
Württembergisches Landesmuseum, Stuttgart

The phallic-shaped base of a sandstone pillar from Pfalzfeld in western Germany shows four disembodied male heads staring blankly forward (fig. 49).[32] Two balloon-like shapes (so-called 'leaf-crowns') emerge from the heads, perhaps attached to the leaf-decorated caps they each wear; three buds sprout from the chins. Another leaf-crowned head once topped the pillar, while the theme of plant decoration covers the rest of the stone in the flowing lines of S-scrolls. 'Leaf-crowns' were a widely shared motif throughout Europe for about a hundred years, depicted on men, women and mythical creatures.[33] For instance, two harness discs from a burial at Hořovičky in the Czech Republic have concentric circles of heads wearing leaf-crowns (fig. 48).[34] Such crowns were real, not imagined: an example survived in one of the Glauberg warrior graves (fig. 3).[35] Who wore such head gear? Did it mark out leaders, or perhaps people who were able to connect to other worlds?

Changing styles

Early-Style Celtic art (fifth to early fourth century BC) was gradually transformed. Recognizable humans and animals did not last long. Instead they morphed into much more elusive beasts. From around 350 BC, the regular scrolls of the Early Style became meandering curves resembling a wandering line of vegetation with tendrils curling off it. Often hidden faces

Fig. 48 (opposite, far left)
Circles of heads

The disc comes from a set
of horse harness, which was
buried with a chariot in a
richly equipped grave. The
two circles of disembodied
heads all have curious 'leaf-
crowns', indicating special or
supernatural status.

Hořovičky, central Bohemia, Czech
Republic 450–400 BC
Bronze, iron; D 12 cm
National Museum, Prague

Fig. 49 (opposite)
The Pfalzfeld pillar

The surviving base of this
sandstone pillar is dominated
by staring heads wearing a
leaf-crown headdress. The
rest of the pillar is covered in
stylized vegetation. Originally
it was around twice this height,
and topped by another head
with a leaf-crown.

Pfalzfeld, Rheinland-Pfalz, Germany
450–400 BC
Sandstone; H 1.48 m
Rheinisches Landesmuseum, Bonn

of humans or animals lurked within. This is known as 'Vegetal Style' after
its plant-like form, or 'Waldalgesheim Style' after a famous find: a rich burial
found in Germany, west of Mainz, in 1869 (see p. 56).[36] An important
woman had been buried with lavishly decorated items around 320 BC. They
show what people thought were the key areas of her life to commemorate.

    She was adorned in magnificent jewellery: a gold torc and two
bracelets, all decorated in Vegetal Style, and a twisted gold arm-ring (fig. 50).
Two bronze anklets also carried a variation on this curling decoration: a
series of palmettes. She wore rare glass beads and two tiny cowrie shells
from the Mediterranean, probably on a necklace: markers of distant contacts
or unusual amulets to protect her. A gold earring and a black arm-ring of
lignite (a stone similar to jet) completed her jewellery. Small bronze rings
and spirals that preserved traces of textile hint at the finery of her vanished
costume. The exotic materials (gold, cowrie shells and glass) and complicated
decoration marked her out as special. These items must have carried
messages about her age, her gender and her power to control or persuade
people, to mediate with other groups or with other worlds, but the subtleties
of this are now lost.

Fig. 50 **Gold jewellery
from Waldalgesheim**

The torc and bracelets from
the burial are decorated with
flowing tendrils of vegetation.
The two bracelets are so
similar that they were probably
made by the same person.
All the jewellery is fabricated
from hollow gold tubes, with
decoration hammered in
repoussé from the rear and
chased from the front. The
torc is made from ten separate
components.

Waldalgesheim, Rheinland-Pfalz,
Germany 340–300 BC
Gold; torc D 21.1 cm
Rheinisches Landesmuseum, Bonn

Fig. 51 (above left and centre) **A richly decorated flagon**

Today the viewer's attention is drawn to the figures on the flagon from Waldalgesheim: the rather static horse on the lid and the decorated handle. Originally the vessel's body would also have caught the eye: it has rows of punched decoration, dominated by two bands of carefully laid-out interlocking scrolls. These are now hard to see due to corrosion. The decoration is in the Early Style, and it was probably an heirloom over fifty years old at the time of burial. The base of the handle shows a man with a long beard and a leaf-crown between two beasts with gaping jaws.

Waldalgesheim, Rheinland-Pfalz, Germany
Made c. 400–350 BC; buried c. 340–300 BC
Bronze; H 35 cm
Rheinisches Landesmuseum, Bonn

Fig. 52 (above) **A Greek import**

This two-handled bucket was made in the Greek colony of Tarento in southern Italy around 340 BC. It was intended for mixing wine. The symmetrical floral motifs on the handle fitting inspired the person who decorated the torc from the same burial (fig. 50).

Waldalgesheim, Rheinland-Pfalz, Germany
Made c. 340–320 BC; buried c. 340–300 BC
Bronze; H 23 cm
Rheinisches Landesmuseum, Bonn

She was also accompanied by feasting gear. A locally-made flagon was engraved with subtle decoration that still used the Early Style of Celtic art, its S-spirals very regular compared to the new Vegetal Style. A horse stood impassively on the lid, while the handle had a fierce ram at the top and a bearded male face wearing a leaf-crown at the base, flanked by two beasts (fig. 51). The Celtic flagon was accompanied by a bucket imported from the Greek world, intended for mixing wine; the bucket's decoration may have inspired the ornament on the gold torcs (fig. 52).[37] The vessels might have been for feeding the woman in the afterlife, but could also have marked her role in life as a generous host, as in the earlier grave at Kleinaspergle, discussed above.[38]

Most of the other finds at Waldalgesheim came from a richly decorated chariot that was buried with her in the grave. The vehicle itself, of wood and leather, had long vanished, but ornate bronze fittings survived: curving terminals for the yoke, strap fasteners and fittings, some formed of interlocking strands mimicking vegetation. There are also two remarkable mounts, probably from the yoke. On one, a ring carries vegetal decoration, with gaps originally filled with coral (fig. 53, left). In the centre is an openwork design of two birds facing one another. It has been argued that in the myths of the Bronze Age and earlier Iron Age birds pulled the sun on its heavenly course.[39] Were these sun-birds to pull this chariot on its journey? But the most striking find is a double-sided mount with a portrayal of a woman in low relief (fig. 53, below). Holes symbolizing her breasts were inlaid, possibly with coral. On her head she wears a giant leaf-crown, which marked a special status, while a torc adorns her neck. Her body is covered by writhing tendrils of vegetation: was this a tattoo or body painting? Was this woman thought to be transforming from human to plant, or vice versa? Was she a deity, or a character from a myth? Could this even be a depiction of the special woman buried in the chariot? Other rich burials around this time included very individual jewellery: maybe the dead person was not just the wearer of these things but also part of the stories or myths that they

Fig. 53 (above and right)
A chariot covered in stories

These two ornate mounts once decorated the yoke of a chariot. The two birds and the woman with the ornate headdress must have been characters in lost Iron Age myths or beliefs. The twisting tendrils over the woman's body and round the edge of the bird-ring are typical of the Vegetal or Waldalgesheim style.

Waldalgesheim, Rheinland-Pfalz, Germany 340–300 BC
Bronze, coral; both mounts H 9 cm
Rheinisches Landesmuseum, Bonn

represented. We can never know what these decorated objects meant, but their exceptional nature suggests a remarkable person: perhaps with earthly power, or with an ability to arbitrate with the gods.

The Waldalgesheim burial is isolated. There is nothing quite like it in the local area: the heartlands of this Vegetal Style lay elsewhere, in northern France, the Swiss Alps and northern Italy.[40] The style reached British shores as well, though only rarely. A cauldron from Chiseldon has its iron rim marked with a curving tendril, while on a curious pair of scoops from Weston (near Bath) the pattern seems to writhe within the limiting space of the handles (fig. 90). Foliage curves up and down the bronze protective spine of a shield from Ratcliffe-on-Soar and animals burst out of the intertwined tendrils: early traces of what would develop into a dominant feature of this art in Britain.[41]

Art across Europe

A key element of these Iron Age Celtic art styles was their range: similar habits were found across large parts of Europe. During the third century BC, Celtic art reached its broadest extent, with examples from the Black Sea to the Baltic and the British Isles. It continued to change. Widely separated craftworkers in northern France and central Europe transformed the Vegetal Style: at one level simplifying it; at another making it more complex.[42] Interlinking tendrils became fewer, fatter, higher relief and less intricate, creating bold spirals and bosses known as 'Plastic Style' (see p. 56; named from a German word that means sculpted or three-dimensional, referring to the way the shapes were modelled in high relief). But in these simpler styles were complex stories: hidden faces of humans and animals lurked in the curves and coils, visible only to the observant or from the corner of an eye (figs 54–6). Paul Jacobsthal, who was the first to study this art systematically, referred to this phenomenon as 'Cheshire Style' after the cat in Lewis Carroll's *Alice in Wonderland* that gradually vanished, leaving only its grin behind.[43] This device of hidden faces is one that runs throughout Iron Age Celtic art: it can be seen from the earliest examples of the fifth century BC to the art of the Roman period in Britain, although it is particularly common in the fourth to third centuries BC (in the Vegetal and Plastic Styles).

Not all animals were hidden, however. Vincent Megaw coined the phrase 'Disney Style' to express the ability of craftworkers using Plastic Style to convey an animal or a human with just a few simple shapes.[44] This is seen powerfully on a chariot linchpin from the river Erms near Urach in south-western Germany, where bronze scrolls coil over the surface like baroque icing on a cake, and two rather mournful horses' heads stare wide-eyed from the corners (fig. 54).[45] Such unambiguous animals contrast with the elusive 'Cheshire cats'.

Fig. 54 **Bronze horses on a linchpin**

This iron linchpin once slotted through the axle of a chariot to hold the wheel in place. A bronze terminal was cast onto the top, its decoration including two horse heads.

River Erms near Urach, Baden-Württemberg, Germany
300–200 BC
Bronze, iron; H 10.7 cm
Württembergisches Landesmuseum, Stuttgart

Fig. 55 **The Roissy dome**

The function of this unique domed mount is unclear, but the circling decoration of distorted semi-humans and animals is a masterpiece.

Roissy-en-France, Val d'Oise, France 300–200 BC
Bronze; D 21 cm
Musée d'Archéologie Nationale, St Germain-en-Laye

Fig. 56 (below) **A Plastic-Style zoo**

Fittings from the yoke of the Roissy chariot are decorated with a wide variety of strange, staring creatures.

Roissy-en-France, Val d'Oise, France 300–200 BC
Bronze; L 5.8 cm
Musée d'Archéologie Nationale, St Germain-en-Laye

A recent find from Roissy-en-France, north-east of Paris, shows Plastic Style at its best. Excavations in advance of an extension to Roissy airport in 1999 uncovered a small Iron Age cemetery of the early third century BC. Among the burials was a person accompanied by a highly decorated chariot.[46] The wheels were held in place by linchpins adorned with bug-eyed faces. Along the yoke was a series of ornate fittings with coil stacked upon coil, forming intense swirling designs (fig. 56). Other fittings came from the harness. Within this were figures: humans, birds and fantasy creatures. Most striking of all was a unique openwork dome (fig. 55), perhaps the lid of a box or the centrepiece of a ceremonial hat. Two bands of figures circle a central boss of spirals. The inner band has three creatures that resemble horses, their snouts touching the central boss, with globe-like spirals linking them. The outer band alternates between screaming animals, their mouths wide open, and silent figures that look almost human, but with elongated bulbous noses. It is a fantasy masterpiece, a glimpse into an alien world.

Who was the person in this grave? We are conditioned to expect only the rich and powerful to be buried in this way, but this was no wealthy woman bedecked with gold jewellery, nor a mighty warrior with his decorated weaponry. The grave seems poor by those standards, but it is intriguing: simple jewellery (a plain bronze bangle, an ordinary iron brooch); a few iron tools and fittings (including a pair of shears, some fine-bladed implements and an enigmatic hooked object); a natural banded pebble (possibly a charmstone); and two unremarkable pots for serving and eating an everyday meal. The answer may lie not in the secular world but a ritual one. The unusual tools and items suggest this may be a healer or a religious specialist: perhaps one of the mysterious figures called druids in classical sources.[47] Maybe this was someone who dealt with the otherworld, and when they were sent there in death they were protected by complex, enchanting decoration evoking many different beings: human, animal, bird, insect and fantastical creatures of the mind (figs 55–6). Iron Age Celtic art was connected with making sense of their universe, hinting at beliefs that we cannot grasp.

The Roissy chariot burial is one of a series of finds near Paris, and it seems there was a workshop specializing in Plastic-Style art in the area. A mount from Cambridgeshire in the same tradition shows there were links across the Channel at this time (fig. 57). Although it is concentrated in France and Bohemia, the Plastic Style was widespread. For instance, heavy cast bronze knobbed anklets, often with Plastic-Style decoration, were typical female ornaments of the time (fig. 58). They are commonly found from south-west Germany through Bohemia to Hungary, with outliers in south-west France, Greece and Turkey.[48]

Fig. 57 **Plastic Style in the Fens**

This bronze mount from Cambridgeshire is very similar to Plastic-Style decoration in the Paris area, and may well be an import. It is cast, with remains of an iron fitting in the hollow underside, and was probably the head of a linchpin or a decorative fitting from a chariot yoke.

Cambridgeshire 300–200 BC
Bronze; L 4.3 cm
British Museum, London

Fig. 58 **A wide-ranging fashion**

The bold Plastic-Style decoration is typical of such anklets of the third century BC in central Europe. Outliers to east and west show the movement of people or fashions.

Plañany, Bohemia, Czech Republic 300–200 BC
Bronze; H 4 cm
National Museum, Prague

Histories and alternatives

Such far-flung finds create challenges in interpretation. Greek and Roman writers recorded histories of this period, long after the event. They spoke of the Celts or the Gauls (the terms were used interchangeably) invading Italy, Greece and the Balkans in the fourth and third centuries BC, with some groups eventually ending up in Turkey. They wrote of warrior bands and massive movements of people. But we must be cautious. The classical authors were not necessarily wrong but they simplified a complex situation. They were affected by their own biases. They saw these people from the north as barbarians, who were expected to behave in certain stereotyped ways: fickle and unreliable, footloose and fancy free, unpredictable and unsettled; in fact, the exact opposite of people in the stable urban worlds of Greece and Italy. Everything they recorded was seen through this lens.

It is very tempting to link our archaeological evidence to this 'proto-history', and see mass migrations and war bands everywhere. In northern France and western Germany, the areas in which the Early Style of Celtic art thrived from *c.* 475 to 350 BC, there were few rich burials and little evidence of such creativity and wealth in the succeeding generations, *c.* 350 to 200 BC. This has been taken as a marker of abandonment and movement, with populations migrating to northern Italy or eastern Europe. Connections between objects in northern France and northern Italy, or Plastic-Style art in both Bohemia and the Paris basin, have also been used to argue for migrations.[49]

But there are strong biases in our evidence. The rise and fall of rich burial rites is a poor guide to the movement of people, although they offer tremendous insights into their social and emotional needs and beliefs. Burial traditions evolved, but did not disappear; these landscapes were not abandoned at the end of the fourth century BC. Instead, the decline in rich burial suggests a change in society. Perhaps the uncertainties and competition of the previous century had come to an end, with winners and losers played out and a social pecking order established. Once positions were cemented, there was no longer the same need to show off with wealthy burials.[50] Celtic art was not needed to the same degree. Instead, from the third century BC, major regional ritual sites developed in many areas. These would have served to bring different groups together in ceremonies.[51]

We should not doubt that people moved around: objects cannot move by themselves. The styles of art and Mediterranean imports show there were connections. People made journeys for adventure, marriage, or trade and exchange of valued goods; they served in war bands, eager for glory and booty, or as mercenaries for the city states of the Mediterranean. But connections were nothing new; they had been taking place across Europe for thousands of years. Contacts do not need to mean mass migrations. Certain groups of people are inherently mobile: youths seeking marriage partners or adventure; young men out to make their name in travel and war;

Fig. 59 **European styles and local variants**

Continental art styles had an influence on British tastes. The technology of this brooch shows it was made in Britain, but the coiled decoration is typical Plastic Style, indicating knowledge of Continental fashions.

Balloch Hill, Kintyre, Argyll and Bute 300–200 BC
Bronze; L 5.8 cm
Glasgow Museums

leaders seeking connections to support them against their enemies. In a world where travel was an effort, where there were no trains or planes to whisk you from one area to another, and where every move into a neighbouring territory had to be negotiated or disputed, travellers were special people. They returned as tellers of tales and possessors of strange knowledge and objects.[52] Travel bestowed status or mystique, and the items they brought back were the markers of their journey. Celtic art can be seen as an international badge that distinguished its owners as people who had both connections and the arcane knowledge to understand these decorated objects. Art acted as a bridge between different societies.

In time, we may get clearer answers about how many people moved, and to where. Scientific analysis is starting to reveal a person's travels from the isotopes in their teeth and bones.[53] But results so far are proving entertainingly complicated and refusing to conform to the straightforward pictures from classical sources. Some people moved, and some barely strayed from home turf; some probably moved and returned, while others moved on and on.[54]

Finds of Celtic art remind us that objects were not just blindly carried around as tokens of contacts, but also affected the areas where they ended up. Only a few British artefacts carry the typical Plastic-Style art known from the Continent, but it was clearly familiar as it was adapted for local brooches and pins. From Balloch Hill in Argyll comes a unique brooch (fig. 59). Its construction shows it is British but the arched bow is decorated with coiled bosses typical of Plastic art.[55] In Ireland, home-grown pins were decorated with Plastic-Style motifs.[56] Wider ideas were adjusted to local habits.

A Europe of the regions

This idea of regional habits and wider connections is seen in the other dominant art style of the third century BC. Intricately engraved patterns developed from the earlier Vegetal Style are found across Europe. This is termed 'Sword Style' although the name is wrong on two counts. The art is typically found on scabbards, not swords, and it was not a single style but several related ones.[57] Some of the most spectacular examples come from Hungary, Slovakia and Slovenia, where a diagonal swathe of decoration dominated the front of the scabbard (see p. 57).[58] The same ideas were found in France but with subtle variations, suggesting a series of related regional styles (fig. 60).[59] In Switzerland a more restrained style was used, with only the top of the scabbard decorated.[60] Eastern Britain was home to another regional style: scabbards from burials in Yorkshire featured local variants of these scrolling patterns, which covered the whole of the front (fig. 69).[61] People in the north of Ireland produced a further distinctive variant (fig. 61).[62]

Fig. 60 (opposite) **Scabbard beasts**

Both the front and back of this ornately engraved scabbard from a French cremation burial carried complex scrolling decoration with an animal head emerging from it. Similar beast heads on a scabbard from Slovakia show the wide connections across Europe at this time.

Cernon-sur-Coole, Marne, France 300–250 BC
Iron; W 5.2 cm, L 62 cm
Musée des Beaux-arts et d'Archéologie, Châlons-en-Champagne

Fig. 61 (above) **Ulster scabbards**

A distinctive group of bronze scabbards from northern Ireland uses a regional version of the widespread Sword Style. All come from rivers or bogs, where they were probably placed as deliberate offerings.

Lisnacrogher, Co. Antrim 300–200 BC
Bronze; L 55.4 cm
British Museum, London

Britain in Europe

Britain and Ireland were part of these connections across Europe. The earliest phases of Celtic art have left little trace on these islands,[63] although an ornate headdress from Cerrig-y-drudion in north Wales and a few hints of Vegetal-Style material show there were contacts to this wider European world. But the third century BC saw clear engagement with pan-European styles, such as the decorated scabbards of Yorkshire and Ulster. Most striking is a distinctively British style known, rather inelegantly, as the 'Torrs-Witham-Wandsworth Style' after three of the key finds: a pony cap and horns from Torrs in south-west Scotland (fig. 86), and a series of shields from the rivers Witham and Thames in eastern England (p. 1; figs 1, 31, 39, 62 and 67). These took elements of the Vegetal, Plastic and Sword Styles and fused them into something new. All share high-relief raised patterns, which often seem to take wing as they transform before your eyes into stylized birds or dragons.[64] Incised ornament carries similar echoes of animals or birds. On a round copper-alloy shield boss recovered from the Thames at Wandsworth before 1849, two fantastical birds with hooked beaks and staring eyes chase one another around the circumference, their wings and bodies morphing into scrolls (fig. 62). Fine engraved decoration within the repoussé wings includes another small bird, while two stylized birds or beasts race round the raised centre of the boss (p. 57). These are local versions of the paired beasts that occur repeatedly in the Celtic art on sword scabbards and belt hooks, and seem to represent some wide-ranging warrior belief in their protective powers (see Chapter 4).

Complex art for complex times

Iron Age Celtic art was part of a complicated story. It tells us about the history of Europe during the later first millennium BC: a time of immense changes across the Continent, as powerful city states developed in the Mediterranean and complex societies waxed and waned to the north.[65] Celtic art emerged on the northern fringes of the unstable late Hallstatt societies of eastern France, southern Germany and Switzerland, with their immensely rich burials, proto-towns and strong links to the Greek and Italian worlds. This new art style was born to the north of these groups in the fifth century BC out of the mixture of local traditions, Mediterranean and eastern influences: a creation of societies that wanted to make something novel and visibly their own, perhaps linked to changing religious beliefs.

This early Celtic art was created in different regional centres across Europe that had extensive contacts with one another. We have traced how the styles and the centres changed over the following 300 years. Sometimes there were clear connections across the Continent, sometimes strong regional differences. The archaeological record produces very little evidence

for large-scale tribal structures or major power-centres in the fourth or third centuries BC: it seems these were small-scale societies where travel and connections became a way for someone to gain power and influence. Rather than the massive 'Celtic migrations' recorded by later Greek and Roman historians (who were distant in space, time and culture from the phenomena they recorded), this Celtic art suggests fewer well-connected individuals, moving for adventure, to make contacts or gain knowledge, for marriage, warfare or wealth. They used Celtic art styles on important objects to mark their wide connections, and probably to express shared ideas or beliefs in this restricted, complex art that gave up its meanings only to the initiated.

But the rhythms of European societies were changing by the second century BC. The emerging power of Rome was becoming dominant around the Mediterranean, casting its eyes greedily over its neighbours and increasingly looking north of the Alps into temperate Europe. Here, the smaller-scale societies of the past few hundred years had become progressively bound into larger regional groups, initially with shared meeting places or ritual sites, but growing into more substantial settlements where specialist craftworkers catered for these increased demands. In this changing world, an individual's connections were becoming less significant as there were larger markets and stronger links into wider economic and political worlds. Celtic art was adapted to new roles and communicated in new ways. The focus now was on mass production and trade, not the small-scale fabrication of a few beautiful items (see Chapter 5).

As this creative, complicated art became less dominant on the Continent, in Britain and Ireland curvilinear art flourished in novel ways. From the second century BC onwards, the stories of Britain and the Continent diverged markedly, and so from Chapter 5 our focus tightens from a pan-European one to Britain and Ireland, and takes us into these changing worlds. But first we shall explore what this earlier art was used for. It was not just decoration; it changed the objects that it adorned and the people who carried it, making them potent and marking them out from others.

Fig. 62 **A shield boss takes wing**

Stylized birds in the 'Torrs-Witham-Wandsworth style' circle this shield boss.

River Thames at Wandsworth, London 300–200 BC
Bronze; D 33 cm
British Museum, London

Fig. 63 **Image of a warrior**

An Iron Age warrior springs to life on this richly decorated gold brooch from Iberia (see p. 83).

Braganza collection, Iberia 250–200 BC
Gold, enamel; L 14 cm
British Museum, London

Chapter 4

Powerful Objects:
the Uses of Art in the Iron Age

Fraser Hunter

Around 400 BC at Somme-Bionne in north-east France a dead man was led past mourners in a decorated two-wheeled chariot. Its yoke tips were adorned with openwork bronze mounts. Bronze discs with complicated cut-out patterns highlighted the harness of the two ponies (fig. 44). The animals were led away from the grave but the harness and chariot were left there to take the dead man on a final journey. With him were the things his people thought he needed: an ornate sword in its decorated scabbard, a gold finger-ring and feasting gear (fig. 64). Some objects were imported from the Mediterranean; some were decorated with early Celtic art. The art and connections gave these objects power.

These finds show the areas of life where Celtic art was most commonly employed during the Iron Age: the body, the battlefield, the chariot and the feast. Here we will look at these different spheres and how they linked and differed across Iron Age Europe. We will also consider why so much of this high-value material was committed to the earth, for this tells us something else about its perceived power.

Fig. 64 **Finds from the Somme-Bionne burial**

The selection of finds from this rich burial includes feasting gear, weaponry and jewellery. The locally made jar, Etruscan bronze flagon and Greek cup would have been used at the feast. The knife was probably a tool for butchery or sacrifice, while the iron skewer served to roast meat. The warrior's iron sword is held in a decorated bronze scabbard, once suspended from a belt with a decorated fastening hook; the rings come either from the belt or from chariot harness. An iron handle is all that is left of his shield. Of his costume, all that survives is a plain gold ring.

Somme-Bionne, Marne, France 450–400 BC
Sword L 90 cm
British Museum, London

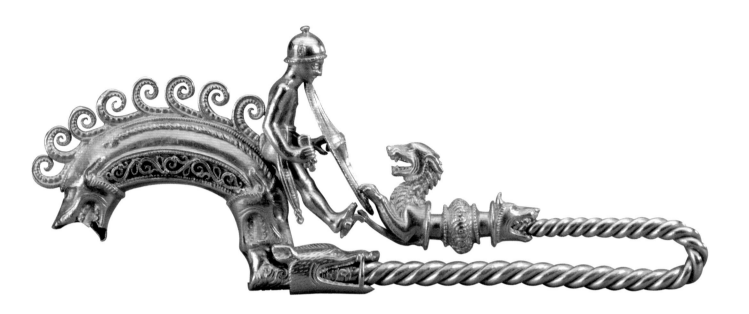

Fig. 65 The Braganza brooch

A spring once fitted under the left end of the
brooch, supporting a pin that was clamped in
place by the sliding beast's head on the lower
strut.

Iberia 250–200 BC
Gold, enamel; L 14 cm
British Museum, London

The clash of arms

A magnificent gold brooch from the Iberian peninsula brings an Iron Age
warrior to life (figs 63 and 65).[1] He faces a ferocious dog, protected by his
helmet and large oval shield, with sword drawn; otherwise, he is naked.[2]
Other fierce beasts lurk around him. This unique brooch may show a lost
myth: some forgotten hero and his adventures. Or perhaps this was a rite of
passage: a young man overcoming a trial to become a warrior. Alternatively,
was the dog a companion rather than an opponent: a hound that would help
in battle, captured in a moment of boisterous play?

In a grave from Gäufelden-Nebringen in south-western Germany, we
meet an Iron Age warrior in death (fig. 66).[3] His iron helmet has decorated
plates to protect the cheeks and a long spike that once held a plume or some
other ornament. His iron sword lies by his right side in an iron scabbard,
slung from his belt with iron rings. No shield survives – it may have been
entirely wooden – but he also carried a spear with an iron tip. His only
jewellery is a plain gold ring.

Fig. 66 **A warrior's farewell**

The grave goods from this man's burial
were dominated by weaponry: a sword in its
scabbard, rings to suspend it from a belt, a
spiked helmet (the spike is shown separately)
and a long spear. The only jewellery is a plain
gold finger-ring.

Gäufelden-Nebringen grave 11, Baden-Württemberg,
Germany 400–300 BC
Iron, gold; sword L 64 cm
Württembergisches Landesmuseum, Stuttgart

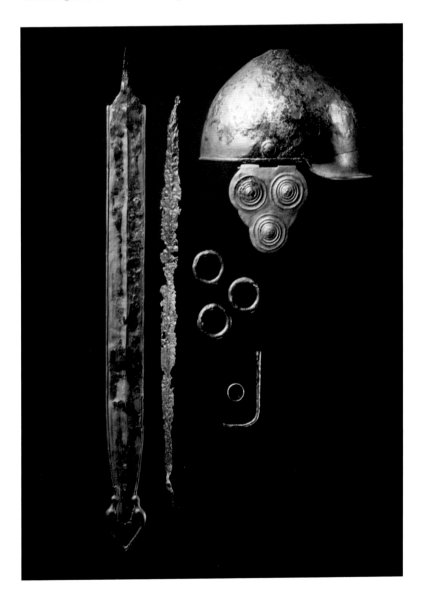

Fig. 67 **Shields for show**

The spine of this bronze shield carries intricate
repoussé decoration with engraved details,
highlighted in red coral, heads of cows, bulls or
horses at the ends of the spine and birds' heads
in the terminal roundels.

River Witham, Lincolnshire 300–200 BC
Bronze, coral; L 110 cm
British Museum, London

Fig. 68 **A protective handle**

The front of this bronze shield from the old course of the river Thames is undecorated, but the metal itself made it a spectacular object. Its handgrip ends in pairs of serpents. Paired animals had a protective function in Iron Age beliefs; they are also found on other objects such as sword scabbards and belt hooks.

Chertsey, Surrey 300–200 BC
Bronze; shield L 84 cm, handle L 23.5 cm
British Museum, London

These were three warriors from different times and places: north-east France around 400 BC; Iberia around 200 BC; and south-west Germany around 300 BC. Warfare was a fact of life throughout most of prehistory, and being seen as a warrior was an important part of being a free man in much of Iron Age Europe.[4] Often the weaponry was decorated: to intimidate the enemy, impress peers or invoke the protection of the gods.

Shields usually had only subtle decoration, such as a delicate pattern on a fastening rivet or a handgrip, but there was a peculiarly British habit of shields made entirely of bronze or with large and ornate bronze facings. These would have been little use in pitched battle. They were for showing off, for posturing in ceremonies or formal duels. One, from the river Witham, had the figure of a wild boar attached to it, perhaps to transfer the animal's strength and courage to the warrior (fig. 67; see also p. 1 and figs 1 and 9). This may have been removed when the spine was added, but the two could have been contemporary, with the boar removed before the shield was consigned to the river. An ornate spine covers the hand grip, with stylized birds and horses lurking in the designs. Another bronze shield, from the old course of the river Thames at Chertsey, is plain on the front, but the hand grip on the rear ends in pairs of serpents (fig. 68).[5] These beasts might have been intended to protect the wearer; they are an emblem we will meet again.

Helmets could also be highly decorated. Another find from the Thames, at Waterloo Bridge, has two fat horns sticking from the sides and fine patterns covering the cap (fig. 70). This may look impractical, but practicality was not the point. The aim was to impress. A helmet from Tintignac in central France is in the shape of a swan, its head curved back to its tail.[6] Another, from Ciumeşti in Romania, has an eagle attached to the top, its wings flapping as the warrior moved.[7] Similar bird- and animal-headed helmets can be seen in use on the silver cauldron from Gundestrup in Denmark (see fig. 258). From the river Seine near Amfreville came a bronze helmet decorated with curving foliage in red glass, iron and gold (fig. 71).[8] This is more like the functional helmet seen on the Iberian brooch discussed earlier, but its ornate embellishment marked it and its wearer out as special.

Fig. 69 **A treasured weapon**

There are over seventy separate components in this iron sword and bronze scabbard. Red glass inlays form patterns in the iron grip; the pommel and guard were of horn, with decorated rivets. The engraved scrolling decoration is a regional version of the trans-European Sword Style. Repairs to the lower scabbard show the sword was old when buried.

Kirkburn, East Yorkshire 300–200 BC
Bronze, iron, glass, horn; L 70 cm
British Museum, London

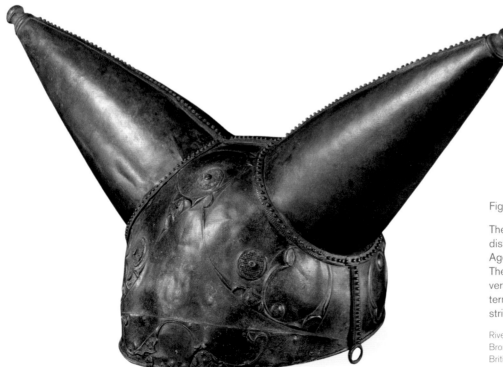

Fig. 70 **A horned helmet from the Thames**

The horns on this bizarre helmet would be a distinct handicap on a battlefield, but much Iron Age warfare was about posturing and prestige. The spindly decoration is a stretched-out version of ornament found on contemporary torc terminals (see fig. 30); the roundels once had striking red glass inlays.

River Thames at Waterloo Bridge, London 200–100 BC
Bronze, glass; W between horns 42.5 cm
British Museum, London

Fig. 71 **The Amfreville helmet**

Almost every part of this bronze helmet is decorated with gold, glass or iron. It would originally have been strikingly colourful, and even more impressive when the lost cheek-piece was present (the leaf-shaped outline of the attachment plate is visible).

Amfreville, Eure, France 350–300 BC
Bronze, iron, gold, glass; H 17.5 cm
Musée d'Archéologie Nationale, St Germain-en-Laye

Decoration on weaponry and armour was intended to impress and intimidate. Sword scabbards often carry complex twisting patterns. The light playing off the intricate markings would have confused and stunned the onlooker, whether opponent or friend. A very elaborate sword from a man's burial at Kirkburn in East Yorkshire has a beautiful handle inlaid with patterns in red glass.[9] Its bronze scabbard is also highly decorated, with a tendril of stylized foliage snaking its way down to the tip. The scabbard has been repaired and was clearly a highly valued weapon (fig. 69).

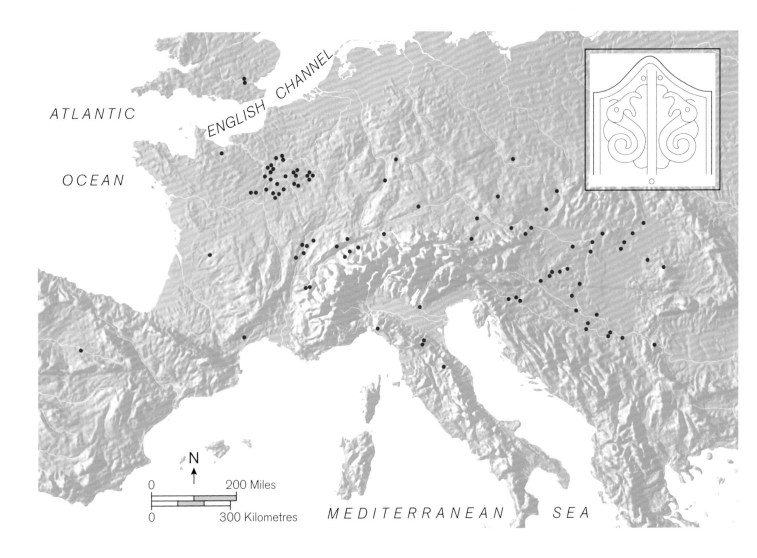

Fig. 72 **Warrior symbols**

All across Europe, the mouths of sword scabbards were decorated with pairs of fantastical beasts (inset). This international symbol of the warrior probably had a protective role. They are called 'dragon-pairs' by modern scholars, but the beasts defy easy identification. While some are very obvious, others hide within decorative patterns.

Scabbards like this are found across Europe in different regional styles (see p. 57), and regional variety is seen in other aspects of sword-play. In most of Europe the sword was slung from the shoulder and drawn at the hip, but in central Britain it was typically worn on the back and drawn theatrically over the shoulder. Chalk figurines from East Yorkshire show swords worn in this way.[10]

Scabbards were very visible markers of a warrior's power, position and potential threat, but a lot of their decoration was hidden. It was not for the sight of friend or foe, but for the warrior himself or for the gods. Small stamped motifs, typically showing humans, animals or solar symbols, were occasionally added to sword blades in the later Iron Age.[11] On some swords the designs were so faint that they would be almost impossible to see unless you were too close for comfort: the scabbard from the Somme-Bionne burial

has very delicate punch-marked motifs.[12] These may have been protective images designed to be seen by gods, not humans.

Other symbols probably had a protective role as well. From Hungary to Britain, scabbards were decorated with pairs of fierce animals facing one another (fig. 72).[13] These fantastical creatures represent a widespread warrior symbol. They are rare in Britain, but the pair of serpents on the handle of the Chertsey shield (fig. 68) may have had a similar effect.[14]

Such widespread habits remind us of the contacts across Europe during the Iron Age: contacts that imply moving warriors, perhaps as mercenaries seeking glory in the service of different leaders. Shared ideas are seen in other sword styles as well. Swords with very long narrow blades are found from western France through southern Germany to Switzerland; heavy knobbed hilts act as a counterbalance. They seem impractical weapons, but nicks on their edges show they were used (fig. 73). This speaks of ritualized duels rather than the mêlée of battle: heroes and champions fighting for a prize.[15]

Another widespread tradition was short swords with bronze hilts in human form; examples are found from Ireland to Hungary (fig. 74).[16] These are much smaller than normal swords, and some carry unusual patterns on the blade. One from Munich-Untermenzing in southern Germany is decorated with circles, crescents and dots inlaid with gold and copper alloy, which probably represent phases of the moon, or perhaps the moon, sun and stars. Like the duelling swords, these must have had a special role, perhaps in sacrifice rather than war.

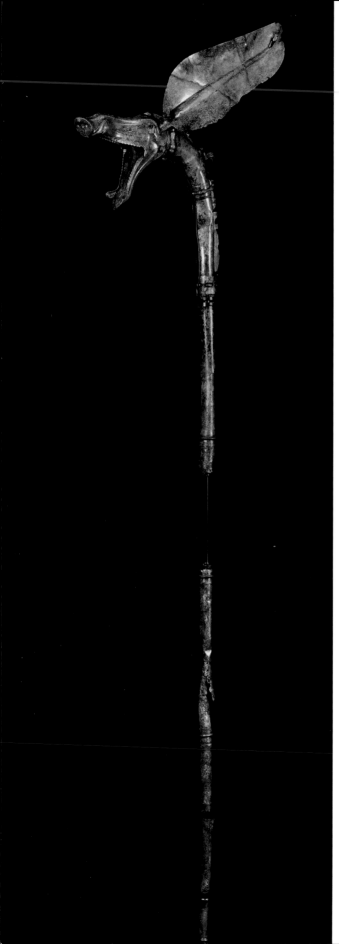

Sound and fury

The impact of a battle lay not just in sight but also in sound: the tumult of the warriors, the thumping of shields, the screams of the fallen and the blare of musical instruments. Across large parts of Europe, a kind of animal-headed horn called a *carnyx* was used in war and ceremonies. This long-lived habit (from *c.* 300 BC to AD 300) extended beyond the bounds of the 'Celtic world' into northern and south-east Europe; carnyx-players are even recorded on sculpture from India.[17] One of the finest examples comes from Deskford in north-eastern Scotland.[18] Only the head survives, deliberately removed from the rest of the instrument and buried in a sacred bog as an offering. It evokes a wild boar with its wrinkles of skin and upturned snout (fig. 76).

At Tintignac in central France fragments of several carnyces from a temple site give a vivid impression of their original appearance (fig. 75). Again, most resemble boars, a fighting animal, but the decoration here is very different. While the idea of the carnyx was widely shared, people in each area made it according to their own style. Once again, we see a Europe of the regions lurking behind this shared Celtic art.

Fig. 75 (left and opposite below)
The Tintignac carnyx find

Excavations in an Iron Age sanctuary uncovered a hoard of valued items dismantled and buried when the sacred site was rebuilt in the Roman period. They included fragments of seven carnyces, which showed for the first time that these remarkable large leaf-like sheets were actually massive ears. They would act like loudspeakers when the instrument was blown.

Tintignac, Limousin, France 250–50 BC
Bronze; H 1.80 m
Institut National de Recherches Archéologiques Préventives, Paris

Fig. 76 (opposite above) **The Deskford carnyx**

The head of this boar-headed horn once looked even more impressive. When it was discovered it had a moveable wooden tongue, and the eyes were probably once filled with brightly coloured enamel. Scientific analysis shows that today's green colour is misleading: different components were made in bronze or brass to create a colour contrast.

Deskford, Aberdeenshire AD 75–200
Copper alloy; L 21 cm (excluding rear disc)
National Museums Scotland, Edinburgh
(on loan from Aberdeenshire Heritage)

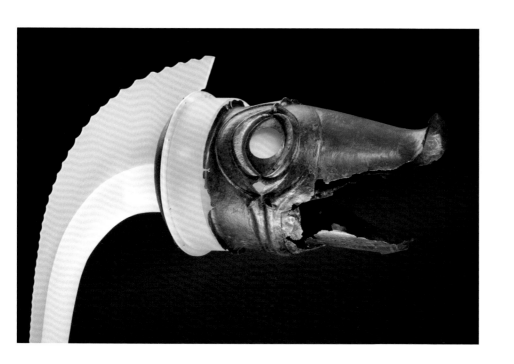

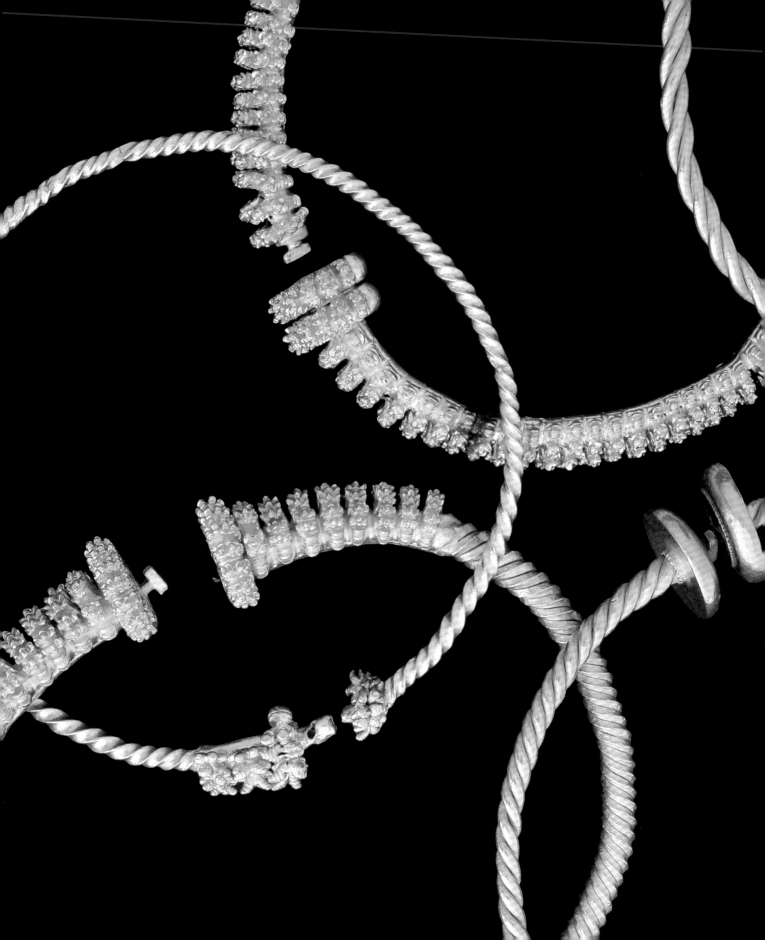

Fig. 77 (left) The Fenouillet hoard

Two different traditions of torc were buried together. Those with twisted hoops and buffer terminals are widespread across Europe in the later Iron Age. The others are a speciality of south-west France. Some or all of the hoop has a knobbly, expanded, almost floral appearance. On these torcs this is achieved by a very fine casting process; other such objects used hammered sheet.

Fenouillet, Haute-Garonne, France 300–200 BC
Gold; internal D of left torc 11 cm
Musée Saint-Raymond, musée des Antiques de Toulouse

Fig. 78 (above right) Far-flung gold

The Blair Drummond torcs are a real mixture. The two at the rear are local styles. They look deceptively simple but are virtuoso pieces made by repeated hammering and coiling to create the double-helix form. The fragmentary torc on the left is modelled on French examples, while the front torc used Mediterranean technologies in its decoration. Did these more exotic torcs travel from southern Europe, or did craftworkers move with these skills in their heads and hands?

Blair Drummond, Stirling 300–100 BC
Gold; D of loop-terminal torc 15 cm
National Museums Scotland, Edinburgh

Dressing up

This similarity and difference is seen in many kinds of Celtic art. In a grave in south-western Germany, a well-dressed woman was laid to rest. Her clothes were fastened with three pairs of brooches, suggesting a complex costume. She wore rich jewellery: a gold finger-ring, and anklets, arm-ring and neck-ring (torc) of bronze (fig. 79). Torcs were a recurring feature of the Iron Age. Classical authors saw them as the sign of a Celt, but such decorated neck ornaments were common across the European Iron Age and beyond. Some styles were widespread; others were local. Sometimes they were worn by men, sometimes by women, sometimes gods. The idea was shared, but developed differently in different areas.[19]

In 2009, a hoard of gold torcs was found at Blair Drummond in central Scotland by a metal detectorist on his very first outing (p. 3 and fig. 78). Excavations showed they had been buried inside a timber building, probably a shrine, in an isolated, wet location. These four torcs show widespread connections across Iron Age Europe. Two are made from spiralling gold ribbons, a style characteristic of Scotland and Ireland. Another, in two fragments, forms half of a tubular torc with an ornate knobbly appearance. This style is found in south-western France – there are close parallels from a hoard at Fenouillet (fig. 77) – although analysis of the Blair Drummond gold suggests it was made locally based on French styles rather than being an import.[20] The final torc is a real mixture. Its form, with

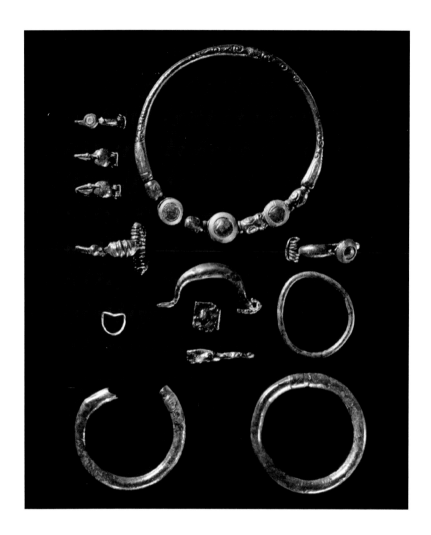

Fig. 79 (left) **A well-dressed woman**

This jewellery accompanied a middle-aged woman to her grave: six brooches from an ornate costume, a belt hook, arm- and foot-rings and a finger-ring. The style of torc is typical of south-western Germany and western Switzerland.

Gäufelden-Nebringen grave 4, Baden-Württemberg, Germany 400–300 BC
Bronze, iron, gold, glass; torc D 16.2 cm
Württembergisches Landesmuseum, Stuttgart

Fig. 80 **Different fashions**

Different styles of torc were popular in different areas: what you wore marked where you came from. This torc with three decorated zones is typical of southern Champagne and north-west Burgundy. It is very different from the Swiss/southern German style of torc in fig. 79.

Pleurs, Marne, France 350–250 BC
Bronze; D 15.3 cm
British Museum, London

a rope-like hoop and expanded terminals, is typically Iron Age, but the embellishment of the terminals is not. Their fastening chain and decoration made up from small gold balls and complex coiled wires are typical of Mediterranean workshops. It shows technological skill, a familiarity with exotic styles, and connections to a craftworker or workshop with the expertise to make such an object. The Blair Drummond find brings together the local and the highly exotic in one hoard.

Torcs show considerable variations in style, material and meaning. In France and western Germany, bronze torcs are found in many female graves, with different styles in different areas (figs 79–80).[21] Iron was also used occasionally, though it rarely survives and would have been difficult to forge into complex forms. Over large areas of Europe, prestige torcs were made in gold, like the ones at Blair Drummond. However, in parts of Spain

Fig. 81 **The silver bull-torc**

This unique torc has an iron core under the decorated silver sheet. The weight (almost 7 kg) and inflexibility suggest it was not intended for human wear. It may have been worn by a statue or passed around at ceremonies.

Trichtingen, Baden-Württemberg, Germany 200–50 BC
Silver, iron; D 29.5 cm
Württembergisches Landesmuseum, Stuttgart

and Portugal silver was much more common.[22] Silver was also used in eastern Europe. A unique massive silver neck-ring on an iron core from Trichtingen in south-western Germany was probably imported from this area (fig. 81). It has terminals in the shape of bulls' heads, while the bulls themselves wear miniature torcs.[23]

But torcs were not just a Celtic thing, as the classical authors thought. They were found across Bronze Age Europe, and in the Iron Age their distribution stretched from the Near East to northern regions beyond the Celtic world. Denmark, for example, produced a local style of bronze torc

with strong links to the south: the terminals were often decorated with versions of Celtic art styles (fig. 83).[24] A Danish gold torc from Dronninglund also shows long-range connections in form and technology – but to the Black Sea, not the Celtic world. Similar connections across northern Europe are seen in a distinctive style of bronze torc that looks like a crown, although it was worn round the neck (fig. 82). These are found from Scandinavia to Ukraine.[25]

Torcs remind us of the complexity of Iron Age Europe. They were a concept that was shared widely, from the Atlantic to the Black Sea and from the Baltic to the Mediterranean. In this connected world, some styles were very local, others very international.

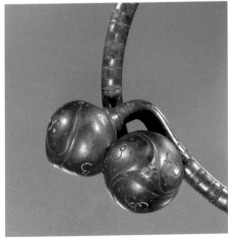

Fig. 83 Celtic art influences in Denmark

Celtic art styles had an influence far beyond the Celtic world. This distinctively Danish style of torc used Plastic-Style decoration on its ball terminals, often in triple-legged (triskele) patterns.

Gammelborg (Møn) and Eggeslevmagle (Zealand), Denmark 250–100 BC
Bronze; upper torc D 18.5 cm
National Museum of Denmark, Copenhagen

Fig. 82 Torcs beyond a Celtic world

Neck ornaments were common in many Iron Age cultures. This Danish example, which hinges to allow it to open, is a type found widely across northern Europe.

Rødmose, Jutland, Denmark 250–100 BC
Bronze; D 16.5 cm
National Museum of Denmark, Copenhagen

Travelling in style

It was not just people who wore ornaments. Horses and the two-wheeled chariots pulled by them were kitted out with decorated fittings. Just like cars today, chariots were about more than getting from A to B. Some were fast, light vehicles; others were heavier and more ornate, where being seen on the journey was as important as the destination. Chariots were another widely shared concept that was adapted in different areas. The one from the Somme-Bionne burial is a stately affair, with lots of bronze decoration and iron suspension fittings for a gentle ride.[26] At the same time on the other side of the North Sea, someone was buried in a chariot at Newbridge, near Edinburgh.[27] The body has decayed, so we cannot tell if it was a man or a woman, but the chariot remains were well preserved. It would have been a light, fast vehicle, very different from its contemporaries in France in style and technology (fig. 84). It has no suspension fittings, for instance, and the wheels are made differently. The idea of burial in a chariot shows a connection to wider Continental concepts – it was a very rare habit in Britain at that time – but the vehicle itself is local.

Different again are the later chariots from East Yorkshire. This area developed a tradition of chariot burial around 200 BC, which used elaborate fittings in a distinctively British style.[28] A man was buried at Kirkburn under a dismantled, richly adorned chariot.[29] Five decorated rings ran along the yoke to hold the reins. A pair of strap fasteners was also embellished, as were the heads of the linchpins that secured the wheels. The bridle bits for the horses were plain in this burial, but ornate bits are known from elsewhere.

Fig. 84 **Reconstructing a chariot**

The chariot burial at Newbridge is the oldest known example from Britain. As the iron corroded it seeped into the surrounding organic components, fossilizing their traces. This informed a detailed reconstruction by Robert Hurford. The wheel rim is a single piece of wood bent into a circle, gripped by an iron tyre that is heated up and then shrunk to fit. This precision engineering seems to have been a British habit – there is no evidence of it on the Continent at this time.

Newbridge, City of Edinburgh. Original 450–380 BC; reconstruction made 2007
Wood, rawhide, skin, iron; L 3.8 m
National Museums Scotland, Edinburgh

Among the finest of such chariot gear is a set from Mezek in Bulgaria, which includes masterpieces of the Plastic Style (see p. 56), covered in cartoon-like figures (fig. 85). The bases of the five rein-rings are decorated with surprised-looking human faces, while birds peer from the bronze linchpins.[30]

The most spectacular piece of horse ornament from around this time is the pony cap from Torrs, dating to the third century BC (fig. 86). There has been a long debate over whether the horns were originally attached or were joined after its nineteenth-century discovery to improve its market value.[31] This has now been solved thanks to an exciting find, not in the field but in the archives.[32] The *Caledonian Mercury* for 17 December 1812 records the discovery of the cap with the horns still attached, and mentions bridle bits and decorative harness fittings, now lost. The cap would fit on the pony's head – the holes are for the ears, not the eyes – with the horns projecting forwards. A similar cap is worn by a winged horse on an Iron Age coin from south-east England.[33]

Fig. 85 **Lively chariot fittings**

The decorated chariot fittings from Mezek seem to come alive, with very human faces staring from some. This has been termed Disney Style as it resembles the cartoonist's ability to evoke faces with curves and coils. These fittings were fastened to the chariot yoke, guiding the reins which ran through the hole in the circle.

Mezek, Svilengrad district, Bulgaria 300–200 BC
Bronze; rings D 7.5–8.4 cm
National Institute of Archaeology with Museum, Sofia

Fig. 86 **Dressing up the horses**

This cap was for a pony, with its ears fitting through the holes and its muzzle facing right. Recent research shows the horns were attached to the cap when it was found. They would have given the animal a dramatic appearance, but may not have been a primary feature – decorated patches show that the cap had been heavily modified.

Torrs, Dumfries & Galloway 300–200 BC
Bronze; cap L 23.4 cm
National Museums Scotland, Edinburgh

The Torrs cap had been heavily repaired, and the horns cut down and refastened in the Iron Age. They may once have come from the ends of a chariot yoke. Their decoration speaks of wider worlds. The repoussé ornament on the cap is a British version of the Plastic Style found on the Continent at this period, while the engraving is in the same style as contemporary decorated scabbards (see pp. 76–7); a small human face peers from the spirals. The effort spent on it emphasizes how important fine horses and chariots were at the time.

Feasting – the cauldron and the cup

Today, what we eat, where we eat it and who we share it with are significant parts of our social lives. Large meals mark special occasions such as birthdays or Christmas, bringing families and friends together. Or we might eat out at a smart restaurant to impress someone, or hold a lavish party to show off to our guests.

These different approaches are seen in prehistory too. Food and drink were used to bring people together or to set some people apart. The big feast is represented by massive cauldrons of paper-thin bronze. These are impressive feats of technology, and evidence of repairs shows that they were utilized regularly to cook food for major gatherings. But they were rarely decorated. A hoard of cauldrons found at Chiseldon was buried after one such prodigious meal.[34] At least 17 vessels were present, representing a massive 800 litres of food or drink (analysis of surviving residues suggests they were filled with stew), but only three bore any adornment, including a striking cow's-head handle. Such feasts marked communal events, perhaps to carry out a joint task such as building a new house or creating the banks and ditches of a hillfort. People would be paid for their efforts in food and drink.

Fig. 87 **Bestiary on a beer mug**

Simple painted pottery is found quite widely in Europe in the second century BC, but this decorated pot from central France is in a different class. Animals have been distorted to create very striking images. The creatures are deliberately hard to identify: many resemble deer, but antlers, legs and ears are often stretched or blown up far beyond nature. (See also fig. 263.)

Clermont-Ferrand, Puy-de-Dôme, France 150–100 BC
Ceramic; H 43 cm
Le Musée Bargoin (Musée Archaeologique), Clermont Ferrand

Fig. 88 **An animated handle**

This handle was fastened to a concave-sided wooden drinking tankard (like that in fig. 27). The simple decoration of rings and bosses brings the handle alive by giving it a zoomorphic character.

Carlingwark, Dumfries & Galloway AD 50–100
Copper alloy; L 12.6 cm
National Museums Scotland, Edinburgh

Fig. 89 **A mysterious knife**

This curious small bronze knife evokes a ferocious bird in its form and decoration. Bronze is an unusual choice for a knife – iron was the norm – so it probably had a special function. It is decorated in the same style as the Torrs pony cap (fig. 86) and shield bosses from the rivers Thames and Witham (figs 39, 62 and 67).

Chiswell Green, Hertfordshire 300–200 BC
Bronze; L 11 cm
British Museum, London

By contrast, smaller, personal items of feasting gear were more often decorated. Flagons like those from Basse-Yutz or Kleinaspergle (figs 35, 40, 41, 45 and 46) would have served drink to the few, not the many. [35] In Britain a form of wooden tankard developed, often with bronze handles which provided touches of ornamentation (fig. 27): a handle from Carlingwark looks like two elephants to the modern eye (fig. 88). [36] In central France, in the second century BC, distinctively painted drinking vessels carried wonderful contorted animal figures within complex patterns (figs 87 and 263). [37] These large mugs and tankards were probably passed around a small group in restricted gatherings rather than at large-scale feasts (see pp. 44–6). Decoration, it seems, served to distinguish the vessels used in these more private settings. It created haves and have-nots.

Magic and ritual

Many objects from the past puzzle us. We struggle to work out what they were for. Sometimes this is because they are fragmentary, or represent skills and crafts that are now unfamiliar to most of us, such as ploughing with animals or making chariots. Sometimes they seem genuinely odd. Were these items used in the religious beliefs and ceremonies of the Iron Age? Such enigmatic objects often feature Celtic art. A bronze knife from Chiswell Green in south-east England takes the shape of a stylized flying bird, its vicious hooked beak forming the blade (fig. 89). [38] But why was it made of bronze? Iron was the standard material for tools by this time. The unusual material and decoration suggest this was no kitchen knife but a blade with a less everyday use, perhaps for sacrifices or healing ceremonies, or gathering ingredients for medicines. A similar question arises with curious pairs of bronze scoops found occasionally across Britain and Ireland (fig. 90), with one example from France. [39] These are no ordinary spoons: they have ornamented handles and carefully made bowls with a cross in one and a small off-centre hole in the other. Their role remains a puzzle. Were they

used for fortune-telling or prophecy, perhaps as something poured from the hole onto the quadrants of the cross? We can but speculate.

Another puzzling group of objects may also have a ritual purpose: highly decorated bronze dishes (fig. 91), also found in pairs, which are known across Ireland but nowhere else.[40] These have a small, deep hollow near the centre and a broad rim embellished with slender scrolling trumpets. Again, their function is obscure. Perhaps we reach too quickly for the idea of a religious or magical purpose, but it is hard to see everyday uses for them.[41] The same is true of a cylindrical bronze box found in a woman's burial at Wetwang Slack in East Yorkshire (fig. 92).[42] The box is attached to a fine chain and its exterior is decorated in a style just like that of the sword scabbards from this area. But the box is sealed; there is no way to open it without destroying it. Whatever was held within was not coming out. What is this mysterious container? Is it an ornate rattle, with the rattling element long decayed? Did it contain some special or magical substance, now lost? Did it have some symbolic significance, holding a spirit or essence? Only one related item is known: a canister from a grave at Ballydavis in Ireland, similarly sealed, similarly mysterious.[43]

Fig. 90 Strange scoops

These enigmatic scoops are typically found in pairs, with a cross on one and an offset hole in the other. This pair has a cast design of twisting vegetation on the handles, in Vegetal or Waldalgesheim Style. Their function is uncertain.

Weston, Somerset 350–300 BC
Bronze; L 11 cm
National Museums Scotland, Edinburgh

Fig. 91 Enigmatic discs

The function of these decorated discs remains a puzzle. The focus is the central hollow, surrounded by high-relief repoussé decoration. Depending on its orientation, it can resemble a face. The deliberate roughening of the background makes the raised decoration visually dominant.

Ireland 100 BC–AD 400
Copper alloy; D 27.2 cm
British Museum, London

Fig. 92 **Hidden contents**

This curious cylinder from a woman's burial
in Yorkshire is a real puzzle. It has no obvious
function, and there is no way to open it:
whatever it contained was sealed in for good.
The carrying chain suggests it was a personal
item, or perhaps a musical instrument such as a
rattle. The style of decoration resembles sword
scabbards from the same area.

Wetwang Slack, East Yorkshire 300–200 BC
Bronze; D 9 cm
Hull and East Riding Museum

These unusual items take us to another subject: the druids, who were
religious specialists of the Iron Age in Britain and France, according to
Roman writers.[44] This topic encouraged all kind of conjecture among earlier
scholars trying to reconstruct ancient religions and remains a popular area
for wild speculation today. Hard evidence is very limited indeed, though
hints may lie in some unusual headgear that cannot easily be explained as
helmets. From an unknown location in Ireland comes a bronze contraption
that seems to be part of a ritual headpiece or crown: a decorative bronze
band with discs and horns attached.[45] Some of the more unusual 'helmets'
(fig. 70) could equally have been religious headdresses.[46] More convincing
material comes from a temple complex at Roseldorf-Sandberg in Austria,
where finds include an unusual iron cap made from straps and an antler
whose base had been modified so it could be fitted to a headpiece and worn
by a human.[47]

We should hesitate to associate these things with druids, for the term's
ancient implications are poorly understood, and classical writings give no
indication of any particular sets of objects that might denote this special
status. However, there was a recurring idea in the Iron Age that unusual
headgear marked out people who undertook a special role: for instance, the
leaf-crown headdresses of the fifth and fourth centuries BC were clearly
more than just fancy hats (see p. 68). This role could have been to take
charge of religious rituals, or as a secular leader; we cannot tell. However,
there are hints here of a shadowy world of beliefs where the decoration of
these items was a key part of their power and magic.

Buried treasure, sacrificed wealth

In 1855, labourers pulled a magnificent decorated shield from the river
Thames at Battersea (figs 17 and 26). One of the most spectacular pieces of
Iron Age Celtic art from Britain, its front is decorated with panels of curling
foliage and lurking animals, embellished with red glass.[48] Many of our finest
pieces of Celtic art are chance finds like this, often from wet or out-of-the-
way locations such as rivers, bogs, lakes or mountains. These were not just
casual losses: it is unlikely people would be so repeatedly careless with such
valuable things. It is also unlikely they were buried for safekeeping: a river is
not a good place in which to hide something. These items were deliberately
deposited, perhaps as sacrifices to unknown gods, during rites of passage, or
to seal agreements between individuals or groups.[49]

These sacrifices and offerings did not just include spectacular objects
like the Battersea shield. They could also feature everyday items. Sometimes
these deposits took place on settlement sites – for example, a quernstone
might be deliberately broken up and buried when a house was abandoned
– but often they occurred in special locations. One of the most famous such

sites in Europe is La Tène on Lake Neuchâtel in western Switzerland.[50] From the mid-nineteenth century, people began to fish iron objects out of its waters. Excavations in a branch of the river Thielle flowing out of the lake revealed two bridges and a huge number of finds, most dating to the late third century BC.[51] This included swords in decorated iron scabbards, many spearheads and shields, part of a carnyx, everyday iron tools, brooches and preserved wooden items such as pieces of carts and wooden vessels. There were also human and animal remains. The finds were so numerous that they were employed as type-specimens by scholars: the name of La Tène is still used by archaeologists to refer to the later Iron Age and the styles of art that were represented at the site. There continues to be much debate over exactly what happened at La Tène – in particular, whether the bridge was a platform for sacrificing items to the water, or whether they were displayed on the bridge and only later fell in – but it seems clear these were deliberate offerings.

Another dramatic landscape location has only recently been examined. On the island of Skye in western Scotland, on a low-lying river valley with spectacular views to the Cuillin mountains, cavers exploring a blocked passage at Uamh An Ard Achadh (High Pasture Cave) came across large quantities of animal bones (fig. 93). Excavations showed that the cave had been the focus of rituals throughout the Iron Age, from *c.* 800 to 100 BC. Animals were slaughtered, massive feasts held and offerings deposited there. Perhaps it was seen as an entrance to the underworld, as the passage leads to an underground stream. Offerings were left around the cave mouth, on the boundary of dark and light: mostly everyday objects such as bone jewellery, stone spindle whorls and an iron axe, but also much rarer items like parts of a wooden lyre. When the site was abandoned, a massive feast was held and the remains of fifteen butchered young pigs were left in the cave. The entrance was then blocked up, but 200 years later, around AD 100, a young woman, a foetus and a newly-born infant were buried in the infill, suggesting that the cave retained some kind of significance.[52]

These examples show that everyday objects as well as spectacular ones could be used as offerings, bringing people and groups together at special places, probably at particular times of the year. There must have been many such sites across Iron Age Europe where people gathered. Most had local or regional significance, but some had much wider importance. One of those lay in north-west Norfolk, at Snettisham.

The golden hoards

The Norfolk landscape lacks the obvious drama of Skye's hills or the waterscape of La Tène, but the low promontory at Snettisham is a significant feature in the surrounding area.[53] No trace of ancient activity was known from the site until 1948, when gold torcs were picked up after ploughing.

Fig. 93 (above and below) **Everyday offerings**

High Pasture Cave on Skye is dramatically situated with views to the Cuillin mountains. It was a focus of offerings throughout the Iron Age. Most were very practical tokens of people's lives, such as spindle whorls: spinning yarn was an everyday, endless task. The rearmost four whorls pictured below were buried together. They cover all stages in a whorl's life from partly-made through well-used to broken.

High Pasture Cave, Skye, Highland 800–700 BC
Steatite; front right whorl D 3 cm
National Museums Scotland, Edinburgh

Fig. 94 **Golden pits**

Careful excavation of a find can reveal vital information about how it was buried. Here, the dramatic contents of one pit at Snettisham are revealed for the first time in over 2,000 years. Gold and copper alloy torcs were carefully placed in this lower pit; a layer of earth separated them from an overlying deposit of silver torcs.

Snettisham, Norfolk 300–50 BC
Gold; D of decorated torc at bottom of picture 16 cm
British Museum, London

Further discoveries were made over the years, culminating in a series of magnificent finds in 1990 when several large hoards were unearthed, buried carefully in pits: gold, silver and bronze torcs, complete and in fragments.[54] In one pit, the torcs had been buried in two batches with a layer of soil between them, the gold examples at the bottom (fig. 94). Other tantalizing finds have been lost to unscrupulous treasure hunters. A hoard of some 6,000 silver and gold coins, buried in a silver bowl, was plundered and sold without any record.[55]

The torcs show a wide range of styles and periods, but it seems most date from between the third and first centuries BC.[56] Some hoards include cut-up fragments and ingots. Perhaps production took place nearby, although incomplete items may have been considered equally appropriate offerings. Some torcs are clearly from further afield. A hoard of four 'tubular torcs' (see p. 106) are made from hollow tubes of gold sheet, in a style shared with northern France: they are probably imports.[57] The coins from the site also speak of wide-ranging connections, to Lincolnshire, Essex and Kent, northern and southern France, and even north Africa and Turkey.[58]

The hoards are set within a massive enclosure.[59] This suggests a major ritual centre, where the community's wealth was brought either for safe-keeping or for sacrifice. The two interpretations need not be exclusive: material could be placed under the protection of the gods, as it would be taboo to take it from their control. This surely was a site of pilgrimage, famous over wide areas. It gives us a vivid insight into how special locations were used and why powerful objects were buried there.

The power of decoration

Decoration gave objects special powers. We have seen how it was used in activities that were critical to people's lives: what they wore, what they fought with, how they travelled, what they ate. These were key to how people and communities defined themselves, gained prestige in relation to other individuals or groups, and sought to control relationships with others. Decorating valued items with this mysterious art gave the objects an edge, making them powerful or mysterious, symbolizing something about the wearer or user, or perhaps invoking the power of the gods.

The potency of these items is seen in their fate: accompanying someone to the afterlife in a burial or being deposited in a special place. The idea of making offerings was widespread in the Iron Age, for religious reasons or for more political ones to do with negotiating relations between groups. Some of the most spectacular offerings were magnificent items decorated with Celtic art. Their decoration gave them power and made them worthy sacrifices.

The Science of Celtic Art:
Scientific Analysis of the Snettisham Torcs

Nigel Meeks, Caroline Cartwright, Duncan Hook and Julia Farley

Scientific analyses carried out at the British Museum have given new insights into how the torcs from Snettisham were constructed. They have been examined using a combination of techniques including X-radiography, optical microscopy, scanning electron microscopy with microanalysis (SEM-EDX), which can achieve a much higher level of magnification and detail than an optical microscope, and X-ray fluorescence analysis (XRF), to reveal the metal composition.

The results have revealed a wide variety of manufacturing techniques, showing that the people who made these objects had sophisticated knowledge of the properties of metals (various alloys of gold, silver and copper), and were skilled in complex, multi-stage metalworking processes.

The X-radiograph of a tubular torc (fig. A) reveals its complex construction. Sheet gold objects like this torc were made from alloys with a high gold content, which were softer and easier to work than alloys that had higher silver

and copper contents. The sheet gold is very thin and would have been hammered out by hand. It would have been formed around a supporting core material, perhaps of clay, sand or wax.

Most of the wire torcs from Snettisham are made from alloys containing gold, silver and copper. Some of the wires have a low precious-metal content, but have been cleverly worked to give them a more golden or silvery colour rather than a copper colour at the surface. The wires would have been hammered out from cast ingots, and annealed (heated) to re-soften the metal between hammering cycles. Heating also oxidizes the copper in the surface of the metal, and the wires would have been

Fig. B
SEM back-scattered electron image of a bronze wire torc. The bright areas are the remains of mercury gilding. This torc also shows extensive wear between the wire strands due to heavy use.

British Museum, London

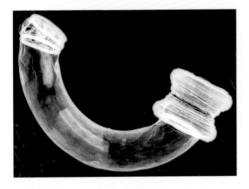

Fig. A
X-radiograph of a gold tubular torc showing the remains of an internal supporting structure, a curved iron rod, now broken, which may also have formed part of a locking mechanism.

Norwich Castle Museum

'pickled' after each cycle in an acidic solution to remove the black copper oxide before hammering again to elongate the wires further. Repeating this process of annealing, pickling and hammering removes much of the copper from the outside of the wire, creating a surface enriched in gold and silver.

In some cases, another advanced technique had been used to change the surface colour of the wires. Fig. B shows twisted bronze wires that have been mercury gilded. Mercury gilding is a complex process that would have involved making an amalgam, or 'butter', of mercury and

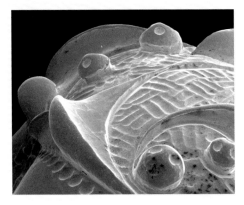

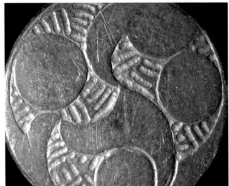

Fig. C (far left)

SEM backscattered electron image of the Snettisham 'Great Torc'. (See also p. 41 and fig. 30.)

British Museum, London

Fig. D (left)

Buffer terminal torc from Snettisham.

British Museum, London

gold, applying this to the surface of the bronze wires, and then heating the torc to evaporate the mercury. This leaves a layer of gold on the surface that is then burnished to give it a high shine. Some of the mercury-gilded torcs are twisted wire forms, which are typically British types. Where local craftworkers might have sourced the mercury remains a mystery, but it was probably imported from the continent, most likely from Spain. The mercury gilding process was previously thought to be unknown outside China and the classical world at this time.

Microscopic examination of the torcs can reveal further insights into the manufacturing process. The torc terminals were often finished with the addition of punched and chased designs and embellishments. Figs C and D show similarities between the punched decoration on the terminals of the 'Great Torc' and a buffer terminal from a separate hoard. Perhaps these objects were made in the same workshop?

Metal was not the only material used in the construction of the Snettisham torcs. Fig. E shows how bronze wires have been twisted around an organic core to create the neck-ring of the torc. SEM examination of the charred core shows that originally it was a length of coppiced hazel wood, which would have prevented the wires collapsing during twisting and been flexible enough to bend while forming the curved torc.

Torcs were complex objects with many different elements which could be constructed and decorated in a number of different ways. The complicated manufacturing processes revealed by scientific analyses show that Iron Age goldsmiths working in Britain around 2,000 years ago produced some of the most accomplished and elaborate precious metal objects in the ancient world.

Fig. E
SEM backscattered electron image of a bronze wire torc fragment revealing an organic core.

British Museum, London

Chapter 5

Fig. 95 **Decorated mirror (detail)**

On the Continent the swirling designs of Celtic art gradually declined from the second century BC. In Britain and Ireland the use of these motifs continued to develop. Some of the finest British examples of Celtic art, including the beautifully engraved mirror, were made in the century before the Roman conquest (see pp. 124–7).

Desborough, Northamptonshire 50 BC–AD 50
Copper alloy; L 35 cm
British Museum, London

A Changing World, *c.* 150 BC–AD 50

Ian Leins and Julia Farley

On a September day in 2013 Jonathan Barrett uncovered a small, mundane-looking copper-alloy cylinder as he searched with his metal detector in a field in the parish of Bredgar, Kent. The sides and upper face of the object offered little clue to its function, but its exquisitely decorated lower face served to identify it as a late Iron Age coin-die. The die (fig. 96) would have been one of a pair of punches required to stamp the designs into an ancient coin. The Bredgar die carries the distinctive galloping horse pattern of the so-called 'Gallo-Belgic A' gold coins of the later second century BC, a design reminiscent of the white chalk horse that adorns the hillside at Uffington in Oxfordshire. As the name implies, these coins are conventionally thought to have been manufactured in Belgic Gaul (modern northern France and Belgium), although it is clear from findspots that they circulated widely on both sides of the Channel. It is the third and easily the finest example of a coin-die from Britain, but the real significance of the discovery stems from the intriguing possibility that these early coins were produced in Britain as well as on the Continent. This innocuous object may have struck Britain's first coinage, pushing the introduction of this technological development to the British Isles back by at least one generation.

The introduction of coinage was one of the great changes of the late Iron Age in Europe. The process usually involved an initial reliance on coins imported from distant or neighbouring communities, followed by the adoption of the technologies of coin manufacture. The spread of coinage coincided with a rapid decline in the production of unique and ornately decorated objects: the shields, weapons and torcs that were both symbols of status and power, and the canvases for earlier Celtic art. As small, mass-produced objects, coins are undoubtedly less impressive than the imposing metalwork that had gone before but they offered a new kind of impact. Rapid manufacture and portability allowed powerful images, political messages and a newly transformed stock of Celtic art to be transmitted to a wider audience than ever before.

Coinage appeared in central and northern European communities from the late fourth century BC, under the influence of the classical world.[1] Greek gold and silver coins struck by Philip II of Macedon (who reigned 359–36 BC), his son Alexander the Great (reigned 336–323 BC) and their successors, moved northwards across the Alps and the Balkan Mountains through existing social, political and economic networks and in the hands of warriors and mercenaries. The mechanisms for subsequent imitation, innovation and local manufacture are unclear. In most cases coins appear to have been struck in relatively small numbers. They probably served a restricted role, supplementing or replacing other high-value precious metal objects in the regular negotiations between the emerging elites of late Iron Age society.

Around the same time as the widespread adoption of coinage on the Continent was the emergence of large defended sites, usually referred to by the Latin word *oppidum* (plural *oppida*) or as 'proto-urban centres' in the more

Fig. 96 **Britain's first coins**

This recently discovered die was used as a punch for striking coins. It pushes the date of the earliest manufacturing of coins in Britain back to around 150 BC. Iron Age coin makers created abstract versions of Greek coin designs. The horse and chariot on this die ultimately derive from the gold staters of Philip II of Macedon.

Coin: unknown findspot, *c.* 150 BC
Gold; D 2.1 cm
Coin die: Bredgar, Kent *c.* 150 BC
Copper alloy; L 2.9 cm, D 2.6 cm
British Museum, London

Fig. 97 **Iron Age *oppidum* of Alésia**

This fortified hilltop settlement occupies the plateau of Mont-Auxois in north-eastern France. The sheer limestone cliffs of the hill tower over the valleys below. Alésia was a major regional settlement during the late Iron Age. In 52 BC it was the site of the final stand of Gallic leader Vercingetorix against Caesar's forces.

prosaic language of modern archaeology (fig. 97).[2] These were the settlements described by Julius Caesar in his commentaries on the Gallic Wars of 58–52 BC, which include an account of the siege of the *oppidum* at Alésia, scene of the decisive battle in the Roman conquest of Gaul. Similar sites sprang up across Europe, from Hungary to the Atlantic coast, during the second century BC. They differed from hillforts in Britain like Maiden Castle in their apparent urban characteristics, incorporating discrete spaces dedicated to religious and economic activity, as well as agricultural structures and domestic dwellings. Some of the better excavated *oppida*, such as Manching in Germany and Bibracte in France, reveal areas dedicated to craft production and industry.[3] In addition to the specialist workshops of blacksmiths, bronzeworkers and artisans producing glass beads, jewellery, pottery and textiles, we find workshops that include the tools and materials of coin production.[4] It is clear that by the first century BC some communities were producing coins in gold, silver and bronze on an industrial scale, perhaps signifying the development of a wider economic function. However, these developments were by no means universal: small-scale local production characterized some areas, such as western Britain, into the first century AD.

Coins as treasure and offerings

Few discoveries capture the public imagination like a hoard of gold or silver coins, which are often seen as the ultimate 'buried treasure'. The discovery of an Iron Age coin hoard is usually given the same explanation as hoards of later periods: in a world without bank accounts, hoards were buried for safekeeping during periods of conflict and uncertainty. This was often the case. For example, the epidemic of late Iron Age silver hoards buried in East Anglia shortly after the Roman conquest has a clear link with the revolt of Boudica in AD 60–61.[5] But does this necessarily mean that they were hidden for safekeeping with the intention of recovery? It is equally possible that they were deposited as offerings to local deities, as an appeal for supernatural support in the campaigns against the might of Rome.

Iron Age archaeologists have led the way in suggesting such alternative explanations for coin hoards. Excavations of sites like Hallaton in Leicestershire have demonstrated the highly ritualized manner in which many hoards were deposited. Here, more than five thousand coins were buried in at least sixteen separate clusters. This hilltop location was a focus for ritual activity: a ditch separated the coin deposition from an area where pigs were sacrificed and feasting may have taken place. A gateway linked ceremonies in the two areas.[6] The much smaller Essendon hoard (fig. 98), found in Hertfordshire between 1992 and 1994, lacks such clear archaeological evidence, but was also made up of a series of different deposits comprising gold coins and a hoard of weapons.[7] Multiple deposits like Hallaton, Snettisham (see Chapter 4) and Essendon are unlikely to represent conventional 'emergency hoards'.

Coins as art

Studies of Celtic art have almost invariably ignored coins. The reasons lie in a traditional separation of numismatics (the study of coins) from mainstream archaeology, as well as an apparent difference in the iconographic language of coins and other objects. While there are clear differences – not least the appearance of writing on coins, a feature conspicuous by its absence from contemporary decorated artefacts – it is difficult to ignore the links. The spindly-legged boar on the surface of the Witham shield (see fig. 9 and pp. 84–5) is a frequent subject on coins, while the abstract animals and faces hidden within the swirls and twists of the decoration on the Wandsworth or Battersea shields (figs 31, 62; 17, 26) find many parallels within the motifs employed on late Iron Age coins.

Despite these similarities, it is clear that the artists and engravers of Iron Age coinage chose to focus on a number of subjects that were rare in earlier Celtic art. Heads and figurative representations of human or divine beings, horses, mythical beasts and objects from daily life feature prominently

Fig. 98 Coin hoards from Essendon

Several hoards of Iron Age gold coins were buried at Essendon over a period of about fifty years. They were probably sacred offerings rather than savings buried for safekeeping.

Essendon, Hertfordshire c. 60 BC–AD 40
Gold
British Museum, London

on coinage. They are depicted with a greater degree of realism than on earlier artefacts. In most cases the choice of design owes something to the Greek and Roman prototypes from which the craftworkers drew inspiration. The 'Gallo-Belgic A' gold coin, made in northern France or Belgium in the second century BC, includes a head copied and adapted from that of the god Apollo on the coinage of Philip II of Macedon. There is, of course, no way of telling whether the engraver knew that they were copying an image of Apollo or whether it was immediately imbued with some other meaning, perhaps representing a deity, mythical figure or living ruler. What we can be sure of, however, is that it was every bit as skilfully executed as the

Macedonian original and the attention given to the wild dreadlock-like hair at the expense of the face was deliberate. This was not a crude imitation, but a non-naturalistic reinvention of an image drawn from the classical world.

This same process of deliberately reinventing classical subject matter to satisfy an abstract aesthetic can be seen on coins struck from the shores of the Black Sea in the east to the English Midlands in the west (fig. 99). The beautiful triple-tailed horse design, struck in southern Britain in about 50–30 BC, and the stunning third-century BC silver coin from the area of the Carpathian Mountains in eastern Europe both abandon realism in favour of fluid designs that were intended to fill the circular canvas of the coin-blank. The latter coin is particularly unusual, resulting in a somewhat comic horse.

Ambiguity and hidden meaning, themes of earlier Celtic art, remain a feature of the iconography of coinage. The strange and stylized head depicted on the gold coin struck in France, close to the mouth of the river Seine, in the second or first century BC, is a clear example. Like the earlier gold coin discussed above, its design was derived from a head of Apollo, but an increasing tendency towards abstraction has left an image that is not instantly recognizable as a head to the modern eye. Towards the back of the unknown subject's face, nestled among the hair and folds of clothing, is a small figure of a boar, apparently suspended upside down from the ear and the cheek. The meaning is not clear. The boar may have served to identify the god or human concerned, represent a boar skin or decorative object, convey characteristics of the boar such as strength and ferocity, or possess some other meaning that is lost to today's viewer. Its presence, however, highlights the subtle and hidden meanings added into the design at the point when the die was engraved.

Another coin of the second century BC, from Brittany, features a more realistic head, this time adorned with a boar, positioned within a beaded 'bubble'. A number of smaller heads are attached to the principal portrait by lines of beads, although the heads are not clear on this example. People have speculated that this could relate to headhunting, but in truth the meaning is not known.[8] A similar and equally surprising insight into the mind of the engraver can be gained from the contemporary gold coin from the Moselle Valley (on the border of Luxembourg, France and Germany). The appearance of a human-headed horse dominates a curious scene that also features a half-human rider and a winged man beneath the horse. Together the characters bring to mind the Roman writer Tacitus' description of the reported inhabitants of the ends of the Earth who 'have the faces and expressions of men, with the bodies and limbs of wild beasts'.[9] Whatever the explanation of these images, they provide an insight into the mythology and beliefs of their makers and, like the extraordinary decorative friezes of the Gundestrup cauldron (see Chapter 11), remain to be decoded.

Fig. 99 **Coin designs**

Before the Roman conquest, communities from the Black Sea to the Atlantic minted their own highly distinctive coins. Many included stylized heads with elaborately curled hair (top left) and horses with crescent-shaped or cartoon-like bodies (centre). Artists hid details within abstract designs (such as the upside-down boar behind the bulging cheek on the coin at top right). Other coins depicted more naturalistic faces and animals, but with surprising elements (such as the boar in dotted bubble on the coin at bottom left). Hybrid creatures and strange scenes may reflect local stories and beliefs (like the man-headed horse trampling a winged figure on the coin at bottom right).

Top left and right:
Fenny Stratford, Buckinghamshire c. 200–150 BC, gold, D 2.6 cm; Lens, Pas de Calais, France c. 200–100 BC, gold, D 2.1 cm

Centre left and right:
Ruscombe, Berkshire c. 50–20 BC, gold, D 1.7 cm
Medieşu Aurit, Satmar, Romania c. 300–200 BC, silver, D 2.3 cm

Bottom left and right:
Unknown findspot, Brtittany, France c. 150–50 BC, gold, D 2.1 cm
Unknown findspot, Moselle Valley, France c. 150–50 BC, gold, D 2.1 cm

British Museum, London

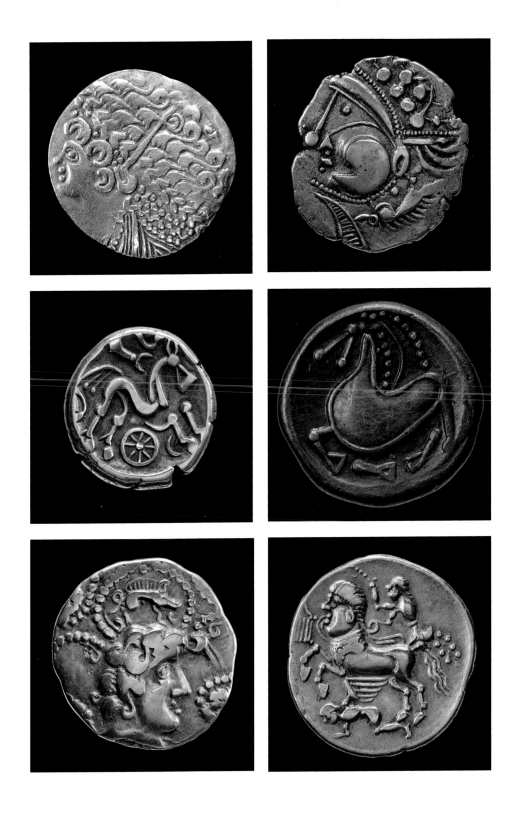

Animals and people: a new way of seeing

Animals and human faces were not new subjects in Celtic art. They had long been incorporated into the details of abstract design as hidden faces (see Chapter 3). But they were now shown in new ways. The strikingly beautiful miniature horse-head mount from Stanwick is a perfect example of the more realistic but distinctively 'Celtic' animal imagery made in the first century BC and first century AD (fig. 29). More realistic representations of animals, similar to those on late Iron Age coinage, also appeared on other objects. Boars were a common choice across much of Europe. Often seen as a symbol of courage in battle,[10] boars feature on carnyx heads (figs 75–6) and in at least one instance on a shield (figs 9 and 67), as well as being a common image on coinage. They also appear as figurines. Although the function of these small boars is unclear, and may have been as varied as their precise form, the curved pose and angled legs of an example from Norfolk (fig. 100) suggests it was mounted on a curved object such as a helmet.[11] Warriors wearing such boar-crested helmets are depicted on the Gundestrup cauldron (figs 258 and 265).

Domestic animals including cattle and sheep, as well as ducks and other birds, appear on mounts, fittings and other objects of the first century BC and first century AD. The handles of vessels and the terminals of firedogs (decorative iron stands possibly used to support logs in a hearth or to hold a spit for roasting meat) were often fashioned into stylized or realistic depictions of animals, such as on the bird-handled cup from the Crownthorpe hoard (fig. 103) and the firedogs from burials at Welwyn (fig. 102) (see below). Cosmetic grinders, a distinctive class of object from the first century AD found almost exclusively in southern Britain, are commonly decorated with finely crafted stylized animal-head terminals (fig. 101).[12] This increasing use

Fig. 100 (below, left) **Boar figurine**

A metal-detectorist discovered this small bronze figurine in a field in Norfolk. It may have been the crest from a helmet. The wild boar is a ferocious animal, and may have been associated with bravery in combat, or perhaps protection in warfare.

Ashmanhaugh, Norfolk 100 BC–AD 100
Copper alloy; L 8.7 cm
Norwich Castle Museum

Fig. 101 (opposite, left) **Cosmetic grinders**

Shortly before the Roman invasion of Britain in AD 43, new types of object appeared that reflected changes in how people dressed and presented themselves. Many of these objects were decorated with animals, such as this pestle and mortar which were used to grind cosmetics.

Cow-headed mortar: Hockwold, Norfolk AD 1–100
Copper alloy; L 10.3 cm
Pestle with duck: Norfolk AD 1–100
Copper alloy; L 4.8 cm
British Museum, London

Fig. 102 (opposite, right) **Firedog**

This wrought iron firedog was found in a richly furnished late Iron Age cremation burial. Firedogs like this one may have been used to spit-roast meat over an open fire. The two uprights have been skilfully forged into smiling bulls' heads with exaggerated horns.

Welwyn, Hertfordshire 50–25 BC
Iron; L 135 cm, H 96.5 cm
British Museum, London

Fig. 103 (opposite, below) **Bird-handled cup**

This cup is one of a matching pair discovered in Norfolk in 1982. They were part of a hoard of seven Iron Age and Roman drinking vessels that were deliberately buried near a Romano-British settlement. Some of the vessels were Italian-made, but the two drinking cups are unique. The form is Roman, but the bird-shaped handles are in a local style.

Crownthorpe AD 40–70
Copper alloy; H 8.9 cm
Norwich Castle Museum

of naturalistic realism may have been a response to the influence of Roman classical art, or a desire to incorporate more obvious and specific animal symbolism into the decoration of these objects, perhaps due to changing late Iron Age beliefs and practices. But once again this was no mindless copying of classical styles: the animals and people were stylized and simplified to their essential elements.

New ways of living and dying

Realistic depictions of humans were rare in earlier Iron Age art, but alongside animal imagery became more common towards the end of the Iron Age. Three bronze faces from a late Iron Age burial at Welwyn in Hertfordshire are fittings that would originally have gazed out from a bucket (fig. 104). Each depicts a mature man, hair neatly combed, clean-shaven except for an exquisitely groomed moustache, his expression now inscrutable. This bucket was buried some time in the first century BC, one of several objects accompanying the cremation of an important man or woman. The deceased was a member of the local elite and many of the burial goods reflect local Iron Age practices: the decorated bucket and a bull-headed firedog (fig. 102). But some of the trappings of the burial are distinctly Roman, including a bronze dish, Roman-style ceramics for eating and drinking, and an amphora that would have contained imported Italian wine.[13] In a nearby burial in what is now Welwyn Garden City, a man buried at around the same time was interred in a large vault with not one but five amphorae, which would have contained around 120 litres of wine (fig. 105).[14] The use of feasting equipment, food and drink as burial goods may have been intended to equip the dead for the afterlife, or it may have been a means of involving the deceased in funeral feasts held by the mourners. The late Iron Age certainly seems to have been a time when new ways of eating and drinking were adopted by the living to show off their wealth, status and connections through fancy tableware and cosmopolitan dining habits. These practices were also reflected in the manner in which the dead were remembered.

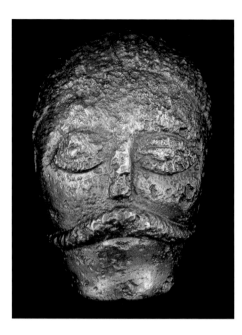

Fig. 104 **Bucket fitting in the form of a human head**

This fitting is one of a set of three which probably once decorated a wooden bucket. They were found in a rich late Iron Age grave. The fitting shows a man with a well-groomed moustache, his hair carefully combed.

Welwyn, Hertfordshire 50–25 BC
Copper alloy; H 3.8 cm
British Museum, London

Fig. 105 **Reconstruction of a late Iron Age burial chamber**

In the century before the Roman conquest of Britain, burial practices changed in south-east England. In the most elaborate of the new funeral rites the cremated remains of the deceased were interred in a richly furnished burial chamber. The man buried in this grave was wrapped in a bearskin before he was cremated. His grave goods include five amphorae of imported Italian wine, as well as tableware, a silver cup, a wine strainer and glass gaming counters.

Welwyn Garden City, Hertfordshire 50–25 BC
British Museum, London

Fig. 106 Goods from a rich late Iron Age burial

This jug, pan and bucket accompanied a late Iron Age cremation burial found in Kent. The bucket was probably used for serving wine, ale or mead in the local style. The imported jug and pan were designed for Roman ways of preparing and serving wine.

Aylesford, Kent 75–25 BC
Bucket: copper alloy, iron, wood; H 34.5 cm
Jug: copper alloy; H 18.8 cm
Pan: copper alloy; L 43.3 cm
British Museum, London

Such elaborate burial traditions were largely restricted to south-east England, the region with closest ties to the Roman world at this time. The Aylesford burial (fig. 106) is much smaller in scale than the Welwyn and Welwyn Garden City graves, but impressive in its own right thanks to the inclusion of a highly decorated bucket. This burial was discovered by chance in 1866 and was one of the first Iron Age burials to be studied by archaeologists.[15]

Fig. 107 **Prancing horses**

The improbable creatures on the upper band of
the bucket have strange lips and human feet.
They may represent people dressed as horses,
or human-animal hybrids like those on coins
made around the same time (see fig. 99, bottom
right).

Aylesford, Kent 75–25 BC
Copper alloy
British Museum, London

The person buried with the Aylesford bucket was accompanied by a
mixture of Iron Age and Roman-style goods. The bucket itself was probably
made locally. Distinctive faces with impressive headdresses or helmets
enhance the handle attachments (fig. 108) and three bronze bands adorn the
bucket itself.[16] The upper band is the most extensively decorated, with
repoussé designs depicting prancing horses (fig. 107) and swirling scrollwork.
The horses have human-looking feet and protruding pursed lips, and it has
been suggested that they were intended to represent humans dressed as
horses, like somewhat sinister pantomime animals.[17] This slippage between
the human and animal worlds echoes some of the designs from Iron Age
coins of the same period (fig. 99). The bucket was probably for serving
alcoholic drinks, perhaps mead, ale or wine, and may have been in use for
decades before it was buried.

Fig. 108 **Enigmatic faces**

Stylized faces with unusual headdresses
stare out from the rim of the bucket.

Aylesford, Kent 75–25 BC
Copper alloy
British Museum, London

The jug and pan in the Aylesford burial were designed for use in Roman drinking practices, which might have been quite different to the Iron Age ways of drinking represented by the decorated bucket. The jug and pan were probably made in Italy or southern Gaul, and were intended for mixing or spicing and serving wine, rather than the more traditional ale or mead. The grave also contained three bronze brooches and at least four wheel-made pots, which may have been local imitations of Roman-style drinking and serving vessels. Similar burials are found throughout south-east England, and also across the Channel in other parts of north-west Europe, at sites such as Goeblingen-Nospelt in Luxembourg (fig. 109).[18]

The individuals buried at Welwyn and Aylesford lived in Iron Age Britain, but they were part of a well-connected elite whose relationships spanned the Channel, perhaps even as far as the Mediterranean. They were familiar with aspects of Roman life, such as drinking Italian wine, but this is not to say that they lived in a Roman style. In the city of Rome and much of Roman Italy, the standard burial rite at this time was cremation of a clothed body and the burial of the remains in an urn, often accompanied by a glass or ceramic libation vessel (used to pour an offering over the cremated bones), and sometimes other items that reflected Roman beliefs: a lamp to light the deceased into the next world, a coin to pay the ferryman across the river Styx and perhaps some jewellery or a drinking vessel.[19] The specific set of objects chosen for Iron Age bucket burials, and especially the richer burials such as those at Welwyn, was unique to Iron Age south-east Britain and north-west Gaul. Interaction with the expanding Roman world was selective, with communities in Iron Age Britain choosing and adapting particular aspects of the Roman way of life that fitted with local ideas and traditions. Nevertheless, the effect was notable, and even generations before the invasion of AD 43 under the emperor Claudius, life was changing dramatically for some communities in south-east England. It is now thought that Caesar's campaigns of 55 and 54 BC had a greater impact than was once believed. As well as new burial rites like those at Welwyn and Aylesford, this period saw changes in settlement forms, the creation of new types of local objects, and an increase in the quantities and range of Continental imports.[20]

Contact with Rome

In Caesar's time, when the Romans first subdued an area it was common for them to take hostages (*obsides*) from among the children of local leaders, who were removed from their families to be educated in Rome. This was not merely a way to ensure that newly conquered subjects would fulfil their obligations, but also a means of exerting a more subtle, longer-term political control. *Obsides* were generally well treated, and often formed connections with important political families in Rome and across the empire; some served as officers in the Roman army. Many eventually returned home,

Fig. 109 **Bucket from a late Iron Age burial in Luxembourg**

This bucket resembles the one found in Aylesford in southern England, but it was found in Luxembourg. These similar burial rites are evidence of a powerful elite with cross-channel connections.

Goeblingen-Nospelt, Luxembourg 30–20 BC
Copper alloy, wood; H (excluding handles) 35 cm
Musée National d'Histoire et d'Art, Luxembourg

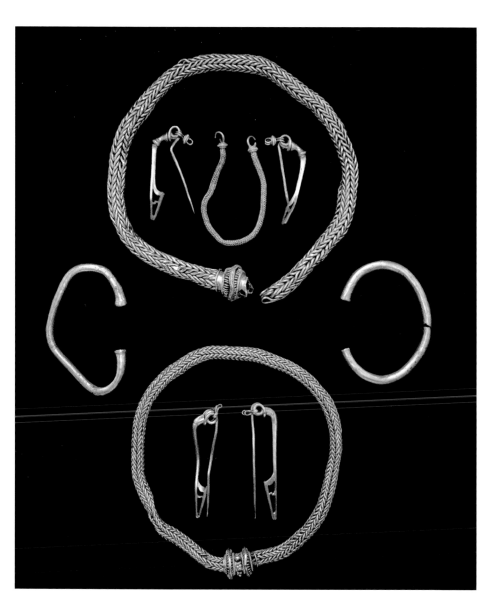

where their Roman education will undoubtedly have influenced their personal and political agendas. It is highly likely that some of the children of British leaders were taken as *obsides*, and their return may lie behind some of the changes that appear in the archaeological record before the Roman conquest of AD 43, including the appearance of classical imagery and inscriptions on coinage.[21] Some of these leaders may even have become 'client kings': local rulers who owed their position to Rome. Client kings and queens protected Roman interests and their kingdoms often acted as a buffer between the empire and more hostile territories beyond. There may have been two such client kingdoms in pre-conquest Britain: the dynasty of Commius ruled a 'Southern Kingdom', while the dynasty of Tasciovanus controlled an 'Eastern Kingdom' to the north of the River Thames.[22] So the individuals buried in Welwyn and Aylesford, or perhaps their descendants, may have lived under Roman client rulers.

This new relationship with the Roman world is reflected in the objects that were adopted to display power and status. In 2000, a metal detectorist searching in a field near Winchester discovered a hoard of gold jewellery that had been buried on a hilltop, probably in the mid-first century BC (fig. 110). Over a kilogram of gold had been used to make a matching set of two necklaces (torcs), two pairs of gold brooches and two bracelets. One of the torcs is slightly larger than the other, and they may have been for a man and a woman. The torc was an Iron Age symbol of power rather than a Roman one (see Chapter 4), but these examples were produced with Mediterranean technology. Most torcs in Iron Age Britain were solid objects made from twisted wires, rods of metal or occasionally tubes of gold sheet. The two from Winchester are different: pick one up and it runs through the hands like a snake, sinuous and fluid. Each of the neck-rings is of fine gold wire, decorated using a technique called granulation, which involves tiny beads of gold so small that they are hard to see with the naked eye.[23] Iron Age metalworkers were highly skilled, but there is no

Fig. 110 The Winchester hoard

The technology used to make the gold necklaces from the Winchester hoard suggests that they were made in a Mediterranean workshop, or by a craftworker with experience of Mediterranean techniques. The matching sets of jewellery were probably imported into Britain.

Winchester, Hampshire 75–25 BC,
Gold; necklaces approx. 15–16 cm in diameter
British Museum, London

evidence for local use of this technology. It is likely that the Winchester hoard jewellery was created in a Mediterranean workshop and perhaps sent to Britain as a diplomatic gift to local rulers. The jewellery could have come to Britain at the time when Caesar was at war in Gaul, reaching out to extend Roman power into Britain, or perhaps a generation later, when Caesar's *obsides* might have been returning home. Wearing these objects would have signalled the owners' power and also their connections to the Roman world.

Celtic art: reflecting a changing world

Across much of Iron Age Europe, the introduction of more realistic imagery and mass-production technologies such as those used to make coinage signalled the beginning of the decline of Celtic art in favour of classical-inspired imagery. In Britain, the reverse was true: the generations before the Roman conquest saw a flourishing of Celtic art. A new, more two-dimensional Celtic art style developed, compressing the fluid organic shapes of the earlier styles into engraved lines that created a harmony of interlocking positive and negative motifs. These designs often appeared on new types of objects associated with changing ways of life, such as the beautiful decorated mirrors that reflect an increased interest in personal grooming and appearance. The connection between mirrors and this late Iron Age Celtic art is so important that archaeologists refer to it as the 'Mirror Style' (see pp. 126–7).

The St Keverne mirror (fig. 111) is one of the earliest decorated Iron Age mirrors, dating to the beginning of the first century BC. It was buried in a stone cist grave, probably that of a woman, in a small Iron Age cemetery on the Lizard peninsula in Cornwall, uncovered during construction of a road in 1833.[24] Like many late Iron Age mirrors, one side of the bronze plate is polished to create a reflective surface, while the other has an engraved design. The latter takes the form of two circles side by side, each filled with a carefully balanced but subtly asymmetric pattern of positive motifs picked out by hatching, and 'empty' negative motifs that fill the spaces between.

Around sixty Iron Age mirrors are known from Britain and Ireland, and the decorated mirror appears to be unique to these islands; only two finds are known from the Continent and these may well have been exported from the British Isles.[25] The Desborough mirror (fig. 114) is one of the finest examples of Celtic art from Britain. On the reverse of its reflective plate is a lyre-loop design, which perfectly balances positive and negative motifs. The complex pattern must have been laid out with a compass and slight traces of the faint guidelines can still be seen beneath the inscribed design. The mirror obviously had a long life before it was buried: the bottom loop of the handle is worn thinner on one side where it might have been suspended from a belt, or where a cover for the mirror could have been attached.[26] Someone could

Fig. 111 (below) **The St Keverne mirror**

In Iron Age Britain, mirrors were rare objects. Instead of glass, they were made from metal plates which were highly polished on one side to create a reflective surface. The reverse was often decorated, as on this example from a grave in Cornwall.

St Keverne, Cornwall 100–50 BC
Copper alloy; L 21.8 cm
British Museum, London

Fig. 112 (opposite, above) **Iron Age comb**

Hair combs first appeared in Britain shortly before the Roman invasion of AD 43, around the same time as tweezers, nail clippers and cosmetic pigment grinders. People were becoming more concerned with their appearance, perhaps using combs to groom beards and moustaches as well as hair. The decoration on this Scottish comb is similar to the designs on mirrors from England.

Langbank, Renfrewshire AD 1–200
Bone; L 3.8 cm
National Museums Scotland, Edinburgh

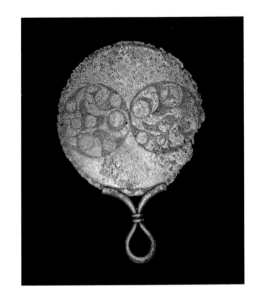

have used this mirror to change and control their appearance, perhaps in combination with other new objects that appear in the late Iron Age: tweezers, shears, nail clippers and cosmetic grinders for preparing pigments used as make-up.[27] But these were not purely cosmetic objects; mirrors might have held a special kind of power in a world where reflections could otherwise only be glimpsed in water. Jody Joy has suggested that the intricate patterns etched into the reverses of the mirrors, with their careful balance between positive and negative, light and dark shapes, might themselves represent the very idea of a reflected 'mirror image': harnessing and reflecting light to create an image that was at once familiar and altered.[28]

Although Mirror-Style Celtic art objects are most common in south-east England, the same motifs appear elsewhere in Britain, and on a wider range of objects. Similar designs can be seen on the small bone comb from the waterlogged site at Langbank crannog in western Scotland (fig. 112).[29] Such small, personal combs were a new type of object in Iron Age Britain, first appearing in the last century BC. They were probably used for grooming the hair, beard or moustache, and again speak of concerns over personal appearance at the very end of the Iron Age.

The crescent-shaped mount (fig. 113) was discovered in a hoard at Balmaclellan in south-west Scotland, where four cloth parcels contained sheet-bronze mounts and a mirror.[30] Rivet holes around the edges suggest that these mounts were once attached to a larger object, perhaps a wooden box. The engraved scrollwork design was made using a compass and the motifs closely resemble those seen on the Desborough mirror. The mount may well have been made in England, but its appearance in a Scottish hoard emphasizes the wide appeal of Mirror-Style Celtic art objects, and the connections that bound northern communities into broader social and exchange networks. These ties reached across Iron Age Britain and beyond, connecting northern peoples to a world that was soon to be rocked by a new upheaval: the Roman invasion of southern Britain in AD 43.

Fig. 113 **Decorated mount from Scotland**

The compass-drawn designs on this mount are so similar to those on mirrors from England that its appearance in a Scottish hoard must reveal connections between communities across Britain. Rivet holes suggest that it was attached to a wooden box. (See also p. 4.)

Balmaclellan, Dumfries & Galloway AD 50–250
Copper alloy; L 38.1 cm
National Museums Scotland, Edinburgh

Fig. 114 The Desborough mirror

This beautifully decorated mirror is one of the
finest examples of Celtic art from Iron Age
Britain. The care that went into the designs on
mirrors suggests that these were important
objects. Their reflective quality may have been
seen as a powerful or magical property.

Desborough, Northamptonshire 50 BC–AD 50
Copper alloy; L 35 cm
British Museum, London

Mirror Style

The designs on the backs of Iron Age mirrors are formed from interlocking positive and negative motifs. Darker areas filled in with engraved texture, such as cross-hatching, stand out against the empty spaces in between. Archaeologists call this type of decoration the 'Mirror Style', although it also appears on other types of objects. Like the decorated mirrors from which it takes its name, this style of Celtic art is almost exclusively found in Britain.

The drawing below deconstructs part of the design of the Desborough mirror (figs 95 and 114), showing how the overall image can be broken up into individual shapes. Similar motifs recur on many Mirror-Style objects at a variety of different scales. In the finest examples of this art style, such as the Desborough mirror, the decorated area is almost entirely covered with positive and negative motifs, with very little filler space. In order to achieve this effect the design had to be carefully laid out with a compass. Faint traces of the original guidelines can still be seen on the Desborough mirror, beneath the finished design.

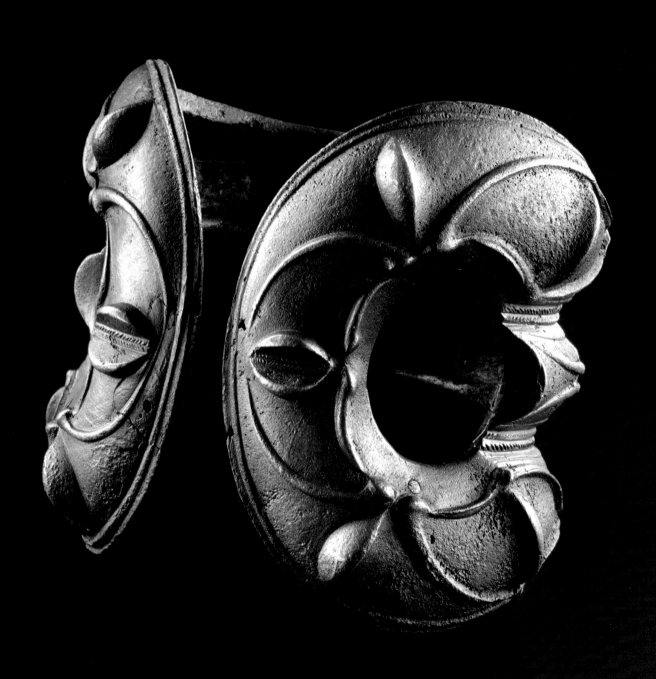

Chapter 6

Fig. 115 **Massive-style armlet**

Even after the Roman conquest of southern Britain, communities in Britain and Ireland continued to produce decorated metalwork that drew on older Celtic art styles. Massive-style ornaments were a distinctive local jewellery tradition made in north-eastern Scotland (see pp. 150–1 and fig. 262).

Belhelvie, Aberdeenshire AD 50–150 Copper alloy; H 11.5 cm
National Museums Scotland, Edinburgh

The Impact of Rome, *c.* AD 50–250

Fraser Hunter

Fig. 116 **Ornate swords, exotic materials**

This sword includes a remarkable variety of materials and decorative techniques. The brass scabbard is decorated with enamelled mounts and openwork plaques. The decayed hilt (right) was once spectacular, with a whale ivory pommel and hilt guard, a grip of elephant ivory and copper-alloy fittings to provide a colour contrast. One of the openwork panels (opposite) looks abstract, but the bosses and trumpets hint at a pair of long-legged cranes standing back-to-back, their necks stretching up and their heads turned down.

South Cave, East Yorkshire AD 50–80
Copper alloy, iron, enamel, whale ivory, elephant ivory; L 60 cm
Treasure House and Beverley Art Gallery, East Riding Museums & Galleries

In a Yorkshire field, a long-buried sword gradually emerged from the earth. The archaeologists hunched over it, slowly clearing away the soil. Its handle was made of whalebone and ivory, the iron blade concealed within an ornate copper-alloy scabbard. Contrasting plates of brass and silver glinted through the mud, decorated in a spiralling repoussé design. Beside it lay another scabbard, and another: five swords in total, their blades sheathed for burial. Beneath lay a bundle of thirty-three iron spearheads: a cache of arms, speaking of troubled times.

This find from South Cave, just north of the Humber estuary, was found by metal detectorists in 2002, carefully excavated by archaeologists and then forensically disentangled by conservators in the laboratory.[1] It contains some of the finest decorated Iron Age sword scabbards from Britain. Swirling openwork or repoussé designs were riveted to the copper-alloy scabbard plates. One shows a pair of stylized water birds, perhaps cranes or herons (fig. 116); another has pairs of interlocked beasts, their jaws gaping, while snakes lurk on one scabbard terminal.

These weapons marked changing times. In earlier centuries swords were rare in Britain, but during the first century AD they became much more widespread. They were often decorated: part of a general explosion of Celtic art at this time. Areas that had barely used such art styles before, like central Britain, rapidly developed the habit. People drew on earlier time-honoured traditions from southern Britain and the Continent, adapting them to adorn the traditional trappings of the status-conscious: weapons, horse and chariot gear, feasting equipment and torcs.

It should be no surprise that such ostentatious symbols developed at

this time. This was the period when the Roman empire became a reality for the occupants of ancient Britain. Societies under threat often resort to grand gestures at times of stress, emphasizing their independence, their power and their virility. This rapidly changing world brought about by contact and conflict with Rome created unsettled conditions where Celtic art was seized upon as a symbol. With these objects, people could mark out their difference from the Romans.

Yet these highly decorated weapons cannot simply be seen as acts of resistance to Rome. The picture is more complicated. The South Cave hoard was buried in a pit lined and covered with Roman potsherds: fragments of amphorae that once held olive oil, a hint that the owners enjoyed some aspects of the Roman lifestyle. The very fabric of the weapons also shows connections to this alien world: two of the hilt fittings are made of elephant ivory, which must have come to Britain via Mediterranean links.[2] The technologies of decoration were also new. Silver sheets, a novelty ultimately derived from the Roman world, were attached to some of the copper-alloy scabbards. Others used brass, another Roman metal: an alloy of copper with zinc, which was not available locally in Britain. Alongside patterns drawn from local traditions and wider Celtic art styles, the sword-bearers wanted the exotic. The power of these weapons lay not just in the edge of the blade but in the mix of materials: the swirling complex patterns, the shining, rare metals, the unusual handles. In combination, these elements gave the swords their strength and attractiveness.

Why were the weapons buried? Was it intended to put them beyond use, a symbol of calmer times as conflict eased? Or were they given to the protection of the earth, ready for retrieval if needed? Could they be trophies of a conflict between local groups, unconnected to the invading Romans? The weapons themselves speak of violence and display, but who used them, in what circumstances, and why they were consigned to the earth, remain opaque.

The threat of Rome may have provoked an increasingly martial society, but these warriors were not just fighting the invading legions. Some chose to do battle alongside the Romans. Similar weapons are mostly found in the conflict zone of central Britain.[3] Their bronze scabbards and hilts, decorated with enamel or curving trumpet motifs, drew on typical British styles. Yet they were not just an indigenous phenomenon. Over a third come from Roman forts, too many to dismiss as trophies or keepsakes. This weaponry became part of the kit for the army of occupation, which probably included local recruits. It offers a glimpse into the complexities of conquest. As the invading army grappled with war and peace on the frontier, and the inhabitants tried to shape and adapt to these unfamiliar realities, the simple certainties of Roman and non-Roman, enemy and friend, had to be rethought. New styles initially developed as an art of resistance, but became adopted by the conquerors. Innovative object types were created as emblems, marking and negotiating how people wanted to be seen as they came to terms with this changing world.

A similar sword comes from Hod Hill in Dorset, where the bloody siege of a hillfort ended in Roman victory.[4] The decoration of the hilt uses local Iron Age styles, but the blade itself is probably Roman (fig. 118).[5] Related examples come from other Roman forts in the area: hybrids created in the conquest period, perhaps for locally-raised troops serving on the Roman side.

A remarkable helmet, probably from northern England, tells a similar story (fig. 117).[6] Its history is distressingly vague. It comes from the collection of the great magpie of early armour, Samuel Meyrick (1783–1848), who omitted to record where he obtained it. However, the object itself gives us clues. The curling repoussé decoration on the side-plates and neck guard is typical of Celtic art styles in central Britain at the time of conquest. One might presume this was the helmet of a warrior who faced the Roman armies. Yet other hints argue against this: the inscription 'II' in Roman numerals on one side, and an omega-shaped design on the neck guard that mimics the carrying handle of a Roman legionary helmet. This was made for an owner familiar with the Roman military. Indeed, the inscription suggests it was someone serving with the Roman army. Here is Celtic art inspired by Roman styles, probably for a local warrior who was serving with Rome. These were complicated times.

Fig. 117 **Mixing styles**

Weaponry is often very fluid in conflict zones, as soldiers adopt enemy styles that have proved efficient or caught their eye. This helmet has both Celtic and Roman features in its form and decoration. The large rivets were once decorated with red glass.

From the collection of Samuel Meyrick;
provenance uncertain AD 50–100
Copper alloy, red glass; H 165 mm
British Museum, London

Fig. 118 **A hybrid weapon**

The blade of this sword may well be Roman – it was most likely carried by a soldier fighting for Rome – but the decoration uses local Iron Age styles. The copper-alloy fittings preserve the outline of a decayed organic hilt. The engraved and dot-decorated trumpets on the hilt guard are typical of the southern English Iron Age.

Hod Hill, Dorset AD 40–60
Iron, copper alloy; hilt L 12 cm
British Museum, London

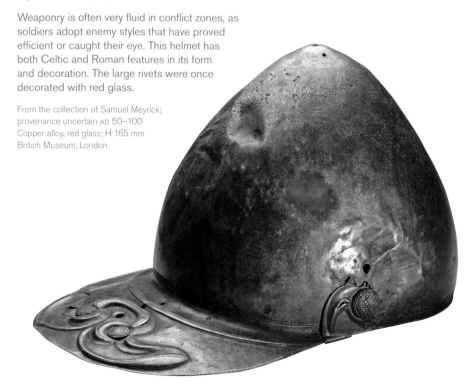

Fig. 119 **The Polden Hill hoard**

This selection of horse and chariot gear from the Polden Hill hoard is typical in style and decoration of the fashions of southern England at the Roman conquest. It includes rein guides which fastened to the chariot yoke (left), strap junctions (right) with curvilinear decoration, and two sliders to tighten or loosen straps. One uses the swirly styles of the Iron Age, the other the neater geometry that became popular in the Roman period.

Polden Hill, Somerset AD 40–60
Copper alloy, enamel; L of object bottom right 14.8 cm
British Museum, London

Art in a changing world

This newly flourishing conquest-period Celtic art is found over large areas of Britain, although it is rare in the extreme south-east. It was concentrated in the trouble spots of the conflict against Rome: south-west England, the scene of extensive fighting; East Anglia, homeland of the restless Iceni; southern Wales, where several Roman governors waged bloody conflict against local uprisings; northern England and southern Scotland, where an extended campaign was fought to bring the area to heel; and north-east Scotland, the land that the general Agricola thought he had conquered at the battle of Mons Graupius, forty years after Britain was invaded, but which was never permanently held.

Metalwork hoards from these areas contain horse and chariot gear in regionally distinctive styles. The find from Polden Hill in Somerset includes elegantly enamelled rein guides and other harness ornaments (fig. 119).[7] A harness hoard from Seven Sisters in Glamorgan (fig. 120) mixed different traditions. Some objects used local styles of ornament, while others took habits from the Roman world: the metal, brass (alien to Welsh traditions), and multicoloured glass inlays.[8] Both these hoards also contained some Roman imports: a couple of brooches in Polden Hill and a rather wider range at Seven Sisters, including cavalry harness fittings. Once again, the boundary between local and Roman was a fluid one. Hoards from East Anglia are dominated by enamelled metalwork (fig. 121). This is true of some central British hoards as well, although others utilized a distinctive native style of raised boss ornament (fig. 122).[9] While the styles may be locally specific, the idea was shared. Spreading this decoration over status items like chariot gear drew attention to it and gave it added power and significance.

Fig. 120 **The Seven Sisters hoard**

This large hoard of chariot gear, tankard handles and metalworking debris includes strikingly different styles of decoration. Some use local fashions of curvilinear Celtic art in traditional materials: bronze and red glass (top left). Some are imported Roman cavalry fittings with classical decoration (bottom right). Others used a new style that was influenced by Roman habits, with small cells containing multicoloured glass settings (centre).

Seven Sisters, Glamorgan AD 50–75
Copper alloy, glass, enamel, niello
National Museum Wales

Fig. 121 **Terrets reunited**

These rein-rings (terrets) from a chariot yoke are so similar that they probably came from the same harness set, but they were found over 20 km apart. We do not know why some chariot sets were buried whole and others were split up, but this was clearly no accident. Such valued metalwork was rarely just 'lost'; it was carefully buried in special places. Terrets with small enamelled platforms are typical of East Anglia and central Britain.

Saham Toney and Carleton Rode, Norfolk AD 40–100
Copper alloy, enamel; D 7.6 cm
Norwich Castle Museum

Fig. 122 **The Middlebie hoard**

Central Britain, between the rivers Humber and Forth, had its own distinctive metalwork style decorated with raised bosses. These chariot fittings, selected from a larger hoard, feature bridle bits, rein guides, strap junctions and fasteners.

Middlebie, Dumfries & Galloway AD 50–100
Copper alloy; bridle bit L 25 cm
National Museums Scotland, Edinburgh

Yet, once again, these were more than an art of resistance. Such local styles of chariot and horse fittings continued into the Roman period. Iron Age vehicle technology had long been a source of envy in the Roman world. Indeed, many of the words for vehicles in Latin were derived from the Celtic language: the modern word 'car' comes ultimately from Celtic chariots.[10] The surviving copper-alloy trappings mark a wider cultural exchange, with advanced local vehicle technologies being adopted and developed: influences between Roman and Iron Age worlds were two-way, not one-way.

Making a new world – becoming Romano-British

These two worlds, Roman and Iron Age, began changing from the moment they came into contact. This is seen in the objects and the art. Some objects, such as coins bearing the emperor's face, were clearly Roman: symbols of imperial power and new economic forces. Others were obviously British, such as the chariot fittings. Many items were modified or created anew as Britain adapted to Rome over several centuries. Mostly this took place in the frontier worlds of northern England, southern Scotland and Wales where the army and the locals came into direct long-term contact, and where there was no strong desire for towns, baths and 'civilized living'. However, it was not just a frontier feeling. Across most of the province and beyond its boundaries, new styles of object were created, melding Roman and local traditions.[11]

Brooches demonstrate this nicely. People in southern Britain already used safety-pin brooches to fasten clothing and this continued into the Roman period. In the north, things were different: the pin, not the brooch, was the normal means of fixing clothes. The Roman arrival introduced people to this new habit, which merged with local artistic traditions to create fresh, regionally distinctive brooch styles.

The classic example is the so-called dragonesque brooch: an S-shape with the ends transformed into stylized animal heads, often decorated with swirling motifs from Celtic art in enamel, relief or openwork (fig. 123).[12] A pin coiled round one 'neck' was fastened through clothing before being slipped over the other 'neck' to retain it. Dragonesques are often considered typically Celtic brooches, with their scrolling zoomorphic patterns and enamel. Their ancestors were plain iron S-shaped brooches of the late Iron Age. Yet dragonesques were creatures of conquest. They flourished in Roman Britain, created by this meeting of an ancestral type, a newly flourishing local artistic style and a Roman habit of using brooches in animal form. The dragonesque brooch was a beast of this changing world.

Dragonesques were a local speciality of Yorkshire, although they proved very popular elsewhere. Other regional types of brooches similarly incorporated elements of local style into their design (fig. 124). Some idiosyncratic special commissions took things to the extreme. From

Fig. 123 (opposite, left and centre)
Ferocious brooches

These animal-headed 'dragonesque' brooches are one of the most distinctive styles of brooch that emerged in the meeting of Roman and Iron Age traditions. Their stylized animal shape and decoration, enamelled or with cast swirling shapes, are typical of contemporary Celtic art, but the idea of animal-shaped brooches was a Roman one, and the explosion of art at this time was due to the changing world of the Roman conquest.

Left: from Faversham, Kent AD 75–175
Copper alloy, enamel; H 5.6 cm
British Museum, London

Right: unprovenanced AD 75–175
Copper alloy, enamel; H 5.9 cm
J. V. S. Megaw (on loan to National Museums Scotland, Edinburgh)

Fig. 124 (opposite, above right)
Romano-British brooches

Distinctive regional styles of brooch developed across most of Roman Britain. These were local reactions to typical Roman brooch styles, and often used motifs of Celtic art or local preferences such as enamelling. This example uses swirling forms from local traditions in its decoration.

Wickham, Hampshire AD 75–200
Copper alloy, tinned, enamel; L 3.8 cm
British Museum, London

Fig. 125 (right) **The Carmarthen brooch**

Brooches with an expanded trumpet-like head were popular in Roman Britain, but this example is exceptional in its ornate decoration and unusual material. Silver was rarely used for brooches; most were of copper alloy. This one is made even more striking by the gilded parts. The ornate loop at the head allowed it to be fastened to a chain and worn as a pair.

Carmarthen, Dyfed AD 50–100
Gilt silver; L 6.2 cm
Carmarthenshire County Museum, Carmarthen

Fig. 126 (far right) **Over the top**

This is one of the largest and most spectacular Romano-British brooches. It comes from 300 km north of Hadrian's Wall and would have been a highly valued item. The craftworker drew on a wide range of Celtic art motifs to create what must have been a special commission. Originally the little cups on the central boss held inlays to add to the spectacular effect.

Auldearn, Highland AD 75–150
Copper alloy, enamel, iron; L 14.4 cm
National Museums Scotland, Edinburgh

Carmarthen comes a 'trumpet' brooch, named from the resemblance of its head to a trumpet (fig. 125).[13] The type is a normal Romano-British one, but its material is attention-seeking: it is made of silver decorated with raised scrolling patterns typical of Celtic art in Britain, with gilding applied to the background. A similarly over-inflated brooch is a recent find from Auldearn (fig. 126). It is more than twice the size of a typical specimen and would have weighed heavy on the owner's cloak. The chequerboard yellow and red enamel designs are combined with virtually every known variant of northern Celtic art motifs. This was a brooch for showing off with; hence its desirability far to the north of Hadrian's Wall.

Such material with Celtic-style decoration could include real luxury items. The hinged gold bracelet from Rhayader in central Wales (fig. 127) is a style known elsewhere in central Britain in bronze.[14] The luxury of this gold bracelet is brought home by the careful use of enamelling in the delicate spiralling designs on the terminals, straight from local traditions of Celtic art.

Enamelling was a technique that originated in the Greek world. It was taken up north of the Alps on a small scale in the later Iron Age, but flourished in Britain from the first century BC into the Roman period, and was recognized as a speciality of the area.[15] The Roman period saw technological changes, with a wider range of colours introduced and a shift

Fig. 127 **A luxury item**

In the Roman period Celtic art is usually found on copper alloys. This gold hinged bracelet is a rare exception. The form is an Iron Age one and the enamelled decoration employs Celtic motifs, but the use of precious metal marks it out as a real luxury. It was found in a hoard with other more typically Roman pieces of jewellery.

Rhayader, Powys AD 100–200
Gold, enamel; H 3.3 cm
British Museum, London

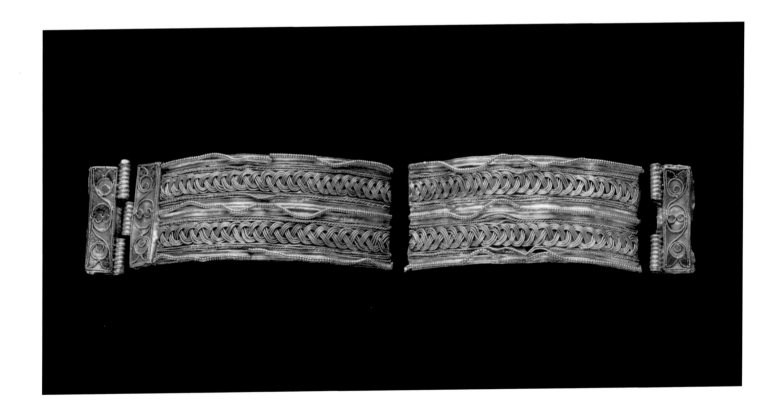

Fig. 128 (right and below)
A souvenir of Hadrian's Wall

The inscription on this small enamelled pan commemorates some of the forts on Hadrian's Wall. Today's tourist attraction was clearly a wonder of the Roman period too. It once had a handle, which is now lost. Below the inscription is a complex scrolling enamelled frieze. At first glance the enamelled design looks like discs with typically Celtic triskeles (triple-legged designs), but a closer look reveals buds and leaves as well. The drawing below restores the original enamel scheme where the blue and turquoise colours ran across the triskele discs, blurring the boundaries and making them less obvious. Different viewers could see either Celtic triple motifs or Roman scrolling vine patterns, depending on their cultural background.

Ilam, Staffordshire AD 130–200
Copper alloy, enamel; D 9.4 cm
British Museum, London / Tullie House Museum, Carlisle / Stoke Potteries

from employing glass inlays (which were heated until soft and pushed into place) to using powder that was transformed into glass at high temperature, fusing to the metal. Among the finest products is a series of enamelled vessels, which took typical Roman forms but often gave their decoration a local twist. The enamelled pan from Ilam (fig. 128) has a frieze listing the names of forts at the western end of Hadrian's Wall along with an inscription of the maker or owner.[16] Such pans were probably souvenirs of Hadrian's great frontier, perhaps for an officer who served on the Wall. The bulk of the design is taken up with an ornate spiralling enamelled frieze. At first glance, this looks Celtic – a swirling colourful interlinked triple-legged (triskele) pattern – but closer inspection shows a different story: it can also be seen as a much more classical running vine-scroll. This one vessel illustrates the coming together of invader and invaded as they adapted to the new world, creating objects that could be read and appreciated in different ways depending on who was looking at them.

The torc reinvented

Time and again in this book we have met the torc: the neck ornament that Greek and Roman authors and artists saw as distinctive of the Celts. We have seen how it was worn far beyond any 'Celtic world' and how its use varied: sometimes it was a male ornament, sometimes female; sometimes for humans, sometimes gods. This idea was reimagined once more in Britain under Roman rule. Earlier torcs were often made in gold or silver, metals that were stripped from the province by the Roman conquerors. In Roman Britain, this iconic item was transformed into a series of impressive neck

Fig. 129 **A regional tradition**

In south-west Britain a distinctive version of Iron Age torcs developed in the early Roman period. These hinged neck collars were often decorated with Celtic art motifs.

Portland, Dorset AD 50–150
Leaded brass, red enamel; internal D 12.2 cm
British Museum, London

Fig. 130 **Changing torcs**

The old idea of the torc was reinvented in Roman Britain. This is the finest of the so-called 'beaded' torcs from central Britain, with a row of ornate beads strung on a bar at the front and openwork Celtic-style decoration round the rear.

Lochar Moss, Dumfries & Galloway AD 75–200
Copper alloy; D 16 cm
British Museum, London

ornaments in copper alloy, a more affordable metal.[17] Torcs from south-western Britain featured styles of Celtic art in their decoration (fig. 129), while others from central Britain took earlier forms of buffer-ended torcs and elaborated them into a row of ornamental beads at the front (fig. 130). Such torcs were alien to traditional Roman ways but became part of being Romano-British across much of the country: a part of an older world, reinvented for new purposes to mark identities in this changed society. It is not clear if they were worn by men, women or both. On other Roman frontiers, women often preserved elements of local tradition while men adopted more outwardly Roman garb,[18] but we cannot find such subtleties yet in our British evidence.

Fig. 131 **A local goddess in Roman form?**

This sculpture of a goddess was found in a shrine outside a Roman fort. The inscription records it was commissioned by Amandus, a military engineer, and dedicated to Brigantia. Her name is local, from the northern English tribe of the Brigantes, but her appearance is entirely Roman. The very idea of giving a god human form is also a classical one: Iron Age beliefs did not usually conceive of gods as humans.

Birrens, Dumfries & Galloway
AD 120–180
Sandstone; H 91 cm
National Museums Scotland, Edinburgh

Fig. 132 **Mixed-up gods**

Worshipping miniature figures of gods was a Roman idea that was modified in Britain. This male is a version of the war god Mars, but the naturalistic style has been simplified, his weaponry swapped for snakes, and his helmet topped with a bird.

Southbroom, Wiltshire AD 50–250
Copper alloy; H 10.7 cm
British Museum, London

Belief and religion: Celtic past or Roman creation?

A few minutes in a good bookshop or on the internet will rapidly turn up works on Celtic religion, full of unusual gods and strange faces staring from the pages or the screen. A closer look will start to reveal some equally strange facts. Almost all the archaeological and historical evidence is Roman in date. Our knowledge of the names of gods, their equation with Roman deities, their roles and their appearance stems mostly from Roman sources: the authors who discussed them, inscriptions that named them and sculpture that showed them. Such evidence is found over much of Roman Europe and is a critical source for understanding religion at that time. But it tells us about the Roman period, not necessarily what went before. The Roman world did not simply make earlier religions visible; it transformed them beyond recognition. It gave gods human form. It opened an Iron Age world to Mediterranean deities and in exposing them to a pantheon of all-powerful strangers led to unusual hybrids.

The female depicted on a Roman sculpture from a fort at Birrens (fig. 131), for example, is clearly a goddess – humans have little need for wings – but she is a curious mix. Her wings link her to the goddess Victory, her armour to the war goddess Minerva and her turreted headgear to the protecting deity of a city. The globe and pointed stone at her feet are symbols of Juno Caelestis.[19] Yet she is none of these. An inscription records that she is Brigantia, the tribal goddess of the Brigantes. This sounds a very local custom – the Brigantes were a group from northern England – but it was a Roman conceit to give the spirits of areas human form, often for political reasons. There is no evidence of such a cult before the Romans and certainly no evidence that deities were conceived as human: hidden faces and figures occur in much Iron Age Celtic art, but recognizable humans were exceedingly rare in pre-Roman Britain. This same Roman view of the world is seen in an altar from Auchendavy on the Antonine Wall, dedicated 'to the spirit of the land of Britain' by a high-ranking Roman officer.[20] There is no hint of any meaningful concept of Britain before the Romans arrived. In these examples we see the perspectives of the Roman world.

This impact of Rome is seen in other areas of religion too: in equating gods from different cultures and finding new ways to depict them. Small bronze figures from a hoard found at Southbroom look alien to our eyes, calibrated as we are to the idealized naturalism of the classical world.[21] The lines of the body have been simplified; decorative folds of clothing are emphasized and hairstyles reduced to patterns. A striking design was more important than a faithful rendering of nature.[22] In part this arose from craftworkers unfamiliar with naturalistic depictions, which are hard to represent in three dimensions,[23] but it also shows a concern for pattern over reality, a mindset continuing from pre-Roman artistic ideas. These gods and goddesses of the provinces were shaped by local ideas but created by Roman rule, with gods taking human form for the first time. One bearded god from

Southbroom wears a helmet, typical of Mars in classical mythology, but this is no war god from Rome (fig. 132). On his helmet perches a bird, perhaps a raven; his hands hold not weapons but ram-horned snakes, an Iron Age fantasy, which coil round his arms and legs.[24] This unknown deity blends elements of classical and more local concepts.

Such ideas were set in stone as well. The sculpture of a lioness from the Roman fort of Cramond, near Edinburgh, served as a tomb guardian on the northern frontier (fig. 133).[25] Her body is naturalistic but her head is exaggerated: a monstrosity of tooth and claw, the mouth distended to fit even more teeth in. Her prey is human: a captive barbarian. Here we see not the normal classical lion, feasting on lamb or calf, but a man-eating beast. The image draws on pre-Roman myths, but from where? It was made locally but the inspiration could have lain elsewhere, for the troops who served at Cramond came from many corners of the Roman world, bringing their own traditions and tales with them.

Fig. 133 **From lioness to man-eating monster**

Stone predators and their prey guarded Roman tombs and reminded onlookers of their mortality. Here, the typical Roman lion devouring a domestic animal is transformed into something much fiercer. The teeth and claws of the lioness are exaggerated, reflecting older Iron Age visions of monstrous beasts. Her prey is a captured barbarian, his arms bound behind his back: this served as victory monument as well as tomb guardian. Snakes on the base symbolize the survival of the soul.

Cramond, City of Edinburgh AD 140–215
Sandstone; L 1.47 m
National Museums Scotland / City of Edinburgh Museums

Fig. 134 The goddess and the bear

This striking sculpture depicts a local bear cult: the name of
the goddess, Artio, means 'bear' in many Celtic languages.
Perhaps the deity could take either human or bear form.
Originally the sculpture comprised only the bear and the tree;
the woman was added later and the composition shuffled to
accommodate her. The inscription records that it was dedicated
by Licinia Sabinilla. It was found in a Roman villa along with
more classically Roman religious sculptures.

Muri, Bern, Switzerland AD 150–200
Copper alloy; plinth L 28.6 cm
Historisches Museum, Bern

Modified images were not just a British phenomenon. From Muri in
western Switzerland comes another mixture of Roman and local ideas (fig.
134). A bronze plinth carries a seated goddess in classical fashion, with fruit
in her lap (her throne is missing), but the rest of the sculpture is more
unusual. At the far end is a tree, and between the two a rather vocal bear, its
patterned pelt more decorative than natural. The inscription shows that this
is no Roman deity, but the goddess Artio, a Celtic word meaning bear.[26]
Here a local cult is represented in Roman form.

Such modified classical images were made widely in the north-western
provinces. A series of copper-alloy heads of gods and emperors from Britain
and Gaul followed good classical models but added a regional twist. Once
again they emphasized patterns, showing hair and beards with coils and spirals

Fig. 135 **An emperor re-imagined**

The half-sized head depicts the Roman emperor Marcus Aurelius in a style typical of Britain and Gaul. It is based on his official portraits but the local craftworker has made significant changes. Both hairstyle and beard are decorative rather than naturalistic, with the coils and curves catching the eye; evidence of local rather than purely classical tastes.

Steane, Northamptonshire c. AD 160–190
Gunmetal (copper-zinc-tin alloy); H 16.2 cm
Ashmolean Museum, Oxford

Fig. 136 **Mars the huntsman**

This votive plaque shows Mars in typical warlike pose standing in a Roman temple. However, the inscription links him to local tradition. He is named as Mars Alator, Mars the hunter, using a local Celtic language term for this most Roman of warrior gods.

Barkway, Hertfordshire AD 200–300
Gilt silver; H 18 cm
British Museum, London

(fig. 135).[27] This was highly accomplished metalworking, deliberately choosing elements of local taste in portraying classical subjects. Yet it did not use the motifs of earlier Celtic art such as complex spirals, trumpets and tendrils. While these designs still appeared on other metalwork in Britain, as we have seen, they are never found on sculpture in bronze or stone.

Mixing and moving gods

Deities were often equated or combined after the conquest. Mars, the Roman warrior god, was regularly linked to local gods on the basis of shared powers. Much of this was driven by the beliefs of the military garrison, although in some cases the dedicator seems to have been local or, at least, not certainly connected to the military.[28] Mars was associated with the deities Toutatis and Alator ('huntsman') on silver plaques from Barkway in Hertfordshire (fig. 136).[29] On an inscription from Colchester, dedicated by a Caledonian, he is connected with the otherwise unknown Medocius.[30] A series of stones from north-west England link him to Belatucadrus, who must have been a native deity,[31] while one from Bar Hill on the Antonine Wall associates him with Camulus, a god better known in Gaul.[32] Some of these names are recorded elsewhere in both Britain and France, suggesting a widely shared deity; others are very regional.[33] Few have any certain time depth before the Roman period. Of course, there is a circularity to this: without written evidence and with so few earlier depictions of deities, how can gods be identified? But we should be wary of back-projecting our Roman sources too far to re-create a Celtic religion. Many of these 'old

Fig. 137 **By Toutatis ...**

A dense cluster of finger-rings inscribed 'TOT' from Roman Lincolnshire reveals a strong regional cult of the god Totatis (or Toutatis), whose name means 'people' or 'tribe'. The distribution links it to the Corieltavi, a Roman administrative unit that may have originated in an Iron Age tribal grouping.

Heckington, Lincolnshire AD 150–300
Silver; L 2.7 cm
British Museum, London

gods' were variations on very general human themes: gods of fertility, war, light and dark. Toutatis, for instance, means people or tribe (fig. 137);[34] Belatucadrus, 'fair shining one', suggests a god of light.[35] Such general concepts are a weak basis for proposing any shared ideology across Europe in the pre-Roman period.

The wide distribution of particular Celtic god names across large areas of Europe has been a playground for people seeking a far-reaching Celtic pantheon. Yet we should be cautious, not just because the evidence is from the Roman period, but because that very proliferation may be a Roman phenomenon. A good example is Epona, often seen as a pan-Celtic horse goddess (her name is derived from the Celtic word for horse).[36] Horses had

Fig. 138 **A goddess for the soldiers**

The goddess Epona sits on a chair with a basket of fruit on her lap, flanked by two horses. This sculpture came from a Roman fort; cavalry troops were particularly devout worshippers because of her association with horses.

Köngen, Baden-Württemberg, Germany c. AD 200
Sandstone; H 43 cm
Württembergisches Landesmuseum, Stuttgart

Fig. 139 Evidence for Epona

Epona occurred widely in sculpture and inscriptions in the Roman world. There are two separate patterns in the distribution. Strong local concentrations in eastern France, the Moselle and the upper Rhine mark areas where the worship of Epona was socially widespread. Secondly, the cult spread with the army into the frontier provinces, west up the Rhine to Britain, east down the Danube, and to Rome itself, where members of the imperial horse guard made many dedications to her.

been seen as special animals in Europe since their introduction in the Bronze Age, often venerated or treated in unusual ways when they died.[37] Epona is named on Roman inscriptions and shown as mistress of the horses (fig. 138). However, the inscriptions and sculpture are concentrated along the Roman frontiers (fig. 139), carried by cavalry troops of very mixed origins for whom the idea of a protective horse goddess had a tremendous personal relevance. The spread of Epona tells us about her popularity in the Roman world, especially with the Roman military, not her hypothetical worship across Europe in pre-Roman times. The same is true for other deities such as Toutatis, whose inscriptions hug the frontier zone.[38]

From this, we can see that the Roman presence reshaped the relationship with the gods for the peoples of western Europe. It provided novel ways of thinking, talking about and portraying deities, and led in some cases to popular new or hybrid gods. The tale of Celtic religion in the Roman world tells us of contemporary concerns, not some earlier pantheon. The peoples of Iron Age Europe undoubtedly had complex religious beliefs, as the designs of early Celtic art suggest (see Chapter 3), but the details are lost to us. We cannot assume that this earlier spiritual world is reflected in the Roman evidence.

Beyond the frontier

Within Roman Britain, we have seen an explosion of art in response to Rome, and the use of art to reshape ideas of identity and belief. Similar processes took place in the worlds beyond Rome's frontier but still within its sphere of interest: Scotland and Ireland.

In both areas, decorated metalwork exploded at this time. The Scottish evidence is better dated and understood. In north-east Scotland, beyond the Antonine Wall, a new style of art developed, drawing on earlier traditions but creating something that was brash, innovative and impressive: massive armlets for men, some with striking enamelled insets; snake-like spiralling bracelets for women, coiling around their wrists; finger-rings, modelled on Roman ideas but using local designs and technologies, such as enamelling; and smaller versions of all of them, so that the children of powerful families could be adorned appropriately (fig. 140).[39]

This art was distinctively local and different, but was once more a response to Rome, and drew on the Roman world for raw materials and inspiration (as with the finger-rings, which adapted the classical model of a gem-set ring; fig. 140, pictured bottom right). The impact of the Roman world extended either side of the border. Both inside and outside, peoples' lives were transformed and their personal belongings were altered to reflect this. The effect of Roman conquest or conflict was not neutral; it drew people in, making them change and create innovative things in response that were not Roman or Celtic but an imaginative mixture. These styles of Celtic art existed because of Rome, spanning the Roman frontier in Britain. It was this interaction between the Roman provinces and beyond that gave birth to the new Celtic art of the early medieval period.

Fig. 140 **Massive metalwork**

The big, bold castings of the 'massive' metalwork tradition of north-east Scotland were used mainly for jewellery: armlets and finger-rings for men, bangles for women. These varied regionally. Bangles are overwhelmingly found around the river Tay, and armlets from this area have a related spiral form. To the north, bangles are almost unknown and armlets had a fold-over symmetry instead. (See also fig. 262.)

Rear armlet: Stanhope, Scottish Borders; right armlet: Seafield Tower, Fife; left bangle: Bunrannoch, Perth & Kinross; front bangle: West Grange of Conan, Angus; ring: Tarnavie, Perth & Kinross. c. AD 50–200
Copper alloy, enamel; D of front bangle 7.4 cm
National Museums Scotland, Edinburgh

Fig. 141 **Pictish silver plaque (detail)**

This decorated silver plaque combines swirling Celtic art motifs with Pictish symbols. It formed part of the largest known hoard of Pictish silver, discoverd at Norrie's Law in 1819 (see pp. 154–7).

Norrie's Law, Fife AD 400–700
Silver, enamel. W 3.2 cm
National Museums Scotland, Edinburgh

Chapter 7

Out of a Roman World, *c.* AD 250–650

Martin Goldberg

Norrie's Law in Fife has long been a special place. The panoramic view stretches out across Largo Bay over the Firth of Forth to the Lothian plain across the southern horizon, punctuated by prominent hills including the great grey hump-back form of Traprain Law. This view made Norrie's Law an important place in the Bronze Age, when it was chosen for the site of a burial mound. Around four thousand years later, in 1819, a labourer was digging into the barrow to quarry out the sandy soil. He probably had little concern for the deep past. But unknown to him, precious possessions had been concealed there over a thousand years ago, by other hands, when the Bronze Age barrow was already an ancient, special place. As he dug, the labourer uncovered the largest Pictish silver hoard ever found,[1] but instead of reporting it to the landowner or declaring it to the Crown he secretly spirited the treasure away and illegally sold it on. Most was bought by silversmiths who melted it down to make the latest fashions in nineteenth-century silverware. What survives now is less than six per cent of the original total.[2] In 1819, the idea of saving treasures from the past was barely established, and there was little concept of using such objects to understand how the people who made them had lived.

Silver

Even in its reduced state, what survives of the Norrie's Law hoard provides an important snapshot of valuable material in the centuries after Roman rule in Britain ended (fig. 142). The raw material, silver, came out of the Roman world: fragments of Roman objects can still be recognized among the pieces.[3] Silver was not mined in Britain or Ireland at the time. The Roman empire had been the only source of silver for these islands, and when links to Roman government were severed at the beginning of the fifth century silver became an increasingly valuable and rare commodity: something to be hoarded, reworked into new symbols of power and carefully diluted over the next few centuries to make the precious metal stretch further. Some of the objects in the Norrie's Law hoard may have been several centuries old when they were deposited sometime in the sixth or seventh century.[4] Many of the fragments are difficult to identify, but they encapsulate two important themes that will be covered in this chapter: different pasts, including connections with the Roman world; and connections and distinctions between the various peoples of these islands.

One silver plate was carefully hammered up using a repoussé technique to create eggshell-thin, high-relief spiral domes that were accentuated with carefully defined trumpet-spiral lines worked in from the front (fig. 143). These are reminiscent of earlier metalwork in form and technique. The closest comparison are pairs of large bronze discs with similar repoussé spiral decoration from Ireland (fig. 91),[5] although they

Fig. 142 **Recycling Rome**

Most of this hoard has been deliberately broken, hacked up and prepared for melting down to make new objects. Some of the silver had already been recycled – the large handpin was made from re-used Roman silver. Above the twisted penannular hoop on the right is a hacked-up triangular fragment of an inscribed Roman spoon.

Norrie's Law, Fife AD 450–600
Silver; largest pin L 16.7 cm
National Museums Scotland, Edinburgh

Fig. 143 **Silver spirals**

The high-relief spirals on this silver sheet have been worked from both sides, creating extra definition for the three-dimensional form. This repoussé technique is also used on the bronze Monasterevin discs from Ireland (fig. 91). These objects were both among the earliest pieces of metalwork labelled as Celtic art by J. O. Westwood in 1853.

Norrie's Law, Fife AD 400–600
Silver; 11.5 x 12.7 cm
National Museums Scotland, Edinburgh

Fig. 144 (below left) **Fine-line spiral decoration on a pin-head**

Bright red enamel would originally have filled all of the finely carved grooves surrounding the silver spiral decoration and enhanced the small equal-armed cross decorating the well-worn central 'finger' of the handpin. Whether this indicated that the original owner was a Christian is difficult to say.

Norrie's Law, Fife AD 400–600
Silver; W 2 cm
National Museums Scotland, Edinburgh

differ in shape and material. The motifs on the Norrie's Law sheet connect to this earlier legacy, while the silver suggests a Roman heritage, coming out of a Roman world.

The tiny well-worn spiral finger-ring in the Norrie's Law hoard is of a type commonly found across Britain in bronze, although silver examples are much rarer.[6] The most distant are a silver pair discovered at Newgrange, a Neolithic tomb in the Boyne valley in the central Irish midlands. In Irish mythology this ancient tomb was the home of pre-Christian gods. The Newgrange silver rings are part of a collection of exotic material that was deposited as gifts to the gods of this ancient place, thousands of years after the tomb itself had fallen out of use. Other objects included late Roman gold and silver coins, and a variety of personal ornaments.[7] Just like Norrie's Law, the past was a prominent element at Newgrange, but so too were connections to distant shores. These brought foreign influences through trade, warfare and raiding. Warriors from beyond the frontier even served in the late Roman armies. Such links explain how valuable Roman objects and materials came to be buried in Ireland and Scotland.[8]

Decoration on silver items provides further links between Scotland and Ireland at this time. The enamelled head of a large silver pin from Norrie's Law (fig. 144) acts as a canvas for fine-line spirals, carved in relief and enhanced using red enamel.[9] These large pins are called handpins because of the projecting 'fingers' along their tops. Both the type and the artistic style had a wide currency across Britain and Ireland. One other item

Fig. 145 (right) **Language connections**

This Welsh standing stone has two inscriptions on it with names in two languages using two different types of script. The ogam inscription on the right-hand edge reads upwards from the bottom MAQITRENI SALICIDUNI '(the stone of) Maqas-Treni Salicidunus'. The same names are inscribed in Roman letters as [M]ACCUTRENISALIC[I]D[U]NI with a simple cross separating the two words. The first name is probably Irish. Differences between the ogam and Roman letter versions show changes in language structure occurring at the time of carving. The second name, Salicidunus, means 'willow fort' in both Old Irish and Old Welsh. Dual inscription stones provide a wealth of early evidence for Celtic languages. They also show that Irish-speaking people had settled in Wales in the fifth and sixth centuries.

Pentre Poeth, Powys, sometimes known as Llywel or the Trecastle stone AD 450–550
Sandstone; H 182cm
British Museum, London

in the hoard carries spirals in red enamel: a plaque incised with a pair of Pictish symbols (figs 141 and 142).[10] These symbols appear elsewhere in silver, on two massive chains from eastern Scotland (figs 158–9),[11] but they were more commonly inscribed on Pictish symbol-stones (fig. 147).[12]

Language, literacy and identity

Inscribed stones record different Celtic languages (Old Irish, Old Welsh and Pictish) using a variety of scripts and reveal something of the diverse regional identities across Britain and Ireland between the fifth and seventh centuries (figs 145–6). They acted as memorials proclaiming lineage and reinforcing ancestral claims over surrounding territories. Those that can be translated mostly record names with occasional extra, often formulaic, phrases. They provide a wealth of evidence for developments in Celtic languages, showing how those languages changed dramatically over a few centuries. They also show connections between the people of these islands.

Literacy was another technology that came out of the Roman world. People in central and western Britain,[13] which had once been part of the Roman empire and remained Christian, often used Latin letters and phrases, but this was not true of all the Celtic-speaking people of these islands. Beyond the imperial frontiers, people developed their own scripts that reinforced local identities.

In Ireland, the ogam alphabet was created to transcribe the sounds of Old Irish through a system of notches carved along a baseline or into the edges of objects.[14] The mobility of Irish-speaking people is seen through the widespread use of ogam. In south-west Britain, Irish settlers raised bilingual inscriptions in Latin and ogam. There are some ogam inscriptions in western Scotland, but surprisingly few given that the origin myth of the Scots says that they invaded from Ireland. However, ogam inscriptions are also uncommon in the Scottish 'homeland' of north-east Ireland, so using this as evidence of migration is inconclusive.[15]

North of the Firth of Forth, the Picts created their own non-alphabetic symbol script, although it has not yet been deciphered.[16] Some of the symbols resemble real objects or animals, but most are geometric shapes that are not obviously recognizable. Messages were usually communicated through a pair of symbols, sometimes with the formulaic addition of mirror and comb symbols. Celtic art was used to elaborate this pictographic script in similar ways to contemporary metalwork, ranging from simple incised decoration to more complex spirals, peltae and scrolls: older 'heritage motifs' that were taken from Roman-period art (fig. 147). The Picts also portrayed stylized animals on their stones, such as boars or bulls. These captured the essence of the animal in a simple outline, with fluid contours showing the animal's muscles and joints.[17]

- Pictish symbol stones
- Ogam inscription
- Pictish and ogam inscriptions
- Roman letter inscription
- Ogam and Roman letter inscriptions

N

0   100 Miles

0   150 Kilometres

Fig. 146 (opposite) **Inscribed stones from Britain and Ireland** AD 400–650

Monuments inscribed with a variety of scripts (ogam, Roman letters and Pictish symbols) are among our earliest evidence for the different language groups (Old Irish, Old Welsh and Pictish) that shaped the history of early medieval Britain. The different distributions reveal emerging regional identities. There is very little overlap between Pictish and Roman letter inscriptions, whereas the distribution of ogam inscriptions shows the mobility of some Irish-speaking groups (e.g. into south-west Wales and England) and connections between Britain and Ireland.

Fig. 147 (right) **Image and text: Pictish symbol stones**

Pictish stones feature a system of paired symbols that was used to communicate messages in a similar way to inscribed stones elsewhere in Britain and Ireland. Uniquely the Picts used motifs otherwise found on metalwork to decorate their stone inscriptions.

St Peter's church, South Ronaldsay AD 400–650
Sandstone; H 166 cm
National Museums Scotland, Edinburgh

Looking to different pasts in the Roman provinces and beyond

Traditionally, discussion of early medieval 'Celtic arts' starts with the light of civilization leaving British shores with the Roman legions in AD 410 and the primitive barbarism of the Dark Ages engulfing these islands, allowing ancient art styles to re-emerge. Objects decorated with curvilinear swirly patterns, trumpet scrolls and triskele spirals are often thought to have been preserved beyond the imperial frontiers by the barbarian Picts and Scots, who were notorious raiders of the empire in late Roman historical sources. These were certainly times of great political and social change, and the virtual absence of historical documents from AD 400 to AD 600 is almost like returning to prehistory: hence the negative term 'Dark Ages'. However, Dark Age decline is not our story. The chapter title has a deliberate double meaning: the art styles that we are tracing came out of the Roman world as much as they existed out of (beyond) the imperial frontiers. The roots for understanding the styles, materials and forms of early medieval objects lie in the Roman period rather than some mystical survival from prehistory.

These roots are not always obvious. Very few types of object carried over unchanged from the Roman period: we no longer see decorated weapons, torcs, chariot gear or distinctive ornaments such as dragonesque brooches. But some of the most important early medieval dress accessories, for example penannular brooches and handpins, were elaborately embellished versions of plainer earlier forms. The distinctive, delicate style that adorns these objects emerged as a result of relationships and connections between people within and beyond late Roman Britannia.[18]

These relationships can be seen in a tiny silver pin from Oldcroft, in the wealthy civilian zone of south-west England (fig. 148). It was found along with scrap silver and over 3,000 low-value Roman copper-alloy coins, buried around AD 359.[19] The pin is far from spectacular – it weighs less than three grams and is only six centimetres long – but it is important because of its material and decoration. It has a minute projecting ring-head, beaded above and enamelled below on a field barely one centimetre across. Chip-carving left a central pelta in silver connected to two fine scrolls ending in stylized bird heads; red enamel highlights the design (fig. 148). This small pin is an ancestor of the handpins found across Britain and Ireland.[20] It shows that these objects decorated with Celtic art have their roots in the late Roman world.

The designs they carry also have earlier origins. During the late second and third centuries a distinctive style of decoration using swirly openwork geometric forms and trumpet-scrolls became popular among soldiers along the Roman frontiers (fig. 149).[21] The motifs were ambiguous, and could be interpreted as classical or Celtic depending on the viewer's preference and background (like the spirals/vine-scrolls on the enamelled Ilam pan; fig. 128). Other designs that are often seen as typically Celtic also survived in

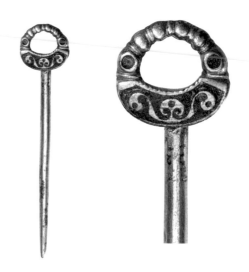

Fig. 148 **Small beginnings**

This tiny pin is illustrated actual size on the left and enlarged on the right to show the detail of the decoration. At this small scale would an observer even notice the subtle ornament?

Oldcroft, Gloucestershire AD 300–360
Silver, enamel; L 6 cm
British Museum, London

Fig. 150 **A Christian mosaic from a Roman villa**

In late Roman art, geometric patterns came to dominate the naturalistic elements of the design. Such patterns influenced the development of new styles of Celtic art in Britain and Ireland.

Hinton St Mary, Dorset AD 300–350
Ceramic mosaic; central roundel
D 86 cm
British Museum, London

Fig. 149 (left) *Trompetenmuster* mount

This style of mount was popular with the Roman military and examples have mostly been found near the imperial frontiers. Known by the modern German name *trompetenmuster* (trumpet decoration), does the triskele and trumpet-spiral design justify the label of 'Celtic art'?

Dormagen, Nordrhein-Westfalen, Germany AD 150–200
Copper alloy; D 9.6 cm
Rheinisches Landesmuseum, Bonn

Roman Britain: for instance, the three-legged (triskele) design is found on Romano-British plate brooches (fig. 24).[22]

The emergence of these trumpet-spiral and triskele decorations was part of a wider, developing trend in the late Roman world. Across a variety of materials and forms – silverware, stone, mosaic and jewellery – there was a growing emphasis on abstract and geometric ornament. These had previously been of secondary importance to classical naturalistic art, but increasingly they occupied more space in designs until they became the dominant feature (fig. 150).[23]

This shift in aesthetic can also be seen in a late Roman military style of the fourth and fifth centuries, especially on military dress ornaments or fittings, usually in bronze, but with the highest quality in silver. They are found along the Roman frontiers and beyond, where they were probably carried by warriors returning home after military service. Examples come from hoards of hacked silver from Ballinrees (fig. 151) and Traprain Law. These hoards may themselves be linked to warriors, though whether as military pay, subsidy or loot from raiding the empire is much debated.[24]

These geometric ornaments influenced the design of objects in Britain and Ireland, such as two great disc-headed Irish pins (fig. 152).[25] Their decoration is shared with the large silver handpins and with enigmatic broken mounts from Norrie's Law (fig. 142 top left). The adaptation of these late Roman fashions into a local style in the fifth and sixth centuries was a legacy of Rome.

Fig. 151 (below) **Military style**

This mount was from a weapon, perhaps a sword-sheath, and was found in an Irish hoard of late Roman hacksilver, ingots and coins. The style of such military fittings influenced the decoration of silver objects made in Britain and Ireland (fig. 152).

Ballinrees, Coleraine, Co. Londonderry AD 350–450
Silver-gilt, niello; L 7.75 cm, W 2.5 cm
British Museum, London

Fig. 152 (above and below)
Insular military-style pins

The upper surfaces of the disc-headed pin (right) are almost completely decorated with 'military-style' abstract and geometric ornament. The front of the disc-head has three pairs of spirals ending in beaked heads like the Gaulcross handpin (top).

Gaulcross, Aberdeenshire AD 400–650
Silver, enamel; pin-head W 1.85 cm
National Museums Scotland, Edinburgh
(on loan from Aberdeenshire Heritage)

Unknown provenance, Londesborough collection
AD 400–500
Silver, enamel; disc-head D 1.9 cm
British Museum, London

Characterizing early medieval Celtic art

This new Celtic art was selective. Just like in previous periods, only certain objects and materials were chosen to be decorated. In Britain and Ireland between *c.* AD 250 and 650, Celtic art occurred predominantly on cast bronze objects (and only very rarely on silver), mostly clothing fasteners including penannular brooches (fig. 155), pins and so-called 'latchets' (figs 153 and 157). Organic materials such as wood, bone, leather and textiles were rarely embellished with these curvilinear, swirly, abstract styles (judging from what few organic objects survive).

As we saw with the tiny Oldcroft pin, designs were often very small-scale and focused on minute, intricate details. Unlike Iron Age and Roman objects, it was rare for entire artefacts to be decorated. More often, only certain components of larger objects were adorned. For example, typical of this period are bronze bowls called 'hanging-bowls' because they were suspended using the distinctive mounts fixed around their rim. These were high-status objects, but the bowls themselves were normally plain, with the elaborate decoration used on the rim and base mounts (fig. 28).[26]

These hanging-bowls highlight a key feature of this period: different techniques and art styles were in use at the same time, sometimes on the same object. The decoration on their mounts ranges from simple incised or punched motifs to incredibly detailed carved designs, with enamel enhancing the fine ornament. Books on Celtic art usually focus on the sweeping lines and compass-drawn patterns of the triskeles and trumpet-spirals (see Chapter 8) because they compare with later Christian illuminated manuscript arts (fig. 169) but these were only the most elaborate examples among a much wider variety of decoration. Many simpler motifs had a Roman inspiration, such as running spirals or marigold designs (fig. 153).[27] For example, the mounts from a bowl that was reused to hold a cremation burial at Sutton Hoo in East Anglia dating to around AD 550 carry motifs that first appeared on third-century Romano-British plate brooches.[28]

Technologies and techniques such as enamelling and carving, raw materials like silver, and common design elements were all part of the legacy of Roman Britain used by the political and social groups emerging in the fourth to sixth centuries AD. Even the form of many of these decorated objects had their roots in Roman times. For this period where historical records are slender, these objects cast fresh light on societies in Britain and Ireland after Rome. They were reinventing habits, styles and materials from previous centuries; renovation of different pasts as well as innovation, in order to create new identities and connections in this post-imperial world.

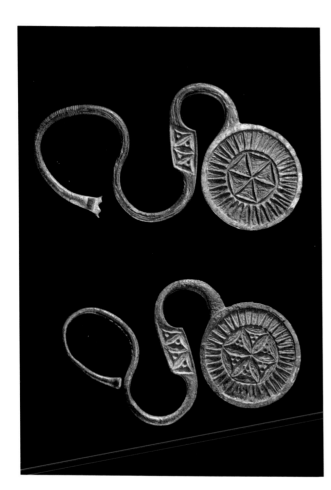

Fig. 153 **Not just swirls and spirals**

Latchets are a type of dress ornament that was distinctive to Ireland. This pair shows the legacy of Rome beyond the imperial frontiers in the variety of geometric and abstract motifs which were used on post-Roman personal ornaments and hanging-bowls.

Near Newry, Co. Down AD 400–600
Copper alloy; L 8.15 cm
British Museum, London

Looking different and looking the same

There were both connections and differences across early medieval Britain and Ireland. What you wore said a lot about who you were. For example, the penannular brooch was the clothes fastener of choice for both sexes in northern and western Britain and Ireland, whereas in Anglo-Saxon areas of eastern and southern England, very different styles of brooch were the norm and were worn only by women. Brooches marked wider cultural connections and differences.[29]

Penannular brooches came to be highly decorated, but were simple in concept. Their basic form is a circular hoop with a gap in the ring and an attached pin. The pin was pushed through cloth (like a modern badge) and tucked through the gap and over the hoop, bracing and fastening the garment in position. The origins of these brooches lie in the Iron Age, but their use (along with all brooch forms) exploded in the Roman period.[30] Numerous related types in a variety of metals demonstrate they were popular across the social spectrum. They are widespread across the Roman province of Britain and beyond, as far as the Northern Isles.

These brooches changed shape over time. The Roman-period ones were quite plain, but some had elaborate zoomorphic terminals (fig. 154). A triangular space behind the creature's head was later expanded to create a small enamelled field. The origin of this variant was in Britain, but more intricately patterned examples were made in Ireland in the fifth to seventh centuries AD (fig. 155). During the seventh to ninth centuries, the terminals became large flattened plates for complex decoration (see Chapter 8). From humble beginnings a millennium before, the penannular brooch became increasingly important as a vehicle for display.

Fig. 154 (below left) An early zoomorphic penannular brooch

Brooches like this, with hints of animal-headed terminals on the ring, lie near the beginning of a long tradition of brooches that became increasingly ornate over the next half millennium (fig. 155). This example was found with a Roman bronze pan and belt buckle in a small hoard.

Longfaugh, Midlothian AD 150–200
Copper alloy; D 5.8 cm, pin L 7.3 cm
National Museums Scotland, Edinburgh

Fig. 155 (below right) The Ballinderry brooch

This is one of the most lavishly decorated zoomorphic penannular brooches known from Ireland. The materials used and the engraved hoop are very similar to mounts on the largest Sutton Hoo hanging-bowl (fig. 28). This brooch was found on a high-status site: an important crannog (artificial island dwelling) whose occupants had connections across Britain and Ireland.

Ballinderry Crannog 2, Co. Offaly AD 600–650
Bronze, tin, millefiori, glass; D 8.6 cm, pin L 18.3 cm
National Museum of Ireland, Dublin

Fig. 156 **From torc to brooch**

This gravestone of a Roman soldier, Cn. Musius, standard-bearer in the 14th legion, shows him wearing his awards for military valour including miniature torcs worn on the chest. This military use could have been a factor in the shift in popularity from penannular neck ornament to the similarly shaped brooch.

Mainz, Rheinland-Pfalz, Germany AD 1–50
Stone; H 1.96 m
Mittelrheinisches Museum, Mainz

A curious quirk of Roman military dress might explain why the penannular brooch became a key marker of people's identity in the Celtic-speaking parts of Britain and Ireland. In the Iron Age, the torc had been a symbol of status, but it declined in popularity during the Roman period. The wearing of a brooch was better suited to the changed worlds of the Roman provinces: they were rather more subtle, and more affordable. However, in the Roman army miniature torcs were also worn on the chest as an award for valour (fig. 156).[31] This may have created an ambiguity between the penannular neck ornament, which had been the primary symbol of status and identity in Iron Age Europe, and the penannular brooch. The Norrie's Law hoard includes a pair of large penannular hoops that embody this duality (fig. 142).[32] They are twisted like torcs, but have large flattened terminals like penannular brooches. One (on the right in fig. 142) is well worn at the point where a pin would have fixed the cloth. Perhaps over time the penannular brooch acquired some of the status that a torc once signalled.

Other ornaments beyond the old Roman frontiers were more regionally specific. In Ireland, people made a distinctive form of bronze dress fastener that archaeologists have called a 'latchet' (because it looked like a door latch). Some latchets are plain, but others carry a range of ornament similar to hanging-bowl designs, from the most accomplished fine triskele spirals (fig. 157) to more classical geometric designs (fig. 153). In contrast, massive silver chains are found only in Scotland. They were a spectacular, conspicuous form of precious-metal neck ornament: a new version of the old habit of a torc (fig. 158). Such chains were very rarely decorated, as the impact of the metal alone was enough to impress. They show just how much silver was available in northern Britain at this time: the largest, from Torvean, weighs nearly three kilograms. Almost all the chains were found in boggy ground during nineteenth-century agricultural

Fig. 158 (opposite) **A wealth of silver around the neck**

Massive silver chains, unique to Scotland, are the last of the tradition of great neck ornaments that were used throughout earlier centuries to mark status. They were made from recycled Roman silver. Two have Pictish symbols carved into the large terminal clasp. As a result, they are mistakenly labelled 'Pictish', although most are plain and have been found in southern Scotland.

Parkhill, Aberdeenshire AD 400–700
Silver, enamel; L 42 cm, approx. internal D 11 cm
National Museums Scotland, Edinburgh

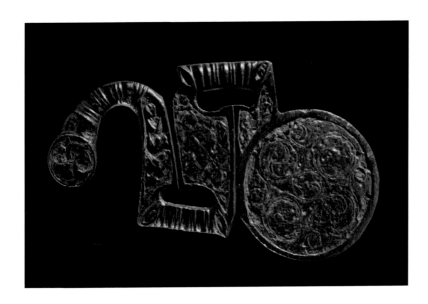

Fig. 157 **A 'latchet' dress fastener**

The disc is filled with curvilinear heritage motifs, while the more angular space in the middle carries lozenges and straight-line patterns. This range of ornament shows the mix of different traditions of decoration that were available for adaptation, even well beyond the former imperial frontiers.

Castle Island, Dowris, Co. Offaly AD 400–700
Copper alloy, enamel; L 7.5 cm
British Museum, London

Fig. 159 **Symbols on silver**

This Pictish symbol carved into the thick silver of a massive chain clasp is spiral-decorated and enhanced with red enamel. The chain was found far to the south of Pictish territory, pulled out of a Lanarkshire bog by a shepherd in 1869.

Whitecleugh, Lanarkshire AD 400–700
Silver, enamel; terminal ring H 2.1 cm
National Museums Scotland, Edinburgh

improvements. They were probably deliberate sacrifices in special places beyond the everyday world, much like the precious metalwork of earlier centuries (see pp. 103–5).[33]

There were also regional variations in the availability of materials. This was especially true of silver, which came ultimately from relationships with the late Roman empire: it was gifted, paid to, and stolen by warrior groups from beyond the imperial frontiers.[34] It seems groups in Scotland acquired more silver than their Irish neighbours, as silver ornaments are much rarer in Ireland than in Britain. For instance, the three known Irish silver handpins are all well worn, while one had its pin replaced in antiquity using bronze rather than silver.[35] Tin (which would have been mined in Cornwall) was often used in Ireland to cover the surface of bronze objects, giving them the appearance of silver (e.g. on the Ballinderry brooch hoop, fig. 155 and Donore disc, fig. 32).[36] Silver was not universally available, even to repair silver objects, and would have been a carefully guarded resource.

Wider connections

Brooch styles show differences between Celtic-speaking areas and Anglo-Saxon England, and these were evident in other ways too. We have seen that designs with trumpet-scrolls and triskele spirals were a defining characteristic of the art of northern and western Britain and Ireland. This swirly curvilinear art, and the objects decorated with it, contrasted strongly with the stylized animals and interlaced designs of Anglo-Saxon art in south and east Britain. There are also clear distinctions in materials and types of object. The Anglo-Saxon world favoured fine goldwork, extensive chip-carved gilded bronze surfaces, minute filigree (golden beads and wires) forming interlaced animals and geometric designs, with garnet cloisonné settings for high-status display (fig. 160).[37] In comparison, the north and west's most precious material was silver; more usually un-gilded bronze was used, with the heritage motifs of trumpet-scrolls and triskele spirals picked out using brightly coloured enamel.

But this difference was not absolute. Other objects show connections between the Celtic-speaking and Anglo-Saxon worlds. There has been extensive academic debate about where hanging-bowls were produced because of their curious distribution.[38] The vast majority have been found in sixth- to seventh-century Anglo-Saxon burials in the south and east of Britain, but there is no evidence they were made there (fig. 161). Production evidence comes from the opposite end of the country. A mould for casting one style of hanging-bowl mount was found at the Pictish hillfort of Craig Phadraig (fig. 164 top). While very few actual hanging-bowl fittings survive from Scotland, this style of mount has been found at several Scottish sites including Castle Tioram and Tummel Bridge, as well as far to the south, in Anglo-Saxon graves in England (fig. 164 bottom).[39]

Fig. 160 **Gold and garnet in Anglo-Saxon metalwork**

Gold and red garnets were used to decorate early Anglo-Saxon metalwork, but are very rare in the north and west of Britain and Ireland where different materials and types of objects were used to mark status, identity and gender. Belt-buckles were very important markers of male status in Anglo-Saxon society and all across early medieval Europe, but they are rarely found elsewhere in Britain and Ireland at this time.

Faversham, Kent AD 600–700
Gold, silver-gilt, niello, garnet; L 8 cm
British Museum, London

Fig. 161 **Hanging-bowls: manufacture and burial**

Although hanging-bowls are mostly found in Anglo-Saxon burials of the sixth–seventh centuries AD, our limited evidence currently suggests they were made in northern Britain.

- Hanging-bowl or hanging-bowl mount findspot
- Hanging-bowl mount production evidence

Craig Phadraig

Castle Tioram

Tummel Bridge

Mote of Mark

Baginton

Hildersham

Sutton Hoo

Lullingstone

N

0   100 Miles

0   150 Kilometres

This surprising distribution pattern largely arises due to biases in the archaeological evidence. In the north and west of Britain and Ireland people were not buried with their possessions, whereas Anglo-Saxon burials in the south and east were furnished with a variety of grave-goods. Consequently, for the north and west we are reliant on the random discovery of hoards and stray finds, or perhaps workshops if we are lucky. Objects might be made in very different places to where they ended up: our picture of the past can be highly skewed by particular cultural habits such as how people were buried. Rich Anglo-Saxon burials gathered valuable items from near and far: the famous ship burial from Sutton Hoo contained grave-goods from all over early medieval Europe, including three particularly fine hanging-bowls (fig. 28). All these objects served to show the wealth and contacts of this Anglo-Saxon king, with the hanging-bowls emphasizing connections to the north and west of Britain and Ireland.[40] It seems that hanging-bowls were indeed a north-western object type, given the evidence for production in Scotland, and it is only because of the quirks of Anglo-Saxon burial practices that they have been recovered almost exclusively in the south.

As we will see in Chapter 8, the distinction between metalwork traditions in the north and west versus the south and east did not remain clear cut for long. One hanging-bowl from Sutton Hoo looks like a hybrid, with unusual openwork mounts more common in Anglo-Saxon traditions.[41] Other hanging-bowls are embellished with interlaced motifs typical of Anglo-Saxon styles. Clay moulds for making axe-shaped interlace-decorated mounts recovered from the Mote of Mark fort in south-west Scotland show connections between this area and the expanding Anglo-Saxon world in the seventh century (fig. 163).[42] Other connections are suggested by animal

Fig. 162 (above left) **Northern connections**

This hanging-bowl has bronze mounts applied to the outside which show links to northern Britain. The animals are reminiscent of Pictish symbols, while the axe-shaped interlace-decorated mounts are similar to ones made at the Mote of Mark (fig. 163).

Lullingstone, Kent AD 550–650
Silver, enamel, copper-alloy; D 24.8 cm
British Museum, London

Fig. 163 (above right) **Early interlace**

This broken clay mould was used for casting bronze axe-shaped interlace-decorated mounts. Similar mounts have been found on objects buried at Sutton Hoo and on the Lullingstone hanging-bowl. The use of interlace decoration shows the growing influence of Anglo-Saxon Northumbria in seventh-century southern Scotland.

Mote of Mark, Dumfries & Galloway AD 550–650
Clay; L 6.2 cm, W 3.7 cm
National Museums Scotland, Edinburgh

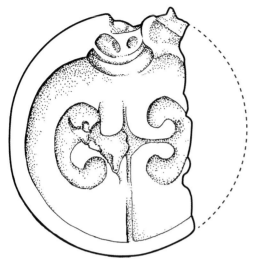

mounts on the hanging-bowls from southern England including finds from Lullingstone and Hildersham, which resemble Pictish animal art: perhaps they are imports or imitations (fig. 162).[43] These examples hint at what was to follow: from the seventh century on, connections between north-west Britain, Ireland and the Anglo-Saxon world fundamentally changed art in these islands.

Looking to the future

This chapter has shown that complex curvilinear, swirly and spiral art was not just some mystical 'Celtic' survival in the misty regions beyond Rome's frontiers. Our story is more complicated than that, and more interesting too. The Roman occupation played a significant part in the history of the Celtic arts that we are tracing, as many of the objects, styles and motifs developed and flourished in the Roman province of Britannia.

Art styles were not the only influence from Rome. Christianity also came out of the Roman world. This new monotheistic religion spread across Europe as Roman imperial power declined.[44] It achieved a more lasting legacy than Roman legions ever did, and an influence that continues today. Christianity altered how people thought about the world and their place in it. In Britain and Ireland from the fifth century onwards, becoming Christian changed the ways in which people used art and depicted their most sacred concepts.[45] In the following chapter we will see that Christianity and wider connections beyond the Celtic-speaking world stimulated this flickering light of artistic brilliance, illuminating the so-called Dark Ages.

Fig. 164 (left, above and below)
From north to south

The clay mould (line drawing, above) from near Inverness shows that mounts with openwork pelta decoration were made in northern Scotland. The actual mount (left) was attached to a hanging bowl found far to the south, in an Anglo-Saxon grave. The bowl is also decorated with appliqué mounts of animals, like the Lullingstone hanging-bowl (fig. 162), which resemble Pictish animal art.

Mould: Craig Phadrig, Inverness-shire AD 500–600
Clay; L 6.6 cm, T 1.4 cm
National Museums Scotland, Edinburgh

Mount: Hildersham, Cambridgeshire AD 500–600
Copper-alloy, enamel; hook D 6 cm
University Museum of Archaeology and Anthropology, Cambridge

Chapter 8

Fig. 165 **Penannular brooch (detail)**

The birds drinking from a fountain on this silver-gilt penannular brooch were a Christian symbol of eternal life. This fine detail could only have been appreciated close-up. (See pp. 196–7 and fig. 191.)

Rogart, Highland AD 700–800
Silver, gilding, glass; central circle D 2.5 cm
National Museums Scotland, Edinburgh

At the Western Edge of the Christian World, *c.* AD 600–900

Martin Goldberg

In 1830, two workmen set about quarrying stone from coastal crags at Hunterston in Ayrshire. They had little time to enjoy the view west out to the islands of Little Cumbrae and Arran, and south towards the Irish Sea. But they did spot something glinting gold where it had rolled out from the rocks: a large circular brooch, with an ornate pin and amber insets. The colour was misleading. The brooch was cast in silver, but its surface was enhanced with intricate gold filigree decoration (p. 2 and fig. 166).[1] The tiny balls and wire created complex designs, including fantastic animals whose interlaced limbs contort to give them an unnatural, otherworldly appearance.[2]

Despite its ornate beauty, what initially caused most interest was the tenth-century runic inscription that had been scratched onto the back of the brooch when it was already several centuries old. The Hunterston brooch was probably made in the early eighth century, and would have been treasured by many generations of owners before one Maelbrigte (a Gaelic name that translates to 'the servant of St Brigit') inscribed their Christian name in Norse runes. It would have been used to fasten the clothing of powerful people throughout most of the period covered by this chapter.

Fig. 166 (above, left and right)
Front and back of the Hunterston brooch

On the back of the brooch, a later tenth-century runic inscription is scratched into the silver naming one owner, Maelbrigte, a Gaelic Christian name. The only use of curvilinear spiral heritage motifs is on the back of the brooch and would have been hidden when worn.

Hunterston, Ayrshire AD 650–750
Silver, gold; D 12.2 cm, broken pin 13.1 cm
National Museums Scotland, Edinburgh

Fig. 167 (above, left and right)
Anglo-Saxon influences

Details of the design and shared techniques show the similarities between the Hunterston brooch (right; detail of pin-head) and Anglo-Saxon metalwork (left).

Faversham, Kent AD 600–700
Gold, silver, niello; L 7.6 cm, W 3.6 cm
British Museum, London

Hunterston, Ayrshire AD 650–750
Silver, gold; pin-head W 4.2 cm
National Museums Scotland, Edinburgh

Chapter 7 highlighted clear differences between the decorated metalwork of Celtic-speaking people[3] in the north and west and their Anglo-Saxon neighbours in the south and east in the fifth to seventh centuries: distinctions in materials (silver, un-gilded bronze and enamel versus gold, gilded bronze and garnet) and styles (curvilinear swirls and spirals versus interlaced designs, especially animals). The Hunterston brooch is an example of new relationships with the Anglo-Saxon world through the exchange of techniques, materials and an elaborate mixture of motifs. When it was created, jewellery decorated in this way with gold, gems and contorted beasts was more common in the Anglo-Saxon kingdoms of south-east Britain (fig. 167). The type of brooch is clearly related to the penannular brooch typical of the north and west of these islands (see Chapter 7), but this was a new, fully circular form that was much more prevalent in Ireland.

The range of influences seen on the Hunterston brooch shows that the most powerful people in society could command resources and skills from across these islands. But these jeweller's arts were not just used on the dress ornaments of influential individuals. They are also found on the finest surviving church metalwork, such as the chalices from the Derrynaflan and

Fig. 168 **The Ardagh chalice**

The jeweller's arts were also used on the finest church metalwork.

Ardagh, Co. Limerick AD 700–800
Gold, silver, glass, rock crystal, amber, enamel;
D 19.5 cm, H 17.8 cm
National Museum of Ireland, Dublin

Ardagh hoards in Ireland (fig. 168).[4] These new relationships expressed through art also appear in completely innovative formats: on a grand scale in ambitious Christian stone sculpture, and in the most minute and intricate detail on illuminated manuscripts. This fusion of styles has become known as 'Insular' art, not because it was inward-looking (quite the contrary), but because it was distinctive to these Atlantic islands.

The Insular fusion

The seventh century AD saw the most dramatic changes in art in these islands since the impact of Rome. This was due to major social upheavals. Motifs, technologies and materials expressed new ideas and relationships. Insular art fused diverse influences from the Mediterranean world, the Continent and Anglo-Saxon society. It also linked the different pasts of people who lived within the former Roman provinces and those from beyond the frontiers. It has been described as 'the most vivid material expression of the collision and fusion of ancient Celtic, Germanic, and Mediterranean cultures'.[5] Complex curvilinear and spiral ornament, the heritage motifs we traced 'out of the Roman world' in Chapter 7, were only one component in this new art style (fig. 169). The other most prominent and varied motifs are interlaced designs: ribbons, ultimately from classical sources, and elongated animals that originated in Anglo-Saxon art (see p. 178).

Fig. 169 **Spiral art as Christian icon**

In keeping with its prehistoric roots, spiral heritage motifs continued to have a deep religious significance in Christian art. On folio 3V of the Book of Durrow a complex spiral motif is treated like a central icon in the same way crosses elsewhere in the Gospel book.

Durrow, Co. Offaly AD 650–700
Vellum; 24.5 x 14.5 cm
Trinity College Dublin

The Insular Fusion

The Insular fusion brought together previously distinct art styles from a variety of sources. Interlace designs, running scrolls, inhabited vine-scrolls and Greek key (or fret) patterns were adapted from classical Mediterranean art (fig. 150). Animal interlace, popular across northern Europe, was adopted from the Anglo-Saxon kingdoms (fig. 167). The complex curvilinear motifs, such as triskeles and trumpet-spirals, came from the artistic heritage of the north and west of Britain and Ireland.

The Insular artistic fusion is most commonly associated with objects of Christian art – in stone, metalwork, and especially illuminated manuscripts – but it can also be seen on brooches and other dress ornaments. Objects were decorated using several of the component elements, creating eclectic compositions, but each motif was usually kept separate in discrete panels or fields of decoration. Only the Picts experimented with running patterns together (fig. 171).

Decorated objects indicate high status, and the bringing together of motifs from various cultural backgrounds hints at elite connections between people across Britain and Ireland. But it would be too simplistic to think of this fusion just as a by-product of the cultural melting pot described by Bede (p. 180). Motifs had specific meanings and were often used in quite distinct ways in different parts of these islands (p. 204). This influenced how and by whom they were used; what objects were chosen for decoration; what motifs were appropriate to enhance certain features; and how those objects could be valued differently and appreciated by different eyes (pp.198–204).

a

b

c

d

e

Fig. 170
A motif-hoard

Three of the main elements of the Insular fusion can be seen decorating the two Pictish symbols at the top of the Hilton of Cadboll cross-slab. Interlace decorates the central connecting bar of the double-disc symbol (a), and triskeles can still be seen in the crescent and V-rod symbol whose centre is filled with a key/fret pattern (b).

Beneath the Pictish symbols are a pair of complex interlace roundels (c). Interlace is often popularly thought of as 'Celtic knotwork', but it is much more than that – part of wider Christian art that became a major feature of the Insular fusion c. AD 650 (p. 184).

The border is an inhabited vine-scroll (d), but unlike Anglo-Saxon versions and the Mediterranean origins of this classical motif, here in Pictland it is populated with fantastical beasts rather than clearly recognizable creatures.

The bottom square panel (e; now broken in half) is filled with a complex design of inter-locking triskeles and trumpet-spirals comparable with the finest of manuscript art, but fifty times larger than the smallest spirals in the Book of Kells (fig. 4).

Hilton of Cadboll, Easter Ross, Highland
AD 700–800
Sandstone; W 144 cm
National Museums Scotland, Edinburgh

What caused this fusion? We have already seen at various points in this book that contact between different groups of people could produce dramatic changes. The hanging-bowls in Anglo-Saxon burials (see pp. 168– 71) mark the beginnings of these contacts, but they also show that the fusion of art styles was just beginning in the early seventh century. Relations between people living in these islands were pivotal: the Germanic-speaking Anglo-Saxons of the south and east of Britain; the Welsh-speaking Britons of the west attempting to retain control of land from Cornwall to the Firth of Clyde; the Gaelic-speaking populations of Ireland who also settled in pockets along the western seaboard of Britain, especially the west of Scotland; and the Picts who occupied northern and eastern Scotland, north of the Firth of Forth. In the eighth century, the Northumbrian monk Bede summarized this mixture in terms of four peoples and four languages, with a fifth, Latin, which united all in Christian faith.[6] In this mix, northern Britain had the ingredients for 'Insular fusion'.

Conversion to Christianity was the other key factor. Christian missionaries, especially those from Ireland who founded St Columba's island monastery of Iona on the west coast of Scotland, claimed responsibility for the conversion of the Picts during the second half of the sixth century, and we can see a corresponding change in art in the area. Earlier Pictish symbol-stones (fig. 147) were decorated in similar style to contemporary hanging-bowl mounts: they never used the Insular fusion of art styles.[7] However, later Pictish cross-slabs *were* decorated with Insular art: evidence that conversion to Christianity was a prime stimulus for the Insular fusion (fig. 171). Missionaries from Iona also founded the island monastery of Lindisfarne, off the Northumbrian coast, in the middle of the seventh century. The meeting of Anglo-Saxon and Celtic-speaking Christians during the conversion of Northumbria established important cultural connections between the two monastic centres of Iona and Lindisfarne. Such monasteries became centres of artistic production, employing this new fusion of art styles to adorn religious objects.

This Insular fusion was a radical departure from what had gone before.[8] These arts were no longer restricted to fine metalwork. Different materials were used, such as religious manuscripts with painted designs, a completely new art form for these islands (fig. 173). Decoration was also employed on a grand scale. Large carved stones no longer carried just an inscription but were often completely covered in ornament, with the Christian cross as the primary symbol. In contrast, manuscripts and metalwork were embellished in minute, intricate detail. No matter what the scale, considerable areas of space were filled with an eclectic mix of motifs.

Archaeological excavations show that the creation of such masterpieces not only occurred at centres like Iona but also at other sites that were not historically documented. Modern excavations at the Pictish monastery at Portmahomack in Easter Ross have provided evidence for glass settings like those on the ecclesiastical treasures in the Ardagh hoard (fig. 168), along with

Fig. 171 **Experimental fusion**

Although small, this cross-slab is highly accomplished in decoration and design. On the shaft the artist has experimented with running the motifs of the Insular fusion together using a single continuous line. The size suggests it may have served as a personal memorial or grave-slab. On the reverse are Pictish symbols and a figure wearing a large penannular brooch – a marker of the highest status.

Monifieth, Angus AD 700–800
Stone; L 76 cm, W 30 cm, T 9 cm
National Museums Scotland, Edinburgh

the tools and technologies needed for manuscript production.[9] The range and quality of the stone sculpture from Portmahomack bears comparison with the finest of illuminated manuscript art, while the relief-carved lettering on a cross-slab fragment from the site is similar to the script in the Lindisfarne Gospels and the Book of Kells (figs 172–3).[10] Yet although these stone carvings and manufacturing debris give hints of the Insular art that could have been made here, no illuminated manuscripts comparable to those in Ireland have survived in Scotland and very few ecclesiastical treasures.[11]

The Insular fusion was not just about religion: much of what is illustrated here would have been made for and used by the social elite. The period when Lindisfarne was founded from Iona (around AD 635) also marked the beginning of almost half a century of Northumbrian political domination over much of northern Britain. The small coastal hillfort of the Mote of Mark in Galloway lay in the contact zone between Anglian Northumbria and the Celtic-speaking west in the seventh century. Excavations produced a variety of moulds for making penannular brooches and interlace-decorated metalwork (fig. 163), along with a fragment of bone with Anglo-Saxon runes on it.[12] At the major hillfort of Dunadd in Argyll, excavations have also provided evidence for mixed artistic traditions. For example, among the range of penannular brooch moulds is an eagle-headed one similar to an Anglo-Saxon type. There are also moulds for making belt buckles, an Anglo-Saxon fashion rare in the north and west.[13] This production evidence at Dunadd shows that a variety of objects were made for much wider distribution, crossing political or linguistic barriers.

Fig. 172 (right) **Manuscript art and letters carved into stone**

An inscription using unusual relief lettering was carved onto the side of this once- massive cross-slab from the monastery at Portmahomack in northern Scotland. The lettering is the same style as that used in the finest Insular gospel books. The tiny surviving portion of the decorated cross on the side of this fragment also uses the complex interlocking triskele spirals of illuminated manuscript art.

Portmahomack, Easter Ross
AD 700–800
Sandstone; H 51.5 cm, T 20 cm
National Museums Scotland, Edinburgh

Fig. 173 (opposite) **Initial page from the Gospel of St Matthew in the Lindisfarne Gospels**

If scribes and artists at the island monastery of Lindisfarne could create magnificent illuminated manuscripts enhanced by complex curvilinear spiral art, why did Northumbrian sculptors not create similarly decorated monuments in stone?

Lindisfarne, Northumberland
c. AD 720
Vellum; 36.5 x 27.5 cm
British Library, London

Interlace – new symbols for a timeless purpose

The conversion of Britain and Ireland to Christianity brought new ways of expressing beliefs through art, and resulted in the creation of some of the finest works of Christian art in early medieval Europe. Many people today think of interlace as 'Celtic knotwork', but it is not just Celtic. Interlace decoration was used far and wide, from Egypt to Ireland (figs 175–9). Interlaced animals were features of Anglo-Saxon metalwork before this style was adopted by Christians, but it was complex ribbon interlace that had the greatest influence on Christian arts. The simple over-and-under of Mediterranean guilloche ornament (fig. 150) may have been one inspiration, but weaving and leatherwork would also have provided practical ways of working out models for the complex interlace knots that characterize the pages of Insular manuscripts and stone crosses.[14] Although its origins were varied, interlace had a consistent purpose: it filled empty spaces and acted as a protective device for warding off evil spirits, entangling them in its dense knotwork (fig. 174).[15]

Fig. 174 **Sword hilt and cone-mount from the St Ninian's Isle hoard**

The entire surfaces of these two small objects are covered with complex interwoven animals depicted in minute detail. The origins of this animal interlace lie in the Anglo-Saxon world. For fine ribbon interlace see figs 165 and 178–9, as well as the manuscript illustrations throughout this chapter.

St Ninian's Isle, Shetland AD 700–800
Silver, gold; sword hilt W 8 cm, cone H 4.3 cm
National Museums Scotland, Edinburgh

Figs 175–7 (opposite)
Interlace across Europe and beyond

Interlace decoration was incredibly widespread across Europe and beyond, as far away as Egypt and the Holy Land. The gold buckle from the Sutton Hoo ship burial is one of the finest pieces of Anglo-Saxon metalwork, but the dense interlace that decorates it is often popularly misunderstood as 'Celtic'.

Fig. 175 **Small buckle**

Akhmin, Upper Egypt AD 500–800
Gilt-copper alloy; L 5.8 cm
British Museum, London

Fig. 176 **Disc brooch**

Linz-am-Rhein, Rheinland-Pfalz, Germany AD 600–700
Silver-gilt, niello; D 4.7 cm
British Museum, London

Fig. 177 **Large buckle**

Sutton Hoo, Suffolk AD 610–640
Niello, gold; L 13.2 cm
British Museum, London

Fig. 178 **Interlace and Christian art**

Interlace decoration can be found in great variety in Christian art across Europe. The Christian monuments from western Britain developed an amazing range of complex knotwork and interlace designs. Why did they not also use the complex curvilinear heritage motifs that were so popular in Pictland and Ireland?

Glenluce, Dumfries & Galloway AD 900–1000
Stone; H 167 cm
National Museums Scotland, Edinburgh

Fig. 179 **Interlace in Anglo-Saxon art**

Interlace designs were the most popular element on Anglo-Saxon sculpture, especially the tall slender cross-shafts such as this fragment. Why did Anglo-Saxon Christian sculpture so rarely use the curvilinear art that decorated their finest manuscripts, such as the Lindisfarne or Lichfield Gospels?

Morham, East Lothian AD 800–900
Sandstone, H 103 cm
National Museums Scotland, Edinburgh

Between beasts – new meanings for ancient symbols

Interlace was used extensively and in varied ways across Britain and Ireland in the period AD 600–900, but it was just one element in early medieval Christian art. The human form reappeared in this new style after being absent from Celtic art for several centuries. This figural art was used to illustrate biblical texts, although the human images are often difficult to recognize because Insular Christian art avoided the naturalism of classical art. For example, on a mount from Crieff the human figure is reduced to its most diagnostic feature, the head, representing the human Christ (fig. 181). However, the biblical context means that for the first time we can relate art to the underlying beliefs that were being communicated.

The human figure between beasts is an ancient motif (see p. 64), but in early medieval Europe it became much more widespread (figs 180–1). In a Christian context this motif was used as a reference to the Canticle of Habbakuk. This was a hymn sung at sunrise in monasteries every Friday, and on Good Friday at that most important ninth hour when Christ died on the cross. The chant for the Canticle includes the line: 'Between two living things you will become known'.[16] The popularity of the human between two beasts motif was due to this association with the recognition of Christ as Saviour, at a time when ever greater areas of Europe were converting to Christianity.

Such religious messages are not just found on crosses or religious metalwork, but also on jewellery, indicating the personal devotion of a Christian who proclaimed this message on their dress-pin. Christ could also be represented by abstract motifs such as a lozenge (for example, on the central mount of the Tara brooch; fig. 182), perhaps symbolizing a book,[17] as well as more familiar devices like the cross (as on the central mount on the Hunterston brooch, fig. 166). These complex connections between art, text and belief can only be disentangled because we understand the Christian framework within which they were created. Such a detailed level of interpretation is astounding after the guesswork often required in understanding prehistoric beliefs.

Fig. 180 **Christ between two living creatures**

This bronze mount that decorates the Tully Lough processional cross (see fig. 185) shows a human between two beasts, an ancient motif reinvented in a Christian context.

Tully Lough, Co. Roscommon AD 700–800
Gilt bronze mounts, tinned bronze backing plate; mount W 4 cm
National Museum of Ireland, Dublin

Fig. 181 **Focusing on the head**

The figure of Christ has been reduced here to
its most potent and recognizably human element
– the head. The rest of the mount may represent
the body, with framing beasts. It is unclear what
sort of object it may have originally decorated.
It is one of a pair, and it has been reused at
least once.

Crieff, Perthshire and Kinross AD 700–800
Gilded copper-alloy, rock crystal, amber-coloured glass;
H 5.8 cm, W 5.5 cm
National Museums Scotland, Edinburgh

Fig. 182 **The Tara brooch**

The closest comparison for the Hunterston
brooch is this brooch found at Bettystown
outside Dublin in 1850. It was purchased
by a Dublin jeweller who re-branded it the
'Tara' brooch, giving it a false link to the site
associated with Irish High Kingship. This made
the replicas that the jeweller produced extremely
popular (see pp. 244–5).

Bettystown, Co. Meath AD 650–750
Silver, gold, glass, enamel, amber; D 8.7 cm, pin L 32 cm
National Museum of Ireland, Dublin

Mobile Christianity: missionaries, metalwork and manuscript art

A key part of the new religion was the conversion of non-believers. This process is seen in rare surviving objects that were the tools of conversion. Among the most important portable Christian objects created in this period are small boxes made with metal plates and fittings, which are shaped like buildings with peaked roofs.[18] They once held religious substances, especially the relics of saints, and some are constructed around hollowed-out solid blocks of wood (fig. 183). The similarities between examples from places as far apart as Ireland and northern Italy demonstrate the impact of missionaries from Britain and Ireland on Continental Christianity. The reliquaries from Monymusk and Copenhagen were both treasured, but with different histories: one, now empty, surviving in Scotland till the present day; the other crossing the North Sea, perhaps as Viking loot, and still containing relics today. Like the Hunterston brooch, the example now in Copenhagen has a later Norse runic inscription (fig. 184).[19] They are miniature metalwork examples of religious structures such as a tomb, shrine or church. Some

Fig. 183 **The Monymusk reliquary**

The form of these objects is meant to signify a shrine or a church, but each example is uniquely assembled from a diverse range of decorated fittings and mounts. It has fine punched decoration (pointillé) depicting interlaced beasts similar to those on bowls from the St Ninian's Isle hoard (fig. 187).

Monymusk, Aberdeenshire AD 700–800
Silver, copper-alloy, gilding, glass, enamel, wood; L 10.8 cm, H 9.8 cm, W 5.1 cm
National Museums Scotland, Edinburgh

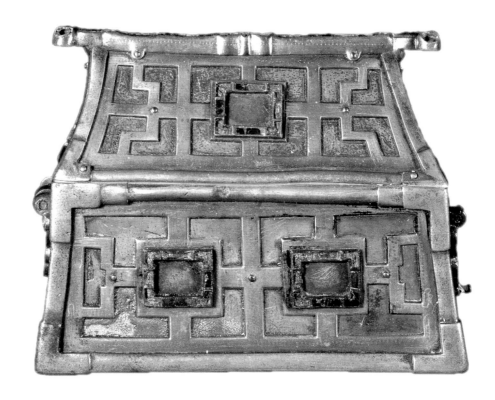

Fig. 184 **The Copenhagen reliquary**

These containers for sacred substances would
have been protected and carried by designated
keepers (see Chapter 9). Fittings on the side
are for carrying straps. This reliquary was carried
to Scandinavia, possibly as a result of a Viking
raid on a Christian monastery. The inscription on
the base reads *Ranvaik a Kistu thasa*, 'Ranvaik
owns this casket', in tenth-century runes.

Norway AD 700–800
Copper-alloy, tin, enamel, wood; L 13.5 cm, H 10 cm,
W 5.3 cm
National Museum of Denmark, Copenhagen

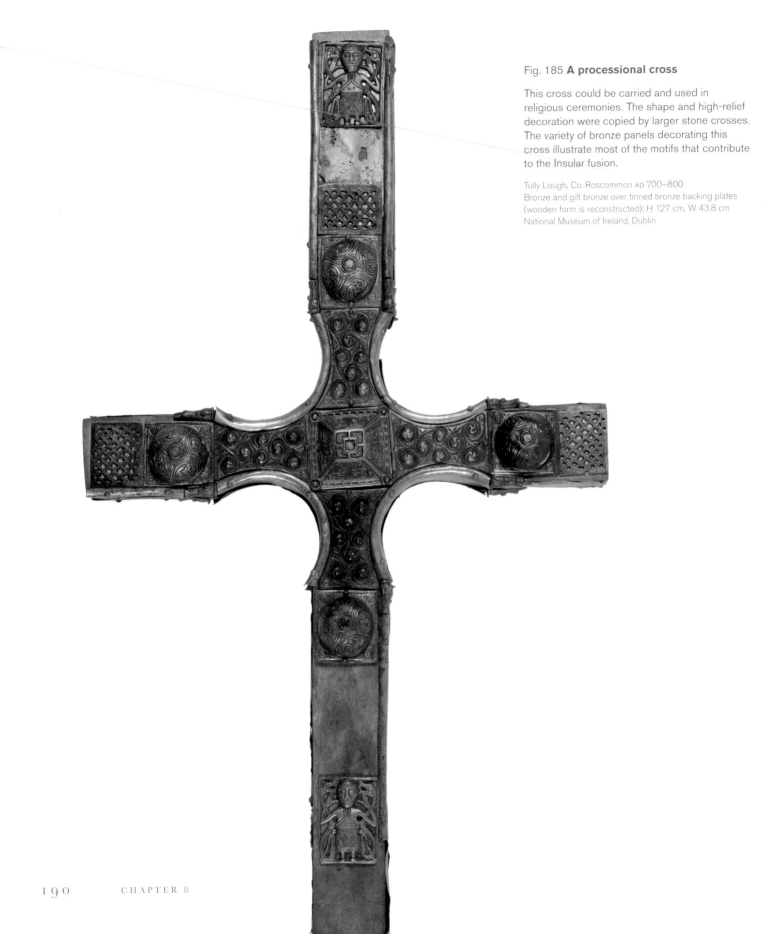

Fig. 185 **A processional cross**

This cross could be carried and used in
religious ceremonies. The shape and high-relief
decoration were copied by larger stone crosses.
The variety of bronze panels decorating this
cross illustrate most of the motifs that contribute
to the Insular fusion.

Tully Lough, Co. Roscommon AD 700–800
Bronze and gilt bronze over tinned bronze backing plates
(wooden form is reconstructed); H 127 cm, W 43.8 cm
National Museum of Ireland, Dublin

Fig. 186 **A mixture of Christian symbols**

The monks beneath the cross appear to be
carrying book satchels which made the gospels
mobile for missionary conversion. The beast
beneath the monks is a lion, the symbol of
St Mark. At the base, the strange bird-men
with a head between them may be one of the
most oblique references to the Canticle of
Habbakuk's recognition of Christ between two
living creatures

Papil, West Burra, Shetland AD 700–800
Sandstone; H 205 cm
National Museums Scotland

have roof beams with a tiny building in the centre between two beast-headed
terminals, another reference to the Canticle of Habbakuk 'between two
beasts', equating the building (probably a church) with Christ.

Other objects helped to transmit the word of God. The Tully Lough
cross is a rare surviving example of a processional cross: a mobile symbol of
Christianity that could be taken beyond the monastic precinct to spread
Christian doctrine. Elaborately decorated with bronze mounts encasing a
wooden core, it shows virtually the full range of Insular motifs (fig. 185).[20]
But the essential tool of conversion was the Bible. A cross-slab from Papil in
Shetland shows four travelling monks beneath a ringed cross, carrying book
satchels that protected the Bible and made it mobile (fig. 186).[21]

Portable objects, especially illuminated Christian manuscripts, took
Insular art onto the Continent through missionary activity from Germany
to Italy. Insular gospels preserved on the Continent are a testament to these
activities. Manuscripts decorated with sacred art travelled widely and so too
did the artists who made them. An Anglo-Saxon monk, Willibrord (who had
also lived in Ireland), was responsible for founding a mission to convert the
Frisians, and one of the twelve disciples he took with him must have been
accomplished in the production of Insular manuscript art. The scriptorium
that Willibrord founded at Echternach in Luxembourg has been linked to
the production of many of the surviving illuminated manuscripts on the
Continent (fig. 210).[22] We should imagine that the scriptorium discovered by
archaeologists at Portmahomack (pp. 180–2), whose products are now lost,
might have had a similarly far-reaching impact. Insular manuscript art was
to have a lasting legacy, influencing later manuscripts in England and on the
Continent in the late eighth and ninth centuries (see Chapter 9).

Fig. 187 **Elements of the St Ninian's Isle hoard**

St Ninian's Isle, Shetland AD 700–800
Silver, gilding, glass
National Museums Scotland, Edinburgh

Fig. 188 (right) **A hanging bowl mount from Deopham**

A recent find from Norfolk is very similar to the mount on the hanging bowl from the St Ninian's Isle hoard (fig. 189), showing the distant connections of the objects that make up the hoard from Shetland.

Deopham, Norfolk AD 700–800
Silver, gilding; H 4.25 cm
Norwich Castle Museum

Fig. 189 (far right) **The hanging bowl from the St Ninian's Isle hoard (detail)**

This hanging-bowl was probably made a century or so after the examples illustrated in Chapter 7. Hanging-bowls from this later period are much rarer as they were no longer buried in Anglo-Saxon graves. This one from St Ninian's Isle is also unusual in that it is made from silver rather than copper alloy.

St Ninian's Isle, Shetland AD 700–800
Silver, gilding; animal mount H 4.9 cm
National Museums Scotland, Edinburgh

The St Ninian's Isle treasure, Shetland

What might you hope to find on your first day on an archaeological site? On 4 July 1958, Douglas Coutts, a sixteen-year-old schoolboy, went to dig on St Ninian's Isle, off the west coast of Shetland, and was set to work in an area that had been heavily disturbed by later burials. He lifted a slab that was lightly incised with the outline of a cross. For once X did mark the spot: underneath was a substantial hoard of silver bowls, penannular brooches, sword fittings and other implements (fig. 187).[23]

The hoard is a remarkable one, and the possible owners and reasons for its burial have been much debated. Was this a church treasury hidden to keep it safe from the Vikings sometime in the early ninth century? If so, why

are there also secular items like sword fittings and brooches? Was it instead the treasure of a local leader, put under divine protection?

Many of the items are unique in early medieval Britain and Ireland. The set of seven nested silver bowls are the only surviving Pictish examples. Their punched decoration is similar to contemporary manuscript art (see the red-dot stippling around letters in the Lindisfarne Gospels, fig. 173) and the silver plates on the Monymusk reliquary (fig. 183). An elaborate silver hanging-bowl, with ornate gilded mounts on the rim and base, resembles the types buried a century earlier in Anglo-Saxon graves, but this one is made from rarer and more valuable material. The rim mounts used for suspension look like animals (fig. 189). A very similar mount found at Deopham in Norfolk suggests that associations with people far to the south of Shetland continued into the eighth and ninth centuries (fig. 188).

The sword fittings include the only known examples of early medieval military equipment decorated with spiral 'Celtic' art (figs 174 right, 190 and 264). The two scabbard terminals (chapes) are similar in form, with opposed beast heads, but variations between them point to rather different histories. One is well worn and was cast in three pieces.[24] Its decoration suggests it was made in the Anglo-Saxon kingdom of Mercia in the English Midlands.[25] The Latin religious inscription invokes the trinity of God the Father, the Son and the Holy Spirit, linking it to a wider tradition of weaponry with Christian inscriptions.[26] Presumably Christian symbols and text were thought to give protection to these 'warriors of God'. In contrast, the other chape is freshly made, cast in two pieces, and decorated with triskele spirals and a cross between the beast heads, evoking the Christian trinity through symbols rather than words.[27] Perhaps it was inspired by the first one. Like the hanging-bowl, the two different chapes emphasize how even in these remote northern islands of Britain both distant and local influences could be brought together.

Fig. 190 **Decorated scabbard fittings**

The chape (scabbard terminal) at the top is older, with the gilding worn away, especially over the Latin inscription; this one is thought to be made in Mercia in the English Midlands. The bottom chape is freshly made and decorated over much of its surface with triskele spirals and a small cross in the middle with an interlaced animal on either side.

St Ninian's Isle, Shetland AD 700–800
Silver, gilding; top chape W 8.1 cm, bottom chape W 8.2 cm
National Museums Scotland, Edinburgh

Jewellery and regional identities

The St Ninian's Isle hoard contains a mix of distant influences, but it also includes items of local production that tell us about regional identities. The range of penannular brooches in the hoard allowed identification of a regional type most common in northern Scotland (fig. 191); moulds for their manufacture have been found at Birsay on Orkney and in the Western Isles.[28] The most elaborate example comes from a hoard found at Rogart, where three-dimensional birds 'drink' from the terminal and at the back of the brooch's ring (figs 165 and 191).[29] In northern Britain the traditional penannular form of brooch continued (see Chapter 7), while smiths in Ireland filled the gap in the ring, making their brooches a complete circle (annular) like the Hunterston brooch. This regional difference had practical implications for how the brooches worked as dress fasteners. The variations were clearly seen as important: in Scotland, Irish-style annular brooches with a closed ring were sometimes opened into penannular form (fig. 192).[30]

Smaller versions of annular brooches (essentially a long pin with a small non-functional 'brooch' head) were also an Irish type, as shown by a lead model for their manufacture from Dooey.[31] However, the finest examples are found far away in Scotland, at Dunipace, and from a ninth-century Viking grave at Westness (fig. 193). This elaborate metalwork was valued as an exotic import far beyond where it was made. It is tempting to try to link objects to particular ethnic or cultural spheres, such as 'Pictish', 'Irish' or 'Mercian', but comparing production sites with distant finds and hoards often reveals widespread connections and relationships between the wealthy and influential people of these islands, continuing after the initial Insular fusion, and ongoing during the eighth and ninth centuries.

Fig. 191 (below left) **Regional tradition**

This type of penannular brooch was popular in northern Britain in the eighth and ninth centuries (see also fig. 165).

Rogart, Sutherland; AD 700–800
Silver, gilt, glass; D 12 cm, pin L 19.3 cm
National Museums Scotland, Edinburgh

Fig. 192 (below) **Adapting to local tastes**

This brooch was originally circular like the Hunterston and Tara brooches, but it has been modified by removing the bar that connected the expanded terminals. This allowed it to function like a penannular brooch.

Scotland AD 700–800
Silver gilt, gold, glass; D 9.8 cm
British Museum, London

Fig. 193 (opposite) **An heirloom from a Viking grave**

This brooch pin is the most finely decorated of its kind and shares many techniques of decoration and design with the Hunterston and Tara brooches. It would have been a treasured heirloom by the time it was buried with a woman in a Viking-age cemetery on the island of Rousay.

Westness, Rousay, Orkney AD 700–800
Silver, gold filigree, amber, glass; D 6.25 cm, pin L 17.5 cm
National Museums Scotland, Edinburgh

Local and international –
exploring the Hilton of Cadboll cross-slab

Hundreds of fragments of carved stone lay smashed among the blackened remains of burnt buildings. Some of Europe's most skilfully carved Christian sculpture had been thrown down and shattered. The layer of ash across the monastery at Portmahomack indicates fire and destruction around AD 800. As with the burial of the St Ninian's Isle hoard, the most obvious explanation is a Viking attack.[32] The sea was the quickest way to travel around Scotland, carrying friends and foes alike, and Portmahomack's position on the Fearn peninsula made it vulnerable to raids. During the eighth century a number of artists had worked stone here, drawing on a range of international influences and using the full repertoire of Insular art. The style of sculpture suggests links with metalworkers and manuscript artists. A series of large cross-slabs, probably carved by sculptors from the monastery at Portmahomack, created a Christianized landscape around the peninsula. The surviving examples are among the most elaborate Christian stone monuments in early medieval Europe: the range of ornament on the Shandwick, Nigg and Hilton of Cadboll cross-slabs bears close comparison with the finest metalwork and the intricacy of the decoration in the Book of Kells.

Fig. 194 **Multiple motifs – the back of the Hilton of Cadboll cross-slab**

Although now broken in half, the spiral panel at the bottom originally had a cross in the middle with four fluid trumpet-scrolls spiralling outward into a complex square composition of interlocking triskeles. The hunt scene above shows a deer being harried by hounds to the point of exhaustion and panting for water – a literal interpretation of Psalm 42:2 'as the deer pants for flowing streams so my soul pants for thee, O Lord'. An inhabited vine-scroll border frames the three square panels (see pp. 178–9).

Hilton of Cadboll, Easter Ross AD 700–800
Sandstone; W 144 cm
National Museums Scotland, Edinburgh

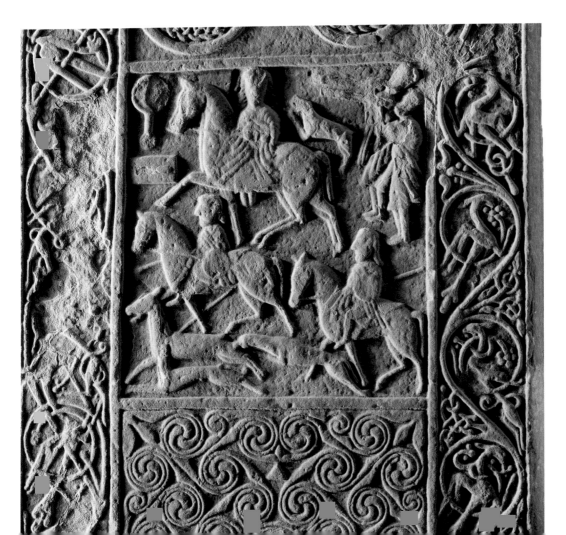

Fig. 195 **The apse mosaic from the church of San Clemente, Rome**

Although very different forms of Christian iconography and from different time periods, this apse mosaic from Rome shares similar elements of composition and themes with the bottom half of the Hilton of Cadboll cross-slab: an inhabited vine-scroll, four rivers of paradise springing out from a cross and the harried deer.

Rome AD 1100–1200
Glass, gold, ceramic; W 13 m
Basilica di San Clemente, Rome

The Hilton of Cadboll cross-slab (fig. 194 and pp. 178–9) can be thought of as a motif-hoard. Like the collections of objects we have seen so often already, the sculptor who carved this cross-slab brought together diverse decorative influences, from the local communication system (the Pictish symbols) to the international symbol of the cross that once dominated the front of the stone, signifying the triumph of Christianity. Both cross and symbols were decorated with the same range of Insular motifs.[33] The cross on the front has been chipped off, and only the back, landward-facing side of the slab is well preserved, with three square panels framed by inhabited vine-scroll. This motif was popular in Anglo-Saxon sculpture, but ultimately of Mediterranean origin. In Christian use it represented the Eucharistic wine and Christ's references to the vine in St John's Gospel.[34] Here among the northern Picts, the vine-scroll has a distinctive local flourish in being inhabited by fantastic beasts. These motifs contrast with the naturalism of the deer-hunting scene in the central panel, a familiar aristocratic pastime across early medieval Europe.

The lower square panel on the back of the Hilton of Cadboll cross-slab is a local elaboration of interlocking trumpet-scrolls (fig. 194): the heritage

motif that came out of the Roman world (see pp. 160–2). Here it was adapted to a large symmetrical format and taken to new levels of complexity, comparable to manuscript designs but on a much grander scale. The central circle within the panel is now broken in half, but we can reconstruct an equal-armed cross from which four trumpet-spirals emerge. Here, on a Christian cross-slab, the fluid forms represent the four rivers of paradise springing from the cross, as depicted on church mosaics in Rome (fig. 195), where such images often also included deer drinking from the four rivers and vine-scroll (fig. 196). These are references to Psalm 42:2: 'as the deer pants for flowing streams so my soul pants for thee, O Lord'. The psalm was sung during the Easter vigil in preparation for the rite of baptism, the most important moment in Christian conversion on the pivotal feast day in the Christian calendar when the community gathered to welcome new members and await Christ's resurrection. St Augustine likened the deer of the psalm to the convert thirsting for the waters of salvation.[35]

On the deer-hunting scene in the central panel (fig. 194), above the stylized, symbolic rivers, the Hilton of Cadboll cross-slab has an even clearer illustration of Psalm 42 than the mosaics of Rome. The method of hunting depicted in Pictish art is harrying, using hounds to exhaust the deer. The harried deer is shown in full flight, panting as the psalm describes. When the hounds are called off, the deer immediately seeks the nearest water where the hunters are pre-positioned, awaiting their quarry.

Fig. 196 **Detail of apse mosaic from the church of San Clemente, Rome.**

The deer, here shown drinking from the four rivers of paradise, are thought to be a visual reference to Psalm 42:2, which was sung during the sacrament of baptism.

Rome AD 700–800
Glass, gold, ceramic; overall W 13 m
Basilica di San Clemente, Rome

The four fluid forms springing out from a cross, combined with the vine-scroll and the harried deer, show careful composition and complex interlocking themes that tie together the bottom half of the Hilton of Cadboll cross-slab across the separate panels. The artist has used a similar device on the top half of the stone too, with Pictish symbols in the central and upper panels operating across panel boundaries: the mirror and comb symbol in front of the majestic rider in the central panel, and a crescent and v-rod in the top panel adjacent to a double-disc and z-rod, which replaced the vine-scroll in the top border. The use of Pictish symbols makes the cross-slabs of Pictland distinct, but the similarity in motifs and themes with the apse-mosaics of Rome shows how these crosses were also part of wider European Christian devotional art. Pictish sculptors used their carving skills and artistic heritage to glorify their God, their beliefs and their understanding of Christianity.

Spiral art as heritage motifs

Complex curvilinear designs using swirls, scrolls and spirals are the recurring theme that we have traced through this book so far. By the early medieval period, they were probably seen as a heritage from earlier times. But, if these curvilinear heritage motifs had religious connotations before Christianity, did these pre-Christian meanings change when they were used to express aspects of these new beliefs?

As the Hilton of Cadboll cross-slab shows, curvilinear art could be used to express specific Christian meanings, but this level of detail is rare and even with our understanding of Christian iconography it is often unclear exactly what these meanings were. Spiral ornament was used in various ways, but often lay at the heart of designs.[36] The Crucifixion plaque from St John's Rinnegan features spiral motifs at key points: at the top of the cross; connecting the angel's wings; on Christ's hem; but most prominently at the centre of the scene, on Christ's breast (fig. 197).[37] Pictish cross-slabs are covered in the full range of Insular motifs, but the curvilinear and spiral motifs often occur at the heart of the cross. Other kinds of objects were dominated by interlace, with the heritage motifs of swirls, scrolls and spirals playing an alternative role. On manuscripts, interlace often filled the letters of illuminated initials; triskeles, spirals and scrolls provided additional, external and background decoration (fig. 198). The front surfaces of brooches were typically covered in a dense mesh of interlace; where spiral motifs were included they were mostly on the back, invisible when worn but closest to the heart, as on the Tara and Hunterston brooches (figs 166 and 182). These swirly spiral heritage motifs were employed in particular ways on early medieval objects. This artistic heritage was reinvented for use within a Christian framework where it could still express concepts that were fundamental to what people believed.

Fig. 197 **Spiral art as an indicator of holiness**

Christ being crucified was a common iconographic scene throughout Christendom. This Irish example may have decorated a shrine or a book cover. Christ and the angels are decorated with three varieties of motif: interlace, spiral and key pattern. The trumpet-spiral and triskele decoration is given extra emphasis through size and placement.

St John's, Rinnagan, near Athlone, Co. Westmeath
AD 700–800
Gilt copper alloy, gold; H 20.7 cm
National Museum of Ireland, Dublin

The idea and realities of 'Celtic arts'

The idea of Celtic art was a Victorian creation and this early medieval material was a key part of it. In 1851 Daniel Wilson, an Edinburgh antiquary, proposed a definition of 'Celtic arts' that made a specific connection to early medieval Christian art in Scotland and Ireland.[38] Tracing a continuity of interlace ornament through the medieval period, he romantically followed the descent of this style onto the decoration of post-medieval Highland circular brooches and Jacobite weapons carried by the Highlanders at the battle of Culloden in 1746. For Wilson this long-lived Scottish legacy of interlace ornament was 'unquestionable proof of the unchanging character of Celtic arts'.[39] The impact of Wilson's definition is still relevant today: most people mistakenly think of interlace as the epitome of 'Celtic' art when it was actually a much more widely used motif, an external addition to the local repertoire introduced through the Insular fusion (pp. 176–80).

The definition of Celtic arts evolved rapidly through the 1850s. European national collections of antiquities were being organized and published, and wide comparisons were made possible through a series of great international exhibitions. The idea of Celtic arts was part of a zeitgeist where early frameworks for understanding the past through material remains were taking shape (see Chapter 10). The logic behind this was often dictated by nineteenth-century nationalist agendas, with many nations tracing their origins back to the post-Roman period or to ethnic groups mentioned by classical authors (such as the Franks and France, or Germans and Germany). Within Britain and Ireland there were tensions about English rule over the rest of the isles that could be traced back through history to the divisions between Anglo-Saxons and Celtic-speaking peoples in the early medieval period. John Obadiah Westwood, a Sheffield scholar and polymath, published a study of Celtic ornament that focused on early Christian material.[40] Like Wilson, Westwood recognized the earliest Christian arts as pre-Viking. Both were keen to dismiss the Scandinavian origins that were attributed to all sorts of antiquities at that time, particularly those decorated with interlace, which was commonly described as 'Runic knotwork'.[41] Westwood referred to interlace as the 'most universal and singularly diversified ornament'[42] of Celtic arts but, unlike Wilson, for him the 'most characteristic'[43] was the curvilinear, spiral ornament that we have been tracing out of the Roman world.

This brings us to the central problem of equating art styles with peoples or languages, which we raised in Chapter 1. Ever since Wilson and Westwood, people have thought of early medieval art as typically 'Celtic'. This is also the historical period from which the best evidence survives for the Celtic languages still spoken today in Britain and Ireland. Yet the evidence for language and art does not match up: some styles are far more widespread, others far more limited, than the language groups would suggest. This should cause no great surprise: the same word 'Celtic' has been used in modern times for very

Fig. 198 **St Chad gospels (Chi-Rho page)**

The Chi-Rho was an ancient Christian symbol (see fig. 150) composed from the two initial letters of Christ's name in Greek. In Insular Gospels they were often chosen for elaboration at Matthew 1:18, in the genealogy of Jesus Christ (compare fig. 4).

Lichfield, Staffordshire AD 700–800
Vellum, pigments; 30.5 x 23.5 cm
Lichfield Cathedral

different ideas. People living in early medieval Britain and Ireland would not have defined either their language or their art as Celtic.

As we have seen, spiral art and interlace had different origins: the former a local element with a long pedigree; the latter introduced from beyond Britain. Both were essential elements in the Insular fusion but they were used differently on particular objects and in particular areas. Interlace was a widespread pan-Christian style found across Britain and Ireland. Curvilinear, spiral ornament is often seen as typically Celtic. Its absence on Anglo-Saxon sculpture is unsurprising,[44] but this 'Celtic art' *was* used on manuscripts created in Anglo-Saxon Northumbria.[45] The complex trumpet-spirals and triskeles do not occur on sculpture in Wales or southern Scotland (where people were speaking Celtic languages), but they were used on Irish and Pictish metalwork and sculpture.

For the first time in our story there is enough evidence to show the complex relationships between art, language, belief and identity. The Celtic arts that we have traced out of the Roman world were a heritage of earlier times. As Britain and Ireland became Christian, they were used in this new religious context as one element in a much wider range of influences. This expanded decorative repertoire (the 'Insular fusion') drew together connections from across these islands and beyond, blurring any simple difference between an 'Anglo-Saxon' south and east, and a 'Celtic' north and west. Styles such as interlace were shared across these islands, and over the whole area complex curvilinear motifs and spirals were used to decorate manuscripts (fig. 198).[46] Yet in some areas where people were speaking Celtic languages, such as Wales and southern Scotland, these curvilinear heritage motifs from the past were otherwise ignored; in contrast, for Pictish and Irish Christians they became a key part of their designs in all formats and must have meant something fundamental to them, perhaps connecting their history with their religion.

This example emphasizes how difficult it is to label art styles as belonging to particular people. Today we see interlace and think 'Celtic knotwork', but its roots come from Germanic areas and the classical world, and it was very widely used. Some people see spirals and think 'Celtic', but these were only employed in certain areas by Celtic-speaking people. The languages people spoke did not dictate the style of art that they created: there were many other complex factors involved.

Back to Hunterston

Although found in Scotland, for the first twenty years after its discovery the Hunterston brooch was often mistakenly identified as a runic brooch of Scandinavian origin until Daniel Wilson's study of it.[47] Similar brooches had been found in Viking graves in Norway, but Wilson rejected a Scandinavian origin and observed that this style of brooch was similar to Irish antiquities

Fig. 199 **Detail from the front of the Hunterston brooch**

A interlaced beast in minute gold filigree.

Hunterston, Ayrshire AD 650–750
Gold, gilt silver; cell W 2.4 cm
National Museums Scotland, Edinburgh

Fig. 200 **Detail from the back of the Hunterston brooch**

The only use of curvilinear spiral heritage motifs is on the back of this brooch and would have been hidden when worn.

Hunterston, Ayrshire AD 650–750
Silver, gilding; W 12.2 cm
National Museums Scotland, Edinburgh

from the early Christian period, before Viking raids began.[48] Wilson recognized in the runic inscription the Gaelic name Maelbrigte, 'the servant of St Brigit', a Christian name that he suggested was 'equally Celtic with the workmanship'.[49]

However, the Hunterston brooch is much more than a 'Celtic' brooch and the workmanship provides the first clue to a wider network of connections. We have seen that the techniques used in making this brooch provide a snapshot of contemporary relationships with the Anglo-Saxon world, boldly presented in gold filigree and the interlaced creatures with which it is decorated (fig. 199).[50] Statements of Christian faith were concealed in its intricate detail and overall design. Hidden on the back of the brooch are small panels of gilded spiral ornament, a heritage motif worn out of sight and closest to the heart (fig. 200). After several centuries, a new owner's Gaelic Christian name was inscribed in the plain silver of the back using a script that had been brought to these islands from Scandinavia. Details of this brooch's manufacture, use and long life tell us how diverse Britain and Ireland were in the early medieval period.

Wilson's concept of 'Celtic arts' would have been meaningless to Maelbrigte. It seems that Wilson's and Westwood's definitions of 'Celtic arts' were flawed from the start, but have been widely used ever since. There is nothing specifically 'Celtic' about interlace, and the lack of spiral ornament in Welsh Christian sculpture breaks the link between this heritage motif and people who spoke languages now defined as Celtic. Artefacts, and what they can tell us about identities in Britain and Ireland, are much more complicated than the concepts of ethnic identity that were developed in Victorian Britain. Celtic art is a difficult and complex label.

Chapter 9

Fig. 201 **St Cuileáin's bell shrine (detail)**

The decoration on this bell shrine drew on both Irish and Scandinavian artistic traditions (see pp. 219–21). The ornate reliquary housed a much older iron bell believed to belong to St Cuileáin.

Borrisoleigh, Co. Tipperary, Ireland AD 1050–1100
Copper alloy, niello, enamel, silver; 30 x 24 x 9.4 cm overall
British Museum, London

Tracing the Celts? Survival and Transformation, *c.* AD 800–1600

Heather Pulliam

In April 1842, Sir Richard O'Donel presented the Royal Dublin Society with a sealed rectangular container made of silver, bronze and gold (fig. 202).[1] Unlike many of the objects in this exhibition, it had not been lost and found, buried and rediscovered. Instead, it had been protected, preserved and repeatedly restored by the O'Donel family.[2] As evidenced by the inscription around the silver openwork design of its back, the family had cared for the shrine since the eleventh century on the understanding that the elaborate container (*cumdach*) housed an ancient relic from the early medieval period that had the power to heal or harm.

Fig. 202 *Cumdach* **of the Cathach of Columba**

The sides of the *cumdach* are from the late eleventh century; the front cover with its central image of Christ enthroned dates from the Gothic period; the bottom of the *cumdach* contains the inscription with its invaluable information about the shrine's commission.

Composite: late AD 1000s; late 1300s; early 1400s
Gilt bronze and silver over wooden core; 24.3 x 19 x 5.5 cm
National Museum of Ireland, Dublin

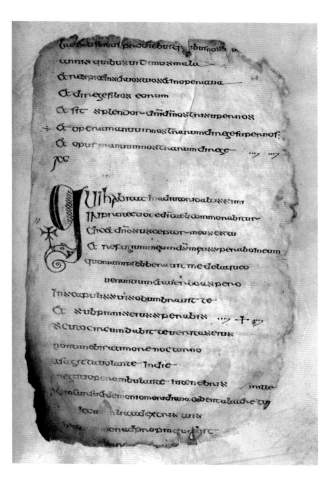

Fig. 203 **Cathach of St Columba**

Found within its *cumdach* (fig. 202) and attributed by some to Columba's own hand. This folio (48r) contains the decorated Q initial that begins Psalm 90 (91), which promises comfort to those who dwell in the shelter of the Lord.

AD 560–600
Vellum; 27 x 19 cm
Royal Irish Academy, Dublin (MS 12 R 33)

As hereditary keepers of the relic, the family had the rights to its protective powers. Written evidence confirms how, shortly before battle, it was processed sunwise (clockwise) around the armies fighting alongside the O'Donels. In one such battle in 1497, the shrine was ineffective: the O'Donel leader was slaughtered and the precious relic seized. It was returned to the family two years later. In 1691, after the end of the war in Ireland between the supporters of William of Orange and the Jacobites, Daniel O'Donel, the head of the clan who had supported the defeated Jacobites, left for France. While there, he commissioned a delicate eighteenth-century silver container to afford the reliquary and its hidden contents further protection. Although long believed to hold a relic of Columba, the shrine had remained sealed until an antiquarian working for the O'Donel family prised open the box, against the family's instruction, revealing the Cathach of Columba (fig. 203), the sixth-century Psalter that some believe was written and decorated by St Columba's own hand.

Celtic traces

Exhibitions and monographs on Celtic art typically end with the invasion of the Vikings.[3] However, while much of the art produced in Britain and Ireland during the high and late medieval periods reflects international Romanesque and Gothic styles, a considerable proportion – especially in Ireland, western Scotland and Wales – continued to make use of Celtic traditions by expanding upon the Insular style and material culture of the early medieval period. As discussed in Chapter 8, this Insular tradition was more than a simple survival from the Iron Age Celtic world; instead it was a new style that incorporated aspects of Mediterranean, Germanic and Celtic art (see pp. 178–9).

In the early medieval period (*c.* 400–900), Insular artists combined spirals, peltae and undulating lines taken from the Celtic-style art of the Roman provinces with Mediterranean and Germanic motifs to create the art style exemplified by the Book of Kells and Hunterston brooch (figs 4 and 166). Artists working during the high and late medieval periods (*c.* 900–1500) blended these Insular traditions with new Scandinavian, Romanesque and even Gothic features. While Iron Age Celtic influences often became more diluted, or were included in a novel way, this aspect survived and even thrived. This artistic inheritance reflects the choices and decisions of later Insular artists. Archaizing features, such as the inclusion of motifs with Iron Age origins, do not necessarily equate to a coarsening or stagnation of art. They may also demonstrate a nostalgic or political reclamation of the past for the purposes of authority and power. A sense of heritage and cultural preservation are not exclusive to the modern world.

The ninth and tenth centuries in Ireland and northern Britain: Viking invasions and Scandinavian style

The Viking attacks of the 790s have traditionally been defined as isolated 'raids', epitomized by the assaults on Lindisfarne in 793 and Iona in 795. More recently, however, it has been observed that the medieval annals from Ireland and Northumbria describe the Viking naval forces as swarming 'like stinging hornets' across Britain and Ireland and portray 'a full scale invasion attempt' rather than a series of 'hit and run' raids.[4] While the significance of the Viking invasions must not be underestimated, it obviously varied in different places and periods. Equally, artists and patrons responded to these events according to their own particular attitudes, desires, abilities and knowledge.

A number of objects offer an almost desperate witness to the turbulence of these centuries. The Book of Deer and the two silver panels from a house-

Fig. 204 **Panels from a house-shaped casket**

AD 900–950
Silver; L 12.6 cm
British Museum, London

Fig. 205 **Book of Deer**

The tenth-century Scottish Book of Deer
juxtaposes exquisite script with awkward but
theologically complex images, as seen here. The
evangelist John carries a book satchel or house-
shaped shrine while a small beast outside of the
frame seems to gesture at the cross beneath
his feet.

Deer, Aberdeenshire AD 900–950
Vellum; 15 x10 cm
Cambridge University Library (Ii.6.32)

shaped casket (figs 204 and 205) stand in striking contrast to the intricacy of
predecessors such as the Lindisfarne Gospels or the Monymusk reliquary
(figs 173 and 183). In the later objects, human anatomy, interlace and
geometrical forms are awkwardly rendered. The extreme skill and beauty
with which the text of the Book of Deer is executed and decorated makes
the waving, irregular lines of the full-page illustrations even more perplexing.
Despite the poor draughtsmanship, recent publications have demonstrated
that the imagery of this manuscript and others like it conveys complex
theological meanings.[5] Perhaps the odd juxtaposition of sophisticated
iconography and poor execution of the imagery indicates that a passive
understanding of past traditions survived long after the skills necessary to
bring them into fruition had been lost.

However, the ninth and tenth centuries also witnessed the carving and erection of some of the most impressive stone monuments in the medieval period across Britain and Ireland: the high crosses of Monasterboice (fig. 206), the Gosforth cross (fig. 209), the carved stones of Govan and the crosses of Margam, to name but a few.[6] A number of these monuments bear the names of their royal patrons: Hywel ap Rhys, king of Glywysing on the

Fig. 206 **Muiredach's cross at Monasterboice**

The inscription on its base, 'Pray for Muiredach who has caused this cross to be erected', probably refers to the Abbot Muiredach who died in 923.

Monasterboice, Co. Louth AD 875–915
Stone; H 5.8 m

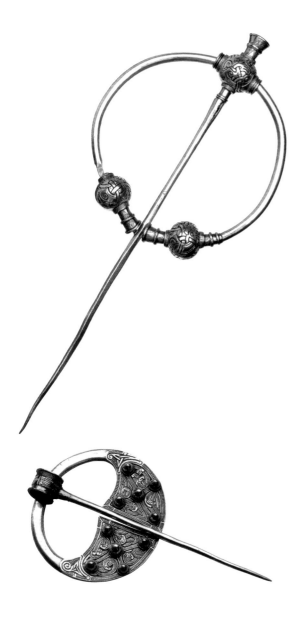

cross of Houelt in Wales; king Flann on the cross of Clonmacnoise in Ireland; and Constantine, son of Fergus, on the Dupplin cross in Scotland.[7] The inscriptions may reflect new models of kingship such as that of Charlemagne, where lands, wealth and powers were consolidated under a single king who in turn served, protected and patronized the church. While some of these monuments lack the refined detail and complexity that exemplify the Insular objects described in Chapter 8, they exhibit a robust physicality, rhythmical patterns and an avid interest in Insular motifs and designs from the earlier period.

Few medieval monuments equal the sophistication of Muiredach's cross at Monasterboice (fig. 206). Its date is debated, but most scholarship places it within the forty-year hiatus between the first and second Viking invasions of Ireland, 875–915.[8] Its iconography and execution compare favourably to earlier Insular masterpieces such as the Book of Kells or Hunterston brooch. Like these objects, the decoration on the cross brings together an extraordinarily wide range of artistic styles. The south-facing side of its shaft incorporates an eclectic and anachronistic mix of intricate and expertly interlaced human figures that reflect some Scandinavian design, Iron Age Celtic spirals and peltae, and a vine-scroll populated with birds and animals that echoes Anglo-Saxon sculpture. Bands of Mediterranean-influenced fretwork and spirals decorate the underside of the curved ring. The west side of the cross includes snake bosses like those found on the eighth- and ninth-century crosses of Iona alongside skilfully rendered narrative scenes in varied relief. The latter draw on Continental sources and are markedly naturalistic in their three-dimensional representation, but the spiral details of the figures' clothing belong to the early medieval Insular tradition.

Much ninth- and tenth-century metalwork exaggerated traditional features, creating larger and bolder designs (figs 207 and 208). Indeed, the pin of a brooch from Skaill has been elongated to such an extent as to endanger the wearer and those around him or her. These objects echo the constant play between abstraction, ambiguity and natural forms so prevalent in Iron Age Celtic art and early medieval Insular objects. Despite their exquisite beauty, rhythmical alteration of light and shadow and sophisticated use of three-dimensional form, these objects have been seen as a 'coarsening' of style reflecting Viking devastation and domination. More recently, scholars have pointed to pre-Viking examples from Ireland and Britain exhibiting characteristics of the new style, suggesting that local tastes were already moving in that direction. Indeed, well-known eighth-century pieces such as the Ardagh chalice suggest an association between silver and bolder, simpler approaches to design.[9] Certainly, though, the substantial influx of Viking silver made it possible to create larger and more three-dimensional pieces such as 'thistle' brooches like the Skaill brooch.

Fig. 207 (top) **Penannular brooch**

Skaill, Orkney AD 900s
Silver; L 37.8 cm
National Museums Scotland, Edinburgh

Fig. 208 (above) **Bossed penannular brooch**

Ireland AD 800s–900s
Silver; hoop D 8.2 cm, L 16.3 cm
British Museum, London

The ninth and tenth centuries in southern Britain: courts and the Continent

From the sixth through to the eighth centuries, missionaries from Britain and Ireland such as Columbanus and Willibrord had established monasteries across much of Europe, populating their attached libraries and schools with Insular scribes and books. It has been suggested, for example, that Willibrord brought one of the most accomplished pieces of Insular illumination, the Echternach Gospels, from Northumbria to stock his new scriptorium at Echternach in Luxembourg (fig. 210).[10] A generation or two later, the same scriptorium produced the Trier Gospels, a manuscript where the Insular, Frankish and Mediterranean elements jostle alongside one another (fig. 211). Two artists were involved: 'Thomas', who worked in an Insular style that embraced Mediterranean naturalism, and an anonymous scribe, who wrote the text and executed the initials in the Frankish tradition.[11] The process of teaching and exchange are made manifest in the pages of this remarkable manuscript.

During the ninth and tenth centuries, the area that constitutes modern-day England underwent political and cultural changes quite distinct from the rest of Britain and Ireland. This is reflected in the development of distinctive local art styles. For the first part of the period, Viking raids and settlement led to hybrid Anglo-Scandinavian styles. The Gosforth cross is perhaps the most striking object produced in this milieu. It is remarkably tall, shows a fusion of styles and a confident mixing of Christian iconography with Norse mythological scenes such as the punishment of Loki (fig. 209). However, Anglo-Scandinavian art altered dramatically in the early tenth century as centres of political power and control were transformed. In 927 the Anglo-Saxon king Aethelstan defeated the Viking kingdom of York, becoming the first king to rule over the whole of England. This new English royal family maintained strong diplomatic relations with the Continent and an avid interest in court culture. Marriages, gifts and diplomatic envoys established a thriving network between Byzantium, Continental Europe and the British Isles.

When Charlemagne became ruler of Francia (France, western Germany and the Netherlands) in 771, he inherited the Insular monastic diaspora whose books and teaching had for generations provided western Europe's educational foundations. These monasteries welcomed manuscripts and scholars from Britain and Ireland well into the eleventh century. While Britain and Ireland struggled through repeated Viking invasions and settlement, the Carolingian court lavished patronage on schools and scribes, making the migration of eminent scholars to the Continent unsurprising. Many of the most highly prized illuminated manuscripts of the Carolingian dynasty – for example, the Godescalc Lectionary, the Harley Gospels, Abbeville Gospels and Saint-Médard de Soissons Gospels – incorporate Insular motifs and letter shapes throughout.[12] In the later ninth and tenth

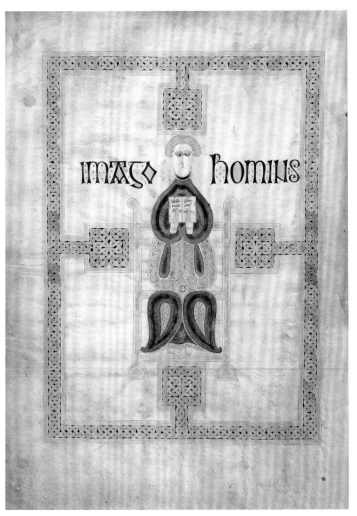

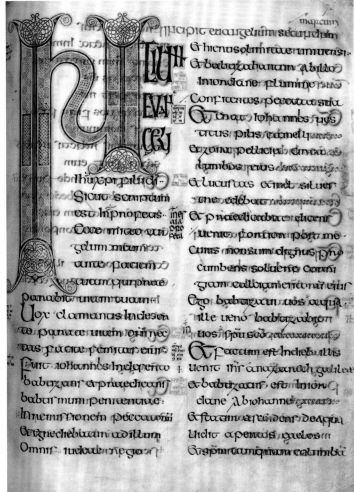

Fig. 209 **Gosforth cross**

The carvings on this slender Viking-period cross are thought to represent scenes from Norse myths, as well as mythical beasts and Christian stories.

Gosforth, Cumbria AD 900s
Stone; H 4.4 m

Fig. 210 **Echternach Gospels**

Each evangelist had his own symbol: Matthew, the man; Mark, the lion: Luke, the ox; John, the eagle. The page on the left (fol. 18v) shows the man of Matthew. The page on the right (fol. 76r) contains the great decorated initials from the beginning of Mark's gospel.

Northumbria (?) or Echternach (?)
AD 650–700
Vellum; 33.5 x 25.5 cm
Bibliothèque nationale de France, Paris (Latin 9389)

Fig. 211 **Trier Gospels**

Four Symbols page (fol. 1v) and Tetramorph
page (fol. 5v): the product of a collaboration
between an unknown Frankish scribe
who worked in a Merovingian style and
an Insular scribe familiar with both Insular
and Mediterranean styles. The latter has
written 'Thomas scripsit' at the bottom of the
Tetramorph page.

Echternach, Luxembourg AD 700–800
Vellum; 30 x 24.5–25 cm
Trier Cathedral (Domschatz 61)

Fig. 212 **The so-called Francis II Gospels**

Made at the end of the ninth century as the Carolingian empire collapsed, this illuminated gospel book combines Insular design, notably in its frames and display script, with Carolingian.

Saint-Amand-en-Pévèle, AD 850–875
Vellum; 30 x 22.5 cm
Bibliothèque Nationale de France, Paris (Latin 257)

century, after the Carolingian empire had fragmented, a new style emerged that was almost wholly dependent upon Insular design, as seen in the 'Gospels of Francis II', made *c*. 850–75 at the Abbey of Saint-Amand (fig. 212). The display script and frames of its illuminated pages seamlessly incorporate intricate elements of Insular style with Byzantine splendour, Late Antique realism and Carolingian clarity. Such manuscripts were almost certainly made by scribes looking to earlier models: either those created by scribes on the Continent who were trained in the Insular tradition; or those created in Britain and Ireland and imported to stock the new Continental Insular foundations.

Gifting richly decorated books was a feature of court culture. Otto I is credited with presenting to Aethelstan a particularly fine example, a lavishly illuminated Carolingian manuscript now in the British Library (fig. 213). Aethelstan, in turn, donated an Irish gospel book, the Book of Mac Durnan from Armagh, to Christ Church, Canterbury, sometime between 924 and 939. A number of other manuscripts suggest that traditional early medieval Insular styles and objects were still prized and respected. Around the year 900, for example, a late Anglo-Saxon portrait of Luke was added to an eighth-century Irish pocket gospel. Tellingly, the older version of Luke was preserved within the manuscript, proclaiming the little gospel's ancient origins and authenticity.[13]

Fig. 213 **Aethelstan Gospels**

As with many deluxe Carolingian manuscripts, Insular motifs and designs are evident within the shape and ornamentation of decorated initials. In this opening, the scribe(s) cleverly use colour to harmonize the abstract Insular style with the more painterly Carolingian image.

Probably made in Carolingian Francia [Lobbes, Belgium (?)], AD 875–925
Vellum; 23 x 17.5 cm
British Library, London (Cotton Tiberius A.II, FF3-218; FF2-7, 9*; and Cotton Faustina B. VI, Vol. 1, ff 95, 98–100)

The eleventh and twelfth centuries: relics, recovery and resistance

Outside of Ireland, traces of Insular cultural inheritance become extremely faint in the eleventh and twelfth centuries, with a few notable exceptions in Wales and the Scottish highlands and islands. A number of factors contributed to the narrowing of influence. The Normans had conquered England. The international styles of the Romanesque and the Gothic arrived, overwhelming more indigenous traditions. The Scottish court turned to Anglo-Norman and Continental culture, due in part to the efforts of the Anglo-Saxon princess Margaret, who after her marriage to Malcolm III of Scotland *c.* 1068 enthusiastically patronized Continental religious orders and art.

In Ireland, the Vikings regained control of Dublin and established new settlements from 914 to 980. Irish chiefs and kings continued to challenge Viking power throughout this period. Cultural amalgamation did take place, however, due in part to the intermarriage between Irish and Norse families. Such alliances caused some internal divisions but helped establish a thriving Hiberno-Norse culture. Insular art incorporated foreign motifs such as foliage as well as new approaches to interlace. The former is visible in the smaller side panels of the *cumdach* of the Cathach (fig. 202). Found in Norwegian, Ottonian and late Carolingian art, it is difficult to establish how this motif was imported into Ireland.[14] Developments within zoomorphic interlace, on the other hand, are recognizable as Scandinavian imports. As seen on the St Cuileáin's bell, animals' whiskers and hair are exaggerated so as to appear as long ribbons (fig. 201). Additionally, the strands of interlace no longer weave over and under but rather bisect one another such as on the side panels of the *cumdach* of the Cathach. Another favoured Scandinavian feature is the combination of thick flat ribbons with intricate, looping narrow strands.

In 1014, the high king Brian Boru defeated an alliance of Norse and Hiberno-Norse forces in the battle of Clontarf. After this victory, Irish lords, kings and scholars consciously set out to restore the culture that had been damaged by over a century of Viking invasion, settlement and rule. The early twelfth-century *Cogad Gáedel re Gallaib* (The War of the Irish with the Foreigners) describes Brian Boru dispatching Irish scholars 'To buy books beyond the sea, and the great ocean; because their writings and their books in every church and in every sanctuary where they were, were burned down and thrown into the water by the plunderers, from beginning to end.'[15]

It is during this time that many of the great relics of the early medieval period – books, body parts and bells associated with local saints such as Patrick and Columba – were carefully housed in ornate reliquaries.

In the late eleventh century, as mentioned earlier in this chapter, the O'Donel family commissioned a metalwork *cumdach* (book shrine) to house the manuscript known as the Cathach of Columba. Only the sides and back of this shrine survive; the figurative cover was added in the late fourteenth

The Hiberno-Norse Style

After the Viking invasions, Insular art changed in a way that was neither homogenous nor cohesive: different areas, artists, patrons and audiences responded to distinct events and exchanges according to their own abilities, needs and resources. Other art styles also played a role in these changes, including Byzantine, Islamic, Carolingian, Ottonian and – eventually – the international Romanesque and Gothic styles.

'Hiberno-Norse' refers to the artistic style that incorporates both Scandinavian and Insular characteristics. The term applies to works produced in Ireland, but it has also been used – rather problematically – to refer to similar works from other Gaelic-speaking areas such as the Western Isles of Scotland. The most recognizable characteristics of the style are: a tendency for lines of interlace to bisect rather than interweave with one another; a bolder, more three-dimensional approach to design; the incorporation of foliage; and the interplay of thin and thick decorative lines. In metalwork, niello and silver were often substituted where previously gold had been used. In manuscripts, a more angular style of script became common, alongside the use of bright pools of colour as backgrounds for decorated initials.

Fig. 214 **St Cuileáin bell shrine**

Also known as the Glankeen shrine, the St Cuileáin bell shrine still houses its original relic, a seventh- or eighth-century iron bell that was associated with its namesake. St Cuileáin founded the monastery at Glankeen and was brother to Cormac, bishop and ruler of nearby Cashel.

Borrisoleigh, Co. Tipperary, Ireland AD 1050–1100
Copper alloy, niello, enamel and silver; 30 x 24 x 9.4 cm
British Museum, London

or early fifteenth century (figs 202–3).[16] Made in Kells, the eleventh-century components display an exquisite fusion of Scandinavian and Insular design, marking the full emergence of the Hiberno-Norse style. The back consists of a plate of bronze covered in silver foil, pierced with openwork crosses, a pattern shared with other contemporary shrines such as St Patrick's bell shrine from Armagh.[17] While the use of silver and bold design reflect newer Hiberno-Norse tastes, the geometric play of positive and negative space and the integration of crosses into the overall composition point to earlier Insular traditions, such as seen in the Durham Cassiodorus (fig. 215) and Lindisfarne Gospels (fig. 173). The open weave, foliage and bisecting ribbon-like bodies were inspired by Scandinavian styles. The distribution of raised round studs that mimic the decorative effects of bosses from Insular carved crosses are also visible in tenth-century silver brooches (fig. 208).

The inscription engraved on the shrine's back reveals a web of connections stretching across church and state, forged from family networks that drew upon early medieval Irish and British saints and their related institutions for authority:

A prayer for Cathbarr Ua Domnaill by whom this cumdach was made
And for Sitric son of Mac Aedha who made it
And for Domnall Mac Robartaigh, coarb of Kells, by whom it was made.[18]

A *coarb* was an abbot who was seen as the spiritual heir and successor of the founding saint, typically chosen from among his blood relations.[19] The Irish Annals record that in 1090 the king of Tír Chonaill (Donegal) gave the relics of Columba and 120 ounces of silver to the monastery in Kells.[20] According to legend, the relics had been given to the Clan Chonaill by a local Donegal saint. The clan Chonaill was headed by none other than Cathbarr Ua Domnaill, the patron named on the back of the *cumdach*. Sitric, the smith described as making the shrine, has a Hiberno-Norse name but the fact that his father, Mac Aedha, is named as an 'artificer' within a charter written directly into the Book of Kells indicates that he belonged to a family of craftsmen who had worked for the ancient Columban foundation for several generations.[21]

From the earliest period of Christianization, bells – like croziers, crosses and books – formed part of the impressive arsenal of the early medieval saint. These too became relics; later generations housed the bells in metal reliquaries as exemplified by St Cuileáin's bell shrine from Ireland and the Guthrie bell shrine from Iona (figs 214 and 216). Gerald of Wales, writing in the twelfth century, observed:

The people and clergy of both Wales and Ireland have a great reverence for bells
that can be carried about, and staffs belonging to the saints, and made of gold and
silver, or bronze, and curved at their upper ends. So much so that they fear to
swear or perjure themselves in making oaths on these, much more than they do
in swearing on the gospels.[22]

The relics and their shrines served as physical conduits of power and wealth between the monasteries, saints and secular rulers. Although forming an intrinsic and regular part of the monastic soundscape, the unexpected, sudden sounding of the bell served as a call to arms, summoning monks to gather with a saint or abbot in order to pray for the defeat of a secular army or host of demons.[23]

From the eleventh to the sixteenth centuries, hereditary keepers commissioned sumptuous shrines for their bells. The miraculous intervention and protection afforded to the keepers and the people they ruled was not free, however, but required tribute. A sixteenth-century poem dedicated to the *Clog-na-Rígh* (Bell of the King) explains the bell's power:

Fig. 215 **Durham Cassiodorus**

Folio 172v shows David standing over a double-headed beast. The figure is surrounded by a bold framework; the design creates spatial ambiguity through the interplay of positive and negative fields.

Northumbria AD 700–800
Vellum; 42 x 29.5 cm
Durham Cathedral Library (B.II.30)

Fig. 217 **Kilmichael Glassary bell shrine**

The figure of Christ is typical of the international styles of this period, whereas the sprawling foliage, especially that on the back of the shrine with its lobes and palmettes, has clear Scandinavian, Insular and Carolingian characteristics.

Torbhlaren, Kilmichael Glassary, Argyll mid-1100s
Copper alloy; 14.8 x 9.5 x 8.5 cm
National Museums Scotland, Edinburgh

Fig. 216 **Guthrie bell shrine**

Ornament added to the bell shows generations of use: the figures of Christ and St John were added in the 12th century, embossed silver designs in the early 13th century and the bishop figures in the 14th century.

Iona, Argyll AD 1150–1500
Iron, copper alloy, silver, gilt; 19.8 x 14.4 x 12.4 cm
National Museums Scotland, Edinburgh

The little bell – it should not be concealed –
He that obeys it will not be judged;
A wretched world he shall sadly find [here]
And yonder, he shall reach much torment.

To the Cinel-Eoghan [O Neills] doth rightly belong
The famous relic, without anguish;
For to them it is strenuously commanded that they obey it, by increasing its tribute …

In every sudden danger in which the tribe may be,
The bell should be borne round them thrice …
'Twill cure every sickness, every disease.[24]

The poem goes on to explain that the kings must fill the bell itself with silver and gold. The zoomorphic interlace and bizarre hybrid animals that decorate the bell shrine of St Cuileáin facilitated and gave testimony to miraculous power, paid tribute and promised protection.

While the evidence from Scotland and Wales is more fragmentary due in large part to the iconoclasm of the Reformation, it reveals both similarities and differences to the situation in Ireland. In Scotland, chieftains governed the western highlands and islands. Here, too, these secular leaders sometimes became keepers of sacred relics, commissioning works such as the shrine of St Fillan's crosier (figs 223–4) and the Kilmichael Glassary bell shrine (fig. 217). Hiberno-Norse, Continental and Scandinavian style elements are all evident within the bell shrine, possibly reflecting the patronage of groups on the Hebrides, which at the time had formed a new 'kingdom' with the Scandinavian dynasty ruling the Isle of Man.[25] In Wales, while Norman and Continental styles and church reforms transformed much of the visual culture, individuals such as Rhygyfarch, bishop of St David's, wrote of the tragic loss of older traditions and commissioned the making of the eleventh-century Rhygyfarch Psalter that consciously references older Insular styles, albeit with clear Scandinavian elements.[26]

Ireland also continued to produce manuscripts in the Hiberno-Norse style. The Corpus Gospel is immaculately preserved, to the extent that its fresh white pages, velvety black script and strong glossy colours appear implausibly fresh (fig. 218). The colour is more striking than in earlier Insular manuscripts. The artists have introduced fields of colour as backgrounds to the zoomorphic decorated initials. Also, because the creatures' bodies, details and interlace are boldly executed, pools of colour become prominent. The Corpus Gospel's Chi-Rho monogram incorporates elements of Hiberno-Norse style, but the initial's shape, interlace and the manner in which the spirals appear to tumble out from the letter's terminals capture the tradition of deluxe Insular manuscripts such as the Echternach Gospels and Book of Kells (figs 4 and 210).

Fig. 218 **Corpus Gospel**

Folio 10r, on the left, contains the beginning of Matthew's gospel. The image on the right shows the reverse of that page, folio 10v, which includes the text of Matthew 1:18. As with earlier gospel books such as the Book of Kells, this verse – especially the χ of χρί, Greek for 'of Christ' – is given decorative emphasis. While following older traditions, new colours and Hiberno-Norse stylistic flourishes have been added.

Probably made in Bangor, Co. Down
AD 1100–1200
Vellum; 22.5 x 14 cm
Corpus Christi College, Oxford (122)

liber generationis
ihu xpi fili dd. fili abraham.
Abraham: genuit ysaac.
Isaac au: genuit iacob. Iacob
autem: genuit iudam 7 fres eius.
Iudas g: genuit phares 7 zaram
de thamar. phares au genuit sipd.
Synom h: genuit aram. aram h: genuit
amminadab. Amminadab h: genuit naayon. Naayon
h: genuit salmon. Salmon h: genuit booz vsia
chab. booz h: genuit obech exruch. Obed h: genuit
iesse. iesse h: genuit dd regem. dd h rex genuit
salomonem exea q fuit uriae. Salomon h: genuit
roboam. Roboam h: genuit abia. Abia h: genuit
asab. asab h: genuit iosaphath. Iosaphath au:
genuit ioram. Ioras h: genuit oziam. Ozias
h: genuit ioachim. ioacham h: genuit achaz.
Achaz h: genuit ezecham. Ezechas h: genuit
manassen. Manasses h: genuit ammon. Am
mon h: genuit iosiam. Iosias h: genuit iechoniam.
7 fres e in transmigratione babilonis. 7 p transmi
gratione babilonis: iechonias genuit salathiel.
Salathiel h: genuit zorobabel. Zorobabel au:
genuit abiud. Abiud h: genuit eliachim. Eliachim
au: genuit azor. Azor h: genuit achim. Achim h:
genuit eliud. Eliud h: genuit eleazar. Eleazar h:

genuit matham. matham h: genuit iacob. Iacob
h: genuit ioseph uirum marie. de qua nat. q ihu
q uocat xps.

Omnes g generationes ababraham usq ad
dauid generationes sunt xiiii. Et adauid
usq; ad transmigrationem babilonis gene
rationes sunt xiiii. Et a transmigratione
babilonis usq ad xpm generationes st xiiii.

Xpi autem generatio sic
erat cum esset disponsata mr eius ma
ria ioseph antequ conuenirent inuenta
e in utero hns despu sco. Ioseph aute
uir eius cum esset homo iustus. 7 nollet ea
traducere uoluit occulte dimittere eam. H au
eo cogitante. ecce angls dni in somnis appaur
it ei dicens. Ioseph fili dd noli timere accipe
mariam coniugem tua. Quod n mea natu q de
spu sco e. Pariet au filiu. 7 uocabis no e ihm.
ipse n saluu faciet plm suu apeccatis eor.
H aute totu factu e ut adimpleretur qd dcm e a dno
per esaiam propheta dicentem. Ecce uirgo in utero con
cipiet 7 pariet filiu. 7 uocabit no e emanuel. qd
e interptatum nobiscum ds. Exurgens aute ioseph
asomno fecit sicut precepit ei angls dni. 7 accepit
coniugem suam. 7 non cognoscebat eam donec peperit
filiu suu primogenitu. 7 uocauit no e ihm.

Cum g natus est ihus in bethlem iude in dieb;
herodis regis. ecce magi aboriente uenerunt
ierosolima dicentes. ubi e q natus e rex iudeor?

The thirteenth to the fifteenth centuries: Gaelic revivals

This period marks the tipping point in which the international Gothic style overtook and in many places completely swamped the Insular-Norse elements of British and Irish art, ending the long story of various Celtic motifs influencing local artistic practice. However, primarily in Gaelic-speaking areas of Ireland and Scotland,[27] Insular-Norse culture not only survived but was also avidly appropriated, revived and refashioned. In Ireland, despite the ebb and flow of Anglo-Norman invasions, Irish chieftains retained reasonable powers beyond the Pale (in those large areas of Ireland not under English control) and in the thirteenth and fourteenth centuries regained considerable wealth and authority. Additionally, a number of aristocratic Anglo-Norman families favoured Irish society and culture. Norse occupation and sporadic political dominance over the Hebrides, Firth of Clyde islands and the Isle of Man (hereafter referred to as 'the Isles') occurred throughout the medieval period, and by the late tenth century the culture might best be described as a hybrid between local and Norse traditions. While power over the Isles was conceded to the Scottish king in the thirteenth century, Gaelic chieftains and culture continued to flourish in the centuries that followed.

In terms of art, while there were obvious distinctions between Anglo-Norman strongholds and areas of Gaelic dominion in Ireland beyond the Pale, the real fault line was between religious and secular. The arrival of Continental religious orders such as the Cistercians and Benedictines saw the decline of the great monasteries of Patrick and Columba. At the same time the authority of bishops replaced that of the traditional abbot and *coarb*. Consequently, religious artworks were now supplied by sister-houses in England and the Continent. Objects made in the Irish churches embraced these foreign styles so completely as to suggest a conscious programme. On the secular side, however, Gaelic chieftains continued to host families of scribes and poets whose eleventh- and twelfth-century ancestors had formerly worked for the monasteries.

A Gaelic chieftain was expected to be in possession of an extremely ancient and noble heritage. A primary function of his retinue of scholars was to celebrate and authenticate the chieftain's claims, deftly weaving material and references from an impressive range of sources: biographies of early medieval British and Irish saints, legal tracts, genealogies, local mythologies, the Bible and even classical epics.[28] These manuscripts – adorned in a notably archaic Hiberno-Norse manner rather than the newer Gothic style – contain the earliest written versions of the great 'Celtic' mythological cycles and heroes such as Finn, Cúchulainn and Arthur. The Book of Ballymote, probably written for Mac Donnchaid of Corann in the late fourteenth century, epitomizes this practice (fig. 219). It has been called 'a miniature library',[29] and even preserves a key for deciphering the ancient

Fig. 219 (opposite) **Book of Ballymote**

Three interlaced creatures on folio 8r (left) form the INI of '*In principio creauit Deus celum et terram*' (In the beginning God created the heaven and the earth), marking the beginning of the Book of Invasions (*Lebor Gabála*). Generations of scribes and scholars have added materials and notes. The detail on the right (from folio 199v) cotains *Dinshenchas*, poems that explain the history and meaning of place names, often incorporating mythological material. The letter F, formed by a human figure, begins a poem about Waterford and describes singing mermaids with golden hair.

Probably Ballymote, Co. Sligo
AD 1300–1500
Vellum; 40 x 26 cm
Royal Irish Academy, Dublin (23 P12)

ogam script.[30] Perhaps the best description of these miscellanies is by a late medieval hand, describing one such manuscript as *bolg an tsholáthair*, 'a collecting sack'.[31]

The Book of Ballymote was purchased in 1522 by Aed Óg O'Donnell, prince of Tír Conaill, bringing it into the orbit of the hereditary keepers of the *cumdach* of the Cathach of Columba. During this period, the family had a Gothic cover made for this talismanic shrine. They also commissioned the writing of a new version of the *Life of Columba*. Two sixteenth-century copies survive. The Oxford *Life of Columba*, which contains a lovely portrait of the saint, is one of the most striking objects from the period (fig. 220). The Gothic delicacy with which the image is drawn and painted makes a decided contrast to the manuscript's size and seal-skin binding with metal fittings that, to modern eyes, resembles a gigantic, tattered sporran. The *Life* interweaves and borrows elements from myth and religious tradition, for

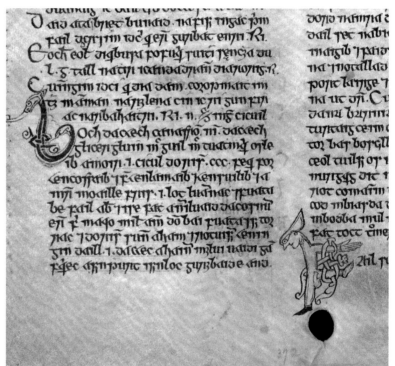

Fig. 220 **Manus O'Donnell's** *Irish Life of St Colum Cille*

Commissioned by a chieftain keen on proclaiming his relationship to the ancient saint, this manuscript's impressive size and unique seal-skin cover sit at odds with the delicate Gothic portrait of a blushing St Columba.

Ireland 1532
Vellum; H 42 cm
Bodleian Library, Oxford (Rawlinson B.514)

Fig. 221 Book of the White Earl

This manuscript with its fine initials includes
the 'Book of the White Earl', written for James
Butler, 4th Earl of Ormond (d. 1452).

Ireland AD 1400–1500
Manuscript, 33.5 x 24.5 cm
Bodleian Library, Oxford (Laud Misc. 610)

example describing none other than the mythical hero Fionn mac Cumhaill prophesying that Columba 'should one day bless the place, and make it a sanctuary'.[32] Most helpfully, the scribe, speaking as the patron, begins by setting out the reasons behind commissioning the text:

> *This* Life *was lost a long while since [when]… the Danes … came to smite Erin … And most specially did they burn and destroy the high churches of Columcille … and destroyed the books concerning him…Be it known to the readers of this* Life *that it was Manus O'Donnell … [who] collected and assembled the part thereof that was scattered throughout the ancient books of Erin … Having conceived the affection and the love of a brother for his high saint and kinsmen by lineage and his dear patron that he was bound to in steadfast devotion.*[33]

The passage shows that the restoration and revival that took place in Gaelic-speaking areas of Scotland and Ireland during the high and late medieval periods was not due to accident or serendipity but rather the resolute efforts of certain Gaelic families. Several Anglo-Irish lords also followed this Gaelic practice. James, the 4th Earl of Ormond, learned Irish and commissioned the Book of the White Earl (fig. 221), a stunning example of revivalist art. Françoise Henry and Geneviève Marsh-Micheli, long recognized as the foremost experts in Irish illumination, describe the manuscript as dazzling, stating, 'The sumptuous initials of this book are not a more or less servile repetition of twelfth-century work. They are, on the old data, new creations'.[34]

Gaelic chieftains became the guardians of Ireland's and Scotland's heritage, preserving genealogies, histories, myths and legends. Many families dutifully watched over these precious survivors until the late nineteenth century and some continue to do so even today. While these 'bags' of knowledge undoubtedly served primarily to validate, authenticate and celebrate the chieftains and their families, they also were and are remarkable repositories of literary, historical, legal and even medical information. Their faded colours, dirty pages and tattered bindings bear witness to their usefulness: to the many fingers and eyes that have scoured their contents looking for a hidden fact, legend or name.

In the fourteenth century, having accepted the overlordship of the King of Scotland, the formerly independent Lords of the Isles sought to consolidate their authority and identity.[35] Unsurprisingly, the inner Hebridean island of Iona – home of Columba and a cradle of the Insular culture that had shaped Britain and Ireland in the early medieval period – became a natural focus. An eleventh-century chronicle states that Scottish kings, beginning with Kenneth MacAlpin in the mid-ninth century and ending with Macbeth in the mid-eleventh century, chose to be buried in the *Rèilig Odhrain* (Oran's Cemetery) on Iona.[36] In the fourteenth and fifteenth centuries, the Lords of the Isles and Highland chieftains such as the Macleans, MacKinnons, MacQuarries, MacDonalds and Macleods followed suit.

In much the same way that Irish kings sought the ancient authority of the relics of Columba and Patrick, Scottish kings and the Lords of the Isles claimed the island most closely associated with Columba. Their children became its abbesses, abbots, nuns and clergy. A grave slab from the *Sràid nan Marbh* (Road of the Dead) commemorates four priors, all brothers from the same clan, probably the clan Campbell; another from the nunnery portrays Lady Anna Maclean, 'prioress of Iona, who died in the year 1543'.[37] A ringed cross covered in interlace and knotwork stands at the juncture of the three medieval streets of Iona, including the *Sràid nan Marbh*. Known as Maclean's Cross, suggesting it may have been erected by the Maclean chieftain, its ringed cross was carved in the fifteenth century, but the form echoes the great eighth-century Insular high crosses that still stood just beyond the cemetery grounds (fig. 222). While incorporating the Romanesque-style foliage that can be found across Europe, the spiral arrangement of the scrolls, geometrical play and integration of interlace invoke the monumental cross's Insular inheritance.

Scotland also produced its share of reliquaries in this period. Perhaps best known is the crosier-shaped shrine, the *Coigreach* or *Quigrich*, which originally housed a smaller shrine, the eleventh- or twelfth-century St Fillan's crosier (figs 223 and 224). Its hereditary keepers, the Dewar family, probably derived their family name from involvement with the reliquary. The Gaelic *deòradh*, anglicized as Dewar, means hereditary keeper.[38] The family gifted the double shrine to the Scottish nation in 1876, and as recently as 1992 Mrs Nilo Wilson, a member of the Dewar family, donated further funds to the museum.[39] The earlier St Fillan's crosier has lost most of its decoration and parts may have been cannibalized in order to construct the newer outer shrine. Bell shrines also survive from Scotland. The Guthrie bell shrine is spectacular due to its composite nature, combining a twelfth-century figure of Christ, thirteenth-century scrollwork, fourteenth-century representations of bishops and fifteenth-century gilt ornaments (fig. 216).[40]

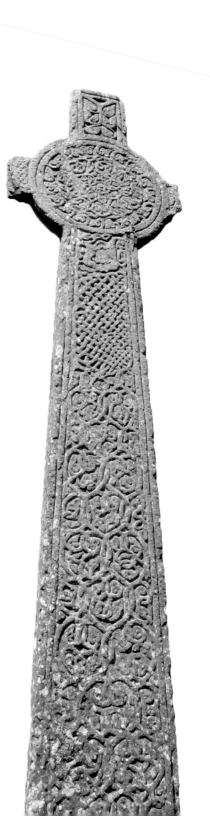

Fig. 222 **Maclean's cross**

This cross stands by a trackway on Iona. Pilgrims filing up from the boats may have paused to say a prayer here before continuing on their journey to the abbey and St Columba's shrine.

Iona, Argyll AD 1400–1500
Stone; H 3.15 m

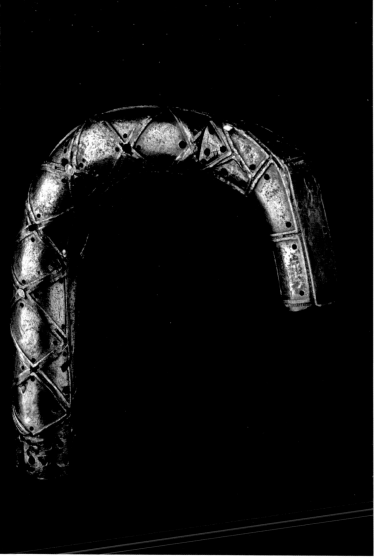

Fig. 223 **St Fillan's crosier**

In 1876 this crosier was removed from its reliquary, the
Coigreach (fig. 224). Most of its ornament has been stripped
from it, probably just before it was placed into the *Coigreach*.

West Highlands AD 950–1050
Copper alloy, niello; 15 cm x 16.8 cm
National Museums Scotland, Edinburgh

Fig. 224 **The *Coigreach***

Made to house the St Fillan's crosier (fig. 223), the decoration of
the shrine includes decorative filigree that originally belonged to
the crosier as well as additional Gothic ornamentation and Insular
interlace.

Probably made in Glendochart, Perth and Kinross AD 1100–1500
Silver, gilt, rock crystal, copper alloy; 23.6 x 20 cm
National Museums Scotland, Edinburgh

'*In my end is my beginning*':[41] history and heritage

Few, if any, objects from the late medieval period so beautifully and expertly incorporate multiple generations' interpretations of the early medieval Insular style as the Queen Mary harp, another product of West Highland culture (fig. 225). Recent technological analyses suggest that parts of the harp were originally coloured bright red so that the fantastical creatures and interlace that decorate it stood out against a vermillion ground.[42] The effect would have been quite similar to that seen in twelfth-century Irish and Scottish illuminated manuscripts such as the Corpus Missal (fig. 218). While the griffin's legs, scales and stubby, pointed wings would not appear out of place in any court in Europe at this time, the contour line of its eye might have been taken directly from the Book of Kells, both in terms of its tear shape and the manner in which it curves down to form the creature's jaw and spiral snout. The spiral arrangement of the split-palmette on the curving fore-pillar reflects the integration of Insular, Norse and Romanesque designs as found on the sculpture of western Scotland and the Isles[43] The double-headed creature that spans the arc of the harp's pillar-arm draws upon multiple earlier traditions. Like its Iron Age, Germanic and Insular artistic predecessors, recognizable anatomical features are scattered and duplicated in an ambivalent, almost riddling fashion. There is a play between form and function, as on the Basse Yutz flagons (fig. 40), where the handles are formed by a wolf-like creature that raises itself up on its hind legs to peer over the stopper, or in the small Pictish spoon from St Ninian's Isle, where the join between the spoon's handle and bowl is formed by a creature cheekily licking the bowl.[44] The curve and lips of the double-headed creature on the harp resemble the handle of the Kilmichael Glassary bell shrine (fig. 217), while its abstracted and almost architectural qualities are not unlike the bell shrine of St Cuileáin (fig. 214).

Like a palimpsest, objects of the high and late medieval period allow us to view multiple layers of history simultaneously. Styles and forms were appropriated and modified, pointing to the past while embodying the present. Preserved and mended through the centuries by their hereditary keepers, these composite and hybrid objects might be seen as imperfect and flawed: unfinished, coarse, incomplete, fragmented, damaged, imitative and impure. They resist classification and categories: St Conall Cael's bell and its shrine are displayed in different galleries within the British Museum and fall under the jurisdiction of separate curators; the Cathach of Columba remains in the Royal Irish Academy while its shrine is exhibited in the National Museum of Ireland. St Fillan's crosier had to be surgically removed from the *Coigreach*. The Gothic cover of the *Cumdach* of the Cathach is welded to the Hiberno-Norse sides and back. Its stylistic discontinuity paradoxically proclaims the consistency of care for the Insular relic that lay within. The awkward repairs and joins show objects that have had multiple uses and lives, revealing not one but many entangled stories.

Fig. 225 **Queen Mary's harp**

Made around 1450, this harp was owned by an aristocratic Scottish family for many generations. The intricate interlace and beasts are inspired by Celtic art from early medieval manuscripts and stone crosses. Noble families in Scotland and Ireland commissioned works in this style to express their powerful heritage and ancestry.

West Highlands *c.* 1450
Wood and brass; H 81.2 cm, W 51 cm
National Museums Scotland, Edinburgh

Fig. 226 **John Duncan, *Riders of the Sidhe* (detail)**

Scottish artist John Duncan combined inspiration from real ancient objects and early medieval myths to produce this colourful masterpiece.

1911
Tempera on canvas; 114.3 x 175.2 cm
The McManus: Dundee's Art Gallery and Museum

Chapter 10

The Celtic Revival in Britain & Ireland:
Reconstructing the Past, *c.* AD 1600–1920

Frances Fowle

In 1890 George Henry and Edward Atkinson Hornel's *The Druids: Bringing in the Mistletoe* (fig. 227) was exhibited at the Grosvenor Gallery in London, where it caused a sensation. The art critic R.A.M. Stevenson described the druidical figures as 'grim, tawdry, and savage . . . glowing with crude colour.'[1] Surrounded by a spectacular gold frame of interlaced snakes, the composition is painted in brilliant vermillion, emerald and gold, recalling the colour range of early medieval illuminated manuscripts. As if stepping out of the

Fig. 227 **George Henry and Edward Atkinson Hornel** *The Druids: Bringing in the Mistletoe*

This painting is almost certainly based on the druidical procession in an account given in William Mackenzie's *History of Galloway*, a copy of which Hornel kept in his library. Mackenzie noted that both female and male druids participated in these sacred rituals, perhaps explaining the figure in the centre of the composition. The white-haired, bearded Archdruid on the left was inspired by an illustration from an 1845 book of costume.

1890
Oil on canvas; 152.4 x 152.4 cm
Glasgow Museums

pages of Pliny,[2] a solemn procession of Celtic priests emerges from a grove of oaks and descends a snow-clad hill. Henry and Hornel constructed a myth around the painting: it was said to have been inspired by the vision of a local shaman and the priests' features were apparently based on close observation of 'druid skulls'.[3] It certainly incorporates references to identifiable sources that were seen as Celtic at the time: a golden lunula-shaped sickle, derived from an early Bronze Age neck ornament; a snake design inspired by Pictish stones; Celtic spirals loosely based on the Battersea shield; and prehistoric cup-and-ring markings linked to recent finds in the local Galloway landscape of south-western Scotland.[4] However, the features of the central druid find their source not in druidical remains, but in photographs of Native Americans that were widely distributed around the time of Buffalo Bill's Wild West show, which performed at the Paris Exposition Universelle in 1889.

Like *The Druids*, the Celtic Revival was a Romantic reconstruction of Britain's ancient past. Drawing on the discoveries of archaeologists and antiquarians, linguists and social anthropologists, it was, at least initially, an attempt by artists to regain contact with their primitive cultural roots and emulate a bygone age. As we shall see in this chapter, the reinterpretation of Celtic artefacts by painters and craftspeople in the eighteenth and nineteenth centuries was often founded in error, ignorance and misconception, or motivated by political and nationalist agendas. Nevertheless, it was also the assimilation of Celtic ornament that helped pave the way for modern movements such as Art Nouveau.

Rediscovering the Celts

The rediscovery of Britain's 'primitive' origins was a focus for antiquarians from as early as the sixteenth century. Geoffrey of Monmouth's entirely unreliable twelfth-century *History of the Kings of Britain* – until then the accepted authority on the genealogy of the British nation – had established a glorious and noble ancestry, dating from the arrival of Brutus (after whom 'Britain' was said to be named) in around 1240 BC. It also made some outrageous claims: that Belinus (legendary king of the Britons) and his brother Brennius had participated in the sack of Rome (390 BC), for example, and that King Arthur had conquered Europe.

In 1582 the poet, playwright and classical scholar George Buchanan published the *Rerum Scoticarum Historia* in which he identified an entirely new set of pagan ancestors: the Britons, an ancient Belgic tribe; the Picts, who came from the Baltic region; and the Celts.[5] Drawing on classical sources, as well as common roots in place names, Buchanan deduced that it was only the Scots and Irish who were descended from the Celts: a tribe originating in an area around Lyons (France), known as *Gallia Celtica*, who travelled to Ireland and Scotland through Spain.[6]

William Camden's *Britannia*, published in Latin in 1586, further undermined Geoffrey's account. Drawing on Caesar's *Commentarii de Bello Gallico* (Commentaries on the Gallic Wars) he asserted that the word 'Briton' derived not from 'Brutus' but from 'brith' or 'brit', meaning 'painted': a reference to the blue-painted men that Caesar had observed.[7] Camden's influential publication coincided with one of the earliest attempts to visualize the ancient people of Britain by the colonialist John White. White produced several likenesses of Picts and ancient Britons following a trip with Thomas Harriot to North America in 1585.[8] These included a nude *Pictish Woman* (fig. 229) and a *Pict Warrior* covered in blue woad, decorated with tattoos and armed with curved swords and spears; and a gruesome *Pictish Warrior holding a human head* (fig. 228), gaily painted with birds, animals and serpents. The latter even brandishes a scimitar, possibly a reference to the Turks, who were then perceived as modern barbarians.[9]

Fig. 228 John White, *A Pictish Warrior holding a human head*

According to early sources the Picts were aggressive, semi-naked warriors who occupied northern Scotland. White's Pict, for all his gruesome appearance, has distinctly contemporary features and adopts a classical pose.

1585–93
Watercolour touched with bodycolour and white over graphite; 24.3 x 17 cm
British Museum, London

Fig. 229 John White, *A Pictish Woman*

With her long flowing hair and elegant pose, this Pictish woman is reminiscent of the Greek goddess Artemis, the huntress. White was keen to show that Britain's ancestors were a dignified and noble people, rather than savages.

1585–93
Pen and brown ink and watercolour over graphite, touched with white (oxidized); 23 x 17.9 cm
British Museum, London

Five engravings by Theodor de Bry – four closely related to White's illustrations and one, *The true picture of a young daughter of the Picts*, after Jacques le Moyne de Morgues – were included as a later supplement to Harriot's *A briefe and true report of the new found land of Virginia* (1588). The text noted that Pictish peoples occupied 'one part of Great Britainne, which is now nammed England'.[10] The comparison with Native Americans was intended to underline the 'primitive' origins of the British people: 'to show how that the inhabitants of the Great Bretannie hau bin in time past as sauuage as those of Virginia'.[11]

Attempts to define the nation's ethnic origins continued into the seventeenth century. Samuel Bochart in his *Geographica Sacra* (1646) proposed that the first Britons were Phoenicians; and in 1676 Aylett Sammes, author of *Britannia Antiqua Illustrata*, linked the Phoenicians to the druids.[12] However, the first published account of the Celts as the original inhabitants of the British Isles did not appear until 1703, in Paul-Yves Pezron's *L'Antiquité de la Nation et la Langue des Celtes*. Translated in 1706 as *The Antiquities of Nations*, Pezron's research was hugely influential. Whereas Pezron proposed that the Celtic language was the root of all European languages, the Welsh linguist and antiquarian Edward Lhuyd – in the first and only volume of his *Archaeologia Britannica* (1707) – argued that the Celts were in fact a small tribe who had influenced only Brittany, Wales, Cornwall and the Gaelic parts of Ireland and Scotland (see pp. 24–5).[13] In time the label 'Celtic' came to describe the people of those areas (with the later addition of the Isle of Man), creating a perceived racial cohesiveness and cultural identity that underpinned the Celtic revival of the Romantic era.

The name 'Celtic' also came to be applied to ancient monuments in the British landscape. One of the most significant figures in this respect was the English antiquarian William Stukeley, working in the first half of the eighteenth century and known by his followers as 'the father of British Antiquities'.[14] Stukeley led the first investigations at Stonehenge and in 1721 drew the archaeological remains of the nearby stone circle at Avebury (fig. 6), describing the site as a 'Celtic temple'. The later publication of this drawing was the first time ancient monuments in the British landscape were linked to the Celts in print.[15] Inspired by the work of his contemporary, the Irish-born philosopher and 'free-thinker' John Toland, Stukeley soon became fascinated by the druids and attempted to revive some of their ancient ceremonies; he even painted a self-portrait in druid's robes and built a druidical folly in his garden.[16] In 1740 he published *Stonehenge: A Temple Restor'd to the British Druids* and three years later *Abury: A Temple of the British Druids, with Some Others ...*. The druids' healing powers and mysterious rituals captured the Romantic imagination and numerous publications would follow, inspiring the first visualizations of these noble Celts.

Fig. 230 **J. Harrison; after P. J. de Louterbourg,** *The Bard*

De Louterbourg's *The Bard* symbolized the potential destruction of Welsh oral culture. Harrison's painting, like the original print, is highly romanticized. The harp-playing bard is set against a dramatic sky and in inhospitable mountainous terrain.

1840
Oil on canvas; 84.6 x 67.5 cm
National Museum Wales

Bards, druids and Ossian

Although research into the origins of Britain's supposed Celtic roots had been ongoing throughout the sixteenth and seventeenth centuries, the Celtic Revival in literature and the visual arts did not really gather pace until the mid-eighteenth century, culminating in Sir Walter Scott's Waverley novels (published 1814 onwards), which created a highly romanticized image of Scotland that has persisted to this day.

Many regard Thomas Gray's *The Bard. A Pindaric Ode*, published in 1757, as the first creative work of the Celtic Revival.[17] The poem relates how the English king Edward I, who invaded Wales and put the bards to death, was challenged by a lone survivor, the last bard, who prophesied the king's downfall before throwing himself to his death in the river Conway. The

poem inspired numerous visual interpretations, not least Thomas Jones's 1774 oil painting *The Bard* and Philip James de Loutherbourg's *The Bard* (*c.* 1784), known through numerous reproductions and copies (fig. 230). Set in an ancient, remote landscape, a bard in druid's robes and long white beard stands on the edge of a cliff. He clutches his harp and turns to curse the invading troops of Edward I before leaping to his death.[18]

The medieval bards were said to be descendants of the ancient druids; they provided access, through poetry and song, to a Celtic past. Their slaughter by Edward symbolized, on one level, the suppression of the imaginative faculties and, on another, the loss of the Celtic histories that constituted British origins and were felt to provide the key to national identity. In the late eighteenth century, under the influence of antiquarians such as William Owen Pughe and Iolo Morganwg (Edward Williams), the bard was adopted as a symbol of the Welsh nation. Pughe illustrated his personal copy of *The Heroic Elegies and other Pieces of Llywarç Hen* (1792) with a frontispiece depicting a Welsh bard creating the world.[19] He also arranged for the engraver Abraham Raimbach to portray Hu Gadarn, Iolo's mythical founder of the Welsh nation, stepping out of his coracle onto Welsh soil.[20]

An engraving of De Loutherbourg's *The Bard* was reproduced as the frontispiece of Edward Jones's *Musical and Poetical Relicks of the Welsh Bards* in 1784. The print was widely disseminated and before long evolved into a druidic 'type'. Around 1797–8, for example, William Blake produced 116 illustrations for Thomas Gray's poem, including on the title page a druidic figure with a long white beard, golden harp and flowing, star-studded robes.[21] When artists began to visualize James Macpherson's *Ossian* they again resorted to this bardic stereotype. MacPherson published his first 'Fragments' of poetry by the Celtic bard Ossian, supposedly translated from the original Gaelic, in 1760. These were followed by *Fingal* in 1761 and *Temora* in 1763.[22] The tales were said to be compiled from mainly oral accounts, gathered in the Scottish Highlands. Macpherson was later exposed as a fraud, but the impact of the hugely popular poems was widespread.

The Danish artist Nikolai Abildgaard's beguiling oil painting of the *Blind Ossian Singing his Swan Song* (1785) (fig. 231) became the standard representation of Ossian as a white-haired, druidic bard clutching his harp. His lack of sight symbolized inner vision, a motif that recalls Homer's characterization as a blind bard. The image was widely disseminated through Johan Frederik Clemens's 1787 engraving and became the frontispiece for numerous translations.

In Scotland Alexander Runciman was the first to bring the tales of Ossian to life, focusing on the hero Fingal.[23] In 1772–4 he was commissioned by Sir James Clerk to paint the staircase and grand saloon (later referred to as 'Ossian's Hall', now destroyed) at Penicuik House in Midlothian, with scenes in a classical style. The suggestion that he should recreate the poems of Ossian appears to have come from Runciman himself, whose imagination extended to including two invented scenes: *Scandinavian Wizards saying their*

Fig. 232 **Alexander Runciman, *Fingal discovers Conban-Cargla at the Cave of Turthor***

Runciman fused classical imagery and a highly Romantic imagination to create his mysterious interpretations of the Ossian cycle. He followed Macpherson's narrative closely. In this scene, the valiant Fingal in pursuit of Starno, King of Lochlin, stumbles across a cave; in the moonlight, Conban-Cargla, her hands tied, shrinks away in fear.

c. 1773
Etching on paper; 16.7 x 26 cm
British Museum, London

Incantations and *Building of a Monument to the Poet*.[24] Runciman later produced three etched variations on one scene, taken from Macpherson's *Cathloda*. *The Finding of Conban-Cargla* (fig. 232) illustrates Fingal's chance discovery, in the Cave of Turthor, of the missing daughter of a tribal chieftain, imprisoned by the Scandinavian King Starno of Lochlin.

Runciman's imagination – as well as his style – was fuelled by the Swiss artist Henry Fuseli, whom he met in Italy around 1767. Fuseli was a key link to Germany and Scandinavia,[25] influencing works such as Asmus Jacob Carstens's *Fingal's Battle with the Spirit of Loda* of around 1797,[26] although Carstens's fascination for the epic poem was also undoubtedly fostered by his master Abildgaard. The Nordic references in the tales of Ossian held an immediate appeal for Danish artists: the principal setting for Fingal's tales was Inistore, the Orkney Islands, which were under Danish rule until 1465.[27]

In France Ossian was used for overtly propaganda purposes. Napoleon Bonaparte was an Ossian enthusiast and is known to have carried a copy with him on his campaigns in Egypt and Syria (1798–1801).[28] In 1801 and 1802 the painters Baron Gérard and Anne-Louis Girodet completed two highly romanticized and theatrical Ossianic pieces for Josephine's château at Malmaison, which Napoleon used as a retreat. Gérard's 1801 canvas *Ossian Evoking Ghosts with the Sound of his Harp on the Edge of the Lora* presents a wild, pagan Ossian, conjuring up the heroes of Celtic legend. Girodet's *Ossian Receiving the Ghosts of French Heroes* of 1802 (fig. 233) is more overtly political. It shows a bearded, god-like Ossian welcoming recently fallen Napoleonic commanders to paradise, visualized as a curious fusion of Christian Heaven and Nordic Valhalla. A radiant French cockerel is held aloft on the right, dominating the Austrian eagle on the left: an allusion to Napoleon's victory over Austria in 1800. This apparently 'Celtic' image is none other than blatant political propaganda, designed to encourage the French to get behind their leader.

Fig. 233 **Anne-Louis Girodet, *Ossian Receiving the Ghosts of French Heroes***

Girodet's extravagant vision shows how Ossian's poetry was used by Napoleon to promote his own political agenda. The poems appealed to the Romantic imagination, providing a northern equivalent of the classical myths.

1802
Oil on canvas; 192 x 184 cm
Musée National du Château de Malmaison, Rueil

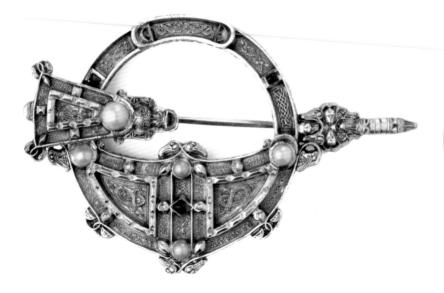

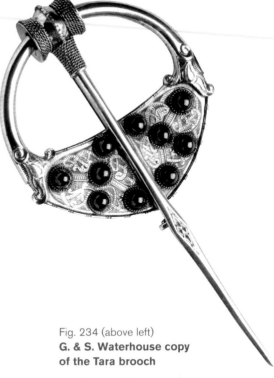

The Irish Celtic Revival: 'finds', copies and Celtomania

With the dawn of the nineteenth century the Celtic Revival spread to Ireland, ignited by a flurry of archaeological discoveries. These were carefully conserved and recorded for posterity through the painstaking work of individuals such as the artist George Petrie and the antiquarian and oculist Sir William Wilde, both of whom were on the committee of the Royal Irish Academy.[29] Petrie was responsible for the acquisition of important Irish manuscripts and significant examples of Insular metalwork, such as the Cross of Cong, now in the National Museum of Ireland. Wilde was a keen Celtic Revivalist and named his soon-to-be notorious son 'Oscar Fingal' after two Ossianic heroes. He produced a three-volume catalogue of the antiquities owned by the Academy, among which were recent discoveries of important Insular metalwork, including the Ardagh chalice (fig. 168) and the Tara brooch (fig. 182).[30]

The discovery of the eighth-century Tara brooch near Bettystown in 1850 opened the eyes of the Victorians to the beauty and sophisticated craftsmanship of early Christian metalwork.[31] The *Art Journal* commented in 1853 that the Tara brooch had been 'made at a period when the Arts in Ireland had reached perfection'.[32] Its sheer scale eclipsed all earlier finds, and the Dublin jewellers G. & S. Waterhouse were quick to exploit the commercial potential of the object, which they acquired and copied.[33] They even named the original 'Tara' after the hill in County Meath where early high kings held court, some twenty-five kilometres from the actual findspot.

This was the era of international exhibitions and the brooch was shown at London's first Great Exhibition at the Crystal Palace in 1851, at

Fig. 234 (above left)
G. & S. Waterhouse copy of the Tara brooch

The Tara brooch was one of the most celebrated penannular brooches discovered in Ireland in the mid-nineteenth century (fig. 182). The design was copied by Waterhouse who exhibited several facsimiles alongside the original at the Great Exhibition of 1851. Queen Victoria's acquisition of one of the replicas established a fashion for such items.

c. 1851
Oxidized silver, parcel-gilt, set with pearls, iron pyrites (known as 'Irish diamonds') and amethysts
Victoria and Albert Museum, London

Fig. 235 (above) **Clarendon brooch**

Created by Edmond Johnson for West & Son, one of the most prominent jewellers in Dublin, this brooch was named after Lady Clarendon, wife of the Viceroy of Ireland, who was one of the first to wear this particular design, based on a ninth-century prototype.

1849–50
Silver, garnets; 13.6 x 7.2 x 1 cm
Royal Collection Trust, London

Fig. 236 **Edmond Johnson,
the Queen's brooch**

Based on the ninth-century Cavan brooch, this
unique piece was designed by Johnson for
West & Son. It was presented to Queen Victoria
when she visited Dublin in 1853.

1849
Gold and pearl; L 9.5 cm, W 6.7 cm
National Museum of Ireland, Dublin

the Dublin Exhibition of 1853 and the Paris Exposition Universelle of 1855, before being sold in 1868 to the Royal Irish Academy.[34] Smaller facsimiles and copies of the Tara brooch (fig. 234) and other recent finds of Irish eighth-century brooches such as the Moor brooch, the Kilmainham or Knight Templar brooch, and the Arbutus berry brooch were created by Waterhouse and examples were acquired by the Museum of Manufactures (now the Victoria and Albert Museum) at the 1851 and 1853 exhibitions.

In 1853 Waterhouse produced a detailed catalogue setting out their range of reproductions for the potential buyer. His commercial venture was considerably boosted by Queen Victoria, who had acquired a facsimile of the Tara brooch at the Great Exhibition, triggering a fashion for such items. Victoria and Prince Albert had visited Trinity College, Dublin, in 1849 and had admired the Book of Kells and the harp of Brian Boru, as well as 'some ancient gold fibulae with silver and bronze brooches, the workmanship of which she particularly noticed'.[35] Prince Albert secretly acquired two brooches, one of which was a shawl pin, designed for Waterhouse by the goldsmith Edmond Johnson. Albert presented it to Victoria at Christmas, much to her delight. Now known as the Clarendon brooch (fig. 235), it is a variant of a ninth-century brooch found in Ballyspellan in 1806.[36] The original is engraved with interlace and has silver bosses, while the royal version is enriched with garnets.

Victoria's love of 'Celtic' brooches was well known and when she visited the Dublin Exhibition in 1853 she was presented with the so-called Queen's brooch (fig. 236), a copy by West & Son of the ninth-century Cavan brooch, discovered in Lough Ramor. Scottish items were also on display at the Dublin Exhibition, including an annular brooch by William Acheson of Dublin, inspired by the Hunterston brooch (fig. 166). Typically these Scottish designs incorporated indigenous gemstones such as agate, while the Irish designs favoured iron pyrites (also known as 'Irish diamonds') and bog oak, an ancient material almost synonymous with Irish crafts, which was used in jewellery in place of jet.[37]

Edmond Johnson was one of Waterhouse's favourite designers and his skill in reproducing Insular objects was honed by his close association with the Royal Irish Academy.[38] As early as 1868 he was employed by the Academy to restore the Ardagh chalice, one of the most important examples of Insular craftsmanship, dating from the eighth century and rediscovered in 1868 (fig. 168). He went on to produce facsimiles of 'Celtic' objects, often restoring rather than simply conserving the original artefacts. This tendency to 'improve' the original material is a common feature in Celtic Revival design, but has the effect of destroying the mystery and associative qualities of the original. Taken out of context and seen as pure pattern, the stylized figures and animal forms lose their symbolic meaning.[39]

Johnson worked in partnership with Joseph Johnson Junior, who was either his brother or first cousin; for around thirty years, they controlled the leadership of the Company of Goldsmiths.[40] A good example of Joseph Johnson's skill at adapting ancient objects to more modern purposes is a dish now in the National Museum of Ireland. Partly gilt, with insets of crystal, glass and enamel, the design is based on the foot of the Ardagh chalice.

Sources of inspiration

Johnson had direct access to the original Ardagh chalice, but the majority of designers relied on illustrated catalogues or pattern books such as Owen Jones's highly influential *Grammar of Ornament* (1856), which included three pages of brightly coloured Celtic motifs, based on designs observed in sculpted crosses and Insular manuscripts, isolated from their original context (fig. 237). They were clearly categorized as examples of 'lapidary ornamentation', 'interlaced style' and 'spiral, diagonal, zoomorphic and later Anglo-Saxon ornaments'. An accompanying essay by John Obadiah Westwood outlined the sources of Celtic art and the 'peculiarities of Celtic ornament'.[41]

A more archaeological approach is evident in John Kemble's *Horae Ferales or Studies in the Archaeology of the Northern Nations* (1863), brought to publication after his death by Robert Gordon Latham and Augustus Wollaston Franks. The text accompanying the plates, written by Franks, drew on his expertise as curator at the British Museum, and was not only the first publication to use the name 'Celtic' to refer to Iron Age rather than early medieval art, but also led to the wider application of the term 'Celtic' on the Continent.[42] A key feature of *Horae Ferales* was the illustration of recent discoveries such as the Battersea shield (fig. 10). Decorated with spiralling repoussé work, engraving and inlaid glass, the shield is one of the most significant pieces ever found in Britain. Indeed, it was referenced along with other finds nearly fifty years later by the Scottish artist John Duncan in his *Riders of the Sidhe* (fig. 238), where the fairy folk of Irish mythology, the Tuatha Dé Danann, are shown riding out on Beltane (May Day) or Samhain, a Gaelic festival marking the end of harvest and the beginning of winter.

Fig. 237 **Owen Jones, *The Grammar of Ornament***

The Grammar of Ornament pattern books provided a rich source of inspiration to British designers in the second half of the nineteenth century. The new chromolithographic process meant that the original Celtic designs were reproduced in brilliant colour, overshadowing the accompanying text.

1856, Plate LXIV, Celtic No. 2, published by Day & Son
Chromolithograph; H 87 cm

Fig. 238 John Duncan, *Riders of the Sidhe*

The riders and their steeds are equipped
with 'Celtic' weapons and armour, such as a
version of the Battersea shield. One carries the
legendary cauldron of Dagda and another the
sword of Nuada. Along with the spear of Lugh
and the *Liath Faill* (Stone of Destiny) these were
the four Treasures of the Tuatha Dé Danann, the
supernatural deities of Irish mythology.

1911
Tempera on canvas; 114.3 x 175.2 cm
The McManus: Dundee's Art Gallery and Museum

Westwood's *Facsimiles of the Miniatures & Ornaments of Anglo-Saxon and Irish Manuscripts* (1868) was another important source for designers in the late nineteenth century and, like the *Grammar of Ornament*, the reproductions were made using chromolithography.[43] As early as 1843–5 Westwood had reproduced coloured illuminations from the Book of Kells in his *Palaeographia sacra pictoria: being a series of the ancient versions of the Bible*. Vivid colour is also a striking feature of Margaret Stokes's illustrations for Samuel Ferguson's poem *The Cromlech on Howth* (1861), which was published in a plush green and gold cover decorated with Celtic interlace. The text was embellished by Stokes with knotwork designs and stylized forms, meticulously transcribed from the Books of Kells and of Durrow.[44] The illuminations were coloured in reds and greens, far more vivid in tone than the originals.

Such brilliance is greatly at variance with the delicate faded tones of the manuscripts as they appear today. It may explain why vivid colour – and

more importantly iridescence – is a feature of the work of later nineteenth-century Revivalists such as Phoebe Traquair (who claimed to have been influenced by the Book of Kells) and John Duncan. Perhaps ironically, however, it was only once designers were able to be less perfectionist – and more inventive – in their approach that they were able to produce objects that retained the beauty and essence of the original.

Celtic modernism in Scotland and Ireland

The emphasis on skill, as well as design, was an important aspect of the Celtic Revival, especially in Scotland and Ireland.[45] One of the crafts to enjoy an upsurge in Ireland around the turn of the century was woodcarving, often using indigenous materials, particularly bog oak. This brought about a revival of vernacular pieces such as settles (high-backed benches) decorated with knotwork and Irish mythological scenes. However, Irish designers and craftworkers had a tendency to ignore ornament such as interlace in favour of more clichéd symbols of Irish identity: in 1883 Dr William Sullivan, President of Queen's College, Cork, criticized the use in Irish decorative art of 'supposed national emblems' such as harps, round towers and shamrocks, praising instead the application of Celtic ornamentation.[46]

In his *Studies in Design* (1876) the (Scots-born) English designer Christopher Dresser touched only briefly on Celtic ornament, which he categorized as 'a class of grotesque', due to the stylization of natural forms: 'In some cases the neck of a bird, or the body of a beast is formed of strapwork; and two animals are not unfrequently twined together in a curious and intricate manner . . . the whole composition is ornamental and not naturalistic, and the effect produced is highly humorous'.[47] This stylization of forms was what fascinated the most gifted 'Celtic' designers of the late nineteenth and early twentieth centuries, some of whom were able to incorporate earlier Celtic features in their work, while also responding to avant-garde styles and movements on the Continent.

The Honan Chapel at St Finn Barr, Cork, with stained glass by Harry Clarke (1916), is surely the most outstanding example of Irish Celtic Revival craftsmanship.[48] However, it perhaps lacks the subtlety of Mary Seton Tyler's innovative designs for the Watts Memorial Chapel, at Compton in Surrey (1896), and Charles Rennie Mackintosh's radical experiments at Glasgow School of Art (1897–1909). Indeed it was among Scottish designers that Celtic modernism reached its apogee.[49]

In 1890s Scotland the Celtic Revival manifested itself as the Glasgow Style, epitomized by the work of Mackintosh, Herbert McNair and Margaret and Frances Macdonald, known as 'The Four'. Among the most iconic images to emerge from this period were the Drooko Umbrella Poster, designed by Margaret and Frances Macdonald in 1895, and the poster for the Glasgow Institute of the Fine Arts (fig. 239), created jointly by McNair

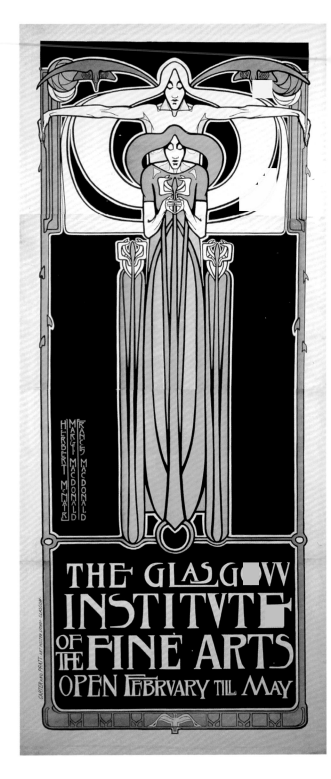

Fig. 239 Herbert McNair, Margaret and Frances Macdonald, *Poster for the Glasgow Institute of the Fine Arts*

Known as 'The Four' (along with Charles Rennie Mackintosh), these artists were celebrated for their bold and innovative designs, which drew on a variety of sources, including stylized 'Celtic' forms. In January 1895 they exhibited their posters in Glasgow alongside the work of Toulouse-Lautrec and Aubrey Beardsley.

c. 1894
Lithograph: ink on paper; 236 x 102 cm
Printer: Carter & Pratt, Glasgow
The Hunterian, University of Glasgow

Fig. 240 Frances Macdonald, *Programme of music for the Glasgow School of Art Club 'At Home'*

This design combines stylized female figures, Celtic interlace and symbolic motifs such as the 'Tree of Life'. The Macdonald sisters' attenuated forms earned them the title 'The Spook School'.

25 November 1893
Green ink on paper; 13.1 x 11.8 cm (sheet, closed)
The Hunterian, University of Glasgow

and the Macdonald sisters. The elongated figures and attenuated plant forms in both works derived from early medieval Insular manuscripts and metalwork, as well as from William Blake and perhaps even more esoteric sources such as Indian and Egyptian art. They caused tremendous consternation among the critics, who described the posters as 'spooky' and 'calculated to cause serious qualms of conscience to the nocturnal reveller'.[50]

For The Four, as for many Scottish artists of the avant-garde, the stylized forms of Celtic art provided a pathway to Modernism. It represented an indigenous, national equivalent to the kind of 'primitive' sources that inspired European artists such as Paul Gauguin, whose radical 'Synthetist'

style derived from Japanese prints, Breton popular prints known as *images d'Epinal* and stained glass. The Macdonald sisters worked in a variety of media, including gesso and glass beads, as in Margaret Macdonald's Celtic-inspired *The May Queen* of 1900 (fig. 241). They also created brilliantly innovative designs in materials such as beaten copper and brass, finding inspiration in Insular metalwork. On occasion they injected humour into their work: Frances Macdonald's design for the music programme for the Glasgow School of Art Club 'At Home' on 25 November 1893 (fig. 240) shows two women curled under an apple tree, an unusual configuration that recalls the attenuated hybrid figures in the Book of Kells, as well as the formal elements of early medieval penannular brooches.[51]

The Macdonald sisters attended Glasgow School of Art, overseen by the charismatic Fra Newbery and his wife Jessie, who taught embroidery. Under Jessie Newbery and her successor Ann Macbeth the Glasgow Style flourished, producing a generation of highly talented women designers.[52] Another advocate of Celtic art and the Glasgow Style, Margaret Gilmour, established a studio in West George Street, Glasgow, where she taught a variety of crafts, including metalwork and enamelling (fig. 242). Meanwhile in Edinburgh the Celtic Revival flowered under the inspirational leadership of the biologist and utopian visionary Patrick Geddes. Geddes's socialist leanings inspired him to support the Edinburgh Social Union, whose programme of urban renewal resulted in the outstanding murals devised by

Fig. 241 **Margaret Macdonald, *The May Queen***

Macdonald was inspired by Celtic folklore, imagery and symbolism. Working in a variety of media she shows here the crowning of the May Queen, seen as an ancient Celtic goddess of fertility and growth, who symbolized the coming of summer. The panel was exhibited at the Vienna Secession in 1900, along with Charles Rennie Mackintosh's *The Wassail*.

1900
Gesso, hessian, scrim, twine, glass beads, thread, mother-of-pearl, tin leaf; 158.8 x 457 cm
Kelvingrove Art Gallery and Museum, Glasgow

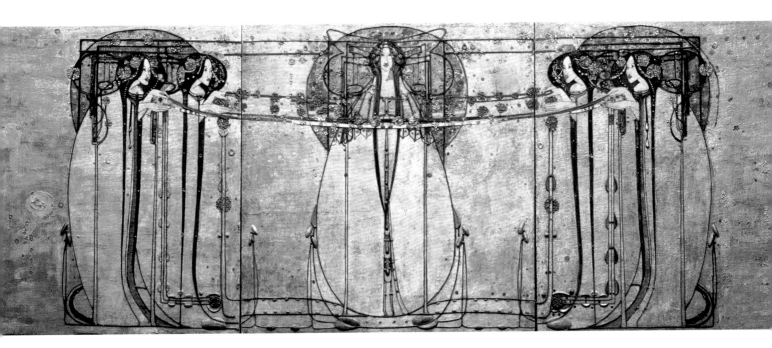

Fig. 242 **Margaret Gilmour, *Alms dish***

Gilmour designed a number of alms dishes of this type, often for domestic rather than ecclesiastical use. This particular dish is embellished with Celtic knot work and coloured enamel roundels, creating a complex and highly decorative design.

c. 1900
Brass and enamel; 58.2 x 58.2 cm
Glasgow Museums

Phoebe Traquair for the Sick Children's Mortuary Chapel, St Mary's Cathedral Song School and the Catholic Apostolic Church in Mansfield Place, Edinburgh.[53] As early as 1885, stimulated by Insular enamel work and medieval manuscripts, Traquair employed brilliant colour and gold leaf as well as foliated initials in her studies for the mortuary chapel scheme (fig. 243), which explores the theme of the journey of the soul to Heaven. In 1889 the art historian Gerard Baldwin Brown described the murals as a piece of 'illumination enlarged'.[54]

Geddes commissioned male and female artist-designers to paint decorative mural schemes, invited artists and scientists to his annual 'summer schools' in Edinburgh, and encouraged Scottish and French writers and artists to contribute to his creative journal, *The Evergreen: a Northern Seasonal*, published in four volumes from 1895 to 1896.[55] The journal included Celtic-inspired illustrations and head and tailpieces, probably based on sources such as J. Romilly Allen's *Notes on Celtic Ornament* (1885).[56] *The Evergreen* also included translations of Breton and Irish legends and the poetry and writings of Fiona Macleod, the Celtic alter ego of the writer William Sharp. Geddes himself contributed an essay entitled 'The Celtic Renascence', a plea for cultural creativity and national revival, underscored by more than a touch of social utopianism.

Among the most striking images in the first edition of the journal (the *Book of Spring*) is John Duncan's *Anima Celtica* (fig. 267), which celebrates cultural revival and the creativity of the Celtic (specifically female, instinctive) imagination. A woman embodying the 'Celtic Mind' or 'Celtic Soul' has conjured up ancient Gaelic tales on regenerative themes, such as the 'Birth

of Ossian' and the 'Awakening of Cúchulainn'.[57] Spirals and interlace emerge from an incense burner, dividing each scene, and the illustration is punctuated by a variety of supposedly 'Celtic' objects: a late Bronze Age sword, an Iron Age armlet, an early medieval penannular brooch, and a later Highland dirk (figs 266–7).[58] A closely related oil painting by Duncan[59] features a different selection of scenes from Irish mythology, including 'Deirdre of the Sorrows' and the 'Children of Lir', painted in a style that owes much to the French symbolist Pierre Puvis de Chavannes, whose work Duncan had admired in Paris.[60]

Geddes's friend, the painter Charles Mackie, designed the cover for *The Evergreen* with a Celtic 'Tree of Life' motif, symbolizing creative evolution, revival and interconnectedness. The Tree of Life soon became a *leitmotif* of the Celtic Revival. Traquair created a stylized Tree of Life on the embossed wing panels of her *Motherhood* triptych of 1901, and in 1906 Alexander Fisher produced a Tree of Life 'Morse' in gold, emerald and enamel.[61] Certain aspects of Fisher's work are comparable to that of Traquair, who was taught by one of Fisher's pupils, Lady Carmichael. Like Traquair, Fisher created beautifully designed objects inset with brilliant coloured enamels, such as his *Triptych in the Form of a Celtic Shrine* of *c.* 1903 (fig. 244).

Fig. 243 (opposite) Phoebe Traquair,
Three Studies for the Decoration of the
first Mortuary Chapel, the Royal Hospital
for Sick Children, Edinburgh

Traquair employed bright colours and gold leaf
in her designs, which combine Celtic, Byzantine,
Gothic and Baroque features. These three
studies depict 'An angel escorting an angel
towards heaven', 'The Virgin and Child with
angels' and 'The Holy Spirit awakening the spirit
of the deceased'. The studies are enclosed in
a frame designed by Traquair and inscribed in
her hand, 'For he that will save his life shall lose
it and he that will lose his life for My sake shall
find it'.

1885
The three studies: 24.8 x 20 cm;
25.1 x 21.9 cm; and 24.8 x 20 cm
Oil and gold leaf on canvas
Scottish National Gallery, Edinburgh

Fig. 244 (opposite, below) Alexander Fisher,
Triptych in the form of a Celtic Shrine

This enamelled triptych shows St Patrick
converting Eithne the fair and Fedelm the red,
the beautiful daughters of the fifth-century King
Laoghaire (or Léogaire). The girls were tutored
by two druids at Cruachan, the ancient palace
of the kings of Connaught.

c. 1903
Gilt brass inlaid with silver and painted enamels; H 45.5 cm
National Museum of Ireland, Dublin

Fig. 245 (above right) Archibald Knox,
Tea Set

Knox designed this tea set in 1903 for the firm
of Liberty & Co. in London. The teapot, milk
jug, sugar bowl and tray are all decorated with
Celtic interlace and stylized Honesty plants,
which were favoured by designers due to their
shape and symbolism.

Pewter; pot H 21.6 cm
British Museum, London

The Manx designer Archibald Knox (of Scottish parentage) also
incorporated Tree of Life motifs into some of his designs for Liberty's of
London.[62] From around 1898 he produced designs for Liberty's 'Cymric'
range of silver (from *Cymru*, the ancient name for Wales), along with Jessie
M. King, Oliver Baker, Kate Harris and Arthur Silver. His designs included
'runic' clasps, chalices, bowls, tea sets (fig. 245) and the occasional vase (fig.
15), often decorated with coloured enamels and stones. His 'Tudric' range
clocks were inspired by the carved stone crosses on the Isle of Man and his
jewellery designs frequently incorporated Celtic interlace, but in general his
highly abstracted designs make only subtle reference to the Celtic ornament
that inspired them. Some of the titles of his early designs for bowls *c.* 1900
point to his Manx origins: the 'Fergus' (a thirteenth-century Isle of Man
king), for example, and the 'Somerled', named after a mid-twelfth-century
warlord of Norse-Gaelic origin who ruled the Kingdom of the Isles,
including the Isle of Man, the Scottish Hebrides and the islands of the Firth
of Clyde.[63]

Fig. 246 **John Duncan, *Tristan and Isolde***

The legend of Tristan and Isolde addressed
the universal theme of adulterous love and was
extremely popular at the end of the nineteenth
century. Decorated with Celtic knotwork, the
lovers' costumes suggest the iridescence of
Insular manuscripts as well as the vivid colours
of Modernist painting.

1912
Tempera on canvas; 76.6 x 76.6 cm
City Art Centre, Edinburgh

Celtic heroes and British nationalism

Archibald Knox was a first cousin of Alexander Carmichael, author of the
Carmina Gadelica (1900), a compendium of Gaelic prayers, hymns and poetry,
amassed over forty years. In the late nineteenth and early twentieth centuries,
translations and versions of Celtic poetry and mythology by the likes of Lady
Charlotte Guest in Wales, Marie Henri d'Arbois de Jubainville in France, W.
B. Yeats and Lady Gregory in Ireland, and Fiona Macleod in Scotland gave
inspiration to artists such as John Duncan, who produced a whole series of
paintings influenced by Celtic mythology in the period leading up to the First
World War.[64] Among the most striking of these is his *Tristan and Isolde* (1912)
(fig. 246), in which the Cornish knight Tristan and the Irish princess Isolde
prepare to drink the love potion that will cause their downfall.

The proliferation of Celtic literature resulted from a wave of
nationalism that swept across Britain (and indeed Europe) in the late
nineteenth century. This heightened consciousness of national identity was
partly a reaction to industrialization, and to the potential homogenization
of British culture, but also emerged from long-standing debates around
language and the concept of a Celtic 'race', a notion fostered above all by

Fig. 247 **Sir Hubert von Herkomer,**
Hwfa Môn, Archdruid of Wales

Commonly known by his bardic name 'Hwfa
Môn', the Welsh clergyman Rowland Williams
(1823–1905) served as Archdruid of the
National Eisteddfod from 1895 to 1905.
Herkomer was fascinated by the Gorsedd
ceremony and in 1899 designed the Grand
Sword, which is still in use today.

1896
Pencil and watercolour set in gilded hinged frame with
mistletoe and snake carvings; watercolour 59 x 37 cm
National Museum Wales

the poet and cultural critic Matthew Arnold.[65] Historians engaged enthusiastically in the debate and often cast the Celts in a negative light. In his seven-volume *History of Scotland*, published in 1870, John Hill Burton described the Celts (defined as Gauls, Welsh, Irish and Scottish Gaels) as a degenerate race, lazy and improvident.[66] They were also associated with pagan rather than Christian practices and were seen as feckless and intransigent in contrast to the disciplined and rational-thinking Teutons. Indeed, some Scottish Lowland commentators were at pains to dissociate themselves from the Celtic north: in his *The Origin of the Aryans* (1889), for example, the Reverend Isaac Taylor went so far as to boast that the Lowland Scot was even 'more purely Teutonic than the English'.[67]

More positively, however, the Celts were regarded by many as a creative and even noble race. 'In a prosaic and utilitarian age', wrote one commentator, 'the idealism of the Celt is an ennobling and uplifting influence both on literature and life'.[68] Artists, writers and musicians identified with the reimagined Celtic past and enthusiastically adopted and promoted a shared sense of Celtic identity.

A growing desire to preserve ancient customs and languages, as well as vernacular crafts, poetry and music, resulted in the establishment of disparate Celtic groups and associations, such as the Royal Celtic Society, founded in Scotland in 1820, and the Pan-Celtic Society, formed in Dublin in 1888.[69] In Wales the medieval festival of music and poetry known as the Eisteddfod was revived as early as 1792 by Iolo Morganwg. The unlikely setting for the revival of this ancient ceremony (known as the Gorsedd) was Primrose Hill in London, where a group of Welsh bards gathered at the autumn equinox.[70] The Welsh Gorsedd became a regular event and similar ceremonies were held in Cornwall and Brittany. The first Inter-Celtic 'Congress' was held at the Eisteddfod in Abergavenny in 1838, but it was not until 1858 that John Williams ab Ithel held the first 'national' Eisteddfod at Llangollen, complete with music, poetry and dance.

A number of Celtic Revival objects were produced in association with the Eisteddfod and the sculptor William Goscombe John modelled the medals that were awarded as prizes. A keen supporter of the annual event was the artist Hubert von Herkomer who, in 1896, depicted the Archdruid of Wales, Hwfa Môn, in full regalia (fig. 247). Wales was not the only country to celebrate its Celtic origins and this period culminated in the first triennial Pan-Celtic Congress, held in Dublin in 1901, at Abergavenny in 1904 and in Edinburgh in 1907, including representatives from the six Celtic 'nations': Scotland, Wales, Ireland, the Isle of Man, Cornwall and Brittany.[71]

National identity was also celebrated through depictions of patriotic 'Celtic' heroes such as Tewdric Mawr, Cúchulainn or Caratacus. The Welsh king Tewdric Mawr was ruler of Gwent and Morgannwg. In 610 he successfully defended his realm against the invading Saxons, but was mortally wounded. John Evan Thomas's *Death of Tewdric Mawr* (fig. 248), the original plaster for which was shown at the Abergavenny Eisteddfod in

1848, shows the warrior in his dying moments, comforted by his daughter Marchell, while an ancient bard sings and plays his harp.

The equivalent in Irish visual culture is Oliver Sheppard's moving bronze *The Dying Cúchulain* (1911) (fig. 249), which shows the mythical Irish hero, fatally wounded in battle and bound to the Clochafarmore Stone, like Christ on the cross. On his shoulder sits Morrígan, the Celtic goddess of war, awaiting the moment that his life is finally extinguished. This image of the dying Cúchulainn became a metaphor for the resolve of the Irish people, desirous of independence from the British: in 1935, at the request of political leader Éamon De Valera, the statue was moved to the General Post Office in Dublin, as a national memorial to the 1916 Easter Rising.

Cúchulainn was also adopted by Geddes's circle in Edinburgh as a more universal pan-Celtic hero and a symbol of cultural renaissance. Duncan depicted *The Awakening of Cuchulain* both in *The Evergreen* and in his mural scheme for Ramsay Lodge. He also produced a drawing, now in the Scottish National Gallery (fig. 250), which depicts this Ossianic figure as a wonderful fusion of mythical and archaeological sources. Fearless and strong, his chiselled features and interlaced hair are seemingly carved from Pictish stone, while his tartan plaid is secured by an ornate penannular brooch based on early medieval examples.

English Iron Age heroes such as Caradog or Caratacus (commonly termed 'Caractacus'), king of the Trinovantes, and Boudica, queen of the Iceni, also enjoyed a revival, especially during the Victorian period. Such figures allowed artists to promote British imperialism through a historical reimagining of the nation's patriotic past since, in their different ways, they symbolized the bravery and tenacity of the British people and their determination to protect their native land against foreign (Roman) invasion.

Caratacus was son of the Catuvellaunian king Cunobelinus. He ruled over a large part of southern Britain and from AD 43 to 47 led the local resistance against the Roman general Aulus Plautius. He was eventually forced to withdraw into southern Wales, from where, according to the Roman historian Tacitus, he led the tribes of the Silures and Ordovices against forces headed by the governor Ostorius Scapula.[72] In AD 50 he was defeated and fled north, only to be handed over to the Romans by Cartimandua, queen of the Brigantes. In Rome he was sentenced to death, but persuaded the emperor Claudius to spare his life. Caratacus's speech to Claudius was a popular subject in late eighteenth-century art, painted by Fuseli and Blake and captured in numerous prints. In the Victorian period Caratacus was regarded increasingly as an inspirational figure, symbolizing national loyalty and patriotism: in 1862 a horse named Caractacus was winner of the Epsom Derby, and in 1898 Sir Edward Elgar composed his uplifting *Caractacus* cantata, a wonderfully romantic choral piece celebrating the British chieftain and his defence of the nation.[73]

The most characteristic nineteenth-century image of the Iron Age hero was by the Irish sculptor John Henry Foley, who later sculpted Prince

Fig. 248 (opposite) John Evan Thomas and William Meredyth Thomas, *Death of Tewdrig Mawr, King of Gwent*

This was one of the most significant works of art to result from the Welsh national revival and the largest work exhibited by Elkington, Mason & Co. at the Great Exhibition in 1851. The figure of the bard derives from the well-known print by De Loutherbourg (fig. 230).

1848–56
Bronze; 167 x 127 x 63 cm
National Museum Wales

Fig. 249 (opposite below) Oliver Sheppard, *The Dying Cúchulain*

Sheppard's iconic sculpture was partly inspired by the success of *Cuchulain of Muirthemne*, a version of the Cúchulainn legends, based on oral and written legends, collected and translated by Lady Gregory and published in 1902.

1911
Bronze
General Post Office, Dublin

Fig. 250 (right) John Duncan, *Cucchulain*

The Irish hero Cúchulainn was the central figure of the Ulster cycle (of the early centuries AD), but also featured in Scottish and Manx folklore. A symbol of tenacity, stoicism and nationhood, he was a major figure in the Celtic Revival of the late nineteenth century.

c. 1917
Pencil on paper; 37.5 x 27.5 cm
Scottish National Gallery, Edinburgh

CUCHULAINN
I care not though I last but a day if my name and my fame are a power for ever!

Albert for the Albert Memorial in London. In 1851 he was commissioned by the Corporation of London to produce sculptures of Caratacus and the nymph Egeria – the legendary counsellor and consort of Numa Pompilius, second king of Rome – for the Egyptian Sculpture Hall at the Mansion House.[74] In the finished work (fig. 251), *Caractacus* stands with legs astride and his left arm raised aloft, in a defiant gesture of command, while his right hand grasps his battle axe and his shield rests by his side.

With Victoria on the throne, Boudica also enjoyed a revival and was used to promote the empire and to encourage loyalty to the monarchy.[75] Boudica was queen of the Iceni, a British tribe who lived in the area that now covers Norfolk, parts of Suffolk and Cambridgeshire. She successfully led a revolt against the Romans, destroying Colchester, London and St Albans, until she was finally defeated by the Roman governor Gaius Suetonius Paullinus and probably took her own life.

'Boudica' was said to mean 'victory', providing a symbolic semantic link between Queen Victoria and the Celtic queen. Among the earliest images was Henry Courtney Selous's *Boudica Harangued by the Iceni* of 1843, a cartoon for the competition to decorate Westminster Hall.[76] The English sculptor Thomas Thorneycroft – who had made a larger than life-size equestrian statue of Victoria for the 1851 Great Exhibition – was later commissioned by Prince Albert to create a monumental bronze *Boadicea and her Daughters*. The finished piece was inspired by lines from Tacitus,[77] and also by Tennyson's 1864 poem *Boadicea*, in which the Icenian queen stands 'loftily charioted . . . maddening all that heard her in her fierce volubility'. The ambitious bronze sculpture, now on the Thames Embankment, was cast only in 1902, a year after Victoria's death. It features Boudica standing tall, brandishing her spear and driving a chariot, complete with rearing horses, and remains to this day an enduring example of British imperial propaganda (fig. 252).

Fig. 251 **John Henry Foley, *Caractacus***

Although adopted in the Victorian period as a symbol of British courage, Caractacus can also be considered Wales's first national hero because he used Wales as a base for resistance against the Romans. His idealized form and commanding pose find their source in Roman imperial sculpture.

1859
Marble; H 266 cm
Guildhall Library and Art Gallery

Fig. 252 **Thomas Thorneycroft, *Boadicea and her Daughters***

Thorneycroft worked on the sculpture from 1856 until just before his death in 1885. Boadicea bears some resemblance to the young Queen Victoria and Prince Albert lent two horses as models. The chariot was based on Roman, rather than British or Iceni prototypes.

1902
Bronze
Westminster Pier, London Embankment

The legends of Britain's primitive past provided inspiration in multifarious ways to the artists of the Celtic Revival, who responded very differently, often according to specific national agendas. In general both Wales and Scotland took a politically neutral route, celebrating their origins through the revival of myth, poetry, art and song, but they were also concerned to establish an identity distinct from their English neighbour. In England the Celtic past was used frequently for propaganda purposes, to promote and celebrate the empire; while in Ireland, the land of the Celtic heroes, the Tuatha Dé Danann, the revival took a political turn, as the Irish people fought to establish their independence. The debates that surround the Celtic Revival – issues of nationalism, identity, 'race' and notions of 'authenticity' – are still entirely relevant today and perhaps explain why this period in art history continues to fascinate.

Fig. 253 **The Gundestrup cauldron**

Discovered in a Danish bog in 1891, the silver panels on the Gundestrup cauldron are richly decorated with scenes from Iron Age life and legends. There is no other object quite like it.

Gundestrup, Jutland, Denmark *c.* 150–50 BC
Silver; D 69 cm
National Museum of Denmark, Copenhagen

Chapter 11

Celtic Arts in the Long Term:
Continuity, Change and Connections

Fraser Hunter, Martin Goldberg, Julia Farley and Ian Leins

Silver from the bog

The changeable weather made for unpleasant working, and the labourers cutting peat at Gundestrup in northern Jutland (Denmark) on 28 May 1891 were starting to think of home. Suddenly, a spade struck something hard and shiny. The workers gathered round, eager to see what they had found. As the peat was cleared away, the edge of a massive silver cauldron was revealed, with a series of decorated plates carefully stacked inside it. The Gundestrup cauldron had returned to this world (figs 253–8 and 260).[1]

Few single items from ancient Europe have proved as contentious as this cauldron. Where was it made? When was it made? What did the magnificent, puzzling decoration represent? Opinions broadly divide in two.[2] Many people see it as a western European Celtic object, and identify among the imagery Celtic gods like the antlered Cernunnos, or scenes known from Irish early medieval heroic tales.[3] But others see different roots, and argue its style and technology place its origin in south-eastern Europe, the world of the Thracians.[4] From this perspective, different gods can be recognized on the cauldron, such as Kybele, Hercules and Orpheus from the eastern Mediterranean. It seems that you can find more or less anything you look for in its scenes. It probably dates to *c.* 150–50 BC, although this too is debated.

The cauldron is often used as an icon of Celtic art. No book on the Celts is complete without it; every exhibition desires it. It is familiar from a hundred book covers and websites. Gundestrup is enchanting. And yet it is not Celtic, or, at least, not just Celtic. It brings us back to some of the key topics we have looked at in this book.

Let us start with a description. The cauldron is a massive, imposing vessel. It dominates the darkened room in Copenhagen's Nationalmuseet where it is usually displayed. The shallow bowl that forms the base is hammered from a single sheet of silver. A framework fastened to its top edge supported a double skin of ornate silver plaques, so that both the inside and outside were decorated (fig. 256). This was not swirling, ambiguous early Celtic art: here the style was more narrative and the figures more recognizable,[5] although their meaning remains a mystery.

First the viewer sees a row of gods glaring from the outer panels of the cauldron. Originally there were eight square plates, each with the bust of a deity in relief, but only seven survive: four males and three females (figs 254–5). Their staring eyes once held glass insets and parts of the decoration are gilded. The ornate hairstyles, beards and moustaches are carefully hammered up from the silver, with detail chased in from the front. They are naked, although some wear torcs. They must be gods rather than humans for they perform superhuman acts, such as grasping a deer in each hand; human figures around them are diminutive by comparison. Animals, real and fantastic, flank the deities: dogs, deer, eagles and boars; winged horses, double-headed wolves and mythical beasts with horses' heads, wings and serpents' tails.

Fig. 254 **Outer plate from the Gundestrup cauldron**

A large male figure, perhaps a god, raises his arms in a symbolic gesture, the meaning of which is now lost. The 'jumping' posture of the smaller female figure on the right is similar to that of a female warrior on the cauldron base (fig. 260), and may have carried a particular significance, or have been connected to a specific individual or story.

Gundestrup, Jutland, Denmark *c.* 150–50 BC
Silver; H 21 cm
National Museum of Denmark, Copenhagen

CELTIC ARTS IN THE LONG TERM

Fig. 255 Outer plates from the cauldron

The plaques from the outside of the cauldron show oversized male and female figures, probably gods and goddesses, in a range of scenes. One goddess (opposite, top left) is having her hair braided by a small human figure. A god with a carefully groomed beard (below right) towers over the two stags he holds in his raised arms. Another god (opposite, top right) holds fantastical serpents, while below him a double-headed beast devours small human figures.

Gundestrup, Jutland, Denmark *c.* 150–50 BC
Silver; H 18.5–21 cm
National Museum of Denmark, Copenhagen

As you approach the cauldron, the interior reveals five rectangular plaques with more complex scenes (figs 256–8). Two of them have god-busts similar to those on the outer frieze. A goddess is surrounded by animals: a wolf, a pair of fantastical griffins and two rather confused-looking elephants. A god and a warrior grasp a wheel while wolves (or lions?), griffins and a ram-horned snake surround them. Two further plaques (fig. 258, left) have narrative scenes. On one, three warriors kill three horned beasts, helped by hunting dogs. Another has a military scene with cavalry above and foot soldiers below, some wearing ornate boar- and bird-crested helmets. Three musicians bring up the rear, blowing animal-headed carnyces, as the foot soldiers and a dog approach a giant figure who dips (or drowns) a warrior in a bucket-like cauldron. Is this a sacrifice scene? Or bringing the dead back to life? Are the warriors transformed in the cauldron? Like so much else on the Gundestrup cauldron, there is no easy answer. The final plaque is less warlike (fig. 258, right). An antlered god sits in an odd pose, which suggests a knowledge of yogic practices.[6] He holds a torc and a ram-headed snake, while around him are a wide range of wild animals and a man riding a sea creature, set among patterns of leaves.

Fig. 256 (below) **Angled view of the cauldron**

The inner panels of the cauldron would have been hidden until the viewer was close. These larger panels show more complex narrative scenes.

Gundestrup, Jutland, Denmark *c.* 150–50 BC
Silver; D 69 cm
National Museum of Denmark, Copenhagen

Fig. 257 (opposite) **Inner plates from the cauldron**

Many of the inner panels show people or deities surrounded by wild animals and fantastical beasts.

Gundestrup, Jutland, Denmark *c.* 150–50 BC
Silver; H 21 cm
National Museum of Denmark, Copenhagen

Fig. 258 **Inner plates from the cauldron**

On one, three warriors or hunters and their hounds are
slaying three beasts, perhaps bulls (opposite, above).
Here, the leaf-like designs may represent blood, hinting at
a deeper meaning for this filler motif in the other panels.
Another panel (opposite, below) shows a martial scene, with
a horned snake above the three boar-headed war horns.
The last (above) shows an antlered god holding a horned
serpent surrounded by wild beasts and, curiously, a small
human figure riding a sea creature.

Gundestrup, Jutland, Denmark c. 150–50 BC
Silver; H 21 cm
National Museum of Denmark, Copenhagen

The drama of the vessel is not over. In its base, covering an area of ancient damage, is an ornate circular plate depicting a bullfight (fig. 260). A dying bull dominates the picture, with a female warrior brandishing the sword that has despatched it. Three dogs circle the beast: one triumphant, one wary, one dying from its wounds.

The cauldron is a visual feast. You can understand why scholars have been dazzled by its complexity and have sought all kinds of explanations for it. But this puzzle defies easy solutions. This is because it cannot simply be labelled 'Celtic'. Recent research has made a convincing case that the cauldron was manufactured in south-east Europe, probably in Bulgaria or Romania. Here, around the Danube, groups using Celtic styles from western and central Europe came into contact with local Thracians, who had their own distinctive art styles.[7] Silver is typical of elaborate metalwork in south-east Europe in the late Iron Age (fig. 259), but its use is extremely unusual for Iron Age Celtic art objects. The style finds many parallels in Thracian art, both for repoussé figural scenes and in minor details such as how the shoes or the animal pelts were depicted. But the overall design is more than just Thracian. We have seen that some of the objects shown, like torcs, were widespread across Iron Age Europe, but others were most common in Celtic art: the carnyx, the ram-headed snake, the god holding a wheel and the antlered god. Other elements take us into Asia, like the elephants or the yogic pose of the antlered god. This one object shows artistic influences from Celtic, Thracian and Asian styles, was made in south-east Europe, and ended up in a Danish bog. We are dealing here with a connected world, not just a Celtic one.

Fig. 260 (opposite) **Basal plate from the cauldron**

The base of the Gundestrup cauldron is decorated with another bull-slaying scene, this time depicting a female warrior and three hounds.

Gundestrup, Jutland, Denmark. *c.* 150–50 BC
Silver; D 25 cm
National Museum of Denmark, Copenhagen

Fig. 259 **Thracian mount decorated in a similar style to the Gundestrup cauldron**

The style of the designs on the cauldron suggests a connection to Thracian silversmithing traditions. The cauldon may have been produced in south-east Europe, like this silver mount discovered in Romania.

Sǎliştea, jud. Alba, Romania 50 BC–AD 50
Silver; H 16.8 cm
Kunsthistorisches Museum, Vienna

Connections and variations

Our story has tracked decorated objects across Europe. At times they were widespread and at others much more regional. The earliest Celtic art originated in the fifth century BC, in various centres from western France to the Czech Republic. It was temperate Europe's first complex art. At its greatest extent in the third century BC, related styles stretched from Ireland to Bulgaria, from Denmark to Italy (Chapters 3–4). In the second and first centuries BC, Britain and Ireland developed different styles from the rest of Europe (Chapter 5). This difference between the islands and the mainland ran through the rest of our story, with an increasingly tight geographical focus on the north and west of Britain and Ireland (Chapters 6–10), although the objects were still part of a broader European story.

These arts were no mere decoration, but a potent skin on an object that gave it extra significance. Early Celtic art was dominated by what look like abstract curves to our eyes (fig. 261). These reflect different ways of seeing the world, where creatures and plants lurked within these shapes. They also hint at different beliefs: a mythology lay behind these patterns, and an idea that they could protect the object and its user, and enchant or affect people who saw it (Chapter 2). The messages that were carried are largely lost to us. However, we can recognize complex meanings and allusions on early Christian decorated objects, where we have more historical background to help interpret them (Chapter 8). We must assume similar stories from the lost beliefs of prehistory lay behind Iron Age Celtic art.

Celtic art objects had power. They gave the user a status or importance. This was normally a very socially restricted art, for the few rather than the many, because it was complex to make and to understand. At times, certain styles broke out of these social constraints: for example, decorated brooches became relatively common in the fifth to third centuries BC, when they may have been seen as amulets. Later, during the early Roman period in Britain, Celtic art motifs were used widely, especially on jewellery, and such embellishment became much more a part of people's everyday lives. But this was a short-lived democratization. In the early medieval period, decoration moved once more onto rare and special objects like lavish brooches and church metalwork.

A thread running through the story of Celtic art is the entanglement between the Mediterranean and temperate Europe. The reinvention of new Celtic art styles often occurred at times of contact and change, and Mediterranean cultures were frequently the catalyst. The art of the Greeks and Etruscans was a vital stimulus for the earliest Celtic art in the fifth century BC. The first Celtic coins of the third century BC transformed Greek portraits and figures into fantastical stylized images. Increasingly naturalistic depictions of the second and first centuries BC were a response to the image-world of Rome. The threat of Roman invasion in the first century AD stimulated a flourishing of Celtic art in Britain and Ireland, perhaps to

Fig. 261 **Sword scabbard terminal**

In the Iron Age and Roman period, Celtic art was often used to decorate martial equipment, such as this sword scabbard. The designs may have imparted powerful and protective qualities onto the object and its owner.

Mortonhall, Midlothian AD 50–150
Copper alloy; W 3.3 cm.
National Museums Scotland, Edinburgh

Fig. 262 **Zoomorphic spiral armlet**

The tradition of massive-style metalwork, which flourished in north-east Scotland during the Roman occupation of southern Britain, may have been a way for communities to emphasize their independent identities. This spiral armlet resembles a stylized double-headed serpent. The ends would once have been decorated with glass or enamel insets (see pp. 150–1).

Culbin Sands, Moray AD 50–150
Copper alloy, glass; H 8.9 cm
National Museums Scotland, Edinburgh

signal their difference from this alien culture (fig. 262). But this became more than an art of resistance to Rome. Artistic interplays within the Roman empire, between soldier and civilian, frontier and centre, led to new provincial styles in Britain that became the foundations of later Celtic art in the isles. In the centuries after Roman rule, Christian communities in early medieval Britain and Ireland still drew inspiration from Rome, the centre of this new religious world; this led to new artistic creations, merging classical and local styles. The long-term entwining of two worlds, north and south of the Alps, over 1,500 years sparked with creativity.

But the Mediterranean was not the sole focus for peoples north of the Alps. There was no simple dependence on southern inspiration: it came from many sources. External and local images were repeatedly combined and reimagined, from western Germany in the fifth century BC to western Britain and Ireland in the seventh century AD. We should not see this imaginative fusion as a 'Celtic thing', though: the fantastical animals of the Scythians on the Eurasian steppe and the twisting beasts of early Germanic art are examples of similar reinventions and creations. These wider patterns also remind us to look further afield for comparisons and connections. In the fifth century BC, the monstrous creatures and swirling patterns of Celtic art were part of a much wider Eurasian phenomenon (Chapter 2).[8] In the fifth to seventh centuries AD, people in northern Germany and Scandinavia drew inspiration from their own encounters with the Roman empire and developed distinctive regional styles.[9] These in turn motivated craftworkers in Britain and Ireland during the 'Insular fusion' of the seventh century AD, with 'Celtic', 'Germanic' and 'classical' influences transformed into a new Christian art. Northern contacts played a key role again in the ninth to eleventh centuries AD, as Viking invasion and settlement hit Britain and Ireland. In the north and west, beyond the blood and violence, there were artistic responses, with the animal-based art of the Viking world and the interlace of the Christian west forming fresh styles.[10]

Contacts and the possibilities they created were a recurring stimulus for innovative styles of decoration, which were transformed in new settings as people responded to changing worlds. But the old was a stimulus as well as the new. In the Celtic art styles of the Iron Age, older motifs were repeatedly reused and reinvented.[11] In Britain and Ireland, the Celtic arts of the early medieval period were drawn upon and reimagined for over a millennium, up to the present day.

A view from Europe's edge

In recent years, Britain has had rather an ambivalent relationship to the wider story of Celtic art. Classic studies of the topic integrated British material as a key element,[12] but this has changed in recent years. The 'Celtosceptic' reaction in Britain, a movement beginning in the 1980s, critiqued the idea of the Celts and stressed local developments, leading to a focus on the British Iron Age and its regional variants.[13] There were clear and significant differences between the Iron Ages of Britain and the Continent in such fundamental issues as the typical form of houses: round in Britain, rectangular on the Continent. Yet these variations and local developments are only part of the picture. Celtic arts clearly show far-reaching links. These islands need to be treated as another region of Europe, not as an isolated margin that can be studied separately. The use of this art in Britain and Ireland can only be understood when viewed in a broader European context.

Let us try to paint a picture of Celtic arts as experienced from our westerly perspective. Their origins lay elsewhere; Britain and Ireland were on the edge of the early developments, and people probably saw only the occasional piece of decorated material in the fifth and fourth centuries BC, from contacts up Atlantic seaways or over the Channel. The story changed markedly in the third century BC: the first great moment of Celtic art in Britain and Ireland. The designs on finds such as the Torrs pony cap (fig. 86), the Kirkburn and Ulster scabbards (figs 61 and 69), and the Wandsworth shield bosses (figs 31, 39 and 62) are regional versions of widespread trans-European styles. Here Britain was very much part of developments that spread across most of Europe: one of many regions creating their own local versions of Celtic art in an increasingly connected Continent (Chapter 3).

But societies across the Continent changed in the second and first centuries BC, as the shadow of the expanding Roman world fell over them. From France through southern Germany and Bohemia to Hungary, more substantial groups began to emerge from the previous small-scale societies, with an increasing focus on markets, big settlements and large-scale craft production. The earlier, complicated art styles fell from use. Some complex art shifted onto mass-produced coinage, but styles became simpler and more influenced by the Roman world. Things were different in Britain (Chapter 5). Societies in the south and east of England shared habits with their neighbours over the water: the production and use of coinage, for example. But the earlier curvilinear styles persisted and developed across much of southern Britain as far north as Yorkshire.

The Roman invasion of Britain in the first century AD was a time of great change, though more so in some areas than others. The extreme south and east had been under heavy Roman influence since the invasions of Julius Caesar in 55–54 BC. They had effectively been drawn into a Roman world for a century by the time of the invasion in AD 43, and Celtic art had been smothered by versions of classical naturalism.[14] But elsewhere in Britain, the invasion sparked a response, not just in how these societies reacted (whether to fight, deal or submit), but also in their visual world. Celtic art exploded across most of the country, often in areas where it had never really taken root before, such as the north. This may have begun as a reaction to Rome in order to emphasize local independence, but it continued

Fig. 263 Ornate painted pottery

Richly decorated painted pots from France
epitomize the ability of Iron Age artists to
suggest shapes with just a few simple lines and
the play of different textures across the surface
(see pp. 100–1 and fig. 87).

Clermont-Ferrand, Puy-de-Dôme, France 150–100 BC
Ceramic; H of right pot 25 cm
Le Musée Bargoin (Musée Archaeologique), Clermont
Ferrand

into the world of occupied Roman Britain (Chapter 6). People used this
newly created art as a way of marking who they were in this changing world:
not just Roman, but people with a different, longer history.

It was in this world of the Roman frontiers that change arose once
more. New materials from the empire – especially silver – became
important, and people drew on a range of influences, from local to
international, to create the frontier styles of the late Roman period (Chapter
7). Many of the seeds for later Celtic art in Britain and Ireland – designs
such as spirals or triskeles, and the use of silver – were sown in these late
Roman styles.

The collapse of Roman government in western Europe in the fifth century AD set societies in turmoil again. Two factors were key in Britain. The first was the invasions, settlements and influences from the Germanic Anglo-Saxon world, initially into southern and eastern England. The second was the spread of Christianity from its Roman roots, surviving beyond the former frontiers, outlasting its imperial origins and going on to play an important part in the conversion of the Anglo-Saxon kingdoms. In northern and western Britain and Ireland, one effect of these upheavals was the fusion of local, Mediterranean and Germanic styles into a new early medieval art style: with its interlace and spirals, today it has become the most widely recognized form of 'Celtic art' in Britain (Chapter 8). But this was not just some local deviancy on the edge of the known world: it was a regional version of a pan-European phenomenon, where art was used for the glorification of the Christian God. In turn this British and Irish art style influenced communities on the Continent when it was taken there by missionaries.

This hybrid, mixed, early medieval Insular style became the dominant artistic influence over the next millennium, reinvented and reimagined in northern Britain and Ireland by successive generations of craftworkers up to the present day (Chapters 9–10). Under Viking influence an interlace-dominated style developed in the lands around the Irish Sea. Versions of this were drawn upon during the later medieval period in these areas, as powerful leaders consciously harked back to their past, stimulated by the visible artistic heritage of ancient stone crosses and surviving religious reliquaries. But this was a shallow past, not a deep one, looking back to surviving objects just a few hundred years old, but not to the depths of the Iron Age. The art we leave our story with is very different in appearance

Fig. 264 **Zoomorphic scabbard terminal** (detail)

The detail on this sword fitting from the St Ninian's Isle treasure shows a vicious, fanged beast with lolling tongue, carefully decorated with scrollwork and geometric motifs drawn from the late Roman world. (See figs 187 and 190 and pp. 193–5.)

St Ninian's Isle, Shetland c. AD 800
Silver, glass; neck W 1.3 cm
National Museums Scotland, Edinburgh

Fig. 265 **Carnyx players on the Gundestrup cauldron**

The Gundestrup cauldron shows Iron Age objects such as carnyces (war horns) in use.

Gundestrup, Jutland, Denmark. *c.* 150–50 BC
Silver; H of carnyx players 14 cm
National Museum of Denmark, Copenhagen

from the one with which we started: a reminder again of why our emphasis has been on *different* Celtic arts, and how much we strain the word 'Celtic' if we stretch it too far.

This long-term story is complex, and different parts of Britain and Ireland were involved at different times. But moments of contact with other cultures were frequently the key times of change. The relationship with other parts of Europe is also an important element in our islands' story. Britain and Ireland were always connected to a wider world; the Celtic arts that developed here were dynamic arts of fusion and creativity, not stylistic fossils preserved in an isolated fringe of Europe.

Simplicity and complexity

We noted in Chapter 1 the complexities that lie behind the apparently simple word 'Celt'. The Gundestrup cauldron exemplifies this: it is often called Celtic, but was made beyond the eastern edge of the Celtic world and buried far to its north, using an unusual material (silver) and showing exotic curiosities such as elephants. Yet it includes many of the objects we have seen in these pages – torcs, carnyces, weaponry, cauldrons, chariot parts – which are normally considered Celtic (fig. 265). This one find emphasizes many of the problems with the term 'Celtic': it may provide a label, but behind this lurk degrees of complexity that make a single word inadequate. There never was a 'pure' Celtic form: everything was a mixture, a developing idea or a reinvention. From one end of Europe to another, artistic styles were shared at certain periods, but clear imports or identical objects are rare. Closer inspection shows modifications and alterations: local variations and interpretations rather than imports. There were real connections, links and shared habits across large areas of Europe at various points over 1,000 years or more, but there was no single art style, no single culture, no single people. Ancient arts, languages and identities are separate strands of evidence that are given the name 'Celtic', but this is a modern term, not the legacy of a unified ancient Celtic past.

One could argue that the words 'Celt' and 'Celtic' have become too broad-ranging to be useful, but they are difficult to avoid because they have been so widely used over the last 400 years for different materials, evidence and concepts. They are embedded in people's minds. They were also widely used in the ancient world, again with little clarity or precision. People have been talking about the Celts for 2,500 years now, with varying degrees of success. And something does lurk behind the word, some hint of ancient connectivity. So we stick with the words we have, but they need qualifiers and context. The idea of 'Celtic arts' – plural – is subtly different from 'Celtic art' or the 'art of the Celts'. 'Celtic art' is a modern definition of temperate Europe's first complex art style. The 'art of the Celts' evokes an overly simplistic idea of a single people who lived across most of Europe, spoke the same language and decorated objects in the same way. This is a generalization with too many flaws in it. Studying different 'Celtic arts' seeks a way beyond this.

Popular views of Celts and Celtic art today are often based on generalization and stereotype, creating an imagined, romantic past. But as knowledge has developed and evidence has grown dramatically in recent decades, debate has sharpened and new ideas have appeared. We need to revise long-held ways of understanding the past, to comprehend some of the myths that have arisen about the Celts and to see what realities lie behind them. This approach is neither Celtosceptic nor Celtomaniac, but accepts both connections and differences, changing in space and time.[15] Our book has tried to take steps towards this. We have re-examined artefacts of great beauty, but they are more than just beautiful objects: they had a tremendous significance to people when they were made and used, and are of great importance now because they tell us about those distant times. We have tried to let those objects tell different stories for different times and places: different Celtic arts.

A Celtic spirit?

The fading paper from 1895 bears the black and white imprint of an artist's vision: 'Anima Celtica' – Celtic Soul (fig. 267).[16] A dark-haired woman looks beyond the picture's edge. Around her are scenes of a mythical past: standing stones from deep prehistory, the blind bard Ossian (invented by a Scottish patriot in the eighteenth century), the heroes Fingal and Cúchulainn from Irish tales of the early medieval period. The muse herself wears a penannular brooch (*c.* AD 800) and an armlet (*c.* AD 100). In front of her lies a Bronze Age sword (*c.* 800 BC), and an eighteenth-century dagger and bonnet with a white cockade, marking Jacobite sympathies (fig. 266).

The artist, John Duncan, has deliberately gathered 3,000 years of archaeology, history and myth from across Scotland and Ireland into a single timeless scene. For him, these objects were all symbols of Celts, used to create a work of art that spoke about contemporary nineteenth-century views of a pan-Celtic past and present.[17] For us, they represent different Celtic arts, different histories. Each element has its own stories that should not be thrown together so readily. Duncan's vision is too broad and yet also too narrow, for it ignores the rest of Europe, a key element of these decorated objects and the people who used them. In this, he reflected a wider modern view from these islands, where Celts were a phenomenon of the Atlantic fringe. Duncan reimagined the past to suit the present, a process that has taken place repeatedly since the Iron Age. But 'Celts' need to be set in a place and time in this past if we are to understand them, not bundled together into a single group. 'Celts' are complicated.

Fig. 266 (below) The objects that acted as inspiration for *Anima Celtica*

John Duncan's inspiration came from illustrations in the recently published *Catalogue of the National Museums of Antiquities of Scotland* (1892).

Clockwise from top left: Rogart (Highland); Belhelvie (Aberdeenshire); unprovenanced; Leadburn (Borders); Walston (South Lanarkshire)1000 BC–AD 1700.
Sword L 63.5 cm
National Museums Scotland, Edinburgh

Fig. 267 (opposite) John Duncan, *Anima Celtica*

This drawing, which appeared in Patrick Geddes's Celtic Revival journal, *The Evergreen*, shows a woman conjuring scenes from a mythical, romanticized Celtic past. The title means 'Celtic mind' or 'Celtic soul'. (See pp. 251–2.)

The Evergreen, Book of Spring, 1895
Image H 22.5 cm
National Museums Scotland, Edinburgh

List of Exhibited Objects

Objects exhibited are listed by broad period, then by country, city, lender and findspot. Inventory numbers are given at the end of each entry. The symbol * indicates the object was shown at the British Museum only; ** at the National Museum of Scotland only. List correct at time of going to press.

IRON AGE

Bulgaria: Sofia, National Museum
Mezek, Svilengrad, BG**: terrets and linch pins, copper alloy. 6411-6413 (see fig. 85)

Czech Republic: Prague, National Museum
Chýnov, Bohemia, CZ: anthropomorphic brooch, copper alloy. H1-229108 (see fig. 18)
Hořovičky, Bohemia, CZ: harness mount, copper alloy. H1-85028 (see fig. 48)
Jikev, Bohemia, CZ: shoe-shaped pot, ceramic. 224 681 (see fig. 33)
Kšely, Bohemia, CZ: anklet, copper alloy. H1-65845
Panenský Týnec, Bohemia, CZ: zoomorphic brooch, copper alloy. H1-111936
Plaňany, Bohemia, CZ: pair of anklets, copper alloy. H1-52425, 52426 (see fig. 58)
Přemýšlení, Bohemia, CZ: zoomorphic brooch, copper alloy. 65 779
Stradonice, Bohemia, CZ: anthropomorphic-handled sword terminal, copper alloy. H1-126977
Stradonice, Bohemia, CZ: decorated comb, bone. 212 509
Stradonice, Bohemia, CZ: statuette of a horn-blower, copper alloy. H1-105612
Želkovice, Bohemia, CZ: anthropomorphic belt hook, copper alloy. 201 825

Denmark: Copenhagen, National Museum of Denmark
Dronninglund, Jutland, DK: torc, gold. C1416
Gammelborg, Møn, DK: ball-terminal torc, copper alloy. MCDLXXII (see fig. 83)
Rødmose, Jutland, DK: crown torc, copper alloy. C18317 (see fig. 82)

France: Clermont-Ferrand, DRAC Auvergne
Clermont-Ferrand, Auvergne, F: painted pot, ceramic. 1103-9
Clermont-Ferrand, Auvergne, F: painted pot, ceramic. 1103-11 (see fig. 263)
Clermont-Ferrand, Auvergne, F: painted pot, ceramic. Gandaillat 2001 SRA 1189 (see fig. 87)

France: St-Germain-en-Laye, Musée d'Archéologie nationale
Euffigneix, Haute-Marne, F: statuette of man wearing torc, cast. 78243*
Mandeure, Doubs, F: bangles, glass. 52491.115, 136, 137
Mandeure, Doubs, F: beads, glass. 52491.289, 298, 301, 304, 405
Plouhinec, Morbihan, F: jar, ceramic. 72933
Roissy-en-France, Val-d'Oise, F: chariot yoke fittings, copper alloy. 89206.001-2, 004-6, 010, 012 (see fig. 56)
Thuisy, Marne, F: pot, ceramic. 27668

France: Toulouse, Musée Saint-Raymond
Fenouillet, Haute-Garonne, F: torc hoard, gold. 25045-25049 (see fig. 77)

Germany: Bonn, Rheinisches Landesmuseum
Niederzier, Nordrhein-Westfalen, D: torc, gold. 79.1348,03
Waldalgesheim, Rheinland-Pfalz, D: rich female grave group, gold, copper alloy, glass, cowrie shell. A 785 (see figs 50–3)

Germany: Glauberg, Keltenwelt am Glauberg
Glauberg, Hessen, D: warrior statue, cast. 1996/23/01-01K (for picture of original see fig. 3)

Germany: Stuttgart, Württembergisches Landesmuseum
Dürmentingen, Baden-Württemberg, D**: torc, iron. A30/265
Eislingen an der Fils, Baden-Württemberg, D**: knobbed-pommel sword, iron. 13791 (see fig. 73)
Gäufelden-Nebringen, Baden-Württemberg, D, grave 11: male warrior grave assemblage, iron, gold. F59/12 (see fig. 66)
Gäufelden-Nebringen, Baden-Württemberg, D, grave 14: neck-ring, copper alloy, glass. F59/14
Gäufelden-Nebringen, Baden-Württemberg, D, grave 4: female grave assemblage, copper alloy, iron, gold, glass. F59/6 (see fig. 79)

Giengen an der Brenz, Baden-Württemberg, D, grave 12: sword and scabbard with dragon-pair decoration, iron. Gi V85/18
Giengen an der Brenz, Baden-Württemberg, D, grave 13**: pair of knobbed anklets, copper alloy. Gi V85/19
Heubach-Rosenstein, Baden-Württemberg, D: zoomorphic brooch, copper alloy. V71,1 (see fig. 42)
Holzgerlingen, Baden-Württemberg, D: statue, stone. A 28,37 (see imprint page)
Ingelfingen-Criesbach, Baden-Württemberg, D: anthropomorphic brooch, copper alloy. 11837
Kleinaspergle, Baden-Württemberg, D*: rich burial assemblage (selection), copper alloy, gold, ceramic. 8723 (see figs 45–7)
River Erms near Urach, Baden-Württemberg, D: linch pin, copper alloy, iron. A1054 (see fig. 54)
Trichtingen, Baden-Württemberg, D: bull-headed torc, silver, iron. A28,61 (see fig. 81)

Ireland: Dublin, National Museum of Ireland
Grange, Co. Sligo, IRE: ring-headed pin, copper alloy. 1932.6455
Ireland: decorated headgear (the 'Petrie Crown'), copper alloy. P869, 870

Switzerland: Bern, Historisches Museum Bern
Bern-Schosshalde, Bern, CH**: Brooch, silver. 11719
Münsingen, Bern, CH**: brooch, copper alloy, coral. 24797

UK: Cardiff, National Museum of Wales
Llyn Cerrig Bach, Anglesey, UK: decorated plaque, copper alloy. 44.294.31
Snowdon, Gwynedd, UK*: bowl with zoomorphic handle, copper alloy, enamel. 74.20H

UK: Edinburgh, National Museums Scotland
Auldearn, Highland, UK: torc, copper alloy. X.FA 135
Balmaclellan, Dumfries & Galloway, UK: decorated quern, stone. X.BB 7
Cawdor, Highland, UK**: bead, glass. X.FJ 4
Blair Drummond, Stirling, UK: torc hoard, gold. X.FE 109-112 (see fig. 78)
Borness, Dumfries & Galloway, UK**: toggle, bone. X.HN 37
Carlingwark Loch, Dumfries & Galloway, UK: zoomorphic tankard handle, copper alloy. X.DW 80 (see fig. 88)
Deskford, Aberdeenshire, UK: carnyx head, copper alloy. IL.2011.1.1 (on long-term loan from Aberdeenshire Heritage) (see fig. 76)
Deskford, Aberdeenshire, UK: carnyx reconstruction, copper alloy, enamel. X.FA 118
Inishowen, Co. Donegal, IRE: ribbon torc, gold. X.FF 24
Kincardine Moss, Stirling, UK**: cauldron, copper alloy. X.DU 1
Leadburn, Scottish Borders, UK**: Late Bronze Age sword, copper alloy. X.DL 42 (see fig. 266)
Newbridge, Edinburgh, UK**: reconstruction chariot, wood, hide, rawhide, iron, antler. X.2007.10 (see fig. 84)
Rathcormac, Co. Cork, IRE: ribbon torc, silver. X.FD 33
Torrs, Dumfries & Galloway, UK: pony cap, copper alloy. X.FA 72 (see fig. 86)
Weston, Somerset, UK**: pair of scoops, copper alloy. X.FB 3-4 (see fig. 90)

UK: Glasgow, Glasgow Museums
Balloch Hill, Argyll, UK: brooch, copper alloy. A.1985.7.95 (see fig. 59)

UK: Hull, Hull and East Riding Museum
East Yorkshire, UK*: figurine, chalk. KINCM:1987.81
Wetwang Slack, East Yorkshire, UK*: decorated canister, copper alloy. KINCM:2010.8.38 (see fig. 92)

UK: London, British Museum
Basse-Yutz, Lorraine, F*: pair of flagons, copper-alloy, coral, glass. 1929,0511.1-2 (see figs 35, 40, 41)

Blackborough End, Norfolk, UK*: torc, gold alloy. 1985,0303.1

Brackley, Buckinghamshire, UK*: tankard, copper alloy. PELoanIn.33
    (On loan from Mr and Mrs Paterson)

Braganza collection, Iberia: warrior brooch, gold. 2001,0501.1 (see figs 63, 65)

Broadway, Worcestershire, UK*: Late Bronze Age sword, bronze-copper alloy. WG.1241

Bugthorpe, East Yorkshire, UK*: decorated scabbard, iron, copper alloy. 1905,0717.1

Burton Fleming, East Yorkshire, UK: clothing fragments, mineral-impregnated textile.
    1978,1202.37

Cambridgeshire, UK**: decorated fitting, copper alloy. 2013,8044.1 (see fig. 57)

Castle Field, Kent, UK: long-handled comb, antler. 1938,0507.151 (see fig. 34)

Chertsey, Surrey, UK*: shield, copper alloy. 1986,0901.1 (see fig. 68)

Chiseldon, Wiltshire, UK: decorated cauldron fragment, iron. 2007,8034.7

Chiseldon, Wiltshire, UK*: decorated cauldron fragment, iron. 2007,8034.10*

Chiswell Green, St Albans, Hertfordshire, UK: zoomorphic decorated knife, copper alloy.
    1993,1104.1 (see fig. 89)

Crosby Ravensworth, Cumbria, UK: pair of decorated scoops, copper alloy. 1869,1211.1-2

Dunaverney, Co. Antrim, UK*: flesh hook, copper alloy. 1856,1222.1 (see fig. 36)

Fontvannes, Champagne-Ardennes, F**: torc, copper alloy. ML.1714

Hallstatt, Oberösterreich, A*: decorated bucket, copper alloy. 1916,0605.356

Hallstatt, Oberösterreich, A*: zoomorphic brooch, copper alloy. 1939,0501.7

Heiltz l'Evêque 'Charvais', Marne, F**: knobbed bracelet, copper alloy. ML.1900

Ireland: decorated disc, copper alloy. 1841,1110.1 (see fig. 91)

Ireland*: Early Bronze Age lunula, gold. 1845,0122.1

Italy*: Etruscan flagon, copper alloy. 1844,0708.6

Kirkburn, East Yorkshire, UK, burial K3*: sword and scabbard, iron, copper alloy,
    horn, glass. 1987,0404.2 (see fig. 69)

Kirkburn, East Yorkshire, UK, burial K5: terrets, strap fittings and linch pins, copper
    alloy, iron. 1987,0404.12-13, 18-24

La Tène, Neuchâtel, CH: spearheads, sword, sickle, axehead, iron. 1867,0701.1;
    1867,0702.1, .4, .5; 1880,1214.6-7

Lisnacrogher bog, Co. Antrim, UK: decorated scabbard, copper alloy.
    1880,0802.115 (see fig. 61)

Loiret area, F: torc, gold. GR1867,0508.477

Luristan, western Iran: twisted torc, copper alloy. 1936,0613.161

Marson, Marne, F, grave 25: beads, glass. ML.1535

Molino de Marrubial, Córdoba, E: torc, silver. 1932,0706.2

Olympia, GR*: Greek helmet, bronze. 1824,0407.32

Orense (probably), Galicia, E: torc, gold. 1960,0503.1

Pleurs, Marne, F: torc, copper alloy. ML1621 (see fig. 80)

River Thames at Battersea, UK: decorated shield, copper alloy, glass. 1857,0715.1
    (see figs 10, 17, 26)

River Thames at Walthamstow, UK*: cauldron, copper alloy. OA.10954

River Thames at Wandsworth, UK: two decorated shield bosses, copper alloy.
    1858,1116.2-3 (see figs 31, 39, 62, p. 57)

River Thames at Waterloo Bridge, UK: horned helmet, copper alloy. 1988,1004.1 (see fig. 70)

River Witham near Lincoln, Lincolnshire, UK: decorated shield, copper alloy. 1872,1213.1
    (see p.1, figs 1, 9, 67)

Sainte-Foi, Rhône-Alpes, F*: helmet, copper alloy. 1851,0813.46

Salon, Champagne-Ardenne, F**: anthropomorphic sword, iron, copper alloy.
    ML.1669 (see fig. 74)

Snettisham, Norfolk, UK: selection of hoards D-H, J-M, gold, gold alloy, silver, copper alloy.
    1990,1101.ff, 1991,0407.ff, 1991,0501.ff, 1991,0702.ff, 1992,1203.7-10
    (see figs 22, 30, 94, pp.106-7)

Somme-Bionne, Champagne-Ardenne, F**: chariot burial grave goods (selection)
    ML.1338.b, ML.1339, ML.1347, ML.1367-9, ML.2713 (see figs 43, 44, 64)

Wetwang, East Yorkshire, UK*: chariot reconstruction, wood, leather, iron. CRM.1128

Yorkshire?, UK**: anthropomorphic sword, iron. 1888,0719.36

UK: Norwich, Norwich Castle Museum

Snettisham, Norfolk, UK: Hoard A, gold, stone. Torcs: 1949, 79.1-4;
    pebble: Clarke 1954: p. 39, fig. 6

Snettisham, Norfolk, UK: torcs, silver. 1965.30.1, 1969,55.3

Austria: Vienna, Kunsthistorisches Museum

Sălişţea, Transylvania, RO**: hoard (selection), silver. VII A 201, 203-5, 211a-b,
    213, 215, 217 (see fig. 259)

LATE IRON AGE & EARLY ROMAN PERIOD

Czech Republic: Prague, National Museum

Prague-Šárka, Bohemia, CZ: boar figurine, copper alloy. H1-229109

Denmark: Copenhagen, National Museum of Denmark

Aarhus, Jutland, DK: zoomorphic brooch, copper alloy. 5970
Gundestrup, Jutland, DK: cauldron, silver. C 6562-6576 (see figs 253–8, 260, 265)
Rynkeby, Funen, DK: decorated cauldron plate, copper alloy. 8900

Germany: Bonn, Rheinisches Landesmuseum

Plaidt, Rheinland-Pfalz, D: horse-shaped comb, copper alloy. 0O.34348

Germany: Stuttgart, Württembergisches Landesmuseum

Köngen, Baden-Württemberg, D: sculpture of Epona, stone. RL 416 (see fig. 138)

Switzerland: Bern, Historisches Museum Bern

Muri, Bern, CH**: Deo Artio statue group, copper alloy. 16170

UK: Beverley, The Treasure House

South Cave, East Yorkshire, UK: sword and scabbard, copper alloy, iron, glass, ivory.
    2005.99.1-3 (see fig. 116)

UK: Cardiff, National Museum of Wales

Seven Sisters, Glamorgan, UK**: hoard (selection), copper alloy, glass, enamel, niello.
    04.125, 126, 128, 131, 134-6, 140-1, 143

UK: Edinburgh, National Museums Scotland

Auchenbadie, Aberdeenshire, UK*: massive-style armlet, copper alloy. X.FA 15
Auldearn, Highland, UK: massive trumpet-variant brooch, copper alloy, iron, enamel.
    X.FA 136 (see fig. 126)
Balmaclellan, Dumfries & Galloway, UK: decorated mount, copper alloy. X.FA 2 (see fig. 113)
Belhelvie, Aberdeenshire, UK: massive-style armlet, copper alloy. X.FA 16 (see figs 115, 266)
Binn Hill, Moray, UK**: zoomorphic brooch, copper alloy, enamel. X.FA 128
Birrens, Dumfries & Galloway, UK: altar dedicated to Brigantia, sandstone.
    X.FV 5 (see fig. 131)
Culbin Sands, Moray, UK: zoomorphic armlet, copper alloy, glass. X.FA.89 (see fig. 262)
Langbank, Renfrewshire, UK: decorated comb, bone. X.HC 105 (see fig. 112)
Longfaugh, Midlothian, UK**: penannular brooch, copper alloy. X.FT 3 (see fig. 154)
Middlebie, Dumfries & Galloway, UK: hoard (selection), copper alloy. X.FA 49, 54, 56,
    59, 69, 71 (see fig. 122)
Stichill (?), Scottish Borders, UK: hinged collar, copper alloy. X.FA 37 (see fig. 12)
Tarnavie, Perthshire, UK: finger ring, copper alloy, enamel. X.FA 109 (see fig. 140)
Unprovenanced, UK: dragonesque brooch, copper alloy. IL.2009.6 (on loan from
    Vincent and Ruth Megaw) (see fig. 123)

UK: London, British Museum

Alfriston, East Sussex, UK*: terret, copper alloy, glass. 1853,1212.1
Asby Scar, Cumbria, UK*: sword and scabbard, copper-alloy, glass, wood, iron. 1994,0204.1
Aylesford, Kent, UK: bucket, jug and handled pan, copper alloy. 1886,1112.1-3
    (see figs 106–8)
Backworth, Northumberland, UK**: trumpet brooch, gilt silver. 1850,0601.16
Barking Hall (?) or Baylham Mill (?), Suffolk, UK: statue of Nero, copper alloy, silver.
    1813,0213.1
Barkway, Hertfordshire, UK: votive plaques of Mars Toutatis and Mars Alator,
    silver and gilt silver. 1817,0308.2-3 (see fig. 136)
Bredgar, Kent, UK: Iron Age coin die, copper alloy. 2014,4014.1 (see fig. 96)
Brough, Cumbria, UK: triskele-decorated disc brooch, copper alloy, enamelled,
    ?tinned. 1857,1214.29 (see fig. 24)
Brough, Nottinghamshire, UK**: horse and rider figurine, copper alloy. 1990,0101.1-2
Castle Newe, Aberdeenshire: pair of massive-style armlets, copper alloy, enamel.
    1946,0402.1*, 1946,0402.1.2
Colchester, Essex, UK: votive plaque to Mars Medocius, copper alloy. 1892,0421.1
Desborough, Northamptonshire, UK**: mirror, copper alloy. 1924,0109.1
    (see fig. 95, 114, pp.126-7)
Drummond Castle, Perthshire, UK: pair of massive-style armlets, copper alloy, enamel.
    1838,0714.3a**, 1838,0714.3a b
Essendon, Hertfordshire, UK: coin hoard, gold. CM1994,0403.1-18, 21, 32-34, 36-41,
    111, 116-7, 122, 153; 1995, 1014.1-2, 4, 6, 32, 35-7, 41, 44-5, 49, 53, 55-6;
    1997,0140.4-7, 32 (see fig. 98)

Farnsfield, Nottinghamshire, UK*: strap fitting, copper alloy, enamel. 2008,8026.1

Faversham, Kent, UK: pair of dragonesque brooches, copper alloy, enamel.
1088.70 a, b (see fig. 123)

Fenny Stratford, Buckinghamshire, UK: Iron Age coin, gold. 1919,0213.17 (see fig. 99)

Heckington, Lincolnshire, UK**: ring inscribed 'ToT', silver. 2004,0702.1 (see fig. 137)

Hockwold, Norfolk, UK: cosmetic grinder, copper alloy. 1977,0403.1 (see fig. 101)

Hod Hill, Dorset, UK*: sword with decorated hilt, copper alloy, iron.
1892,0901.452 (see fig. 118)

Ilam, Staffordshire, UK: decorated pan, copper alloy, enamel. 2005,1204.1
(jointly owned with Tullie House Museum and Stoke Potteries) (see fig. 128)

Ingleton, North Yorkshire, UK: zoomorphic mirror handle, copper alloy. 1945,1103.1

Kings Langley, Hertfordshire, UK*: linch-pin, copper alloy, iron, glass. 1940,0203.1

Lens, Pas de Calais, F: Iron Age coin, gold. 1918,0704.3 (see fig. 99)

Lincolnshire, UK: Aesica-type brooch, copper alloy. 1978,0401.1

Lochar Moss, Dumfries & Galloway, UK: hinged torc, copper alloy. 1853,1105.2 (see fig. 130)

London, UK*: strap mount, copper alloy, glass. 1856,0701.998

Medieşu Aurit, Satmar, RO: Iron Age coin, silver. 1920,0105.2 (see fig. 99)

Norfolk, UK: cosmetic grinder, copper alloy. 1999,0802.52 (see fig. 101)

Polden Hill, Somerset, UK: hoard (selection), copper alloy, glass. 1889,0706.77-78;
1846.0322.94, 96**, 98**, 142-3** (see fig. 119)

Pompeii, IT*: Roman snake bracelet, gold. 1946,0702.2

Portland, Dorset, UK: hinged collar, copper alloy, glass. 1963,0407.1 (see fig. 129)

Rhayader, Powys, UK**: hinged bracelet, gold, enamel. 1900,1122.1 (see fig. 127)

Rise, East Yorkshire, UK: bridle-bit, copper alloy, enamel. 1866,0714.2

Ruscombe, Berkshire, UK: Iron Age coin, gold. 1854,1012.1 (see fig. 34)

Southbroom, Wiltshire, UK: figurine of a warrior god, copper alloy. 1811,0309.2 (see fig. 132)

St Keverne, Cornwall, UK: mirror, copper alloy. 1873,1011.1 (see fig. 111)

Stanwick, North Yorkshire, UK: terret and mount in form of horse head, copper alloy.
1847,0208.36, 82 (see fig. 29)

Unprovenanced UK: ox-head, perhaps from a firedog, copper alloy, iron. 1946,1010.1

Unprovenanced (Meyrick collection): helmet, copper alloy. 1872,1213.2 (see fig. 117)

Unprovenanced: selection of Gaulish Iron Age coins, gold. 1841,B.687,
EH,p39.25.Brit, EH,p261.9.Phill (see figs 96, 99)

Welwyn, Hertfordshire, UK: head-shaped mount from a bucket, copper alloy.
1911,1208.5 (see fig. 104)

Westhall, Suffolk, UK: terret and strap fitting*, copper alloy, glass. 1855,0519.1, 9 (see fig. 23)

Wickham, Hampshire, UK: fantail brooch, copper alloy, tinned, enamelled.
1878,1101.266 (see fig. 124)

Winchester, Hampshire, UK**: jewellery hoard, gold. 2001,0901.1-10 (see fig. 110)

UK: London, Society of Antiquaries of London

Cotterdale, North Yorkshire, UK**: sword and scabbard, copper alloy, iron.
LDSAL 700 (on long-term loan to British Museum)

UK: Norwich, Norwich Castle Museum

Ashmanhaugh, Norfolk, UK: boar figurine, copper alloy. 2011.311 (see fig. 100)

Crownthorpe, Norfolk, UK: bird-handled cup, copper alloy. 1982.464.5 (see fig. 103)

Needham, Norfolk, UK: zoomorphic drinking horn terminal, copper alloy. 2008.483

Ringstead, Norfolk, UK: pair of bridle bits, copper alloy. 1950.77

Thetford, Norfolk, UK: finger-ring, copper alloy, enamel. 1995.60.577:A

LATE ROMAN & EARLY MEDIEVAL

Denmark: Copenhagen, National Museum of Denmark

Norway: house-shaped reliquary, copper alloy, enamel, yew wood. 9084 (see fig. 184)

Germany: Bonn, Rheinisches Landesmuseum

Dormagen, Nordrhein-Westfalen, D: openwork *Trompetenmuster* mount, copper alloy.
1934.329.01 (see fig. 149)

Ireland: Dublin, National Museum of Ireland

Ballinderry, Co. Offaly, IRE: penannular brooch, copper alloy, glass. E6:422 (see fig. 155)

Ballynaglough, Co. Antrim, UK: penannular brooch, copper alloy, amber, glass. 1930:495

Ballyspellan, Co. Kilkenny, IRE: penannular brooch, silver. R 89 (see fig. 208)

Donore, Co. Meath, IRE: hoard of decorated door fittings, tinned copper alloy, glass.
1985:21.1, 2, 4, 5 (see figs 13, 32)

Grousehall, Co. Donegal, IRE: brooch-pin, copper alloy, amber. 1931 16

Newtownbond, Co. Longford, IRE: proto-handpin, silver. 1944:95

St John's Rinnagan, Co. Westmeath, IRE: crucifixion plaque, copper alloy, once gilt.
R554 (see fig. 197)

Tully Lough, Co. Roscommon, IRE: processional cross, copper alloy, gilt and tinned, oak.
1998.9 (see figs 180, 185)

UK: Edinburgh, National Museums Scotland

Aldclune, Perthshire, UK**: penannular brooch, gilt silver, glass. X.FC 304

Crieff, Perthshire, UK**: pair of mounts, gilt copper alloy, crystal, glass. X.FC. 3-4 (see fig. 181)

Croy, Highland, UK**: penannular brooch, silver, amber. X.FC 12

Dupplin, Perthshire, UK*: cross, cast. X.IB.332

Gaulcross, Aberdeenshire, UK; handpin; silver, enamel. IL.2011.1.2 (on long-term loan
from Aberdeenshire Heritage) (see fig. 152)

Hilton of Cadboll, Highland, UK**: spiral-decorated cross slab fragment, sandstone. X.IB 355

Hunterston, North Ayrshire, UK: annular brooch, silver, gold, gilding, amber. X.FC 8
(see figs 166, 199, 200)

Invergowrie, Perthshire, UK**: cross slab, sandstone. X.IB 251

Iona, Argyll & Bute, UK*: St John's cross, cast. X.IB 331

Monifieth, Angus, UK: cross slab, sandstone. X.IB 27 (see fig. 171)

Monymusk, Aberdeenshire, UK: house-shaped reliquary, wood, copper alloy, silver, enamel.
X.KE 14 (see fig. 183)

Mote of Mark, Dumfries & Galloway, UK: mould for hanging-bowl mount, ceramic. X.HH 104
(see fig. 163)

Mull, Argyll & Bute, UK**: penannular brooch, copper alloy. X.FC 6

Norrie's Law, Fife, UK: selection of hoard finds, silver. X.FC 26-7, 29, 31, 34-7, 53, 64,
68, 90, 93, 102 (see figs 141-4)

Papil, Shetland, UK: cross slab, sandstone. X.IB 46 (see fig. 186)

Parkhill, Aberdeenshire, UK: double-link chain, silver. X.FC 147 (see fig. 158)

Rogart, Highland, UK**: penannular brooch, gilt silver, glass. X.FC 2 (see figs 165, 191, 266)

Skaill, Orkney, UK: penannular thistle brooch, silver. X.IL 1 (see fig. 207)

St Ninian's Isle, Shetland, UK: hoard (selection), silver. X.FC 268, 273-5, 278-83, 286, 292-3,
295 (see figs 25, 174, 187, 189, 190, 264)

St Peter's Church, South Ronaldsay, Orkney, UK: Pictish class I stone, sandstone.
X.IB 2 (see fig. 147)

Tarbat, Highland, UK**: inscribed cross fragment, sandstone. X.IB 284

Traprain Law, East Lothian, UK**: double-link chain, silver. X.FC 248

Ulster, UK**: penannular brooch, copper alloy, enamel. X.FD 2

Walston, South Lanarkshire, UK**: decorated sphere, copper alloy. X.AS 39 (see fig. 266)

Westness, Orkney, UK: brooch-pin, silver, gold, amber. X.IL 728 (see fig. 193)

Whitecleugh, South Lanarkshire, UK: double-link chain, silver. X.FC 150 (see fig. 159)

UK: Lichfield, Lichfield Cathedral

Lichfield, Staffordshire, UK*: St Chad Gospels, manuscript. (see fig. 198)

UK: Littlehampton, Littlehampton Museum

Patching, West Sussex, UK*: hanging-bowl mount, copper alloy, enamel. SUSS-F9E7AA

UK: London, British Museum

Akhmîm, Egypt**: buckle with interlace decoration, gilt copper alloy. 1891,0512.21
(see fig. 175)

Ash, Kent, UK*: Anglo-Saxon pendant, gold. 1862,0701.16

Dowris, Co. Offaly, IRE: latchet, copper alloy, enamel. 1854,0714.97 (see fig. 157)

Faversham, Kent, UK**: Anglo-Saxon buckle, gilt silver, gold, garnet, niello. 1098.'70
(see fig. 160)

Faversham, Kent, UK**: Anglo-Saxon buckle, gilt silver, gold. 1097.'70 (see fig. 167)

Faversham, Kent, UK*: Anglo-Saxon pair of Anglo-Saxon square-headed brooches,
gilt silver, gold, garnet, niello. 1054.'70, .1054.a.'70

Faversham, Kent, UK**: hanging-bowl, copper alloy, enamel. .1292.'70

Fintona (?), Co. Tyrone, IRE*: hand-bell, copper alloy. 1945,1102.1

Icklingham, Suffolk, UK: openwork *Trompetenmuster* mount, copper alloy. 1935,0416.1

Linz am Rhein (?), Rheinland-Pfalz, D**: brooch with interlace decoration, gilt silver, niello.
1894,0217.3 (see fig. 176)

Lullingstone, Kent, UK**: hanging-bowl, copper alloy, silver, niello. 1967,1004.1 (see fig. 162)

Nassington, Northamptonshire, UK**: Mercian disc brooch, gilt silver. 2012,8034.1

Oldcroft, Gloucestershire, UK: proto-handpin, silver, enamel. 1973,0801.1 (see fig. 148)

Pentre, Powys, UK: stone inscribed in ogam and Latin, sandstone. 1878,1102.1 (see fig. 145)

Perthshire?, UK (Breadalbane Collection): penannular brooch, gilt silver, gold, glass.
1919,1218.1 (see fig. 192)

Smithfield, London, UK: late Roman chip-carved buckle, copper alloy. 1856,0701.1470

Sutton Hoo, Suffolk, UK: hanging-bowl, copper alloy, silver, enamel. 1939,1010.110
(see fig. 28)

Unprovenanced (Londesborough collection): large decorated pin, silver, enamel.
1888,0719.100 (see fig. 152)

Unprovenanced*: Byzantine Christian panel, ivory. 1923,1205.2

UK: Norwich, Norwich Castle Museum
Deopham, Norfolk, UK: hanging bowl mount, silver. 2011.409 (see fig. 188)

UK: Oxford, Bodleian Library
MacRegol Gospels**, manuscript. MS Auct. D. 2. 19

MEDIEVAL & POST-MEDIEVAL

Ireland: Dublin, National Museum of Ireland
Book-shrine for the Cathach of St Columba, gilt copper alloy and silver over wooden core.
    R2835 (see fig. 202)

UK: Edinburgh, National Museums Scotland
Ballindalloch Castle, Moray, UK: Highland dirk, iron, copper alloy, leather, wood. H.LC 69
St Fillan's crosier head and shrine, copper alloy, gilt silver, niello. H.KC 1-2 (see figs 223-4)
Unprovenanced: Highland brooch, copper alloy. H.NGA 246
Unprovenanced: Highland dirk, wood, leather. H.LC 14 (see fig. 266)
 'Queen Mary's Harp'*, wood, brass. H.LT 1 (see fig. 225)
Unprovenanced*: powder horn, horn, pewter. H.LK.60
Unprovenanced*: targe, wood, leather. H.LN.41
Unprovenanced**: Fife Casket, whalebone, brass. K.2002.982

UK: London, British Museum
Glankeen, Co. Tipperary, IRE*: bell shrine of St Cuilean, copper alloy, silver, iron,
    niello, enamel. 1854,0714.6.A&B (see figs 201, 214)

UK: Oxford, Bodleian Library
Book of the White Earl*, manuscript. Laud Misc. 610 (see fig. 221)
Life of St Columba*, manuscript. Rawlinson B.514 (see fig. 220)

RENAISSANCE & REVIVAL

Denmark: Copenhagen, Statens Museum for Kunst
Nicolai Abraham Abildgaard, *Blind Ossian Singing his Swan Song*, 1785*, oil on canvas.
    KMS395 (see fig. 231)

Ireland: Dublin, National Museum of Ireland
Alexander Fisher, *Triptych in the form of a Celtic shrine*, c. 1903*, gilt brass inlaid with
    silver, enamel. 650.1903 (see fig. 244)
Edmond Johnson, The Queen's Brooch, 1849, gold, pearl. NMIDT 1902.302 (see fig. 236)
Joseph Johnson Jnr, dish based on the foot of the Ardagh Chalice, 1869-70, copper alloy,
    partly gilt, crystal, glass, enamel. NMIDM 1983.1

UK: Cardiff, National Museum of Wales
Bardic armchair awarded at Eisteddfod, 1887*, wood. A 50695
H. Herkomer, *Hwfa Mon, Arch-druid of Wales*, 1896**, watercolour in gilt wooden frame.
    A 24393 (see fig. 247)
J. Harrison, after P. J. de Loutherbourg, *The Bard*, 1840*, oil on canvas. A3492 (see fig. 230)
John Evan Thomas and William Meredyth Thomas, *Death of Tewdrig Mawr – King of Gwent*,
    1848-56*, bronze. A 25991 (see fig. 248)
Arch-druid robes*, 1986, fabric. F2012.12.1-2
Arch-druid regalia and banner*, bronze, fabric, glass, gold, horn (on loan from the
    Gorsedd of the Bards)

UK: Dundee, McManus Galleries
John Duncan, *Riders of the Sidhe*, 1911*, tempera on canvas. 178-1912 (see figs 226, 238)

UK: Edinburgh, National Library of Scotland
James Macpherson, *Poems of Ossian*, 1777**, book. Oss.22
Napolean's copy of *Ossian* by James Macpherson**, book. Ossian Bdg.s.792
Owen Jones, *Grammar of Ornament*, 1856**, book. LC1405 (see fig. 237)
James Macpherson, *Die Gedichte Ossians*, 1768**, book. NG.1168.g.21

UK: Edinburgh, National Museums Scotland
19th-century copy of the Ardagh chalice**, silver, copper alloy, glass. A.1882.50.1
Celtic Revival harp display case made by Whytock and Reid, Edinburgh*, wood, glass. H.KNM 2
Daniel Wilson, *Archaeology & Prehistoric Annals of Scotland*, 1851**, book. ZA 1623 WIL
Edward Lhuyd, *Archaeologia Britannica*, 1707**, book. PB LHU (N)
John Kemble, *Horae Ferales*, 1863**, book. CC990 KEM (see figs 9, 10)

Mid-19th century annular brooch inspired by the Croy brooch**, silver, glass. H.NGB 171
Patrick Geddes (ed.), *The Evergreen: Book of Spring*, 1895, book. ZA 1040 EVE (see fig. 267)
Samuel Rush Meyrick, *The Costumes of the Original Inhabitants of the British Isles*,
    1815**, book. OS768(41)/M
Catalogue of the National Museum of Antiquities of Scotland, 1892**, book.
    069.194134 NMA

UK: Edinburgh, National Trust for Scotland
John Duncan, *Anima Celtica*, c. 1895**, oil on canvas. 78.48

UK: Edinburgh, Scottish National Gallery
John Duncan, *Cucchulain*, c. 1917, pencil on paper. D 5120 (see fig. 250)
Phoebe Anna Traquair, *Motherhood*, 1901*, oil on panel, copper alloy, enamel,
    stone inlays. NG 1871
Phoebe Anna Traquair, *Three studies for the decoration of the first mortuary chapel,
    the Royal Hospital for Sick Children*, 1885*, oil on canvas. NG 1867 (see fig. 243)

UK: Edinburgh, University of Edinburgh
Theodor de Bry, *Virginia*, 1590**, book. JY601
William Stukeley, *Abury*, 1743**, book. D.S.b.2.16 (see fig. 6)

UK: Glasgow, Glasgow Museums
George Henry and Edward A. Hornel, *The Druids - Bringing in the Mistletoe*, 1890,
    oil on canvas. 1534 (see fig. 227)

UK: Glasgow, Hunterian Art Gallery
Frances Macdonald, Margaret Macdonald and James Herbert McNair, *Poster for the
    Glasgow Institute of Fine Arts*, mid-1890s*, poster. 41056 (see fig. 239)

UK: London, British Library
Caesar, *de Bello Gallico*, 1569, book. 1306.b.14
Caesar, *de Bello Gallico*, 1609, book. 1305.l.12
James Macpherson, *Poems of Ossian*, 1762, book, T.667.(10.)
Prints from Theodor de Bry, *A briefe and true report of the new found land of Virginia*,
    1590*. C.38.i.18
Samuel Rush Meyrick, *The Costumes of the Original Inhabitants of the British Isles*,
    1815**, book. G.9776
William Stukeley, *Abury*, 1743*, book. G.6042.(2.) (see fig. 6)

UK: London, British Museum
Alexander Runciman, *Finbar and Conban-Cargla*, c. 1751-1785*,
    print. 1854,0812.84 (see fig. 232)
Archibald Knox, tea set, 1903, pewter. 1980,0511.1-5 (see fig. 245)
Edward Lhuyd, *Archaeologia Britannica*, 1707*, book. KL 115T
Johan Frederik Clemens after Nicolai Abraham Abildgaard, *Ossian*, 1787,
    etching and engraving. 1879,1011.1316
John Kemble, *Horae Ferales*, 1863*, book. BEP Rare books collection, 29e,
    Shelf SC.4.12.1-7 (see figs 9, 10)
Owen Jones, *Grammar of Ornament*, 1856*, chromolithographs from book.
    (On loan from private lender) (see fig. 237)

UK: London, Guildhall Library and Art Gallery
John Henry Foley, *Caractacus*, 1859*, marble. 10139 (see fig. 251)

UK: London, Royal Collection
Edmund Johnson, Clarendon Brooch, 1849-50*, silver, garnets. RCIN 4833 (see fig. 235)

UK: London, Victoria and Albert Museum
West and Son, Dublin, variation of The Queen's Brooch, c. 1853*, gilt silver, gold filigree.
    2750-1853
West and Son, Dublin, variation of The Queen's Brooch, c. 1853*, gilt silver, gold filigree.
    2751-1853
19th century Tara Brooch replica*, bronze, glass. 230.1881
Archibald Knox, vase, 1906-9*, pewter. CIRC.936-1967 (see fig. 15)
G. and S. Waterhouse copy of the Tara brooch, c.1851*, gilt oxidised silver set
    with semi-precious stones. 920-1852 (see fig. 234)

Notes

Chapter 1

1 Mattei 1991.
2 Guggisberg 2009a; Megaw and Megaw 2001a, 258; Fitzpatrick and Schönfelder 2014, fig. 31.6. Excavations revealed a complex of monumental, rich graves outside a large fortified Iron Age settlement; see Baitinger and Pinsker (eds) 2002.
3 Symbolizing the host, the sacred bread believed to represent the body of Christ (Megaw and Megaw 2001b, 209).
4 Giraldus Cambrensis (Gerald of Wales), *Topographia Hibernia* 71 (trans. O'Meara 1982, 84).
5 McCone 2008, 2–3; Koch 2009; 2014, 8–9.
6 Koch and Carey (eds) 1995, 5; Koch 2014, 6–7.
7 Caesar, *De Bello Gallico (The Gallic Wars)* I:1
8 Woolf 2011, 20.
9 For example, Ireland 2008, 11–14. Archaeologists (e.g. James 1999, 17; Collis 2003, 11) set more store on this absence of Celts than linguists (notably McCone 2008; Koch 2014, 9). The latter argue such broad terms could be vulnerable to loss at times of political change, but this does raise the question of what real significance the word had if it was so easily discarded.
10 Such as their religious beliefs, languages and attitude to war; Tacitus, *Agricola* I:11.
11 Buchanan 1582; Collis 1999; 2003, 37–40.
12 Rowley-Conwy 2007, 7.
13 Pezron 1703; Collis 2003, 48–9; Morse 2005, 21–4.
14 Morse 2005, 67, pl. 6.
15 See Sims-Williams (1998; 2013) and, for a taste of the debate, the first few papers in Carr and Stoddart (eds) 2002.
16 On mainland Europe modern Celtic identity remains strong only in Brittany and to a lesser extent Galicia.
17 Cunliffe 1997, 21, 24; Koch 2010; Wodtko 2013, 186. The languages are local but the idea of carving and the script are products of contact with the literate Mediterranean world.
18 Koch 2013.
19 Cunliffe and Koch 2010; Cunliffe 2010; Koch 2010; 2014.
20 Koch 2014, 8.
21 Ibid., 7–8.
22 Charles-Edwards 2000, 163–76; Swift 2001; 2007.
23 Adomnán, *Life of St Columba*, 2.33.
24 Wilson 1851, 504–5.
25 Westwood 1856; Collis 2014. The book is still in print today.
26 Published posthumously (Kemble 1863, 79); the motif is termed the 'trumpet-spiral'.
27 Franks 1863.
28 Notably Ferdinand Keller in publishing Swiss finds from La Tène (1866, 257–8).
29 Déchelette 1914, 1506–27; Collis 2014, 21–2.
30 Wells 2012, 153.
31 Pion and Guichard 1993; Diepeveen-Jansen 2001, 147–9.
32 Although claims have been made to study 'Celtic genetics', there are innumerable practical problems with the science of this approach (e.g. Røyrvik 2010; Sims-Williams 2012). From our perspective, the key problem is that the phenomena we are considering here are cultural, not genetic.

Chapter 2

1 I am grateful to Alice Blackwell, Julia Farley, Martin Goldberg, J.D. Hill, Fraser Hunter and Ian Leins for helpful comments on earlier versions of the text.
2 See Elsner 2007.
3 Green 1996, 17.
4 Gell 1992; 1998.
5 Giles 2008.
6 Olivier 2014.
7 Megaw 1970b.
8 Olivier 2014.
9 Bradley 1990.
10 Garrow and Gosden 2012, 17.
11 Megaw and Megaw 2001a and Stead 1996 provide an excellent impression of the range of material from Europe and Britain respectively.
12 Garrow 2008, 30–36; Gosden and Hill 2008, 2.
13 Johns 1996, chapter 7.
14 Henig 1995, 13.
15 Megaw and Megaw 2001a, 228.
16 Davis and Gwilt 2008; Hunter 2008; Joy 2014a.
17 Laing 2005; Joy 2014a, 320.
18 Read 2011.
19 Wilson 1973.
20 Youngs (ed.) 1989 provides an excellent overview of the material, especially the decorated metalwork.
21 Bradley 2009; Joy 2011.
22 Stöllner 2014a, 121.
23 Horn, in preparation; Brun *et al.* 2009, 194–5
24 Youngs 2009a.
25 Joy 2014b.
26 For example, in Green 1996, 108.
27 Giles 2008.
28 Wells 2008, 42–7.
29 Spratling 2008, 192.
30 Giles 2008, 68; Joy 2011, 213; Blackwell 2012, 22–4.
31 Evans 1989, 184; Wells 2008, ii.
32 Wells 2012, 8–9.
33 Joy 2011; Sharples 2008.
34 Wells 2012, 1.
35 Garrow and Gosden 2012, 5.

Chapter 3

1 Megaw and Megaw 1990; Guggisberg 2009b. The circumstances of discovery make it impossible to be certain if they came from a grave or a hoard. No other burial of this period has two pairs of vessels, but a grave seems the most likely explanation as such flagons are typically found in burials rather than hoards. They date to the early fourth century BC.
2 Megaw and Megaw 2001a, chapter 1.

3 Hoppe 2009a.
4 Wells 2012, 206.
5 Cunliffe 2001, 313–15. It seems increasingly complex societies are developing locally before any visible Mediterranean impact; for instance, at the proto-town of Heuneburg in Germany, Mediterranean imports occurred late in the sequence (Fernández-Götz and Krausse 2013, 481–3).
6 Megaw and Megaw 2001a, chapter 2. For Atlantic France as another centre, see Milcent 2006; Gomez de Soto 2001. Connections from here to Britain are proposed by Cunliffe (2001, 325–6). Evidence remains sparse; the best demonstration of British involvement in Early-Style art is the unusual headdress from a grave at Cerrig-y-Drudion in north Wales (Jope 2000, pls 29–31). The burial has been radiocarbon-dated to 420–350 BC (at 88% probability; Garrow *et al.* 2009, 87).
7 Megaw and Megaw 2001a, chapter 2; Megaw and Megaw forthcoming, chapter 2.
8 Champion 1976.
9 Megaw and Megaw 1990, 47.
10 Ibid., 50.
11 Ibid., fig. 21.
12 Ibid., 46.
13 Wells 2012, 201–9; the point was made originally by Jacobsthal (1944, 162).
14 See, for instance, Megaw 2005 arguing strongly against direct connections; Pare 2012 for connections; Müller 2009a, 100 for a summary.
15 Cunliffe 2001, 315–16.
16 Such as the Veneti in north-east Italy and the Golasecca culture in northernmost Italy, who controlled the Alpine passes; Cunliffe 1997, 66; Frey 2004, 114–17.
17 Cunliffe 1997, 63–7; Krausse and Beilharz 2012, fig. 257.
18 This section uses the arguments of Diepeveen-Jansen 2001. For background, see Cunliffe 1997, 51–67.
19 For examples of recent interpretations of specific items, see Waddell 2009; Kaul 2014.
20 Hoppe and Schorer 2012, 238 and illus. 311.
21 Binding 1993.
22 The great unknown is organic materials such as textiles, leather or wood. These are very rarely preserved, but surviving textile fragments show no trace of such art styles at this time, using far more geometric patterns (e.g. Crowfoot 1991; Bender Jørgensen 1992, 104–6; Bartel 2002); surviving wood fragments likewise rarely carry Celtic art (see, for example, Evans 1989).
23 The finds from the burial are published in Stead and Rigby 1999; see Stead 1991c for a summary.
24 Stöllner 2014b. This human between beasts motif was a long-running one that became popular again (with very different meanings) in the early Christian period; see Chapter 8 in this volume.
25 Lenerz-de Wilde 1977, 117–18, Taf. 20–21; Stead and Rigby 1999, 160–61; Bacault and Flouest 2003.
26 Kimmig 1988; Hoppe 2009b. It is the most southerly of these rich fifth-century BC graves and the only one from the same area as the late Hallstatt rich burials of the previous century.
27 Discussed in a wider context in Waddell 2014, 118–22.
28 Schaaff 1988, 191; Beilharz and Krausse 2012, 197, fig. 241.
29 It was these very pots, with their combination of Greek

and Celtic elements, which inspired the great scholar of Celtic art, Paul Jacobsthal, to start his study (1944, vi): 'in the cold and hungry winter of 1921 . . . I was studying Greek vases in Stuttgart . . . what struck me was the fact that a Greek cup had been found in this Hyperborean country, and the gold plaques of a strange style mounted on it'.

30 For example, Lambrechts 1954; Ross 1958; Megaw 1970a, 20.

31 This discussion largely follows Armit 2012.

32 Megaw 1970a, no. 75.

33 Megaw and Megaw 2001a, 74. The motif was taken from classical plant designs and transformed into a crown; some scholars argue that it represents mistletoe.

34 Megaw 1970a, no. 47.

35 Guggisberg 2009a, fig. 252.

36 Joachim 1995; Guggisberg 2009c.

37 Frey 1995, 180–94.

38 Waddell 2014, 118–22.

39 Sprockhoff 1955.

40 Megaw and Megaw 2001a, 117–21; Müller 2012; Megaw and Megaw forthcoming, chapter 3. There is extensive debate over where the style developed, but the French evidence seems strongest as there are objects decorated with both Early and Vegetal Style (Verger 1987).

41 Watkin et al. 1996.

42 Jacobsthal 1944, 97–103; Megaw and Megaw 2001a, 135–44; Megaw and Megaw forthcoming, chapter 4.

43 Jacobsthal 1941, 308; 1944, 19, 162.

44 Megaw 1970b, 273–5.

45 Jacobsthal 1944, 184, no. 159; Guggisberg and Hoppe 2012, fig. 28.

46 Olivier 2012.

47 Piggott 1968; Fitzpatrick 1997; Hutton 2009; Aldhouse-Green 2010. The topic is discussed further in Chapter 4 in this volume.

48 Jacobsthal 1944, 99–101, nos 266–75; Schaaff 1972a and b; Megaw and Megaw 2001a, 139; Megaw and Megaw forthcoming, chapter 4.

49 For example, Kruta 1991; Szabó 1991, 307; Megaw and Megaw 2001a, 67; Ginoux 2009, 125–6.

50 Diepeveen-Jansen 2001, 212.

51 Wells 2012, 153; good examples are the site of La Tène in Switzerland (see Chapter 4 in this volume), where offerings were made into a river, and the ritual enclosures of Gournay-sur-Aronde and Ribemont-sur-Ancre in Picardy, northern France (Brunaux 1988, 13–23).

52 Helms 1987.

53 The study uses the fact that elements of what we eat and drink become absorbed into our teeth and bones; data from teeth are better as they are much more stable than bone. The signature from teeth reflects childhood location, when the teeth were developing. Comparison with data for the place of burial can indicate whether a person is buried in the same area in which they grew up. Strontium isotopes absorbed from food reflect the underlying geology where the plant or animal grew or grazed, while oxygen isotopes absorbed from water vary geographically according to factors such as climate. For background, see Budd et al. 2004; Bentley 2006; Evans et al. 2012. Such work detects differences between birthplace and burial place, but not any travels a person made during their life.

54 Research on Iron Age skeletons is still in early stages. For an overview of ongoing work, see Hauschild 2010. Among recent studies, work on people buried with chariots in Yorkshire showed that all bar one were local (and the exception had probably not moved far), although the burial rite indicated knowledge of wider worlds (Jay et al. 2013). A comparative study of cemeteries from Nebringen (Germany) and Monte Bibele (Italy) suggested most people did not move far. Exotic goods were found with both local and non-local individuals (Scheeres et al. 2013).

55 Hull and Hawkes 1987, 150, no. 3800, pl. 43. The use of a hinged pin was a typically British feature at this time, as people on the Continent preferred pins held with coiled springs.

56 Raftery 1983, 153, fig. 135, no. 408.

57 Megaw and Megaw 2001a, 126–35; Lejars 2012; Megaw and Megaw forthcoming, chapter 4.

58 Szabó and Petres 1992.

59 Lejars 1994, 89.

60 Müller 2009a, 111–13. It was probably a slightly later development (Lejars 2012).

61 Of bronze, rather than the iron scabbards typical on the Continent. Other finds suggest this style was shared across much of eastern England (Stead 2006, nos 33–5, 53).

62 Raftery 1994.

63 Megaw and Megaw 2008.

64 Fitzpatrick 2007a.

65 Cunliffe 2008, 270–363.

Chapter 4

1 Stead and Meeks 1996; papers in Perea (ed.) 2011.

2 Opinion is divided on interpretation of the brooch (called the Braganza brooch after the Portuguese family who once owned it). Some see the beast as a dog, some a wolf, some a monster; it seems markedly more dog-like to this writer. Some authors see the scene as a warrior facing a monster, others a man with his boisterous hunting dog (noting the less than ferocious demeanour of the beast and the unthreatening pose of the man). The form of the brooch has strong Iberian links, but the iconography and technology (such as blue enamel decorating the goldwork) imply a Hellenistic craftworker or influence from the Greek world. See references in note 1.

3 Krämer 1964, 27, grave 11.

4 We must be cautious not to make unsubstantiated assumptions about gender roles in prehistory (Pope & Ralston 2011). For instance, a study of Iron Age female skeletons from Dorset showed they were regularly exposed to or involved in inter-personal violence (Redfern 2008). But this is rather different from the idea of 'the warrior', marked out in death with weapons such as swords. There is very little evidence for females taking such a role: osteological study of burials with weapons and other strands of evidence such as iconography suggest this 'warrior image' was almost exclusively a male identity across Iron Age Europe, especially in death (Hunter 2005, focusing on British evidence).

5 Stead 1991a.

6 Maniquet et al. 2011.

7 Rusu 1969; Megaw 1970a, no. 211.

8 Jacobsthal 1944, no. 140; Megaw and Megaw 2001a, 112.

9 Stead 1991b, 66–70.

10 Stead 1988.

11 Deutscher 2012.

12 Stead and Rigby 1999, figs 146–7, no. 1349; Baitinger and Pinsker (eds) 2002, illus. 118 and 121. The scabbards from the Glauberg burials in Germany (see chapter 1 in this volume) have similarly subtle decoration (Frey 2004, 114).

13 Ginoux 2007.

14 Stead 1984; Fitzpatrick 2007a, 348–50.

15 Krämer 1962; Wyss et al. 2002, 39–40; Paysan 2005. The dating of such swords has been disputed as they are very rarely found with other datable finds. Moritz Paysan argues for an earlier date, starting in the fifth century BC, but René Wyss and colleagues note associated finds from France that strongly suggest a later La Tène date (later second or early first century BC).

16 Fitzpatrick 1996; Megaw 2002.

17 Hunter 2001.

18 Deskford sits late within the tradition; the use of recycled Roman brass in its manufacture dates it to the period c. AD 75–200.

19 Adler 2003; Hautenauve 2005.

20 Ongoing research at National Museums Scotland.

21 See, for example, Charpy 2009.

22 Almagro-Gorbea 1991, 398; García Vuelta 2002, fig. 1; see Barril Vicente 2002, fig. 7.

23 Hoppe 2009c.

24 Many are decorated with a version of the Plastic Style, often using triskeles; Kaul 1991a.

25 Kaul 2007.

26 For the chariot, see Stead 1991c; Stead and Rigby 1999, 129–36; for the reconstruction of such chariots, see Metzler 1986; Furger-Gunti 1991.

27 Carter et al. 2010.

28 Jay et al. 2012. For the chariots, see Stead 1979, 20–29; 1991b, 58–61.

29 Stead 1991b, 30–33, 42–54.

30 Emilov and Megaw 2012. This find was buried far from home in the Hellenistic-style tomb of a rich Thracian. It might reflect a wanderer's grave or booty from a vanquished war band, and emphasizes again the scale of contacts in third-century BC Europe (see Chapter 3 in this volume). It seems only the fittings, not the chariot itself, were deposited in the tomb.

31 Atkinson and Piggott 1955; Megaw 1983; Jope 1983; Harding 2002; Hunter 2009a.

32 Briggs 2014.

33 Henig 1974; Cottam et al. 2010, no. 2637.

34 Joy and Baldwin forthcoming.

35 Megaw 1970a, nos 50, 60–61, 72; Megaw and Megaw 2001a, 76–80; Baitinger and Pinsker (eds) 2002, 242–5.

36 MacGregor 1976, vol. 2, no. 287.

37 Guichard 1994; 2009; Deberge 2010.

38 Megaw et al. 1999.

39 Fitzpatrick 2007b, 290–99.

40 Raftery 1984, 276–82; Ó Floinn 2009, 204–6.

41 A number of authors have interpreted the decoration on these bronze dishes as 'sunships', a long-lived motif of the ship that was thought to take the sun on its daily voyage; Sprockhoff 1955; Waddell 2009. One might also see hidden faces in them.

42 Jope 2000, no. 89c; Giles 2012, 157–8.
43 McGarry 2008, 219.
44 See Piggott 1968; Fitzpatrick 1997; 2007b; Hutton 2009; Aldhouse-Green 2010.
45 Raftery 1984, 268–75.
46 Fitzpatrick 2007b, 299–305.
47 Holzer 2007; 2008.
48 Stead 1985.
49 Bradley 1990.
50 Dunning 1991; Müller 2009b.
51 Vouga 1923.
52 Information from the excavator, Steven Birch; publication is in progress.
53 Hutcheson 2004, 44–6.
54 Stead 1991d.
55 Stead 1998, 147–8.
56 Stead 1996, 26–7; Hautenauve 2005, 238–55; Garrow et al. 2009, 103.
57 Hautenauve 2005, 82–7, 95.
58 Marsden 2011.
59 It is not closely dated, but is probably contemporary with the hoards; Stead 2014.

Chapter 5

1 Nash 1987.
2 Collis 1984; Cunliffe 1997, 223–31; Fichtl 2005; Rieckhoff and Fichtl 2011.
3 Romero 2006; Sievers 2003; Wendling 2013.
4 Romero 2006, 67–9.
5 Allen 1970, 16–18; Talbot and Leins 2010, 14; for alternative argument, compare Creighton 1994, 326–7.
6 Score (ed.) 2011.
7 Stead 2006, 51.
8 Allen 1980, 135–6.
9 Tacitus, Germania, 46.3–4.
10 Green 1992a.
11 Davies 2011.
12 Jackson 2010.
13 Smith a1911.
14 Stead 1967.
15 Evans 1890.
16 Stead 1971.
17 Jope 1983; Aldhouse-Green 2004, 166.
18 Metzler et al. 2009.
19 Wells 1999, 159.
20 Pitts 2010.
21 Creighton 2000.
22 Creighton 2006.
23 Hill et al. 2004.
24 Rogers 1873; Joy 2010, no. 47.
25 Joy 2010.
26 Joy 2010, no. 24.
27 Eckardt 2008.
28 Joy 2010, 40.
29 MacGregor 1976, vol. 2, no. 275.
30 MacGregor 1976, vol. 1, 159–62; vol. 2, no. 342

Chapter 6

1 Evans 2006. The find was excavated by Humber Archaeology Partnership and block-lifted by conservators from York Archaeological Trust. It was fully conserved by Museum of London Archaeology, and is being prepared for publication (Evans et al., forthcoming). I am grateful to Michael Marshall (MoLA) for advance sight of his work on the find.
2 O'Connor 2013.
3 Piggott 1950, 17–2; Stead 2006, 75–7; Hunter forthcoming, a and b.
4 Brailsford 1962, 1, pl. IIA. A Roman fort was then built into the earlier hillfort.
5 Manning 1985, 149.
6 Jackson 1995.
7 Brailsford 1975b.
8 Davies and Spratling 1976; Davis and Gwilt 2008.
9 MacGregor 1976, vol. 1, 184.
10 Piggott 1983, 230–34; Müller 2009a, 24–5.
11 Hunter 2008.
12 Hunter 2010.
13 Boon and Savory 1975.
14 Cool 1986; see MacGregor 1976, vol. 2, nos 211–12.
15 Philostratus, writing in the third century AD, referred to it as a habit of 'the barbarians living by Oceanus' (Imagines I, 28, 3).
16 See papers in Breeze (ed.) 2012. Martin Henig (2010) has suggested such pans were not simple souvenirs but religious items, perhaps made in a temple in the Wall zone. He argues this area had a religious significance because it was seen as the edge of the known world; there are parallels at other 'edges' of the Roman empire.
17 Hunter 2010.
18 For instance in costume and jewellery on the Danube frontier; Rothe 2012, 173.
19 Keppie and Arnold 1984, no. 12.
20 RIB I, 2175; Keppie 1998, 103 no. 34.
21 Brailsford 1964, 54, pl. XVII; Green 1976, 191; Durham 2014.
22 See Lindgren 2003, 52–4, although she over-simplifies this into pan-Celtic habits, and Aldhouse-Green 2003.
23 Johns 2003.
24 Durham 2012, no. 371.
25 Hunter and Collard 1997; Hunter 2003.
26 Schreyer 2009.
27 Walker 2014.
28 Zoll 1994, 38.
29 Daubney 2010.
30 RIB I, 218.
31 Ibid., 191.
32 Zoll 1994; Green 1992b, 42.
33 Keppie 1998, 99–100; RIB I, 2166. This nicely illustrates the complexities behind such objects. The inscription was erected by a unit who were raised originally in Syria, to a god found mostly in Gaul, on the northern edge of the Roman world.
34 Jufer and Luginbühl 2001.
35 Green 1992b, 42, 208–9.
36 Ibid., 90–92.
37 For example, Creighton 2000, 24–6.
38 Daubney 2010, fig. 2.
39 Hunter 2014.

Chapter 7

1 As discussed in Chapter 1, no classical author describes the ancient inhabitants of Britain as Celts. Instead, a series of more regionally specific names were used – such as Picti, the peoples of north-east Scotland. Modern scholars use the terms 'Picts' and 'Pictish' to refer to these peoples in the period c. 300–900.
2 Graham-Campbell 1991, 246.
3 Stevenson 1955. Late Roman silver was refined for quality and consistency; typically it was around 96% pure, which is better than the modern Sterling standard of 92.5%. Beyond the frontier, the silver was increasingly diluted over successive generations of recycling to make it go further (Goldberg 2012, 181–90).
4 The dating of the hoard is much debated (Graham-Campbell 2002) with the second half of the seventh century generally accepted (Graham-Campbell 1991, 255; Henderson and Henderson 2004, 88; Youngs 2013a, 414–15). Future work by the writer will propose a sixth-century date.
5 Raftery 1983, although the dating of the bronze discs is uncertain and could be later than traditionally dated. The spirals on these objects were among the first to be described as Celtic art by Westwood (1853; see Chapter 8).
6 Clarke 1971.
7 Carson and O'Kelly 1977.
8 Rance 2001.
9 This would have been created in a soft wax model, not directly into the harder silver.
10 A second silver plaque and pin that have long been associated with the Norrie's Law hoard have recently been shown to be nineteenth-century fakes (Goldberg and Blackwell 2013).
11 From Whitecleugh and Parkhill; Youngs 2013a.
12 Fraser 2008.
13 Central Britain is used to mean the lands between the Humber and the Forth–Clyde isthmus.
14 Like the Germanic runic script, the incised notches of ogam were better suited and probably developed for wood. Consequently many ogam texts have probably been lost as wood rarely survives. Those on stone are easily damaged as they are often on exposed edges. The distribution of ogam stones is uneven, with most in the southern half of Ireland (Charles-Edwards 2000, 172–6).
15 Campbell 2001.
16 Forsyth 1997; Lee et al. 2010. There are some ogam inscriptions that record the Pictish language in northern and eastern Scotland, but they are difficult to translate and have not helped yet with deciphering the symbols.
17 This style of depicting animals was later influential on the evangelist animal symbols used in Insular Christian manuscripts (Henderson and Henderson 2004, 31–5; see fig. 8.25 the Trier Gospels).
18 Laing 2005; 2010.
19 Johns 1974.
20 Youngs 2005.
21 Scholars use the German term Trompetenmuster ('trumpet decoration'); Macgregor 1976, vol. 1, 186–9.
22 Laing 2005.
23 Swift 2009.
24 Painter 2013.

25 Gavin and Newman 2007.
26 Bruce-Mitford 2005.
27 Ibid., Table 3. These designs can also be seen on some dress fasteners (Youngs 1989, no. 21).
28 Youngs 2013b.
29 See Ó Floinn 2001; Webster 2012 for Anglo-Saxon brooch types.
30 Fowler 1960.
31 Originally taken as booty: see Maxfield 1981.
32 Laing 1994, 24–5.
33 Youngs 2013a. The only exception is one from the major hillfort settlement of Traprain Law.
34 Painter 2013.
35 Ó Floinn 2001, 5 and fig 1.4; Gavin 2013, 434.
36 Youngs 1989, no. 19; Gavin 2013, 435.
37 Webster 2012.
38 Summarized in Youngs 2009a.
39 For example, at Baginton; Youngs 2009a, 209–13.
40 Bruce-Mitford 2005, no. 88–90. The similarity between the use of millefiori and enamel on the mounts for these bowls and some of the finest Irish zoomorphic penannular brooches, like that found at the high-status crannog of Ballinderry, has led to the suggestion that both could have been made in the same workshop .
41 Ibid., 268–9.
42 Similar interlace mounts can be seen on the Lullingstone hanging-bowl and harness mounts from Sutton Hoo (Laing and Longley 2006, 148).
43 Youngs 2009a.
44 Brown, P. 2003.
45 Youngs 2011.

Chapter 8

1 See Chapter 2 for discussion of this technique.
2 The key publication for the Hunterston brooch is Stevenson 1974; see also Youngs 1989, no. 69; Blackwell 2011.
3 We differentiate between Celtic as a term for a language group as opposed to an artistic style; as discussed later, the two are not coincident.
4 Ryan 1990.
5 Werner 2003; Netzer 2001 gives a useful summary of scholarship.
6 Bede, *HE* (*The Ecclesiastical History of the English People*), Book 1, Chapter 1.
7 Henderson and Henderson 2004, 60.
8 Werner 2003.
9 Carver 2008, 134; Carver and Spall 2004, 193–4.
10 Higgitt 1982; Brown 1972.
11 Even before the recent excavation evidence for parchment production Portmahomack had been suggested as one possible place for the production of the Book of Kells (Brown 1972), although Iona and Kells itself are more widely accepted possibilities.
12 Laing and Longley 2006.
13 Lane and Campbell 2000.
14 Adcock 1974; Cramp 1999.
15 Kitzinger 1993, 3; Wamers 2009.
16 Ó Carragáin 2005.
17 Blackwell 2011.

18 Ryan in Youngs 1989, 129 and nos 128–32.
19 Youngs 1989, no. 131.
20 Kelly 2003.
21 Scott and Ritchie 2009, 4.
22 Netzer 1994.
23 Small *et al.* 1973; Graham-Campbell 2002; Clarke 2008.
24 Wilson 1973, 64; Clarke *et al.* 2012, 126.
25 Webster (ed.) 1991, nos 178 a and b.
26 Such as a helmet from York; Ibid., no. 47 and recent finds in the Staffordshire hoard.
27 Wilson 1973, 65–6.
28 Campbell and Heald 2007.
29 Wilson 1973. Brooches in this style have also been found in Ireland and in Viking graves in Norway, where they were imports or loot.
30 Whitfield 2004.
31 Youngs 1989, no. 185. It is remarkably similar to a finished example found at Lagore crannog; Youngs 1989, no. 186.
32 Carver 2008.
33 The front was chiselled away in the post-medieval period and although thousands of fragments were recovered during recent excavations we do not know precisely what it looked like (James *et al.* 2008).
34 John 15: 1–17.
35 Goldberg 2012, 154–60.
36 Youngs 2009b.
37 Youngs 1989, no. 133; the range of motifs, including spirals, that differentiate the right-hand figure's robes suggest a degree of emphasis is also being placed on the role of Longinus.
38 Wilson 1851, 504–5.
39 Ibid., 220–21.
40 Westwood 1856; for his earlier studies, see Westwood 1843–5; 1853. See Collis 2014 for an assessment of his contribution to Celtic art studies.
41 Wilson 1851, 445
42 Westwood 1856, 92.
43 Ibid., 93.
44 This was first observed by Westwood (1853, 300); over 150 years later and with thousands of sculpture fragments now available for study, these observations still hold true (Cramp 1999), apart from a few fragments in Mercia (Webster 2012, 105) and a few later monuments in Wales, where the spirals are simple and are certainly not the complex curvilinear heritage motifs we see on manuscript art (for example, Edwards (ed.) 2007, 81).
45 Brown, M.P. 2003.
46 Why would spiral art be used on manuscripts created at Lindisfarne and not on the stone monuments? Were they created at different times? Or perhaps its use had become more important than its origin, with the complex curvilinear heritage motifs becoming so closely associated with the manuscript format that in England and Wales it was considered as simply one component of a highly mobile Christian manuscript art?
47 Wilson 1851, 524–30.
48 Ibid., 527.
49 Ibid., 528–9.
50 Stevenson 1974.

Chapter 9

1 The best account of both the shrine and the events that follow remains Lawlor *et al.* 1916.
2 Over the many centuries during which the O'Donel family served as guardians of the shrine, their name was alternately spelled O'Donnel or O'Donnell.
3 For example, Laing and Laing 1995; Moscati *et al.* (eds) 1991; Megaw and Megaw 2001a; Bardiès-Fronty and Dectot (eds) 2008; Müller 2009a.
4 Woolf 2007, 43–7.
5 Henderson 2008; Pulliam 2013.
6 Berg 1958; Ritchie (ed.) 1994; Lord 2003.
7 Manning 1994, 72–4; Forsyth 1995; Lord 2003, 37.
8 Stalley 2014; Henry 2000; Harbison 1992, vol. 1, 146–52.
9 Wallace and Ó Floinn 2002, 215.
10 This scenario is likely, but tentative. For an overview of literature, see Netzer 1989.
11 Netzer 1994. Thomas 'signed' two miniatures 'Thomas scripsit'. Additionally he wrote his name next to a small portrait of the apostle Thomas (ibid., 35).
12 Digitized versions of the Harley Gospels are accessible via http://www.bl.uk/manuscripts/ and the other manuscripts may be accessed at http://www.europeanaregia.eu/en/manuscripts/. Both websites accessed 1 April 1 2015.
13 Farr, 2003, 122–4 and Ben Tilghman, pers. comm.
14 Henry 1970, 190–200.
15 Quoted in Henry 1970, 2.
16 Wallace and Ó Floinn 2002, 269; Hourihane 2003, 117–19.
17 The back and front of the Shrine of St Patrick's bell is reproduced in Wallace and Ó Floinn 2002, cat. 6:26.
18 Lawlor *et al.* 1916, 391. The inscription lists both the craftsman and patrons responsible for the construction of the shrine.
19 Seymour 1932.
20 Henry 1970, 89–90.
21 Ibid.
22 Giraldus Cambrensis (Gerald of Wales), *Topographia Hibernia*, 108.
23 Caldwell *et al.* 2012, 227–9.
24 Hennessy (ed.) 1875, 243.
25 Caldwell *et al.* 2012, 225–7.
26 Lord 2003, 59.
27 Parts of Ireland and mainland Scotland as well as the islands of the west coast that spoke Gaelic as opposed to Scots, English or Anglo-Norman.
28 See Cunningham and Fitzpatrick 2013.
29 Henry and Marsh-Micheli 1987, 798.
30 See p. 157.
31 Carey 2009, 23.
32 O'Kelleher and Schoepperle 1918, xvi.
33 Ibid., 7.
34 Henry and Marsh-Micheli 1987, 802.
35 The title 'Lord of the Isles' (*dominus Insularum*) first appears in a document from 1336 and is used throughout the rest of the fourteenth century, but its adoption may be a conscious gesture to Somerled's rule (d. 1164). Steer *et al.* 1977, 201.
36 Skene (ed.) 1867, 206.
37 RCAHMS 1982, nos 179 and 204.

38 Glenn 2003, 109.
39 Ibid., 111.
40 Ibid., 97–8.
41 The motto of Mary Queen of Scots.
42 Loomis *et al.* 2012, 24.
43 Steer *et al.* 1977, 185.
44 Wilson 1973, 57.

Chapter 10

1   *The Saturday Review*, 10 May 1890, 565; cited in Smith 1997, 60.
2   Pliny the Elder, *Historia Naturalis* XVI, 95.
3   Hartrick 1939, 59 and the painter Robert Macaulay Stevenson's notes, cited in Smith 1997, 59.
4   John Morrison suggests other sources such as the Aylesford bucket (British Museum) and the Dunnichen stone in Angus. See Morrison 2003a; 2003b, 192–7; also Billcliffe (ed.) 2010, 68–70.
5   Collis 2003, 40.
6   Morse 2005, 16.
7   Camden 1586 (quoted here from the English translation of 1610, 26); Morse 2005, 17.
8   See Smiles 2009.
9   As Smiles (2009, 107) has noted, the depictions are based on descriptions of ancient Britons by Caesar, Pliny and Herodian, and of Picts and Scots by Claudian.
10 Ibid., 108.
11 Ibid.
12 Morse 2005, 17–18; Hutton 2009, 69.
13 Morse 2005, 22–8.
14 On Stukeley, see Haycock 2002.
15 Stukeley 1743, plate XV.
16 Morse 2005, 77; Hutton 2009, vi. The portrait is in Bristol University Library, Special Collections.
17 On Gray's poem and related works of art, see McCarthy 1965.
18 On the Welsh bard in visual culture, see Fairclough *et al.* 2001.
19 Lord 2000, 247.
20 Ibid., 248.
21 Now in the Yale Center for British Art.
22 A revised version of the texts appeared in 1773 as 'a new edition, carefully corrected and greatly improved'.
23 On Runciman and Ossian, see Macmillan 1986, chapter IV ('An Ossian's fancy and a Fingal's fire'), 42–62. For a view of Ossian in culture and material culture, see Cheape 1997.
24 Macmillan 1986, 55.
25 Macdonald 2002, 401.
26 Statens Museum for Kunst, Copenhagen.
27 Hugh Blair, writing in 1795, observed of the Orcadians: 'Their ancient language . . . is called the Norse; and is a dialect not of the Celtic, but of the Scandinavian tongue' (Blair 1795, 324).
28 Healey 1959, 127.
29 For a comprehensive discussion of the Celtic Revival in Ireland, see Sheehy 1980.
30 Wilde 1857–62.
31 Gere and Rudoe 2010, 444–53.
32 *Art Journal* 1853, 39; cited in Ibid., 444.

33 On this see further McCrum 1993.
34 Gere and Rudoe 2010, 444.
35 *The Times*, 9 August 1849, 4; cited in Ibid., 446.
36 Youngs 1989, no. 89.
37 Kirschke 2003, 36.
38 On Johnson, see Washer 1992.
39 On this see Camille 1992.
40 Washer 1992, 110.
41 Westwood 1856.
42 When the Swiss archaeologist Ferdinand Keller published on the now iconic site of La Tène in 1866, he openly stated that the attribution of the finds as 'Celtic' was thanks to 'Mr. Franks' work in *Horae Ferales*, where he "very justly lays claim to these swords as products of art by the Celtic nations, and especially by the inhabitants of the British Isles and of Northern Gaul.'" Keller 1866, 258; Morse 2005, 140.
43 On the development of chromolithography and its impact, see Edelstein (ed.) 1992, 123.
44 Sheehy 1980, 24–5. By the late 1880s and 1890s Celtic Revivalists could also refer to Margaret Stokes's detailed illustrations for *Early Christian Art in Ireland* (1887), which reproduced key Insular objects such as St Patrick's bell shrine in intricate detail.
45 On the Arts and Crafts movement in Ireland and Scotland, see Larmour 1992; Bowe and Cumming 1998; Cumming 2007; Carruthers 2013.
46 *Cork Industrial Exhibition 1883. Report*, Cork 1886, 264; cited in Larmour 1992, 4.
47 Dresser 1876, 33.
48 On the Honan Chapel, see Teehan and Heckett 2004.
49 In the 1920s and 1930s Alexander Ritchie (on the island of Iona) and George Bain were among those who continued to be inspired by Celtic design. See Bain 1951; MacArthur 2008.
50 *Glasgow Evening News*, 4 February 1895, 2; cited in Helland 1996, 60.
51 The stylistic influence of Symbolist artists such as Jan Toorop, Carlos Schwabe and Aubrey Beardsley has also been observed. See, for example, Robertson 2006, 34.
52 On the Glasgow School and women designers, see Burkhauser (ed.) 2001.
53 The main authority on Traquair is Elizabeth Cumming (1993; 2006).
54 Gerard Baldwin Brown, *The Scottish Art Review*, January 1889; cited in Cumming 1993, 13.
55 On Geddes's artistic circle and contacts with France, see Fowle and Thomson (eds) 2004. See also Cumming 1990.
56 Allen 1885. Classes in Celtic ornament were also held at Edinburgh School of Art.
57 The woman was modelled on Ella Carmichael, whose father, Alexander Carmichael, edited *Carmina Gadelica*.
58 On this image, see Macdonald 2003.
59 In the collection of the National Trust for Scotland.
60 On Puvis de Chavannes and other French sources for John Duncan, see Fowle 2004.
61 Victoria and Albert Museum, London, accession no. M.39–1968.
62 On Knox, see most recently O'Neill (ed.) 2014.
63 Bernbaum 2014, 37.
64 Guest 1838–48; d'Arbois de Jubainville 1883; Yeats 1893; Gregory 1904; Macleod 1896.
65 On Arnold, see, for example, Pittock 1999, 64–9.

66 On this, see Fergusson 1998.
67 Taylor 1889, 248.
68 Anon., 'Pan-Celtic Congress', *The Advertiser*, 9 November 1907, 8 (reporting on the Edinburgh Pan-Celtic Congress).
69 Pittock 1999, 72.
70 Hutton 2009, 127.
71 Anon., 'Pan-Celtic Congress', *The Advertiser*, 9 November 1907, 8 (reporting on the Edinburgh Pan-Celtic Congress).
72 On Caratacus, see Tacitus, *Annals* 12:34–40; Webster 2003.
73 This was a year after the publication of Gray 1897.
74 See Anon. 1867, 43–7.
75 Aldhouse-Green 2006; Hagerman 2013.
76 Current whereabouts unknown.
77 Tacitus, *Annals* 14:35. 'Boudica with her daughters before her in a chariot went up to tribe after tribe, protesting that it was indeed usual for Britons to fight under the leadership of women. "But now," she said, "it is not as a woman descended from noble ancestry, but as one of the people that I am avenging lost freedom, my scourged body, the outraged chastity of my daughters."'

Chapter 11

1   For the find circumstances see Kaul 1991b. For the cauldron itself: Klindt-Jensen 1950; Megaw 1970a, nos 209, 214; Kaul 1991c; 1991d; 1995; 1999.
2   Benner Larsen 1987, table 1; Kaul 1999, 201–7.
3   For example, Klindt-Jensen 1950, 119–52; 1959; 1979; Hachmann 1990. Olmsted (1979, 211–28) proposed links to the Irish heroic tale *Táin Bó Cuailnge* (the *Cattle Raid of Cooley*).
4   For example, Powell 1971; Bergquist and Taylor 1987; papers in Kaul *et al.* 1991.
5   This fits broader late Iron Age trends; see Chapter 5 in this volume.
6   Taylor 1992, 70–71.
7   Ibid.; Kaul 1995.
8   Wells 2012, 201–9.
9   Eggers 1964; Vang Petersen 2003; Hedeager 2011, 50–98.
10 Graham-Campbell 2013, 77–80.
11 Note, for instance, the longevity of such features as paired animals ('dragon pairs'; Ginoux 2007), or the brooch from Finlaggan in western Scotland, which drew on Continental styles of several hundred years earlier (Hunter 2009b).
12 For example, Duval 1977; Moscati *et al.* 1991; Megaw and Megaw 2001a.
13 For example, Merriman 1987; Chapman 1992; James 1999; Collis 2003.
14 Creighton 2006.
15 For the use of these terms, see Chapter 1 in this volume.
16 See Chapter 10 for further discussion.
17 A '. . .visual manifesto of the Celtic revival' (Macdonald 2003, 29).

Bibliography

Abbreviations

RIB I: R.G. Collingwood and R.P. Wright 1965 *The Roman Inscriptions of Britain. Volume I: Inscriptions on Stone*. Oxford

Ancient sources

Adomnán, *Vita sancti Columbae* = *Life of St Columba* (trans. R. Sharpe, 1995). London

Bede, *HE* (*Historia ecclesiastica gentis Anglorum*) = *The Ecclesiastical History of the English People* (trans. B. Colgrave, 1999). Oxford

G. Julius Caesar *Commentarii de Bello Gallico* = *The Conquest of Gaul* (trans. S.A. Handford, 1951). London

Giraldus Cambrensis, *Topographia Hibernia* = *Gerald of Wales, The History and Topography of Ireland* (trans. J.J. O'Meara, 1982). London

Philostratus, *Imagines* (trans. A. Fairbanks, 1931) *Elder Philostratus, Younger Philostratus, Callistratus*. London (= Loeb Classical Library 256)

Pliny the Elder, *Historia Naturalis* = *The Natural History* (vol. III, trans. J. Bostock and H.T. Riley, 1855). London.

Tacitus, *Agricola* (trans. M. Hutton, revised by R.M. Ogilvie, 1970). Cambridge, Massachusetts (= Loeb Classical Library 35)

Tacitus, *Annals* (trans. A.J. Church and W.J. Brodribb, 2003). New York

Tacitus, *Germania* (trans. A.J. Church and W.J. Brodribb, 1864–77) *The Works of Tacitus*. Reprinted 1942, London

Other sources/references

Adcock, G. 1974 'A study of the types of interlace on Northumbrian sculpture, unpublished M.Phil. thesis, University of Durham

Adler, W. 2003 *Der Halsring von Männern und Göttern*. Bonn

Aldhouse-Green, M. 2003 'Alternative iconographies: metaphors of resistance in Romano-British cult imagery', in Noelke *et al.* (eds) 2003, 39–48

Aldhouse-Green, M. 2004 *An Archaeology of Images: Iconology and Cosmology in Iron Age and Roman Europe*. London

Aldhouse-Green, M. 2006 *Boudica Britannia: Rebel, War-leader and Queen*. Harlow

Aldhouse-Green, M. 2010 *Caesar's Druids: Story of an Ancient Priesthood*. Yale

Allen, D.F. 1970 'The coins of the Iceni', *Britannia* 1, 1–33

Allen, D.F. 1980 *The Coins of the Ancient Celts*. Edinburgh

Allen, J.R. 1885 'Notes on Celtic ornament: the key and spiral patterns', *Proceedings of the Society of Antiquaries of Scotland* 19, 253–308

Almagro-Gorbea, M. 1991 'The Celts of the Iberian peninsula', in Moscati *et al.* (eds) 1991, 388–405

Anon. 1867 *Catalogue of the Sculpture, Paintings, Engravings and Other Works of Art belonging to the Corporation, together with the Books not included in the Catalogue of the Guildhall Library. Part the First*. London

Armit, I. 2012 *Headhunting and the Body in Iron Age Europe*. Cambridge

Atkinson, R.J.C. and Piggott, S. 1955 'The Torrs chamfrein', *Archaeologia* 96, 197–235

Bacault, M. and Flouest, J.-L. 2003 'Schémas de construction des décors au compass des phalères laténiennes de Champagne', in O. Buchsenchutz, A. Bulard, M.-B. Chardenoux and N. Ginoux (eds) 2003 *Décors, images et signes de l'âge du Fer europeéen*, 145–70. Tours

Bain, G. 1951 *Celtic Art: The Methods of Construction* (reprinted: Dover Publications 1973). New York

Baitinger, H. and Pinsker, B. (eds) 2002 *Das Rätsel der Kelten vom Glauberg*. Stuttgart

Bardiès-Fronty, I. and Dectot, X. 2008 *Celtes et Scandinaves. Rencontres Artistiques VIIe-XIIe Siècle*. Paris

Barril Vicente, M. 2002 'Los torques de plata más representativos an el Museo Arqueológico Nacional', in Barril Vicente and Romero Riaza (eds) 2002, 111–28

Barril Vicente, M. and Romero Riaza, A. (eds) 2002 *Torques: Belleza y Poder*. Madrid

Bartel, A. 2002 'Die verpackten Kannen aus den Gräbern 1 und 2', in Baitinger and Pinsker (eds) 2002, 163–7

Beilharz, D. and Krausse, D. 2012 'Symbole der Macht. Repräsentation in frühkeltischer Zeit', in Röber *et al.* (eds) 2012, 187–99

Bender Jørgensen, L. 1992 *North European Textiles until AD 1000*. Aarhus

Benner Larsen, E. 1987 'SEM-identification and documentation of tool marks and surface textures on the Gundestrup cauldron', in J. Black (ed.) 1987 *Recent Advances in the Conservation and Analysis of Artifacts*, 393–408. London

Bentley, R.A. 2006 'Strontium isotopes from the earth to the archaeological skeleton: a review', *Journal of Archaeological Method and Theory* 13, 135–87.

Berg, K. 1958 'The Gosforth cross', *Journal of the Warburg and Courtauld Institutes* 21, no. 1/2, 27–43 (doi: 10.2307/750485)

Bergquist, A. and Taylor, T. 1987 'The origin of the Gundestrup cauldron', *Antiquity* 61, 10–24

Bernbaum, A. 2014 'Origins of the Liberty Cymric silver range', *Journal of the Archibald Knox Society* 3, 26–43

Billcliffe, R. (ed.) 2010 *Pioneering Painters: The Glasgow Boys*. Glasgow

Binding, U. 1993 *Studien zu den figürlichen Fibeln der Frühlaténezeit*. Bonn

Blackwell, A. 2011 'The iconography of the Hunterston brooch and related comparanda' *Proceedings of the Society of Antiquaries of Scotland* 141, 231–48

Blackwell, A. 2012 'Individuals', in Clarke *et al.* 2012, 3–67

Blair, H. 1795 'A critical dissertation on the poems of Ossian, the son of Fingal' in Macpherson 1795 (vol. 2), 275–376

Boon, G.C. and Savory, H.N.

1975 'A silver trumpet-brooch with relief decoration, parcel-gilt, from Carmarthen, and a note on the development of the type', *Antiquaries Journal* 55(1), 41–61

Bowe, N.G. and Cumming, E. 1998 *The Arts and Crafts Movements in Dublin and Edinburgh, 1885–1925*. Dublin

Bradley, R. 1990 *The Passage of Arms: an Archaeological Analysis of Prehistoric Hoards and Votive Deposits*. Cambridge

Bradley, R. 2009 *Image and Audience: Rethinking Prehistoric Art*. Oxford

Brailsford, J.W. 1962 *Hod Hill Volume One. Antiquities from Hod Hill in the Durden Collection*. London

Brailsford, J.W. 1964 *Guide to the Antiquities of Roman Britain*, 3rd edn. London

Brailsford, J. 1975a *Early Celtic Masterpieces from Britain in the British Museum*. London

Brailsford, J.W. 1975b 'The Polden Hill hoard, Somerset', *Proceedings of the Prehistoric Society* 41, 222–34

Breeze, D. (ed.) 2012 *The First Souvenirs: Enamelled Vessels from Hadrian's Wall*. Kendal

Briggs, S. 2014 'The Torrs *chamfrein* or head-piece: restoring "a very curious relic of antiquity"', in Gosden *et al.* (eds) 2014, 341–55

Brown, M.P. 2003 *The Lindisfarne Gospels: Society, Spirituality and the Scribe* (vol. 1). Toronto

Brown, P. 2003 *The Rise of Western Christendom*. Oxford

Brown, T.J. 1972 'Northumbria and *The Book of Kells*', *Anglo-Saxon England* 1, 219–46

Bruce-Mitford, R. 2005 *A Corpus of Late Celtic Hanging-Bowls*. Oxford

Brun, J.-P., Poux, M. and Tchernia, A. (eds) 2009 *Le Vin. Nectar des Dieux. Génie des Hommes*, 2nd edn. Gollion

Brunaux, J.L. 1988 *The Celtic Gauls: Gods, Rites and Sanctuaries*. London

Buchanan, G. 1582 *Rerum Scoticarum Historia*. Edinburgh (trans. J. Aikman, 1827) *The History of Scotland Translated from the Latin of George Buchanan*. Glasgow

Budd, P., Millard, A., Chenery, C., Lucy, S. and Roberts, C.

2004 'Investigating population movement by stable isotope analysis: a report from Britain', *Antiquity* 78, 127–41

Buist, G. 1839 *Report by Mr George Buist on the Silver Fragments in the Possession of General Durham, Largo, commonly called the Silver Armour of Norrie's Law. To the Fifeshire Literary and Antiquarian Society*. Cupar

Burkhauser, J. (ed.) 2001 *Glasgow Girls: Women in Art and Design 1880–1910*. Edinburgh

Caldwell, D.H., Kirk, S., Márkus, G., Tate, J. and Webb, S. 2012 'The Kilmichael Glassary bell-shrine', *Proceedings of the Society of Antiquaries of Scotland* 142, 201–44

Camden, W. 1586 *Britannia*. London

Camden, W. 1610 *Britain* (trans. P. Holland). London

Camille, M. 1992 'Domesticating the dragon: the rediscovery, reproduction and re-invention of early Irish metalwork', in Edelstein (ed.) 1992, 1–19

Campbell, E. 2001 'Were the Scots Irish?', *Antiquity*, 75, 285–92

Campbell, E. and Heald, A. 2007 'A Pictish brooch mould from North Uist: implications for the organisation of non-ferrous metalworking in the later 1st millennium AD.' *Medieval Archaeology* 51, 172–8

Carey, J. 2009 'Compilations of lore and legend: Leabhar na hUidhre and the books of Uí Mhaine, Ballymote, Lecan and Fermoy', in B. Cunningham and S. Fitzpatrick (eds) 2009 *Treasures of the Royal Irish Academy Library*, 17–31. Dublin

Carr, G. and Stoddart, S. (eds) 2002 *Celts from Antiquity*. Cambridge

Carruthers, A. 2013 *The Arts and Crafts Movement in Scotland*. New Haven and London

Carson, R.A.G. and O'Kelly, C. 1977 'A catalogue of the Roman coins from Newgrange, Co. Meath and notes on the coins and related finds', *Proceedings of the Royal Irish Academy, Section C: Archaeology, Celtic Studies, History, Linguistics, Literature* 77, 35–55

Carter, S., Hunter, F. and Smith, A. 2010 'A 5th century BC Iron Age chariot burial from Newbridge, Edinbugh', *Proceedings of the Prehistoric Society* 76, 31–74

Cartwright, C.R., Meeks, N., Hook, D., Mongiatti, A. and Joy, J. 2012 'Organic cores from the Iron Age Snettisham torc hoard; technological insights revealed by scanning electron microscopy', in N. Meeks, C.R. Cartwright, A. Meek and A. Mongiatti (eds) 2012 *Historical Technology, Materials and Conservation: Scanning Electron Microscopy and Microanalysis*, 21–9. London

Carver, M. 2008 *Portmahomack. Monastery of the Picts*. Edinburgh

Carver, M. and Spall, C. 2004 'Excavating a *parchmenerie*: archaeological correlates of making parchment at the Pictish monastery at Portmahomack, Easter Ross', *Proceedings of the Society of Antiquaries of Scotland* 134, 183–200

Champion, S.T. 1976 'Coral in Europe: commerce and Celtic ornament', in P.-M. Duval and C.F.C. Hawkes (eds) 1976 *Celtic Art in Ancient Europe, Five Protohistoric Centuries*, 29–40. London

Chapman, M. 1992 *The Celts: the Construction of a Myth*. Basingstoke

Charles-Edwards, T. 2000 *Early Christian Ireland*. Cambridge

Charpy, J.-J. 2009 'Three-dimensional decoration in Champagne country', in Müller 2009a, 218–9

Cheape, H. 1997 'The culture and material culture of Ossian, 1760–1900', *Scotlands* 4(1), 1–24

Clarke, D.V. 1971 'Small finds in the Atlantic province: problems of approach', *Scottish Archaeological Forum* 3, 22–54

Clarke, D. 2008 *St Ninian's Isle Treasure*. Edinburgh

Clarke, D. 2012 'Communities', in Clarke *et al.* 2012, 69–139

Clarke, D., Blackwell, A. and Goldberg, M. 2012 *Early Medieval Scotland. Individuals, Communities and Ideas*. Edinburgh

Collis, J. 1984 *Oppida. Earliest Towns North of the Alps*. Sheffield

Collis, J. 1999 'George Buchanan and the Celts in Britain', in R. Black, W. Gillies and R. Ó Maolalaigh (eds) 1999 *Celtic Connections: Proceedings of the Tenth International Congress of Celtic Studies. Volume One: Language, Literature, History, Culture*, 91–107. East Linton

Collis, J. 2003 *The Celts: Origins, Myths and Inventions*. Stroud

Collis, J. 2014 'The Sheffield origins of Celtic art', in Gosden *et al.* (eds) 2014, 19–27

Cool, H.E.M. 1986 'A Romano-British gold workshop of the second century', *Britannia* 17, 231–7

Cooney, G., Becker, K., Coles, J., Ryan, M. and Sievers, S. (eds) 2009 *Relics of Old Decency. Archaeological Studies of Later Prehistory. A Festschrift for Barry Raftery*. Dublin

Cottam, E., de Jersey, P., Rudd, C. and Sills, J. 2010 *Ancient British Coins*. Aylsham

Cramp, R. 1999. *Grammar of Anglo-Saxon Ornament: A General Introduction to the Corpus of Anglo-Saxon Stone Sculpture*. Oxford

Creighton, J. 1994 'A time of change: the Iron Age to Roman monetary transition in East Anglia', *Oxford Journal of Archaeology* 13, 325–33.

Creighton, J. 2000 *Coins and Power in Late Iron Age Britain*. Cambridge

Creighton, J. 2006 *Britannia: The Creation of a Roman Province*. Oxford

Crowfoot, E. 1991 'The textiles', in Stead 1991b, 119–25

Cumming, E. 1990 '"A gleam of Renaissance hope": Edinburgh at the turn of the century', in Kaplan (ed.) 1990, 149–61

Cumming, E. 1993 *Phoebe Anna Traquair 1852–1936*. Edinburgh

Cumming, E. 2006 *Phoebe Anna Traquair 1852–1936*. Edinburgh

Cumming, E. 2007 *Hand, Heart and Soul: The Arts and Crafts Movement in Scotland*. Edinburgh

Cunliffe, B. 1997 *The Ancient Celts*. Oxford

Cunliffe, B. 2001 *Facing the Ocean: the Atlantic and its Peoples*. Oxford

Cunliffe, B.W. 2005 *Iron Age Communities in Britain*, 4th edn. London

Cunliffe, B. 2008 *Europe Between the Oceans 9000 BC – AD 1000*. New York and London

Cunliffe, B. 2010 'Celticization from the west. The contribution of archaeology', in Cunliffe and Koch (eds) 2010, 13–38

Cunliffe, B. 2013 *Britain Begins*. Oxford

Cunliffe, B. and Koch, J.T. 2010 'Introduction', in Cunliffe and Koch (eds) 2010, 1–10

Cunliffe, B. and Koch, J.T. (eds) 2010 *Celtic from the West. Alternative Perspectives from Archaeology, Genetics, Language and Literature*. Oxford

Cunningham, B. and Fitzpatrick, S. 2013 *Aon amharc ar Éirinn: Gaelic Families and their Manuscripts*. Dublin

Curle, C.L. 1982 *Pictish and Norse Finds from the Brough of Birsay 1934–74*. Edinburgh

Cusack, T. and Bhreathnach-Lynch, S. (eds) 2003 *Art, Nation and Gender: Ethnic Landscapes, Myths and Mother-Figures*. Ashgate

d'Arbois de Jubainville, M.H. 1883 *Introduction à l'étude de la littérature celtique* Paris (= Cours de littérature celtique 1)

Daubney, A. 2010 'The cult of Totatis: evidence for tribal identity in mid Roman Britain', in Worrell *et al.* (eds) 2010, 109–20

Davies, J.A. 2011 'Boars, bulls and Norfolk's Celtic menagerie', in Davies (ed.) 2011, 59–68

Davies, J.A. (ed.) 2011 *The Iron Age in Northern East Anglia: New Work in the Land of the Iceni*. Oxford (= BAR British Series 549)

Davies, J.L. and Spratling, M.G. 1976 'The Seven Sisters hoard: a centenary study', in G.C. Boon and J.M. Lewis (eds) 1976 *Welsh Antiquity*, 121–47. Cardiff

Davis, M. and Gwilt, A. 2008 'Material, style and identity in first century AD metalwork, with particular reference to the Seven Sisters Hoard', in Garrow *et al.* (eds) 2008, 146–84

Davis, O., Sharples, N. and Waddington, K. (eds) 2008 *Changing Perspectives on the First Millennium BC*. Oxford

Deberge, Y. 2010 'Nouvel ensemble de vases à décors peints en territoire arverne', *Jahrbuch des Römisch-Germanischen Zentralmuseums Mainz* 57, 123–49

Déchelette, J. 1914 *Manuel d'Archéologie Préhistorique, Céltique et Gallo-Romaine II: Archéologie Celtique ou Protohistorique –*

troisième partie, Second Age du Fer ou Époque de La Tène. Paris

Deutscher, L. 2012 'Latènezeitliche Schwerter mit Stempelmarken', *Jahrbuch des Römisch-Germanischen Zentralmuseums Mainz* 59, 245–363

Diepeveen-Jansen, M. 2001 *People, Ideas and Goods. New Perspectives on 'Celtic Barbarians' in Western and Central Europe (500–250 BC)*. Amsterdam

Dresser, C. 1876 *Studies in Design*. London

Dunning, C. 1991 'La Tène', in Moscati *et al.* (eds) 1991, 366–8

Durham, E. 2012 *Depicting the Gods: Metal Figurines in Roman Britain* (= *Internet Archaeology* 31; http://dx.doi.org/10.11141/ia.31.2)

Durham, E. 2014 'Style and substance: some metal figurines from south-west Britain', *Britannia* 45, 195–221

Duval, P.-M. 1977 *Les Celtes*. Paris

Eckardt, H. 2008 'Technologies of the body: Iron Age and Roman grooming and display', in Garrow *et al.* (eds) 2008, 113–28

Edelstein, T.J. (ed.) 1992 *Imagining an Irish Past: The Celtic Revival 1840–1940*. Chicago

Edwards, N. (ed.) 2007 *A Corpus of Early Medieval Inscribed Stones and Stone Sculpture in Wales: South-West Wales* (vol. 2). Cardiff

Edwards , N. (ed.) 2013 *A Corpus of Early Medieval Inscribed Stones and Stone Sculpture in Wales: North-West Wales*. Cardiff

Eggers, H.J. 1964 'Die Kunst der Germanen in der Eisenzeit', in H.J. Eggers, E. Will, R. Joffroy and W. Holmqvist 1964 *Kelten und Germanen in heidnischer Zeit*. Zürich (= Kunst der Welten 4)

Elsner, J. 2007 *Roman Eyes: Visuality and Subjectivity in Art and Text*. Princeton

Emilov, J. and Megaw, V. 2012 'Celts in Thrace? A re-examination of the tomb of Mal Tepe, Mezek, with particular reference to the La Tène chariot fittings', *Archaeologia Bulgarica* 16(1), 1–32

Evans, A.J. 1890 'On a late-Celtic urn-field at Aylesford, Kent, and on the Gaulish, Illyro-Italic, and Classical connexions of the forms of pottery and bronze-work there discovered', *Archaeologia* (2nd series) 52, 315–88

Evans, C. 1989 'Perishables and worldly goods – artefact decoration and classification in the light of wetlands research', *Oxford Journal of Archaeology* 8, 179–201

Evans, D. 2006 'Celtic art revealed. The South Cave weapons hoard', *Current Archaeology* 203, 572–7

Evans, D.H., George, R., Anderson, K., Cameron, E., Doherty, A., Goodman, E., Marshall, M., Northover, P. and O'Connor, S. forthcoming 'A first century AD hoard of weapons from South Cave, East Riding of Yorkshire', for submission to *Britannia*

Evans, J.A., Chenery, C.A. and Montgomery, J. 2012 'A summary of strontium and oxygen isotope variation in archaeological human tooth enamel excavated from Britain', *Journal of Analytical Atomic Spectrometry* 27, 754–64

Facos, M. and Hirsh, S.L. (eds) 2003 *Art, Culture and National Identity in fin-de-siècle Europe*. Cambridge

Fairclough, O., Gwilt, A. and Lile, E. 2001 *Cambria's Curse: Images of the Bard 1750–1850*. Cardiff

Farr, C. 2003 'Style in late Anglo-Saxon England: questions of learning and intention', in C.E. Karkov and G.H. Brown (eds), *Anglo-Saxon Styles*, 115–31. New York

Fergusson, W. 1998 *The Identity of the Scottish Nation: A Historic Quest*. Edinburgh

Fernández-Götz, M. and Krausse, D. 2013 'Rethinking early Iron Age urbanisation in central Europe: the Heuneburg site and its archaeological environment', *Antiquity* 87, 473–87

Fichtl, S. 2005 *La ville celtique. Les oppida de 150 av. J.-C. à 15 ap. J.-C.*, rev. edn. Paris

Fitzpatrick, A.P. 1996 'Night and day: the symbolism of astral signs on later Iron Age anthropomorphic short swords', *Proceedings of the Prehistoric Society* 62, 373–98

Fitzpatrick, A.P. 1997 *Who Were the Druids?* London

Fitzpatrick, A.P. 2007a 'Dancing with dragons: fantastic animals in the earlier Celtic art of Iron Age Britain', in C. Haselgrove

and T. Moore (eds) 2007 *The Later Iron Age in Britain and Beyond*, 339–57. Oxford

Fitzpatrick, A.P. 2007b 'Druids: towards an archaeology', in C. Gosden, H. Hamerow, P. de Jersey & G. Lock (eds) 2007 *Communities and Connections: Essays in Honour of Barry Cunliffe*, 287–315. Oxford

Fitzpatrick, A. and Schönfelder, M. 2014 'Ascot hats: an Iron Age leaf crown helmet from Fiskerton, Lincolnshire?', in Gosden *et al.* (eds) 2014, 286–96

Forsyth, K. 1995 'The inscription on the Dupplin cross', in C. Bourke (ed.) 1995 *From the Isles of the North: Early Medieval Art in Ireland and Britain*, 237–44. Belfast

Forsyth, K. 1997 'Some thoughts on Pictish symbols as a formal writing system', in D. Henry (ed.) 1997 *The Worm, the Germ, and the Thorn*, 85–98. Balgavies

Forsyth K, 2005 'HIC MEMORIA PERPETUA: the inscribed stones of sub-Roman southern Scotland', in S. Foster and M. Cross (eds) *Able Minds and Practised Hands: Scotland's Early Medieval Sculpture in the Twenty-First Century*. Society for Medieval Archaeology Monograph Series 23, 113–34. Leeds

Fowle, F. 2004 'The Franco-Scottish alliance: artistic links between Scotland and France in the late 1880s and 1890s', in Fowle and Thomson (eds) 2004, 37–44

Fowle, F. and Thomson, B. (eds) 2004 *Patrick Geddes: The French Connection*. Oxford

Fowler, E. 1960 'The origins and development of the penannular brooch in Europe', *Proceedings of the Prehistoric Society* 26, 149–77

Franks, A.W. 1863 'Description of the plates', in Kemble 1863, 123–217

Fraser, I. 2008 *The Pictish Symbol Stones of Scotland*. Edinburgh

Frey, O.-H. 1995 'Das Grab von Waldalgesheim. Ein Stilphase des keltischen Kunsthandwerks', in Joachim 1995, 159–206

Frey, O.-H. 2004 'A new approach to early Celtic art', *Proceedings*

of the Royal Irish Academy, Section C 104, 107–29

Furger-Gunti, A. 1991 'The Celtic war chariot. The experimental reconstruction in the Schweizerisches Landesmuseum', in Moscati *et al.* (eds) 1991, 356–9

García Vuelta 2002 'Los torques áureos más representativos del Museo Arqueológico Nacional', in Barril Vicente and Romero Riaza (eds) 2002, 97–110

Garrow, D. 2008 'The time and space of Celtic art: interrogating the "Technologies of Enchantment" database', in Garrow *et al.* (eds) 2008, 15–39

Garrow, D., Gosden, C. and Hill, J.D. (eds) 2008 *Rethinking Celtic Art*. Oxford

Garrow, D. Gosden, C., Hill, J.D. and Bronk Ramsey, C. 2009 'Dating Celtic art: a major radiocarbon dating programme of Iron Age and early Roman metalwork in Britain', *Archaeological Journal* 166, 79–123

Garrow, D. and Gosden, C. 2012 *Technologies of Enchantment? Exploring Celtic Art: 400 BC to AD 100*. Oxford

Gaskill, H. (ed.) 2002 *The Reception of Ossian in Europe*. London

Gavin, F. 2013 'Insular Military-style silver pins in late Iron Age Ireland', in Hunter and Painter (eds) 2013, 427–39

Gavin, F. and Newman, C. 2007 'Notes on insular silver in the "military style"', *Journal of Irish Archaeology* 16, 1–10

Gell, A. 1992 'The technology of enchantment and the enchantment of technology', in J. Coote and A. Shelton (eds) 1992 *Anthropology, Art and Aesthetics*, 40–63. Oxford

Gell, A. 1998 *Art and Agency: An Anthropological Theory*. Oxford

Gere, C. and Rudoe, J. 2010 *Jewellery in the Age of Queen Victoria*. London

Giles, M. 2008 'Seeing red: the aesthetics of martial objects in the British and Irish Iron Age', in Garrow *et al.* (eds) 2008, 59–76

Giles, M. 2012 *A Forged Glamour. Landscape, Identity and Material Culture in the Iron Age*. Oxford

Ginoux, N. 2007 *Le thème symbolique de 'la paire de dragons' sur les fourreaux celtiques (IVe-IIe siècles avant J.-C.)*. Oxford (= BAR International Series 1702)

Ginoux, N. 2009 *Élites guerrières au nord de la Seine au début du IIIe siècle av. J.-C. La nécropole celtique du Plessis-Gassot (Val-d'Oise)*. Lille

Glenn, V. 2003 *Romanesque and Gothic Decorative Metalwork and Ivory Carvings in the Museum of Scotland*. Edinburgh

Goldberg, M. 2012 'Ideas and ideologies' in Clarke *et al.* 2012, 141–203

Goldberg, M. and Blackwell, A. 2013 'The different histories of the Norrie's Law hoard', in J. Hawkes (ed.) 2013, 326–38

Gomez de Soto, J. 2001 'Monde nord-Alpin et/ou Méditerranée? Actualités de l'art celtique de Gaule de l'ouest (Ve-IVe s. av. J.-C.)', *Revue Archéologique* 2001, fascicule 1, 212–18

Gosden, C. and Hill, J.D. 2008 'Introduction: re-integrating "Celtic" art', in Garrow *et al.* (eds) 2008, 1–14

Gosden, C., Crawford, S. and Ulmschneider, K. (eds) 2014 *Celtic Art in Europe: Making Connections. Essays in Honour of Vincent Megaw on his 80th Birthday*. Oxford

Graham-Campbell, J. 1991 'Norrie's Law, Fife: on the nature and dating of the silver hoard' *Proceedings of the Society of Antiquaries of Scotland* 121, 241–59

Graham-Campbell, J. 2002, *Pictish Silver: Status and Symbol*. Cambridge

Graham-Campbell, J. 2013 *Viking Art*. London

Graham-Campbell, J. and Ryan, M. (eds) 2009 *Anglo-Saxon/ Irish Relations Before the Vikings*. Oxford (= Proceedings of the British Academy 157)

Gray, A. 1897 *The Origin and Early History of Christianity in Britain: From its Dawn to the Death of Augustine*. London

Green, M.J. 1976 *The Religions of Civilian Roman Britain*. Oxford (= BAR British Series 24)

Green, M. 1992a *Animals in Celtic Life and Myth*. London

Green, M.J. 1992b *Dictionary of Celtic Myth and Legend*. London

Green, M. 1996 *Celtic Art: Reading the Messages*. London

Gregory, Lady A. 1904 *Gods and Fighting Men*. London

Guest, Lady C. 1838–48 *The Mabinogion*. London

Guggisberg, M. 2009a 'Warrior, hero or god? Stone statue from the Glauberg, about 400 BC', in Müller 2009a, 190–93

Guggisberg, M. 2009b 'Elegance of technique and form. Two beaked flagons from Basse-Yutz, about 360 BC', in Müller 2009a, 200–1

Guggisberg, M. 2009c 'A style which defined a new era: from the burial mound of a Celtic "princess" at Waldalgesheim, about 320 BC', in Müller 2009a, 210–13

Guggisberg, M. and Hoppe, T. 2012 'Von Zirkeln, Ranken und anderen Dingen. Kunst und Künstler der Kelten', in Röber *et al.* (eds) 2012, 42–51

Guichard, V. 1994 'La céramique peinte des IIe et Ier s. avant J-C dans le nord du Massif Central: nouvelles données', *Etudes Celtiques* 30, 103–36

Guichard, V. 2009 'Imaginative designs from the heart of France. Pottery from Clermont-Ferrand, about 120 BC', in Müller 2009a, 234–7

Hachmann, R. 1990 'Gundestrup-Studien. Untersuchungen zu den spätkeltischen Grundlagen der frühgermanischen Kunst', *Bericht der Römisch-Germanischen Kommission* 71(2), 565–903

Hagerman, C.A. 2013 *Britain's Imperial Muse: The Classics, Imperialism and the Indian Empire, 1784–1914*. New York

Harbison, P. 1992 *The High Crosses of Ireland: An Iconographical and Photographic Survey*. Bonn

Harding, D.W. 2002 'Torrs and the early La Tène ornamental style in Britain and Ireland', in B. Ballin Smith and I. Banks (eds) 2002 *In the Shadow of the Brochs: The Iron Age in Scotland*, 191–204. Stroud

Hartrick, A.S. 1939 *A Painter's Pilgrimage Through Fifty Years*. Cambridge

Hauschild, M. 2010 '"Celticised" or "assimilated"? In search of foreign and indigenous people at the time of the Celtic migrations', in B. Sándor (ed.), *Iron Age Communities in the Carpathian Basin. Proceedings of the International Colloquium from Târgu Mureş 9-11 October 2009*, 171–80. Cluj-Napoca

Hautenauve, H. 2005 *Les torques d'or du second Âge du Fer en Europe. Techniques, typologies et symbolique*. Rennes

Hawkes, J. (ed.) 2013 *Making Histories. Proceedings of the Sixth International Insular Arts Conference, York 2011*. Donington

Haycock, D.B. 2002 *William Stukeley: Science, Religion and Archaeology in Eighteenth-Century England*. Woodbridge

Healey, F.G. 1959 *The Literary Cult of Napoleon*. Geneva

Hedeager, L. 2011 *Iron Age Myth and Materiality. An Archaeology of Scandinavia AD 400–1000*. Abingdon

Helland, J. 1996 *The Studios of Frances and Margaret Macdonald*. Manchester

Helms, M.W. 1987 *Ulysses' Sail: an Ethnographic Odyssey of Power, Knowledge, and Geographical Distance*. Princeton

Henderson, G. and Henderson, I. 2004 *The Art of the Picts: Sculpture and Metalwork in Early Medieval Scotland*. London

Henderson, I. 2008 'Understanding the figurative style and decorative programme of the Book of Deer', in K. Forsyth (ed.) 2008 *Studies on the Book of Deer*, 32–67. Dublin

Henig, M. 1974 'A coin of Tasciovanus', *Britannia* 5, 374–5

Henig, M. 1995 *The Art of Roman Britain*. London

Henig, M. 2010 'Souvenir or votive? The Ilam pan', *Association for Roman Archaeology Bulletin* 20, 13–14

Hennessy, W. (ed.) 1875 *The Book of Fenagh in Irish and English* (trans. D. Kelly). Dublin <http://archive.org/details/bookoffenaghinir00dubl> [accessed 23 October 2014]

Henry, F. 1970 *Irish Art in the Romanesque Period (1020–1170 AD)*. London

Henry, F. 2000 *Irish Art During the Viking Invasions, 800–1020 AD*. Cornell

Henry, F. and Marsh-Micheli, G. 1987 'Manuscripts and illuminations', in A. Cosgrove (ed.) 1987 *A New History of Ireland*, 780–815. Oxford

Higgitt, J. 1982 'The Pictish Latin inscription at Tarbat in Ross-shire', *Proceedings of the Society of Antiquaries of Scotland* 112, 300–21

Hill, J.D., Spence, A.J., La Niece, S. and Worrell, S. 2004 'The Winchester hoard: a find of unique Iron Age gold jewellery from southern England', *Antiquaries Journal* 84, 1–22

Holzer, V. 2007 'Roseldorf/Sandberg (Österreich) – ein keltisches Heiligtum nach dem Modell von Gournay-sur-Aronde', in S. Gron and H. Sedlmayer (eds) 2007 *Blut und Wein. Keltisch-römisch Kultpraktiken*, 77–90. Montagnac

Holzer, V. 2008 'Der keltische Kultbezirk in Roseldorf/Sandberg (Niederösterreich)', in E. Lauermann and P. Trebsche (eds) 2008 *Heiligtümer der Druiden. Opfer und Rituale bei den Kelten*, 32–49. Asparn an der Zaya

Hoppe, T. 2009a 'Strict geometry and colourful contrast: luxurious pottery from Gomadingen, 700–650 BC', in Müller 2009a, 172–3

Hoppe, T. 2009b 'Grimacing demons and compass-drawn patterns. The Kleinaspergle grave, about 430 BC', in Müller 2009a, 184–7

Hoppe, T. 2009c 'A gift to the gods? The Trichtingen torque, about 350–100 BC', in Müller 2009a, 222–3

Hoppe, T. and Schorer, B. 2012 'Dämonenfratzen und Zirkelmuster. Die Geburt der Latènekunst', in Röber *et al.* (eds) 2012, 230–44

Horn, J.A. forthcoming 'Tankards of the British Iron Age', submitted to *Proceedings of the Prehistoric Society*

Hourihane, C. 2003 *Gothic Art in Ireland, 1169–1550: Enduring Vitality*, 117–19. London and New Haven

Hull, M.R. and Hawkes, C.F.C. 1987 *Corpus of Ancient Brooches in Britain. Pre-Roman Bow Brooches*. Oxford (= BAR British Series 168)

Hunt, L.B. 1980 'The long history of lost wax casting: over five thousand years of art and craftsmanship', *Gold Bulletin* 13(2), 63–79

Hunter, F. 2001 'The carnyx in Iron Age Europe', *Antiquaries*

Journal 81, 77–108

Hunter, F. 2003 'Funerary lions in Roman provincial art', in Noelke *et al.* (eds) 2003, 59–65

Hunter, F. 2005 'The image of the warrior in the British Iron Age – coin iconography in context', in C.C. Haselgrove and D. Wigg (eds) 2005 *Ritual and Iron Age Coinage in North-West Europe*, 43–68. Mainz (= Studien zu Fundmünzen der Antike 20)

Hunter, F. 2008 'Celtic art in Roman Britain' in Garrow *et al.* (eds) 2008, 129–45.

Hunter, F. 2009a 'A cap for a pony. Pony cap from Torrs, about 200 BC', in Müller 2009a, 230–31

Hunter, F. 2009b 'Miniature masterpieces: unusual Iron Age brooches from Scotland', in Cooney *et al.* (eds) 2009, 143–55

Hunter, F. 2010 'Changing objects in changing worlds: dragonesque brooches and beaded torcs', in Worrell *et al.* (eds) 2010, 91–107

Hunter, F. 2014 'Art in context: the massive metalworking tradition of north-east Scotland', in Gosden *et al.* (eds) 2014, 325–40

Hunter, F. forthcoming a 'Interpreting Celtic art on the Roman frontier – the development of a frontier culture in Britain?', in L. Vagalinski and N. Sharankov (eds) *Proceedings of the 22nd International Congress of Roman Frontier Studies, Ruse, Bulgaria, September 2012*. Sofia

Hunter, F. forthcoming b 'Iron Age swords and Roman soldiers in conquest-period Britain', in T. Grane and X. Pauli Jensen (eds), *Proceedings of the 18th Roman Military Equipment Conference, Copenhagen 2013*. Copenhagen

Hunter, F. and Collard, M. 1997 'The Cramond lioness', *Current Archaeology* 155, 404–7

Hunter, F. and Painter, K. (eds) 2013 *Late Roman Silver: The Traprain Treasure in Context*. Edinburgh

Hutcheson, N.C.G. 2004 *Later Iron Age Norfolk: Metalwork, Landscape and Society*. Oxford (= BAR British Series 361)

Hutton, R. 2009 *Blood and Mistletoe. The History of the Druids in Britain*. New Haven and London.

Ireland, S. 2008 *Roman Britain: A Sourcebook*, 3rd edn. London

Jackson, R. 1995 'The Meyrick helmet: a new interpretation of its decoration', in B. Raftery, V. Megaw and V. Rigby (eds) 1995 *Sites and Sights of the Iron Age*, 67–73. Oxford

Jackson, R. 2010 *Cosmetic Sets of Late Iron Age and Roman Britain*. London (= British Museum Research Publication 181)

Jacobsthal, P. 1941 'Imagery in early Celtic art', *Proceedings of the British Academy* 27, 301–20

Jacobsthal, P. 1944 *Early Celtic Art*. Oxford

James, H., Henderson, I., Foster, S.M. and Jones, S. 2008 *A Fragmented Masterpiece. Recovering the Biography of the Hilton of Cadboll Pictish Cross-Slab*. Edinburgh

James, S. 1999 *The Atlantic Celts. Ancient People or Modern Invention?* London

Jay, M., Haselgrove, C., Hamilton, D., Hill, J.D. and Dent, J. 2012 'Chariots and context: new radiocarbon dates from Wetwang and the chronology of Iron Age burials and brooches in East Yorkshire', *Oxford Journal of Archaeology* 31(2), 161–89

Jay, M., Montgomery, J., Nehlich, O., Towers, J. and Evans, J. 2013 'British Iron Age chariot burials of the Arras culture : a multi-isotope approach to investigating mobility levels and subsistence practices', *World Archaeology* 45(3), 473–91

Joachim, H.-E. 1995 *Waldalgesheim. Das Grab einer keltischen Fürstin*. Bonn

Johns, C.M. 1974 'A Roman silver pin from Oldcroft, Gloucestershire', *Antiquaries Journal* 54, 295–7

Johns, C. 1996 *The Jewellery of Roman Britain: Celtic and Classical Traditions*. London

Johns, C. 2003 'Romano-British sculpture: intention and execution', in Noelke *et al.* (eds) 2003, 27–38

Jones, O. 1856 *Grammar of Ornament*. London

Jope, E.M. 1983 'Torrs, Aylesford and the Padstow hobby-horse', in O'Connor and Clarke (eds) 1983, 149–59

Jope, E.M. 2000 *Early Celtic Art in the British Isles*. Oxford

Joy, J. 2010 *Iron Age Mirrors: A Biographical Approach*. Oxford (= BAR British Series 518)

Joy, J. 2011 '"Fancy objects" in the British Iron Age: why decorate?', *Proceedings of the Prehistoric Society* 77, 205–29

Joy, J. 2014a 'Brit-art: Celtic art in Roman Britain and on its frontiers', in Gosden *et al.* (eds) 2014, 315–24

Joy, J. 2014b '"Fire burn and cauldron bubble": Iron Age and early Roman cauldrons of Britain and Ireland', *Proceedings of the Prehistoric Society* 80, 327–62

Joy, J. and Baldwin, A. forthcoming *The Bubbling Cauldron: The Iron Age Cauldrons from Chiseldon, Wiltshire*. London

Jufer, N. and Luginbühl, T. 2001 *Répertoire des dieux gaulois: les noms des divinités celtiques connus par l'épigraphie, les textes antiques et la toponymie*. Paris

Kaplan, W. (ed.) 1990 *Scotland Creates: 5000 Years of Art and Design*. Glasgow

Karl, R. 2010 'The Celts from everywhere and nowhere. A re-evaluation of the origins of the Celts and the emergence of Celtic cultures', in Cunliffe and Koch (eds) 2010, 39–64

Kaul, F. 1991a 'The ball torques. Celtic art outside the Celtic world', in Moscati *et al.* (eds) 1991, 540

Kaul, F. 1991b 'Introduction: the history of the find', in Kaul *et al.* 1991, 1–5

Kaul, F. 1991c 'The Gundestrup cauldron – Thracian, Celtic or both?', in Kaul *et al.* 1991, 7–42

Kaul, F. 1991d *Gundestrupkedlen: Baggrund og billedverden*. Copenhagen

Kaul, F. 1995 'The Gundestrup cauldron reconsidered', *Acta Archaeologica* 66, 1–38.

Kaul, F. 1999 'Gundestrup', in R. Müller (ed.) 1999 *Reallexikon der Germanischen Altertumskunde* 13, 195–211. Berlin

Kaul, F. 2007 'Celtic influences during pre-Roman Iron Age in Denmark', in S. Möllers, W. Schlüter and S. Sievers (eds) 2007 *Keltische Einflüsse im nördlichen Mitteleuropa während der mittleren und jüngeren vorrömischen Eisenzeit*, 327–45. Bonn

Kaul, F. 2014 'The not so ugly duckling – an essay on meaning', in Gosden *et al.* (eds) 2014, 105–12

Kaul, F., Marazov, I., Best, J. and de Vries, N. 1991 *Thracian Tales on the Gundestrup Cauldron*. Amsterdam

Keller, F. 1866 *The Lake Dwellings of Switzerland and Other Parts of Europe* (trans. J.E. Lee). London

Kelly, E.P. 2003 'The Tully Lough Cross', *Archaeology Ireland* 17(2), 9–10

Kemble, J.M. 1863 *Horae Ferales; or, Studies in the Archaeology of the Northern Nations* (eds R.G. Latham and A.W. Franks). London

Keppie, L. 1998 *Roman Inscribed and Sculptured Stones in the Hunterian Museum, University of Glasgow*. London

Keppie, L.J.F and Arnold, B.J. 1984 *Corpus Signorum Imperii Romani / Corpus of Sculpture of the Roman World. Great Britain. Volume I Fascicule 4: Scotland*. Oxford

Kimmig, W. 1988 *Das Kleinaspergle. Studien zu einem Fürstengrabhügel der frühen Latènezeit bei Stuttgart*. Stuttgart

Kirschke, A.M. 2003 *Materialization of Irishness in Nineteenth-Century Bog Oak Souvenirs*. Madison

Kitzinger, E. 1993 'Interlace and icons: form and function in early Insular art', in R.M. Spearman and J. Higgitt (eds) 1993 *The Age of Migrating Ideas: Early Medieval Art in Northern Britain and Ireland. Proceedings of the Second International Conference on Insular Art Held in the National Museums of Scotland in Edinburgh, 3–6 January 1991*, 3–15. Edinburgh

Klindt-Jensen, O. 1950 *Foreign Influences in Denmark's Early Iron Age*. Copenhagen

Klindt-Jensen, O. 1959 'The Gundestrup bowl: a reassessment', *Antiquity* 33, 161–9

Klindt-Jensen, O. 1979 *Gundestrupkedelen*. Copenhagen

Koch, J.T. 2009 'On Celts calling themselves "Celts" and related questions', *Studia Celtica* 43, 73–86

Koch, J.T. 2010 'Paradigm shift? Interpreting Tartessian as Celtic', in Cunliffe and Koch (eds) 2010, 185 301

Koch, J.T. 2013 'Ha C1a ≠ PC ("The earliest Hallstatt Iron Age cannot equal proto-Celtic")', in Koch and Cunliffe (eds) 2010, 1–13

Koch, J.T. 2014 'Once again Herodotus, the Κελτοι, the source of the Danube, and the Pillars of Hercules', in Gosden et al. (eds) 2014, 6–18

Koch, J.T. and Carey, J. (eds) 1995 The Celtic Heroic Age. Literary Sources for Ancient Celtic Europe and Early Ireland and Wales, 2nd edn. Andover, Massachusetts

Koch, J.T. and Cunliffe, B. (eds) 2013 Celtic from the West 2. Rethinking the Bronze Age and the Arrival of Indo-European in Atlantic Europe. Oxford

Koch, J.T., Karl, R., Minard, A. and Ó Faoláin, S. 2007 An Atlas for Celtic Studies. Oxford

Krämer, W. 1962 'Ein Knollenknaufschwert aus dem Chiemsee', in W. Krämer (ed.) 1962 Aus Bayerns Frühzeit. Festschrift für Friedrich Wagner zum 75. Geburtstag, 109–24. Munich

Krämer, W. 1964 Das keltische Gräberfeld von Nebringen (Kreis Böblingen). Stuttgart

Krausse, D. and Beilharz, E. 2012 'Alles hat ein Ende. Vom Niedergang der Fürstensitze', in Röber et al. (eds) 2012, 205–7

Kruta, V. 1991 'The first Celtic expansion: prehistory to history', in Moscati et al. (eds) 1991, 194–213

Kruta, V., Lička, M. and Cession-Louppe, J. (eds) 2006 Celts. Belges, Boïens, Rèmes, Volques …,. Mariemont

Laing, L. 1994 'The hoard of Pictish silver from Norrie's Law, Fife', Studia Celtica 38, 11–38.

Laing, L. 2005 'The Roman origins of Celtic Christian art', Archaeological Journal 162, 146–76

Laing, L. 2010 European Influence on Celtic Art: Patrons and Artists. Dublin

Laing, L. and Laing, J. 1995 Celtic Britain and Ireland: Art and Society. London

Laing, L. and Longley, D. 2006 The Mote of Mark: A Dark Age Hillfort in South-West Scotland. Oxford

Lambrechts, P. 1954 L'exaltation de la tête dans la pensée et dans l'art des Celtes. Bruges

Lane, A. and Campbell, E. 2000 Excavations at Dunadd: An Early Dalriadic Capital. Oxford

Larmour, C. 1992 The Arts and Crafts Movement in Ireland. Belfast

Lawlor, H.J., Armstrong, E.C.R. and Lindsay, W.M. 1916 'The Cathach of St. Columba', Proceedings of the Royal Irish Academy, Section C 33, 241–443

Lee, R., Jonathan, P. and Ziman, P. 2010 'Pictish symbols revealed as a written language through application of Shannon entropy', Proceedings of the Royal Society A: Mathematical, Physical & Engineering Sciences 466, 1–16

Lejars, T. 1994 Gournay III: les fourreaux d'épée. Le sanctuaire de Gournay-sur-Aronde et l'armement des Celtes de La Tène moyenne. Paris

Lejars, T. 2012 'Verschlungene Verzierungen. Der Schwertstil', in Röber et al. (eds) 2012, 318–25

Lenerz-de Wilde, M. 1977 Zirkelornamentik in der Kunst der Latènezeit. Munich

Lhuyd, E. 1707 Archaeologia Britannica. Volume I. Glossography. Oxford

Lindgren, C.K. 2003 'The provincialization of Classical form in Britannia', in Noelke et al. (eds) 2003, 49–57.

Loomis, K., Caldwell, D., Tate, J., Ogilvie, T., and Van Beek, E.J.R. 2012 'The Lamont and Queen Mary harps', Galpin Society Journal 65, 113–29

Lord, P. 2000 The Visual Culture of Wales: Imaging the Nation. Cardiff

Lord, P. 2003 Medieval Vision. Cardiff

Lucas, A.T. 1987 'In the middle of two living things. Daniel or Christ?', in E. Rynne 1987 Figures from the Past: Studies in Figurative Art in Christian Ireland in Honour of Helen M. Roe, 92–7. Dun Laoghaire

MacArthur, E.M. 2008 Iona Celtic Art. The Work of Alexander and Euphemia Ritchie. Iona

McCarthy, F.I. 1965 'The Bard of Thomas Gray, its composition and its use by painters', National Library of Wales Journal 14, 105–12.

McCone, K. 2008 The Celtic Question: Modern Constructs and Ancient Realities. Dublin (= Miles Dillon Memorial Lecture, April 2008)

McCrum, E. 1993 'Commerce and the Celtic revival: Irish jewelry of the nineteenth century', Éire – Ireland, Winter 1993, 26–52

Macdonald, M. 2002 'Ossian and art: Scotland into Europe via Rome' in Gaskill (ed.) 2002, 393–404

Macdonald, M. 2003 'Anima Celtica: embodying the soul of the nation in 1890s Edinburgh', in Cusack and Bhreathnach-Lynch (eds) 2003, 29–37

McGarry, T. 2008 'Some exotic evidence amidst Irish late prehistoric burials', in Davis et al. (eds) 2008, 215–34

MacGregor, M. 1976 Early Celtic Art in North Britain. Leicester

Macleod, F. 1896 Lyra Celtica. Edinburgh

Macmillan, D. 1986 Painting in Scotland: the Golden Age. London

Macpherson, J. 1773 The Poems of Ossian. London

Macpherson, J. 1795 Morison's Edition of the Poems of Ossian, the Son of Fingal. Perth

Magnen, R. and Thévenot, E. 1953 Épona: déesse gauloise des chevaux, protectrice des cavaliers. Bordeaux

Maniquet, C., Lejars, T., Armbruster, B., Pernot, M., Drieux-Daguerre, M., Mora, P. and Espinasse, L. 2011 'Le carnyx et le casque-oiseau celtiques de Tintignac (Naves-Corrèze). Description et étude technologique', Aquitania 27, 63–150

Manning, W.H. 1985 Catalogue of the Romano-British Iron Tools, Fittings and Weapons in the British Museum. London

Manning, C. 1994 Clonmacnoise. Dublin

Marsden, A. 2011 'The Iron Age coins from Snettisham', in Davies (ed.) 2011, 49–58

Mattei, M. 1991 'The dying Gaul', in Moscati et al. (eds) 1991, 70–71

Maxfield, V.A. 1981 The Military Decorations of the Roman Army. London

Meeks, N., Mongiatti, A. and Joy, J. 2014 'Precious metal torcs from the Iron Age Snettisham treasure: metallurgy and analysis', in E. Pernicka and R. Schwab (eds) 2014 Under the Volcano: Proceedings of the International Symposium on the Metallurgy of the European Iron Age (SMEIA) held in Mannheim, Germany, 20–22 April 2010, 135–55. Rahden

Megaw, J.V.S. 1970a Art of the European Iron Age: A Study of the Elusive Image. Bath

Megaw, J.V.S. 1970b 'Cheshire Cat and Mickey Mouse: analysis, interpretation and the art of the La Tène Iron Age', Proceedings of the Prehistoric Society 36, 261–79

Megaw, J.V.S. 1983 'From Transdanubia to Torrs: further notes on a gabion of the late Jonathan Oldbuck', in O'Connor and Clarke (eds) 1983, 127–48

Megaw, J.V.S. 2002 'A late La Tène anthropoid gripped sword in New York', in K. Kuzmová, K. Pieta and J. Rajtár (eds) 2002 Zwischen Rom und dem Barbaricum: Festschrift für Titus Kolník zum 70. Geburtstag, 407–18. Nitra

Megaw, J.V.S. and Megaw, M.R. 1990 The Basse-Yutz Find: Masterpieces of Celtic Art. London

Megaw, J.V.S. and Megaw, M.R. 2001b 'A cat-and-mouse game: tracing Iron Age elements in the Book of Kells', in E. Pohl, U. Recker and C. Theune (eds) 2001 Archäologisches Zellwerk. Beiträge zur Kulturgeschichte in Europa und Asien. Festschrift für Helmut Roth zum 60. Geburtstag, 209–53. Rahden

Megaw, J.V.S. and Megaw, M.R. 2008 'A Celtic mystery: some thoughts on the genesis of insular Celtic art', in Garrow et al. (eds) 2008, 40–58.

Megaw, R. and Megaw, V. 2001a Celtic Art from its Beginnings to the Book of Kells (revised and expanded edition). London

Megaw, R. and Megaw, V. forthcoming Early Celtic Art: a Supplement. Oxford

Megaw, R., Megaw, V. and Niblett, R. 1999 'A decorated Iron Age copper alloy knife from Hertfordshire', Antiquaries Journal 79, 379–87

Megaw, V. 2005 'Early Celtic art without Scythians? A review', in H. Dobrzańska, V. Megaw and P. Poleska (eds) 2005 Celts on the Margin. Studies in European Cultural Interaction 7th Century BC – 1st Century AD Dedicated to

Zenon Woźniak, 33–47. Kraków

Merriman, N. 1987 'Value and motivation in prehistory: the evidence for "Celtic spirit"', in I. Hodder (ed.) 1987 *The Archaeology of Contextual Meanings*, 111–16. Cambridge

Metzler, J. 1986 'Ein frühlatènezeitliches Gräberfeld mit Wagenbestattung bei Grosbous-Vichten', *Archäologisches Korrespondenzblatt* 16, 161–77

Metzler, J., Gaeng, C. and Le Goff, I. 2009 *Goeblange-Nospelt: une nécropole aristocratique trévire*. Luxembourg

Milcent, P.-Y. 2006 'Premier âge du Fer médio-atlantique et genèse multipolaire des culture matérielles laténiennes', in D. Vitali (ed.) 2006 *Celtes et Gauloises, l'Archéologie face à l'Histoire 2: la Préhistoire des Celtes*, 81–105. Glux-en-Glenne (= Collection Bibracte 12/.2)

Morrison, J. 2003a 'Nationalism and nationhood: late-nineteenth-century painting in Scotland', in Facos and Hirsh (eds) 2003, 186–206

Morrison, J. 2003b *Painting the Nation: Identity and Nationalism in Scottish Painting, 1800–1920*. Edinburgh

Morse, M.A. 2005 *How the Celts Came to Britain: Druids, Ancient Skulls and the Birth of Archaeology*. Stroud

Moscati, S., Frey, O.-H., Kruta, V., Raftery, B. and Szabó, M. (eds) 1991 *The Celts*. Milan

Müller, F. 2009a *Art of the Celts 700 BC to AD 700*. Brussels and Bern

Müller, F. 2009b 'Le mobilier mis au jour à l'emplacement des ponts de La Tène: offrandes, trophées, objéts funéraires?', in M. Honegger, D. Ramseyer, G. Kaenel, B. Arnold, and M.-A. Kaeser (eds) 2009 *Le site de La Tène: bilan des connaissances – état de la question. Actes de la Table ronde internationale de Neuchâtel. 1–3 Novembre 2007*, 87–91. Hauterive (= Archéologie neuchâteloise 43)

Müller, F. 2012 'Keltische Ornamentik par excellence. Der Waldalgesheimstil', in Röber *et al.* (eds) 2012, 295–9

Nash, D. 1987 *Coinage in the Celtic World*. London

Netzer, N. 1989 'Willibrord's scriptorium at Echternach and its relationship to Ireland and Lindisfarne', in G. Bonner. D.W. Rollason and C. Stancliffe (eds) 1989 *St Cuthbert, His Cult and His Community to AD 1200*, 89–106. Woodbridge

Netzer, N. 1994 *Cultural Interplay in the Eighth Century: The Trier Gospels and the Makings of a Scriptorium at Echternach*. Cambridge

Netzer, N. 2001 'Style: a history of uses and abuses in the study of Insular art', in Redknap *et al.* (eds) 2001, 169–77

Noelke, P., Naumann-Steckner, F. and Schneider, B. (eds) 2003 *Romanisation und Resistenz in Plastik, Architektur und Inschriften der Provinzen des Imperium Romanum. Neue Funde und Forschungen*. Mainz

Ó Carragáin, É. 2005 *Ritual and the Rood: Liturgical Images and the Old English Poems of the* Dream of the Rood *Tradition*. London

O'Connor, A. and Clarke, D.V. (eds) 1983 *From the Stone Age to the 'Forty-Five*. Edinburgh

O'Connor, S. 2013 'Exotic materials used in the construction of Iron Age sword handles from South Cave, UK', in A. Choyke and S. O'Connor (eds) 2013 *From These Bare Bones: Raw Materials and the Study of Worked Osseous Objects*, 188–200. Oxford

Ó Floinn, R. 2001 'Patrons and politics: art, artefact and methodology', in Redknap *et al.* (eds) 2001, 1–14

Ó Floinn, R. 2009 'Notes on some Iron Age finds from Ireland', in Cooney *et al.* (eds) 2009, 199–210

O'Kelleher, A. and Schoepperle, G. (eds) 1918 *Betha Colaim Chille: Life of Columcille, Compiled by Manus O Donell in 1532*. Champagne-Urbana

Olivier, L. 2012 'La tombe à char aux bronzes d'art celtique de Roissy (Val-d'Oise)', *Antiquités Nationales* 43, 79–138

Olivier, L. 2014 'Les codes de représentation visuelle dans l'art celtique ancien', in Gosden *et al.* (eds) 2014, 39–55

Olmsted, G.S. 1979 *The Gundestrup Cauldron*. Brussels (= Collections Latomus 162)

O'Meara. J.J. (trans.) 1982 *Gerald of Wales: The History and Topography of Ireland*. London

O'Neill, L. (ed.) 2014 *Archibald Knox: Beauty and Modernity, a Designer Ahead of his Time*. London

Painter, K. 2013 'Hacksilber: a means of exchange', in Hunter and Painter (eds) 2013, 215–42

Pare, C. 2012 'Eastern relations of early Celtic art', in C. Pare (ed.) 2012 *Art and Communication. Centralization Processes in European Societies in the 1st Millennium BC*, 153–78. Mainz

Paysan, M. 2005 'Im Feuer geboren – dem Wasser geweiht. Technologische Untersuchung und Rekonstruktion der Herstellungstechnik keltischer Knollenknaufschwerter im Hinblick auf deren chronologischen Einordnung', *Fundberichte aus Baden-Württemberg* 28(1), 93–206

Perea, A. (ed.) 2011 *La Fíbula Braganza*. Madrid

Pezron, P. 1703 *Antiquité de la Nation, et de la Langue des Celtes, autrement appellez les Gaulois*. Paris

Piggott, S. 1950 'Swords and scabbards of the British early Iron Age', *Proceedings of the Prehistoric Society* 16, 1–28

Piggott, S. 1968 *The Druids*. London

Piggott, S. 1983 *The Earliest Wheeled Transport from the Atlantic Coast to the Caspian Sea*. London

Pion, P. and Guichard, V. 1993 'Tombes et nécropoles en France et au Luxembourg entre le IIIème et le Ier siècles avant J.-C. Essai d'inventaire', in D. Cliquet, M. Remy-Watt, V. Guichard and M. Vaginay (eds) 1993 *Les Celtes en Normandie. Les Rites Funéraires en Gaule (IIIème – Ier siècle avant J.-C.)*, 175–200. Rennes (= Revue Archéologique de l'Ouest, supplement 6)

Pittock, M. 1999 *Celtic Identity and the British Image*. Manchester

Pitts, M. 2010 'Re-thinking the southern British oppida: networks, kingdoms and material culture', *European Journal of Archaeology* 13(1), 32–63

Pope, R. and Ralston, I. 2011, 'Approaching sex and status in Iron Age Britain with reference to the nearer continent', in T. Moore and X.-L. Armada (eds), *Atlantic Europe in the First Millennium BC: Crossing the Divide*, 375–414. Oxford

Powell, T.G.E. 1971 'From Urartu to Gundestrup: the agency of Thracian metal-work', in J. Boardman, M. A. Brown and T.G.E. Powell (eds) 1971 *The European Community in Later Prehistory: Studies in Honour of C.F.C. Hawkes*, 181–210. London

Pulliam, H. 2013 'Beasts of the desert: marginalia in the Book of Deer', *Journal of the Society for Medieval Archaeology* 57, 83–110

Raftery, B. 1983 *A Catalogue of Irish Iron Age Antiquities*. Marburg

Raftery, B. 1984 *La Tène in Ireland: Problems of Origin and Chronology*. Marburg

Raftery, B. 1994 'Reflections on the Irish Scabbard Style', in C. Dobiat (ed.) 1994 *Festschrift für Otto-Herman Frey zum 65. Geburtstag*, 475–92. Marburg

Rance, P. 2001 'Attacotti, Déisi and Magnus Maximus: the case for Irish federates in late Roman Britain', *Britannia* 32, 243–70

RCAHMS 1982 *Argyll: An Inventory of the Monuments. Volume 4: Iona*. Edinburgh (Royal Commission on the Ancient & Historical Monuments of Scotland)

Read, A. 2011 *The Faddon More Psalter: Discovery, Conservation and Investigation*. Dublin

Redfern, R. 2008 'A bioarchaeological analysis of violence in Iron Age females: a perspective from Dorset, England (fourth century BC to the first century AD)', in Davis *et al.* (eds) 2008, 139–60

Redknap, M. 1995 'Early Christianity and its monuments', in M. Green (ed.) 1995 *The Celtic world*, 737–78. London

Redknap M. and Lewis J. 2007 *A Corpus of Early Medieval Inscribed Stones and Stone Sculpture in Wales: South-East Wales and the English Border*. Cardiff

Redknap, M., Edwards, N., Youngs, S., Lane, A. and Knight, J. (eds) 2001 *Pattern and Purpose in Insular Art. Proceedings of the Fourth International*

Conference on Insular Art Held at the National Museum & Gallery, Cardiff 3–6 September 1998. Oxford

Renfrew, C. 2013 'Early Celtic in the West. The Indo-European context', in Koch and Cunliffe (eds) 2013, 207–17

Rieckhoff, S. and Fichtl, S. 2011 Keltenstädte aus der Luft. Stuttgart

Ritchie, A. (ed.) 1994 Govan and its Early Medieval Sculpture. Stroud

Röber, R., Jansen, M., Rau, S., von Nicolai, C. and Frech, I. (eds) 2012 Die Welt der Kelten. Zentren der Macht – Kostbarkeiten der Kunst (catalogue of Stuttgart exhibitions). Ostfildern

Robertson, P. 2006 Doves and Dreams: The Art of Frances Macdonald and J. Herbert McNair, 34. Glasgow

Rogers, J.J. 1873 'Romano-British or late Celtic remains at Trelan Bahow, St Keverne, Cornwall', Archaeological Journal 30, 267–72

Romero, A.M. 2006 Bibracte. Archéologie d'une ville gauloise. Glux-en-Glenne

Ross, A. 1958 'The human head in insular pagan Celtic religion', Proceedings of the Society of Antiquaries of Scotland 91 (1957–8), 10–43

Rothe, U. 2012 'Clothing in the middle Danube provinces. The garments, their origins and their distribution', Jahreshefte des Österreichischen Archäologischen Instituts in Wien 81, 137–231

Rowley-Conwy, P. 2007 From Genesis to Prehistory. The Archaeological Three Age System and its Contested Reception in Denmark, Britain, and Ireland. Oxford

Røyrvik, E.C. 2010 'Western Celts? A genetic impression of Britain in Atlantic Europe', in Cunliffe and Koch (eds) 2010, 83–106

Rusu, M. 1969 'Das keltische Fürstengrab von Ciumeşti in Rumänien', Bericht der Römisch-Germanisch Kommission 50, 267–300

Ryan, M. 1990 'The formal relationships of insular early medieval eucharistic chalices', Proceedings of the Royal Irish Academy. Section C: Archaeology, Celtic Studies, History, Linguistics, Literature, 90, 281–356

Schaaff, U. 1972a 'Ein keltischer Hohlbuckelring aus Kleinasien', Germania 50, 94–7

Schaaff, U. 1972b 'Zur Tragweise keltischer Hohlbuckelringe', Archäologisches Korrespondenzblatt 2, 155–8

Schaaff, U. 1988 'Zu den antiken Reparaturen der griechischen Schalen', in Kimmig 1988, 191–5

Scheeres, M., Knipper, C., Hauschild, M., Schönfelder, M., Siebel, W., Vitali, D., Pare, C. and Alt, K.W. 2013 'Evidence for "Celtic migrations"? Strontium isotope analysis at the early La Tène cemeteries of Nebringen (Germany) and Monte Bibele (Italy)', Journal of Archaeologicla Science 40, 3614-25

Schreyer, S.B. 2009 'The Celtic bear and the Roman goddess. Deo Artio group, about AD 200', in Müller 2009a, 258–9.

Score, V. (ed.) 2011 Hoards, Hounds and Helmets: A Conquest-Period Ritual Site at Hallaton, Leicestershire. Leicester

Scott, I.A.G. and Ritchie, A. 2009 Pictish and Viking-Age Carvings from Shetland. Edinburgh

Seymour, St J.D. 1932 'The coarb in the Medieval Irish church (circa 1200–1550)', Proceedings of the Royal Irish Academy, Section C 41, 219–31

Sharples, N. 2008 'Comment I. Contextualising Iron Age art', in Garrow et al. (eds) 2008, 203–13

Sheehy, J. 1980 The Rediscovery of Ireland's Past: The Celtic Revival 1830–1930. London

Sievers, S. 2003 Manching – Die Keltenstadt. Stuttgart

Sims-Williams, P. 1998 'Celtomania and Celtoscepticism', Cambrian Medieval Celtic Studies 36, 1–35

Sims-Williams, P. 2012 'Bronze- and Iron-Age Celtic-speakers: what don't we know, what can't we know, and what could we know? Language, genetics and archaeology in the twenty-first century', Antiquaries Journal 92, 427–49

Sims-Williams, P. 2013 'Post-Celtoscepticism: a personal view', in D. Ó Baoill, D. Ó hAodha and N. Ó Muraíle (eds) 2013 Saltair Saíochta, Sanasaíochta agus Seanchais: a Festschrift for Gearóid Mac Eoin, 422–8. Dublin

Skene, W.F. (ed.) 1867 Chronicles of the Picts, Chronicles of the Scots, and Other Early Memorials of Scottish History. Edinburgh

Sloan, K. (ed.) 2009 European Visions: American Voices. London (= British Museum Research Publication 172)

Small, A. Thomas, C. and Wilson, D.M. 1973 St Ninian's Isle and its Treasure. Oxford

Smiles, S. 2009 'John White and British antiquity: savage origins in the context of Tudor historiography', in Sloan (ed.) 2009, 106–12

Smith, B. 1997 The Life and Work of Edward Atkinson Hornel. Edinburgh

Smith, R.A. 1911 'On late-Celtic antiquities discovered at Welwyn, Herts', Archaeologia 63, 1–30

Spratling, M. 2008 'On the aesthetics of the ancient Britons', in Garrow et al. (eds) 2008, 185–202

Sprockhoff, E. 1955 'Central European Urnfield culture and Celtic La Tène: an outline', Proceedings of the Prehistoric Society 21, 257–81

Stalley, R. 2014 'Irish sculpture of the early tenth century and the work of the "Muiredach Master": problems of identification and meaning', Proceedings of the Royal Irish Academy, Section C 114, 141–79

Stead, I.M. 1967 'A La Tène III burial at Welwyn Garden City', Archaeologia 101, 1–62

Stead, I.M. 1971 'The reconstruction of Iron Age buckets from Aylesford and Baldock', British Museum Quarterly 35, no. 1/4, 250–82

Stead, I.M. 1979 The Arras Culture. York

Stead, I.M. 1984 'Celtic dragons from the River Thames', Antiquaries Journal 64, 269–79

Stead, I.M. 1985 The Battersea Shield. London

Stead, I.M. 1988 'Chalk figurines of the Parisi', Antiquaries Journal 68, 9–29

Stead, I.M. 1991a 'Many more Iron Age shields from Britain', Antiquaries Journal 71, 1–35

Stead, I.M. 1991b Iron Age Cemeteries in East Yorkshire. London

Stead, I.M. 1991c 'Somme-Bionne', in Moscati et al. (eds) 1991, 174–5

Stead, I.M. 1991d 'The Snettisham treasure: excavations in 1990', Antiquity 65, 447–65

Stead, I.M. 1996 Celtic Art in Britain before the Roman Conquest, 2nd edn. London

Stead, I.M. 1998 The Salisbury Hoard. Stroud

Stead, I.M. 2006 British Iron Age Swords and Scabbards. London

Stead, I.M. 2014 'Snettisham swansong', in Gosden et al. (eds) 2014, 297–303

Stead, I. & Hughes, K. 1997 Early Celtic Designs. London

Stead, I.M. and Meeks, N.D. 1996 'The Celtic warrior fibula', Antiquaries Journal 76, 1–16

Stead, I.M. and Rigby, V. 1999 The Morel Collection. Iron Age Antiquities from Champagne in the British Museum. London

Steer, K., Bannerman, J.W.M. and Collins, G.H. 1977 Late Medieval Monumental Sculpture in the West Highlands. Edinburgh

Stevenson, R.B.K. 1955 'Pictish chain, Roman silver and bauxite beads', Proceedings of the Society of Antiquaries of Scotland 88, 228–30

Stevenson, R.B.K. 1974 'The Hunterston brooch and its significance', Medieval Archaeology 18, 16–42

Stevenson, R.B.K. and Emery, J. 1964 'The Gaulcross hoard of Pictish silver', Proceedings of the Society of Antiquaries of Scotland 97, 206–11

Stöllner, T. 2014a 'Between ruling ideology and ancestor worship: the mos maiorum of the early Celtic "hero graves"', in Gosden et al. (eds) 2014, 119–36

Stöllner, T 2014b 'Mobility and cultural change of the early Celts: La Tène openwork belt-hooks north and south of the Alps', in P. Barral, J.-P. Guillaumet, M.-J. Roulière-Lambert, M. Saracino and D. Vitali (eds) 2014 Les Celtes et le Nord de l'Italie; Premier et Second Âges du fer, 211–29. Dijon

Stukeley, W. 1743 Abury: A Temple of the British Druids, with Some Others . . . London

Swift, C. 2001 'Irish monumental sculpture: the dating evidence provided by linguistic forms', in Redknap et al. (eds) 2001, 49–61

Swift, C. 2007 'Welsh ogams from

an Irish perspective', in K. Jankulak and J.M. Wooding (eds) 2007 *Ireland and Wales in the Middle Ages*, 62–79. Dublin

Swift, E. 2009 *Style and Function in Roman Decoration: Living with Objects and Interiors*. Farnham

Szabó, M. 1991 'The Celts and their movements in the third century BC', in Moscati *et al.* (eds) 1991, 302–19

Szabó, M. and Petres, E.F. 1992 *Decorated Weapons of the La Tène Iron Age in the Carpathian Basin*. Budapest

Talbot, J. and Leins, I. 2010 'Before Boudicca: the Wickham Market hoard and the middle phase gold coinage of East Anglia', *British Numismatic Journal* 80, 1–23

Taylor, I. 1889 *The Origin of the Aryans*. London

Taylor, T. 1992 'The Gundestrup cauldron', *Scientific American* 266(3), 66–71

Teehan, V. and Heckett, E.W. 2004 *The Honan Chapel: A Golden Vision*. Cork

Thomas, C. 1994 *And shall these mute stones speak?* Cardiff

Tolkein, J.R.R. 1963 *English and Welsh Angles and Britons*, The O'Donnell Lectures. Cardiff

Vang Petersen, P. 2003 'Warrior art, religion and symbolism', in L. Jørgensen, B. Storgaard and L.G. Thomsen (eds) 2003 *The Spoils of Victory: The North in the Shadow of the Roman Empire*, 286–94. Copenhagen

Verger, S. 1987 'La genèse celtique des rinceaux à triscèles', *Jahrbuch des Römisch-Germanischen Zentralmuseums Mainz* 34, 287–339

Vouga, P. 1923 *La Tène*. Leipzig

Waddell, J. 2009 'The elusive image', in Cooney *et al.* (eds) 2009, 341–9

Waddell, J. 2014 *Archaeology and Celtic Myth*. Dublin

Walker, S. 2014 'Emperors and deities in rural Britain: a copper-alloy head of Marcus Aurelius from Steane, near Brackley (Northants.)', *Britannia* 45, 223–42

Wallace, P.F. and Ó Floinn, R. 2002 *Treasures of the National Museum of Ireland: Irish Antiquities*. Dublin

Wamers, E. 2009 'Behind animals, plants and interlace: Salin's Style II on Christian objects', in Graham-Campbell and Ryan (eds) 2009, 151–204

Washer, C. 1992 'The work of Edmond Johnson: archaeology and commerce', in Edelstein (ed.) 1992, 106–21

Watkin, J., Stead, I., Hook, D. and Palmer, S. 1996 'A decorated shield-boss from the River Trent, near Ratcliffe-on-Soar', *Antiquaries Journal* 76, 17–30

Webster, G. 2003 *Rome Against Caratacus: The Roman Campaigns in Britain, AD 48–58*. London

Webster, L. (ed.) 1991 *The Making of England. Anglo-Saxon Art and Culture AD 600–900*. London

Webster, L. 2012 *Anglo-Saxon Art: A New History*. London

Wells, P.S. 1999 *The Barbarians Speak: How the Conquered Peoples Shaped Roman Europe*. Princeton

Wells, P. 2008 *Image and Response in Early Europe*. London

Wells, P.S. 2012 *How the Ancient Europeans Saw the World: Vision, Patterns, and the Shaping of the Mind in Prehistoric Times*. Princeton

Wendling, H. 2013 'Manching reconsidered: new perspectives on settlement dynamics and urbanization in Iron Age central Europe', *European Journal of Archaeology* 16(3), 459–90

Werner, M. 2003 'The beginning of Insular book illumination', in P. Lindley (ed.) 2003 *Making Medieval Art*, 91–103. Donington

Westwood, J.O. 1843–5 *Palaeographia Sacra Pictoria: Being a Series of Illustrations of the Ancient Versions of the Bible, Copied from Illuminated Manuscripts, Executed between the Fourth and Sixteenth centuries*. London

Westwood, J.O. 1853 'On the distinctive character of the various styles of ornamentation employed by the early British, Anglo-Saxon and Irish artists', *Archaeological Journal* 10, 275–301

Westwood, J.O. 1856 'Celtic ornament', in Jones 1856, 89–97

Whitfield, N. 2004 'More thoughts on the wearing of brooches in early medieval Ireland', in C. Hourihane (ed.) 2004 *Irish Art Historical Studies in Honour of Peter Harbison*, 70–108. Dublin

Wilde, W.R. 1857–62 *A Descriptive Catalogue of the Antiquities in the Museum of the Royal Irish Academy*. Dublin

Wilson, D. 1851 *The Archaeology and Prehistoric Annals of Scotland*. Edinburgh

Wilson, D.M. 1973 'The treasure', in Small *et al.* 1973, 45–148

Wodtko, D.S. 2013 'Models of language spread and language development in prehistoric Europe', in Koch and Cunliffe (eds) 2013, 185–206

Woolf, A. 2007 *From Pictland to Alba, 789–1070*. Edinburgh

Woolf, G. 2011 *Tales of the Barbarians: Ethnography and Empire in the Roman West*. Chichester

Worrell, S., Egan, G., Naylor, J., Leahy, K. and Lewis, M. (eds) 2010 *A Decade of Discovery: Proceedings of the Portable Antiquities Scheme Conference 2007*. Oxford (= BAR British Series 520)

Wyss, R., Rey, T. and Müller, F. 2002 *Gewässerfunde aus Port und Umgebung. Katalog der latène- und römerzeitlichen Funde aus der Zihl*. Bern

Yeats, W.B. 1893 *The Celtic Twilight*. London

Youngs, S. (ed.) 1989 *"The Work of Angels": Masterpieces of Celtic Metalwork, 6th–9th Centuries AD*. London

Youngs, S. 2005 'After Oldcroft: a British silver pin from Welton le Wold, Lincolnshire', in N. Crummy (ed.) 2005 *Image, Craft and the Classical World. Essays in Honour of David Bailey and Catherine Johns*, 249–54. Montagnac

Youngs, S., 2009a 'Anglo-Saxon, Irish and British relations: hanging-bowls reconsidered', in Graham-Campbell and Ryan (eds) 2009, 205–30

Youngs, S. 2009b 'From metalwork to manuscript: some observations on the use of Celtic art in insular manuscripts', *Anglo-Saxon Studies in Archaeology and History*, Oxford University School of Archaeology 16, 45–64. Oxford

Youngs, S. 2011 'Cloud-cuckoo land? Some Christian symbols from post-Roman Britain', in F. Edmonds and P. Russell (eds) 2011 *Tome: Studies in Medieval and Celtic History and Law in Honour of Thomas Charles-Edwards*, 1–16. Woodbridge

Youngs, S. 2013a 'From chains to brooches: the uses and hoarding of silver in north Britain in the Early Historic period', in Hunter and Painter (eds) 2013, 403–26

Youngs, S. 2013b 'Histories revealed and pedigrees claimed? New evidence from early medieval metalwork', in Hawkes (ed.) 2013, 134–44

Zoll, A.L. 1994 'Patterns of worship in Roman Britain: double-named deities in context', in S. Cottam, D. Dungworth, S. Scott and J. Taylor (eds) 1994 *TRAC 94: Proceedings of the Fourth Annual Theoretical Roman Archaeology Conference, Durham 1994*, 32–44. Oxford

Illustration Acknowledgements

by Paul Goodhead after Youngs 2009; reproduced
with kind permission of the author

Fig. 162 © The Trustees of the British Museum

Fig. 163 National Museums Scotland

Fig. 164, above: © The Trustees of the British Museum
(artwork by Craig Williams)

Fig. 164, below: Museum of Archaeology and Anthropology
[D 1950.11], University of Cambridge

Fig. 165 National Museums Scotland

Fig. 166 National Museums Scotland

Fig. 167 left: © The Trustees of the British Museum

Fig. 167 right: National Museums Scotland

Fig. 168 Reproduced with the kind permission of
the National Museum of Ireland

Fig. 169 The Board of Trinity College Dublin

Fig. 170 National Museums Scotland

Fig. 171 National Museums Scotland; photo.
© The Trustees of the British Museum

Fig. 172 National Museums Scotland

Fig. 173 The British Library Board

Fig. 174 National Museums Scotland

Figs 175–7 © The Trustees of the British Museum

Figs 178–9 National Museums Scotland

Fig. 180 Reproduced with the kind permission
of the National Museum of Ireland

Fig. 181 National Museums Scotland

Fig. 182 Reproduced with the kind permission
of the National Museum of Ireland

Fig. 183 National Museums Scotland

Fig. 184 © The National Museum of Denmark

Fig. 185 Reproduced with the kind permission
of the National Museum of Ireland

Figs 186–7 National Museums Scotland

Fig. 188 Norwich Castle Museum and Art Gallery

Fig. 189 National Museums Scotland

Fig. 192 © The Trustees of the British Museum

Figs 193–4 National Museums Scotland

Fig. 195 © AA World Travel Library / Alamy

Fig. 196 DeAgostini Picture Library/Scala, Florence

Fig. 197 Reproduced with the kind permission of the
National Museum of Ireland

Fig. 198 Used by permission of the Chapter of the Lichfield
Cathedral, photo. University of Kentucky

Figs 199–200 National Museums Scotland

Fig. 201 © The Trustees of the British Museum

Fig. 202 Reproduced with the kind permission of the
National Museum of Ireland

Fig. 203 By permission of the Royal Irish Academy © RIA

Fig. 204 © The Trustees of the British Museum

Fig. 205 © 2015 University of Cambridge

Fig. 206 © Martin Mullen / Dreamstime.com

Fig. 207 National Museums Scotland

Fig. 208 © The Trustees of the British Museum

Fig. 209 © Werner Forman Archive / Bridgeman Images

Fig. 210 Bibliothèque Nationale de France

Fig. 211 © Cathedral Treasury Trier

Fig. 212 Bibliothèque Nationale de France

Fig. 213 The British Library Board

p. 200 and fig. 214 © The Trustees of the British Museum

Fig. 215 By kind permission of the Chapter of
Durham Cathedral

Figs 216–17 National Museums Scotland

Fig. 218 By permission of the President and Fellows
of Corpus Christi College

Fig. 219 By permission of the Royal Irish Academy © RIA

Figs 220–1 The Bodleian Library, University of Oxford

Fig. 222 Photography by Alan McCaw

Figs 223–5 National Museums Scotland

Fig. 226 Dundee City Council: Dundee's Art Galleries and
Museums, Celebrating 150 Years in 2017/ © Estate of
John Duncan. All rights reserved, DACS 2015

Fig. 227 © CSG CIC Glasgow Museums Collection

Figs 228–9 © The Trustees of the British Museum

Fig. 230 National Museum Wales

Fig. 231 The National Gallery of Denmark, Copenhagen
© SMK Photo

Fig. 232 © The Trustees of the British Museum

Fig. 233 © RMN-Grand Palais (musée des châteaux
de Malmaison et de Bois-Préau) / Franck Raux

Fig. 234 © Victoria and Albert Museum, London

Fig. 235 Royal Collection Trust / © Her Majesty Queen
Elizabeth II 2015

Fig. 236 Reproduced with the kind permission of the
National Museum of Ireland

Fig. 237 © Look and Learn / Rosenberg Collection
/ Bridgeman Images

Fig. 238 Dundee City Council: Dundee's Art Galleries and
Museums, Celebrating 150 Years in 2017/ © Estate of
John Duncan. All rights reserved, DACS 2015

Figs 239–40 © The Hunterian, University of Glasgow 2015

Fig. 241 © Culture and Sport Glasgow (Museums)
/ Bridgeman Images

Fig. 242 © CSG CIC Glasgow Museums Collection

Fig. 243 Scottish National Gallery

Fig. 244 Reproduced with the kind permission of the National
Museum of Ireland

Fig. 245 © The Trustees of the British Museum

Fig. 246 City Art Centre, Edinburgh Museums and Galleries
/ © Estate of John Duncan. All rights reserved,
DACS 2015

Fig. 247 National Museum Wales

Fig. 248 National Museum Wales

Fig. 249 cc, photo: Kman999

Fig. 250 Scottish National Gallery / © Estate of
John Duncan. All rights reserved, DACS 2015

Fig. 251 City of London, Guildhall Art Gallery

Fig. 252 Robert Harding Picture Library,
photo: Walter Rawlings

Figs 253–8 © The National Museum of Denmark

Fig. 259 Kunsthistorisches Museum, Wien

Fig. 260 © The National Museum of Denmark

Figs 261–2 National Museums Scotland

Fig. 263 With kind permission of SRA, DRAC Auvergne
(France), photo: © Bibracte/ Antoine Maillier

Fig. 264 National Museums Scotland

Fig. 265 © The National Museum of Denmark

Fig. 266 National Museums Scotland

Fig. 267 National Museums Scotland/ © Estate of
John Duncan. All rights reserved, DACS 2015

Endpapers (hardback edition only): front, used by permission
of the Chapter of the Lichfield Cathedral, photo. University
of Kentucky; back, © The Trustees of the British Museum

Index